E–Reference Context and Discoverability in Libraries:

Issues and Concepts

Sue Polanka
Wright State University, USA

A volume in the Advances in Library and Information Science (ALIS) Book Series

ALS Series Editor:	Mirela Roncevic
Senior Editorial Director:	Kristin Klinger
Director of Book Publications:	Julia Mosemann
Editorial Director:	Lindsay Johnston
Acquisitions Editor:	Erika Carter
Development Editor:	Myla Harty
Production Editor:	Sean Woznicki
Typesetters:	Milan Vracarich, Jr.
Print Coordinator:	Jamie Snavely
Cover Design:	Nick Newcomer

Published in the United States of America by
    Information Science Reference (an imprint of IGI Global)
    701 E. Chocolate Avenue
    Hershey PA 17033
    Tel: 717-533-8845
    Fax: 717-533-8661
    E-mail: cust@igi-global.com
    Web site: http://www.igi-global.com

Library of Congress Cataloging-in-Publication Data

E-reference context and discoverability in libraries : issues and concepts /
Sue Polanka, editor.
      p. cm.
    Includes bibliographical references and index.
    Summary: "This book consists of over 20 informative chapters by librarians, publishers, and other industry professionals
that propose new ideas for reinventing reference collections and interfaces to fit the needs of today's researchers"--Provided
by publisher.
    ISBN 978-1-61350-308-9 (hardcover) -- ISBN 978-1-61350-309-6 (ebook) -- ISBN 978-1-61350-310-2 (print & perpetual
access) 1. Electronic reference services (Libraries) 2. Electronic reference sources. 3. Electronic information resource
literacy. 4. Libraries and electronic publishing. 5. Electronic reference services (Libraries)--Case studies. I. Polanka, Sue.
    Z711.45.E18 2012
    025.5'24--dc23
                                                 2011017287

This book is published in the IGI Global book series Advances in Library and Information Science (ALIS) Book Series
(ISSN: 2326-4136; eISSN: 2326-4144)

British Cataloguing in Publication Data
A Cataloguing in Publication record for this book is available from the British Library.

All work contributed to this book is new, previously-unpublished material. The views expressed in this book are those of the
authors, but not necessarily of the publisher.

Advances in Library and Information Science (ALIS) Book Series

ISSN: 2326-4136
EISSN: 2326-4144

MISSION

The **Advances in Library and Information Science** (ALIS) book series is comprised of high quality, research-oriented publications on the continuing developments and trends affecting the public, school, and academic fields, as well as specialized libraries and librarians globally. These discussions on professional and organizational considerations in library and information resource development and management assist in showcasing the latest methodologies and tools in the field.

The ALIS book series aims to expand the body of library science literature by covering a wide range of topics affecting the profession and field at large. The series also seeks to provide readers with an essential resource for uncovering the latest research in library and information science management, development, and technologies.

COVERAGE

- Academic libraries in the digital age
- Blogging in libraries
- Cataloging and classification
- Collection development
- Community outreach
- Digital literacy
- Ethical practices in libraries
- Green libraries
- Librarian education
- Mobile library services
- Remote access technologies
- University libraries in developing countries

IGI Global is currently accepting manuscripts for publication within this series. To submit a proposal for a volume in this series, please contact our Acquisition Editors at Acquisitions@igi-global.com or visit: http://www.igi-global.com/publish/.

Titles in this Series

For a list of additional titles in this series, please visit: www.igi-global.com

Robots in Academic Libraries Advancements in Library Automation
Edward Iglesias (Central Connecticut State University, USA)
Information Science Reference • copyright 2013 • 341pp • H/C (ISBN: 9781466639386) • US $175.00 (our price)

Advancing Library Education Technological Innovation and Instructional Design
Ari Sigal (Catawba Valley Community College, USA)
Information Science Reference • copyright 2013 • 339pp • H/C (ISBN: 9781466636880) • US $175.00 (our price)

Recent Developments in the Design, Construction, and Evaluation of Digital Libraries Case Studies
Colleen Cool (Graduate School of Library and Information Studies, Queens College, USA) and Kwong Bor Ng
(Queens College, CUNY, USA)
Information Science Reference • copyright 2013 • 275pp • H/C (ISBN: 9781466629912) • US $175.00 (our price)

Design, Development, and Management of Resources for Digital Library Services
Tariq Ashraf (University of Delhi, India) and Puja Anand Gulati (University of Delhi, India)
Information Science Reference • copyright 2013 • 438pp • H/C (ISBN: 9781466625006) • US $175.00 (our price)

Public Law Librarianship Objectives, Challenges, and Solutions
Laurie Selwyn (Law Librarian [Ret.], USA) and Virginia Eldridge (Grayson County, Texas Law Library, USA)
Information Science Reference • copyright 2013 • 341pp • H/C (ISBN: 9781466621848) • US $175.00 (our price)

Library Collection Development for Professional Programs Trends and Best Practices
Sara Holder (McGill University, Canada)
Information Science Reference • copyright 2013 • 504pp • H/C (ISBN: 9781466618978) • US $175.00 (our price)

Library Automation and OPAC 2.0 Information Access and Services in the 2.0 Landscape
Jesus Tramullas (University of Zaragoza, Spain) and Piedad Garrido (University of Zaragoza, Spain)
Information Science Reference • copyright 2013 • 409pp • H/C (ISBN: 9781466619128) • US $175.00 (our price)

Planning and Implementing Resource Discovery Tools in Academic Libraries
Mary Pagliero Popp (Indiana University, USA) and Diane Dallis (Indiana University, USA)
Information Science Reference • copyright 2012 • 342pp • H/C (ISBN: 9781466618213) • US $175.00 (our price)

Remote Access Technologies for Library Collections Tools for Library Users and Managers
Diane M. Fulkerson (University of South Florida Polytechnic Library, USA)
Information Science Reference • copyright 2012 • 232pp • H/C (ISBN: 9781466602342) • US $175.00 (our price)

www.igi-global.com

701 E. Chocolate Ave., Hershey, PA 17033
Order online at www.igi-global.com or call 717-533-8845 x100
To place a standing order for titles released in this series, contact: cust@igi-global.com
Mon-Fri 8:00 am - 5:00 pm (est) or fax 24 hours a day 717-533-8661

I would like to dedicate this book to my former supervisor at the Radisson Hotel in Dayton, Ohio: thank you for firing me on that fateful day in June. Within thirty minutes of leaving your employment I was placed at the Dayton Metro Library with the help of a temporary agency. Who knew that such a vibrant and fulfilling career was about to blossom? Thanks to Tish Wilson, Assistant Director for Youth Services, for hiring me. Thank you as well to my colleagues who have now retired from the Dayton Metro Library, Jerry Buck, Deputy Director, Glenna Reynolds, Head of Adult Services, and Kay Hodson, Assistant Head of Adult Services, for giving me a chance to prove my skills and abilities as a reference librarian. Your initial support and guidance was crucial to my success in librarianship.

Table of Contents

Section 3
Design and Delivery of Reference Content

Section 4
Solutions for E-Reference Discovery

Preface

Flash back to 1992. *The Thomas Register of American Manufacturers*, all 33 volumes of it, was one of the hottest business sources on the shelf. It was so popular at the Dayton Metro Library, Ohio, where this editor cut her reference teeth, that the alphabetical volumes had sturdy handles book-taped to the cover so that pulling them off the shelf would be easier on users' hands and the spines of books. In addition to *The Thomas Register*, a slew of other print business sources were available to help users verify addresses, employees, sales, and top executives of thousands of companies around the world. While not the only type of reference question, company research was quite popular in 1992 at the "West Reference Desk" of the Dayton Metro Library. But what was still not possible was the availability of company research online. At that time the researcher's best bet was to use a CD-ROM for the *Dun & Bradstreet Regional Business Directory*, loaded on a dedicated stand-alone computer, which provided little more information than the print resources, but focused on a much wider array of local companies.

Enter the World Wide Web in 1993. Little did the librarians at the Dayton Metro Library realize what impact the Web would have on the future of reference collections and formats. And, just what was the Web's impact on the library? Within a few short years, a veritable potpourri of Web sources answered many of the patrons' questions. Today, collections of annual reports, business directories, and telephone books from around the world are gone. The CD-ROM drives and products that librarians so favored for their quarterly updates have now vanished. Hundreds of new print resources produced each year, and the budgets to support them are missing in action. Thanks to HTML, search engines, and dot-coms, much of this front-line print reference material has become unnecessary, and in many cases, all but extinct.

Without question, reference collections have changed. We are in the midst of a paradigm shift where publishers are focusing on a future with electronic content and full-text interfaces; classic reference sources are being transformed into online interactive products; the use of print continues to decline. Despite this relentless shift, some libraries cannot afford a complete transformation to e-reference and depend on print and free Web-based sources for added support. Students, however, are turning to search engines and Wikipedia as starting points for their research, leaving vetted content out-of-sight, and consequently, out-of-mind.

But numerous studies show that students struggle with information overload and a lack of context from general Web searching, pointing to a need for vetted reference sources. Such sources can provide students with the context they need but are difficult, if not impossible, to find in an online environment. Factors such as these elicit many questions: What will become of reference collections in public, academic, and school libraries? How do librarians and reference publishers make e-reference content more discoverable? And, are they doing enough to meet the changing needs of today's researchers?

E-Reference Context and Discoverability in Libraries provides an in-depth analysis of these issues and offers solutions to help vetted reference sources remain integral to research.

This book consists of over 20 informative chapters by librarians, publishers, and other industry professionals that propose new ideas for reinventing reference collections and interfaces to fit the needs of today's researchers. The chapters examine the issues of reference context and discoverability in school, public, and academic libraries as well as within the reference publishing community. Librarians, publishers, and those studying library and information science are the book's primary audience, but others in the information industry, particularly those with an interest in reference, will find significant value here as well.

The collection is organized into five distinct content areas. The first focuses on the rapidly changing landscape of electronic reference, examining the dramatic changes from library, publisher, and end-user perspectives. In Chapter 1, seasoned reference and instruction librarian Jack O'Gorman provides an historical look at the development of reference sources and the paradigm shift to electronic reference services and sources. O'Gorman describes how major changes have impacted traditional reference titles and how libraries and users have adjusted to those changes through history. Peter Tobey, a reference publishing executive, investigates changes in reference publishing, including the shift to electronic publishing, new business models, and challenges publishers face today. Tobey provides detailed and personal discussions about sharing content, simultaneous use, pricing for a fair reward, and the importance of content discovery. The last chapter in this section, written by publisher and researcher Anh Bui, introduces discoverability and sets the stage for how libraries and publishers together might adapt to meet end users' future needs. Bui examines common information seeking practices and the ways in which both discovery and filter failure can play key roles. She also discusses the user's perspective and identifies several value signifiers – i.e., the signals typically used to determine the relevance of discovered resources.

Section 2 explores the value of information literacy in research. James Galbraith, a long-time collection development librarian, and Miriam Matteson, library and information science professor, in Chapters 4 and 5, look at the research habits of undergraduate and graduate students as well as faculty to determine how they conduct their research. Each author summarizes extensive studies addressing the changing habits of students, highlights motivations of researchers as well as their information seeking strategies, and offers suggestions on how to best meet the changing needs of these important user groups.

In Chapter 6, Frank Menchaca, a publishing executive, considers the role of libraries and educational publishers in the information age. Menchaca focuses on information overload and evaluation of resources, proposing new roles for librarians and publishers to help them address these critical issues and remain relevant in a search-engine dominated research process. Jackie Zanghi-LaPlaca, an online reference product developer, explores online research without e-reference sources. She stresses the importance of reference services to increase the value and use of an institution's electronic resources collection, resulting in increased information literacy. Jason Phillips, a social sciences librarian, wraps up Section 2 with his discussion of the underutilization of online resources and the great need for information literacy instruction. Phillips offers insight into these problems by highlighting the results of interviews conducted with undergraduate students at New York University.

Section 3 takes a closer look at the design and delivery of reference content through four informative chapters. In Chapter 9, Tom Beyer, an online product designer, examines interface features available on reference platforms today and suggests innovative ways to reach the end user of the future. Beyer examines the value of adding multi-media content to text, browsing via timelines and maps, developing taxonomies and ontologies, inter-linking products, and delivering content through mobile devices.

Chapter 10, written by two technology consultants, Alix Vance and David Wojick, provides a template of design considerations for mobile applications. Vance and Wojick discuss general theories of content restructuring, strategic planning and tactical execution, with an eye on publisher-based applications. The concepts and issues covered can be applied to library-based applications for reference content delivery.

Chapter 11 examines why medical reference sources frequently lead the way in setting a standard for the design of e-reference products, particularly with e-books and mobile access to content. Two health sciences librarians, Terese DeSimio and Ximena Chrisagis, offer examples of features currently available through medical content aggregators that should be widely adopted. They describe several challenges of e-reference delivery, including ease of access, user-friendliness, mobile delivery, and data security. In Chapter 12, K-12 librarians and educators Terri Fredericka and Jennifer Schwelik examine an INFOhio project that delivers content to today's digital learners. They chronicle the ongoing partnership between INFOhio (Ohio's K-12 library and information network) and a library vendor to create an innovative virtual classroom of reference, research, and discovery material to support student curricular needs.

In Section 4, the focus shifts to possibilities inherent in the discoverability and context of e- reference. Six chapters explore strategies that librarians and publishers can use to improve e-reference discoverability. In Chapter 13, online reference product manager Lettie Conrad challenges today's thinking about discoverability and discusses future publishing tactics that will increase content discoverability. Conrad goes beyond search engine optimization, suggesting that publishers need to investigate business models and existing editorial positions to produce more agile content. In Chapter 14, publishing executive Eric Calaluca covers the indexing of reference content. He begins with an overview of the diminished interaction between end users and librarians and describes how that impacts contextualization for end users. He then examines how new technologies are applied to increase discoverability of subject encyclopedias in particular. Metadata, DOIs, and other discovery tools found in subject encyclopedias are all necessary pieces to this "discoverability" puzzle. John Dove and Ingrid Becker, reference content aggregators, continue the discussion of subject encyclopedias in Chapter 15 by exploring their role in providing context for users. Based on studies of student research behavior, Dove and Becker argue for the contemporary relevance of the subject encyclopedia. They also explore current practices and future possibilities important in the transition of print encyclopedias to digital formats suitable for the open Web.

Information services librarian Chad Mairn goes mobile in Chapter 16, providing examples of the successful implementation of mobile reference products and services in libraries today. He discusses best practices for acquiring, promoting, and using mobile-optimized library resources and services, while attempting to determine if promoting mobile-optimized content is a viable solution to discoverability. In Chapter 17, media consultant Darrell Gunter introduces the Semantic Web and its role in connecting disparate pieces of information. Gunter provides an historical look at the Semantic Web, breaks down the technological pieces that form the Semantic Web with examples of the successful use of semantic technologies in the STM environment. He suggests that many of these technologies could be positioned in most online reference products. Section 4 wraps with a modern view of archival reference. Jane Wildermuth and Laurie Gemmill, archivists and digitization specialists, investigate how the landscape in archival reference has changed from one of protection to one of "crowdsourcing." They propose some new ideas that can be incorporated into a discovery solution for all types of reference sources.

The final section of the book offers a unique glimpse into the inner workings of libraries and publishers through five case studies. Librarians Kathleen Sullivan and Ross MacLachlan give an extensive overview of the shift from print to electronic reference at Phoenix Public Library, highlighting the strategies that helped them achieve quality results while also learning from failed initiatives. In Chapter 20, librarian Wright Rix describes how Santa Monica Public Library's collections and services have adapted and changed to match needs of patrons and available technologies. He surmises that today's library customers exhibit a decreasing tendency to regard the public library as the primary local repository of research information and that the library's services and products must evolve to support the changing needs of patrons.

Chapter 21, written by instructional technologist and library media specialist Buffy Hamilton, examines the positive impact of embedded school librarianship through her Media 21 program at the "Unquiet Library." Her case study chronicles the learning experiences of students who participated in a year-long learning initiative rooted in connectivism, inquiry, and participatory literacy.

In the final two case studies, publishers offer their own perspectives on e-reference. In Chapter 22, publishers Miriam Gilbert and Roger Rosen, describe the creation of the Teen Health & Wellness: Real Life, Real Answers database, review the creative process behind it, and share successes and challenges. Finally, Chapter 23 examines the role of bibliographies in the research process. Online product developers Rebecca Cullen and Robert Faber review the research chain as it is currently understood and discuss both the planned and actual role of Oxford Bibliographies Online on this shifting research process.

Fast forward to 2025. People are using voice-activated personal holographic screens to access information—anywhere, anytime. Scholarly reference content is seamlessly delivered due to technological advances and collaborative business models, licensing agreements, and authentication among libraries, publishers, and search providers. Information seekers are conducting research and connecting to relevant information in ways never imagined. Just as librarians working at the West Reference Desk at the Dayton Metro Library could not anticipate the impact of the Web back in 1993, today we are also unable to anticipate exactly how mobile technology, the Semantic Web, filtering, and the convergence of electronic innovation with scholarly content will impact our own future, be it 2025 or tomorrow. More than anything, this collection of essays, written by information professionals, offers readers an opportunity to think about the future of reference, to explore their own choices, and to act on the ideas that best fit the new generation of researchers they serve.

Sue Polanka
Wright State University Libraries, USA

Acknowledgment

This book would not have been possible without the support, expertise, and guidance of many amazing individuals. First, I thank the thirty-one contributors: Ingrid Becker, Tom Beyer, Anh Bui, Eric Calaluca, Ximena Chrisagis, Lettie Conrad, Rebecca Cullen, Terese DeSimio, John Dove, Robert Faber, Theresa Fredericka, James Galbraith, Laurie Gemmill, Miriam Gilbert, Darrell Gunter, Buffy Hamilton, Jackie Zanghi-LaPlaca, Ross McLachlan, Chad Mairn, Miriam Matteson, Frank Menchaca, Jack O'Gorman, Jason Phillips, Wright Rix, Roger Rosen, Jennifer Schwelik, Kathleen Sullivan, Peter Tobey, Alix Vance, Jane Wildermuth, and David Wojick. Your expertise, dedication to the project, and ability to prepare diverse and informative manuscripts under tight deadlines is greatly appreciated. Second, I thank Mirela Roncevic for her superior editorial skills and guidance. Third, I acknowledge the twelve members of the Editorial Advisory Board for their vision and advice. Fourth, I thank the thirty individuals who participated in the blind review process. Your feedback and direction was critical in developing a successful final product. Finally, I am pleased to recognize three individuals who provided additional support throughout the editorial process, Erik Christopher, Jackie Zanghi-LaPlaca, and Kathryn Reynolds.

As always, I acknowledge the Wright State University Libraries for their generous support of time and freedom, without which I could not achieve my professional and personal goals.

Sue Polanka
Wright State University Libraries, USA

Section 1
The Changing Landscape of E–Reference

Chapter 1
Reference Products and Services:
Historical Overview and Paradigm Shift

Jack O'Gorman
University of Dayton, USA

ABSTRACT

There is a paradigm shift in progress in reference collections affecting the content, format, and use of reference materials. This shift is a result of changing formats for reference products, and it presents challenges to traditional reference services. In order to better understand where reference collections are heading, we must take a look back to see how we got here. This chapter defines a reference paradigm, looks at the history of reference in libraries, and examines the shift from both a reference library product and reference service perspective. It also describes how major changes have impacted traditional reference titles and how libraries and users have adjusted to those changes.

INTRODUCTION

What does "paradigm shift" in reference really mean? To best answer this, we need to also ask a series of related questions. Among them the following questions stand out: What do the rapid changes affecting reference today mean for products on the one hand and the tried-and-true reference service on the other? How are libraries and publishers adjusting to the changes in both areas? What are the key differences between e-reference sources and print reference books, and is there still room for both? Does the format even matter, and is the content still primarily about authority, objectivity, and accuracy?

The emergence of electronic books—especially electronic reference books—presents challenges and opportunities for authors, publishers,

DOI: 10.4018/978-1-61350-308-9.ch001

Table 1.

Clay tablet	First Punctuation	2500 BC
Papyrus Roll	Second Punctuation	2000 BC
Codex	Third Punctuation	150 AD
Printing	Fourth Punctuation	1450 AD
Steam Power	Fifth Punctuation	1800
Offset Printing	Sixth Punctuation	1970
Electronic Book	Seventh Punctuation	2000

librarians, and readers. This chapter presents an overview of how reference publishing is changing and what those changes mean for everyone involved. It provides answers to the questions that emerge while placing reference products and services in the context of library history.

PARADIGM DEFINED

Thomas Kuhn's classic 1962 book, *The Structure of Scientific Revolutions,* first introduces the concept of a paradigm, defining it as a conceptual framework from which common practitioners can discuss and evaluate their discipline. For example, if someone doesn't believe in evolution, then there can be no discussion of the significance of a fossil find. They have no commonality from which to frame their conversation. A classic example of paradigm shift comes from physics. Aristotelian physics led to Newtonian physics, which in turn led to Einstein and relativistic physics. Kuhn also covers a practical dimension of a paradigm, defining it further as not just a set of common principles but also a practice by practitioners. The 1989 edition of the *Oxford English Dictionary* defines paradigm as "a world view underlying the theories and methodology of a particular scientific subject." In short, a paradigm is more than a good model; it presents common standards, common aims, and "a fundamental agreement about the nature of the world and its processes." (Horowitz, 2005, p. 1715)

REFERENCE PRODUCT PARADIGM

Fred Kilgour, founder of OCLC, discusses in his 1998 work, *The Evolution of the Book*, the historical pattern of the book, "in which long periods of stability in format alternate with periods of radical change" (Kilgour, 1998, p. 4). He lays out the seven punctuations of equllibria of the book (see Table 1).

In that same book, Kilgour also identifies five concurrent elements necessary for this radical change to occur: 1) societal need for information; 2) technological knowledge and experience; 3) organization experience and capability; 4) capability to integrate a new form into existing Information Systems; and 5) economic viability.

REFERENCE SERVICE PARADIGM

The history of reference is well documented in books and articles from several giants in the field. Some of the authors who have written on this topic include Bill Katz, Louis Shores, Charles Bunge, Herb White, and Samuel Rothstein. Rothstein's 1953 article, "The Development of the Concept of Reference Service in American Libraries, 1850-1900" seems strangely modern. Several clear articulations of what reference is are presented in this article. Rothstein quotes William Warner Bishop, who wrote in his 1915 work *Theory of Reference Work* that reference was "the service rendered by a librarian in aid of some sort of

Figure 1. Reference Continuum

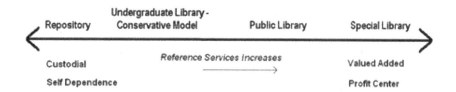

study. It is not the study itself—that is done by the reader…The help given to a reader engaged in research of any sort is what we mean by reference work." (Rothstein, 1953, p. 2)

Rothstein also quotes Lucy Edwards: "Reference work is not only, as the phrase suggests, the use of books on the premises, as against borrowing them for home reading, but an individual and a personal service to each reader, to enable him to obtain the information he requires with the greatest ease, and the least possible delay" (Rothstein, 1953). Reading past the gendered language, Edwards presents a very good point of what reference services are. The article on reference in Garland's 1994 *Encyclopedia of Library History* states: "The distinguishing feature of reference work is the personal assistance rendered by the librarian to patrons in pursuit of information" (Wiegand & Davis, 1994, p. 541).

Rothstein goes on to define reference as:

• The provision by librarians of personal assistance to individual readers in pursuit of information.

• The recognition by the library that such assistance is an indispensable means of fulfilling the duties of the library as an educational institution and the assumption of a definite responsibility to provide it.

• The existence of a specific administrative unit to furnish assistance comprised of personnel specially trained in the technique of reference work… (Rothstein, 1953, p. 3)

The service model can range from a repository or custodial model to a value added model. A custodial model of library services focuses on the books. The stacks may be closed and librarians see their function as guardians. According to Rothstein, "Cast in the role of the keeper of the books, he (the librarian) was naturally disposed to regard the needs of the reader with indifference if not hostility" (Rothstein, 1953, p. 4). In this model, a librarian might greet a patron's request for assistance with a disdainful gesture and the familiar question: "Have you looked in the catalog?" In some circumstances, like a closed archival collection, the custodial model may be appropriate.

A large university library with an undergraduate reference desk in the mid 20th century is a good example of a middle point in service models. "In these academic libraries, as originally in the public libraries, the chief purpose of the reference departments was held to be instruction and guidance. The proper goal of a reference work, according to the 'conservative theory,' which dominated reference thinking at the time, was the self-dependence of the user. This aim would be hindered and the user perhaps 'spoilt' by too much help" (Wiegand & Davis, 1994, p. 542). These university library reference desks may have students or paraprofessionals on the reference desk who make referrals to specialized librarians as appropriate.

Special libraries are, on the other hand, built upon the idea of reference services that create "labor saving, profit increasing" devices (Wiegand & Davis, 1994, p. 543). This is why they were among the first to start providing value-added services. Value added services occur when the librarian assists the users in not only finding information but evaluating and interpreting sources for relevance to their work. This high level of information services is reminiscent of the Elsevier ads where a librarian is assisting a surgeon in the operating room. However impractical it is to search a database in scrubs, this ad capitalizes on the idea of librarian as full partner in the informational endeavor.

Smaller libraries may have staff from different departments doing multiple functions. Reference service at one of these smaller libraries may be more personal, characterized by long-term relationships and even friendships, but hampered by the limited resources of the smaller facility. This reference service model ranging from self-help for undergraduates to personalized and anticipatory support in the departmental or special library has an inherent tension around the level of service for various customers.

The tensions between the levels of service provided and the role of the library in the larger community it serves are as old as reference itself. Discussions about the appropriate level of service and the role of technology are not new. The means of providing reference service including remote users and electronic reference resources is fairly new, but reference comes from a tradition that coalesced in the 19th century.

FROM EARLY REFERENCE TO MODERN REFERENCE

In *Cuneiform to Computers*, Bill Katz makes the case that libraries are exactly as old as history. He says: "The reference book is a universal sign of civilization, of culture, of collective curiosity. Defined in numerous ways, generally a reference work is one filled with specific facts and is not normally read cover to cover. There have been reference sources since the beginning of history" (Katz, 1998, p. xiii). Margaret Landesman states in Frost's book that the ancient libraries of Assyria, Egypt, Greece, and Rome contained "king-lists, genealogies, lists of place names, and dictionaries of foreign words" (Frost, 2005, p. 7). In other words, they had reference books. As history progressed from ancient through medieval and into modern age, technology and society remained closely tied to reference products. In Katz's own words, "The history of reference books parallels both intellectual and technological developments from the first cuneiform tables and papyrus rolls to the present-day digital database" (Katz, 1998, p. xiii).

Modern reference arrives in 1876 with a paper delivered by Samuel Swett Green of the Worcester Massachusetts Public Library at the historic 1876 conference of librarians in Philadelphia. He sees a new kind of library service "unfettered by the custodial tradition" and seeks to make the library more useful and thus contribute to its popularity and support (Wiegand & Davis, 1994, p. 542). This concept of having trained information professionals assist library users and to make it part of the library's mission is an important milestone in librarianship.

At the turn of the 20th century, both reference products and reference services begin to be recognizable. By 1890 the idea of a standard index to popular journal articles is established with the publication of H.W. Wilson's *Reader's Guide to Periodical Literature*. And by 1902, reference comes of age with the publication of Alice Kroeger's *Guide to Reference* (American Library Association). By this time, the reference paradigm in both service and publication is firmly established. Reference is now a recognized part of any library's service. It has its own department, a mission, a staff, and a budget. And with Kroeger's

Guide to Reference, there is a publication that documents this shift and allows libraries to follow its recommendations.

FROM ANALOG TO DIGITAL

One way to look at the development of reference in the 20th century is as a journey from analog to digital. The century begins with ideas like standardized card catalogs, periodical indexes, almanacs, and subject encyclopedias, and it ends with widely available databases and electronic collections of books, journals, and reference publications.

The National Union Catalog Pre 1956 Imprints may seem like a dusty museum piece holding up the wall between cataloging and reference, but it represents an amazing idea in reference services. In 1901, Herbert Putnam, then Librarian of Congress, writes: "The Library of Congress expects to place in each great center of research in the United States a copy of every card which it prints for its own catalogues…" (NUC, 1968, Introduction). What is evident from this powerful statement is the notion of access to information, distributed to libraries and their users in a standardized format. It sounds a lot like the implementation of World-Cat in either its native interface or as worldcat. org. This idea also leads to the development of consortial systems like *OhioLINK* in Ohio or *Melvyl* in California.

These networks are important because of what they bring to the library as well as to its users. Their partnerships transform a smaller library into a statewide resource and allow the shared buying power of the network to purchase or lease materials that otherwise would be too expensive for individual libraries. In the end, users, libraries, and producers of content all benefit from a consortial arrangement.

In addition to the catalog, other sources have an analog start which then grows into an online source. Subject-specific periodical indexes begin in printed form and become databases. Some examples are the Engineering Index which starts in 1884 and eventually grows into Compendex. Psychological Abstracts begins publication in 1872 and becomes PsycINFO. Chemical Abstracts commences in 1902 and evolves into SciFinder Scholar. Similarly, encyclopedias, dictionaries, almanacs, yearbooks, and other reference sources make the journey from initial publication in print to eventual electronic expression.

Subject encyclopedias, with their scholarly articles and in-depth bibliographies also had an early history in print which slowly transitioned to digital. Macmillan's 1937 *Encyclopedia of the Social Sciences* is an early example of a definitive subject encyclopedia. Examples from other disciplines include *The Encyclopedia of Education* (Macmillan, 1971), *The Encyclopedia Judaica* (Macmillan, 1973), and *The Encyclopedia of Religion* (Macmillan, 1986). Today, while many subject encyclopedias are still available in print, most offer an electronic counterpart. The 2010 publications of Greenwood Press's *Toys and American Culture* and SAGE's *Encyclopedia of Motherhood* are also excellent examples of subject encyclopedias available in both formats. The digital versions, however, may stray from their print counterparts. Consider, for example, ABC-CLIO's award-winning Pop Culture Universe database, a regularly updated digital edition consisting of several Greenwood and ABC-CLIO print encyclopedias as well as numerous Web-exclusive features not found in the books.

Today the card catalog is no longer held in the esteem it once was. In its heyday, it was a major reference tool. But the idea of the creation of an accurate description of an item, and a pointer to its location, was an important milestone in the movement from analog to digital. Only when we are able to understand the definition of an analog item and its digital simulacrum, can we begin to understand the shift in reference publishing. The digital item may simulate the analog one, but it is fundamentally different in form and function. It is not limited in physical space, and the orderly systems and assumptions developed over millennia–such as, for example, numeric pages, A-Z order, access in one location only, not available for checkout, et cetera—no longer apply.

REFERENCE BOOKS: OLD MODEL

In order to fully grasp the concept of an electronic reference source, we need to first characterize a printed one. In *Managing the Reference Collection*, Christopher W. Nolan describes some of the key characteristics of a reference collection (Nolan, 1999):

- Reference departments and their collections are usually located in very prominent locations.
- Expenditures for reference materials make up a significant portion of most libraries' budgets.
- Reference librarians use the reference collection and the library's catalog as the principal tools for aiding users who seek help.
- Users ascribe considerable authority to this collection.

In other words, the old model of reference is that the most authoritative sources are in the best real estate in the library, along with a librarian among those stacks waiting to help. There is a certain elegance to this model. Library users of all types—from young students to scholars—have always known where to start their research. "Because many users start their information searches with indexes, encyclopedias, and bibliographies, what they find cited in the reference collection influences what materials they will retrieve from the remainder of the collection (or what items they will request via interlibrary loan). *The reference collection is the demand generator for the entire collection, its leading edge*" (Nolan, 1999, p. 2). The last sentence of Nolan's statement is an actual quote from David Majka's 1996 *Reference Services Review* article.

In the old model, reference books were preferred starting points. They were, in Nolan's own words, surrogates for other sources (Nolan, 1999, p. 10). They functioned as a tertiary literature, to summarize and act as pointers to the primary and secondary literatures. The authority that users ascribed to this collection has always been supported by librarians' use and attitude about the reference collection.

As much as librarians want to ascribe authority and objectivity to reference works, uncertainty, errors, and even nationalism can be found in them. Probably the most notable example of nationalistic misinformation can be seen with the *Great Soviet Encyclopedia*. Originally published in the Soviet Union as *Entsiklopedicheskii muzykal'nyi slovar'* in 1959, Macmillan translated it and published the third edition in 1973, retaining its dubious "facts."

Factual errors in reference books are not common, but still, attitudes and opinions towards reference books have changed. Even by the 1990's, belief in authoritative reference books was declining (Katz, 1998, p. 10). The Internet's promise of fast, easy, and accurate information has made reference sources look like they are hard to use, and there is a perception that they are no more accurate than the general Web. An interesting example of the high regard in which reference books are held appeared in the March 13, 2001 *New York Times*. Zick Rubin Googled himself, and found that Wikia.com had him listed as deceased. The site's editor would not change the listing because the Dictionary of Psychology (Reber and Reber, 2001) had a date of death for him. Rubin goes on to say "Needless to say, I had to take this report seriously. This was not just some unreliable wiki, but a bona fide reference work by a respected publisher that has been around even longer than I have." Finally he was able to convince the site editor that he "was a reliable source on my own existence" (Rubin, 2011, p. 11).

REFERENCE PRODUCTS: NEW MODEL

As previously described, a reference book used to imply an authoritative, printed summary of what is known about a given subject. It was intended to be consulted, not necessarily read cover to cover. "Electronic reference source," on the other hand, is its digital counterpart not intended to be read all the way through but to be used for looking up something specific (technology allows for this). Like the book, which Fred Kilgour describes as "a storehouse of human knowledge intended for dissemination…" (Kilgour, 1998, p. 3), an electronic resource also "stores" knowledge but in a much broader, less-contained way. A key question emerges here: When the item breaks free of its binding, is it still a book?

If we pause here and consider that "reference" is a legacy word, a leftover from the old model, all sorts of new issues come to light. If we were to re-conceptualize libraries with only the new digital model in mind, would there still be a reference section of the physical library? What if there were no libraries and we set out to create them, what would they look like in this new environment?

From 1981 and 2001, Ziff Davis Publishing produced a detailed printed guide to the software and hardware industries called *Data Sources*. What if electronic reference sources were called "data sources," and what if the work of helping users find, evaluate, and use information had a different, more "contemporary" name? A more popular and easier-to-understand name comes to mind here, like, for example, the Geek Squad—the name of the company that fixes computers and electronics. Many people confuse the term "research librarian" with "reference librarian" anyway. Perhaps a whole new approach is necessary to better reflect the new image of the librarian as someone who is more of a "biblio-technician" or simply an "answer guy" rather than a "reference librarian."

Furthermore, a paradigm shift takes a new product into a new venue. To validate this we need not go further than to think of the shift from codex to book. The change in format fundamentally changes the use. With a book versus a codex, the contents are easier to read anywhere. It is easier to refer to, and it achieves wider use. These arguments sound like the same points that e-book reader enthusiasts make in contrast to printed works today, and in all fairness, they are valid ones.

How, then, are the electronic reference sources different from their printed analogs? First, they are not bound to a place—the traditional concept of printed reference collection no longer holds. Traditionally, printed reference books could not be checked out. In some more forward-thinking libraries, reference books may now be checked out, but this is a recent phenomenon. The notion of "checked out" also becomes obsolete. The idea of a monograph or an item that is published once is also changing because electronic products undergo continuous revisions of their content, making them more current. Reference sources are also packaged together online. Good examples of such packages include Oxford Reference Online (a central online place housing many different Oxford University Press reference titles) or Gale Virtual Reference Library (a platform housing thousands of works by a wide spectrum of publishers).

Also noteworthy has been an erosion of free authoritative sources on the Internet. Nolan states that "in light of our knowledge that users will often choose incorrect but convenient information over accurate but inconvenient sources, reference collection selectors must choose only the most authoritative trustworthy sources for this collection" (Nolan, 1999, p. 12). The challenge of ensuring accuracy of information in the Internet age makes the problem of authority in the old model almost quaint.

When "all of the above" is taken into consideration, an electronic reference source may be summed up as followed: It is published electronically and thus available anywhere there is a network connection. Great care has been taken to ensure accuracy and currency of its content.

It may be under continual revision or as part of a package comprising other authored or edited works. It is intended for users to refer to it rather than to read it all the way through. Nolan states that an electronic reference source is "a source designed for consultation rather than continuous reading, predominantly composed of ordered files arranged to facilitate rapid retrieval of pieces of information" (Nolan, 1999, p. 5).

As Keith Webster states in his article in *Refer* on evaluating printed reference sources, "Internet-based resources are available around the clock, irrespective of library opening hours or the location of the end-user. They allow simultaneous use, are not vulnerable to theft or deterioration, are easily updated by publishers and, above all, [they] are located precisely where our users' workflows take place" (Webster, 2010). This change provides an opportunity for better service, but it also presents challenges. Some of them include the following: How do users get to a librarian? How do users discover what their library owns? And finally, how do librarians and publishers make their products and services more visible to users?

Such questions are the crux of the matter for providing reference services in a virtual environment. In for users to "discover" a librarian, libraries need to invest in their marketing and outreach efforts as well as their online and on-campus presence. The library's website should be user friendly and keep up with technological advances and an institution should establish a presence in social networking outlets like Facebook or Twitter. That presence should not just be a "fan page," but it should have a clear focus on trying to connect with the patrons. If possible, a librarian should be assigned to take care of the library's Facebook page and to keep it up to date with current library happenings.

To help users learn about the available resources, the library should continue or expand its library instruction and information literacy programs. Those programs should cover sources relevant to the information needs of the students. For example, business students should learn about EBSCO's Business Source Complete or ProQuest's ABI/Inform, and pre-medical students should be familiar with PubMed. In addition, Libguides (www.libguides.com) have become an increasingly popular venue to let users know about available products. Libraries can customize them to help meet the information needs of their clientele.

A seamless remote access to the library's electronic products is also beneficial for the users. For example, successful linking to online products where a user has a simple login or IP verification of access is preferred. These potential technical pitfalls need to be worked out beforehand, always with the user in mind. To attract patrons, libraries must make it clear how to log into the products online, and they must make it easy for patrons to use their products remotely in order to keep them.

Libraries are still adjusting to all these rapid changes. They now have fewer items in their printed reference collections—many have abandoned print altogether. Materials are regularly weeded and moved to circulating collections or to off-site storage facilities. Libraries are also now more focused on their core services, which now include, among many others, personalized reference service by appointment. They are also more focused on effective information literacy instruction and Reader's Advisory (RA) functions in public libraries. All these new approaches require flexibility in staffing and proficiency in personal and electronic communication styles. They also present challenges to the reference budget. Standing orders for print materials have to be re-evaluated, the costs for packaged sets have to be built into the budget, and allowances need to be made for costly, subscription-based e-reference products.

CONCLUSION

Electronic reference sources may retain some of the characteristics of printed reference books, and they may continue to be sought after because of their authority. Readers may still seek them out for objectivity, accuracy, and content, particularly against the "anything goes" backdrop of general Internet-provided information. However, unlike the physical book, which *The Smithsonian Book of Books* defined as something that "retained its almost magical hold on the imagination and intellect" (Olmert, 1992, p. 19), electronic reference may not hold the same charm as print reference. Therefore, the challenge for the library and publishing industry remains to bring the best features of the old formats into a new model, while enhancing user's access to content from anywhere and at any time.

Much is gained in this transformation from print to electronic, but some things are also undoubtedly lost. The typesetter's craft is a lost art, and many older library users lament the passing of the card catalog. As Elmer Johnson states in the 1995 Scarecrow title *History of libraries in the Western World,* "But somewhere in this midst of this super-mechanization, this Jules Verne world of information storage and retrieval, let us hope that there will always be a place for the ordinary book – and with it the ordinary librarian – the individual who knows books and who finds supreme satisfaction in bringing a book and a reader together. The human element has always been uppermost in the history of books and libraries: let us hope that it always remains that way" (Michael Harris, 1995, p. 498). Indeed, the human element will remain critical as this paradigm becomes the new normal for both reference products and reference services.

REFERENCES

Frost, W. J. (2005). *The reference collection: From the shelf to the web*. Binghamton, NY: Haworth Information Press.

Harris, M. H. (1999). *History of libraries in the western world* (4th ed.). Lanham, MD & London, UK: Scarecrow.

Horowitz, M. C. (2005). *New dictionary of the history of ideas*. New York, NY: Charles Scribner's Sons.

Johnson, E. D. (1970). *History of libraries in the western world* (2nd ed.). Metuchen, NJ: Scarecrow Press.

Katz, B. (1998). *Cuneiform to computer: A history of reference sources*. Lanham, MD: Scarecrow Press.

Kilgour, F. G. (1998). *The evolution of the book*. New York, NY: Oxford University Press.

Kuhn, T. (1962). *The structure of scientific revolutions*. Chicago, IL: University of Chicago Press.

Library of Congress and American Library Association. (1968). *The national union catalog, pre-1956 imprints: A cumulative author list representing Library of Congress printed cards and titles reported by other American libraries*. London, UK: Mansell.

Nolan, C. W. (1999). *Managing the reference collection*. Chicago, IL: American Library Association.

Olmert, M. (1992). *The Smithsonian book of books* (1st ed.). Washington, DC: Smithsonian Books.

Oxford University Press. (1989). *Oxford English dictionary*.

Rettig, J. (1992). *Distinguished classics of reference publishing*. Phoenix, AZ: Oryx Press.

Rothstein, S. (1989). The development of the concept of reference service in American libraries, 1850-1900. *The Library Quarterly, 23*(1), 1–15. doi:10.1086/617934

Rubin, Z. (2011, March 13). How the internet tried to kill me. *New York Times,* p. 11.

Webster, K. (2010). Evaluating printed reference sources: Apostscript. *Refer, 26*(1)

Wiegand, W. A., & Davis, D. G. (1994). *Encyclopedia of library history.* New York, NY: Garland Pub.

Chapter 2
The Impact of Electronic Reference Content and Discovery on Publishers

Peter Tobey
Salem Press, USA

ABSTRACT

The introduction of electronic reference sources has changed the landscape for publishers of traditional, vetted reference content. Sharing content, simultaneous use, pricing electronic content for a fair reward, accountability for product use, patron-driven selection of content, and the importance of content discovery are several of the issues and challenges that publishers are grappling with. These issues and challenges are presented from a publisher's perspective and serve as an introduction to the myriad issues with electronic reference discovery and context.

INTRODUCTION

The purpose of this chapter is to give librarians a view of reference from a publisher's perspective, with special emphasis on how discovery impacts publishing companies. Which is to say, the chapter offers a fairly general description of the reference landscape, especially how it has and will continue to change, grow, and of course,

in part, shrink. These changes impact libraries, librarians, patrons, students and teachers, and as such, cause much discussion. Here though, the focus is on the business of reference from the publishing side of things. The hope is that with an understanding of some of the challenges the business poses, publishers may help librarians make better, more informed choices.

Specifically, questions surrounding the discoverability of content impact publishers in ways that are different from the impact on libraries. The

DOI: 10.4018/978-1-61350-308-9.ch002

influences involved aren't immediately obvious to those who operate outside the business of making and selling reference. So, some sort of brief overview of the business will be helpful as context. Thereafter, there will be some attempt to comment intelligently as to how a) discoverability impacts publishers, and b) how publishers impact discoverability.

The core caveat here is that this is one reference publisher's observations. They bubble out of experiences with print reference, database and e-book publishing, direct selling, and licensing. There is some diversity to this experience, but – like all experience – it is limited. Still, to a certain extent, every publisher is walking in roughly the same direction: toward broader, more effective use of each publisher's content. All this is because broader and more effective use drives the sale of our products.

Put another way, the reference biome is diverse, with product types and distribution channels galore. What's more, the proliferation of electronic formats (for want of a better word) only adds to the diversity. This multiplicity of formats is a complicating factor in collection development efforts of every kind. It is also downright vexing to publishers for a wide variety of reasons.

SHARING

Libraries are about sharing, an admirable tradition whether we're talking about siblings or communities. In times when libraries' primary function was to collect and then make printed things generally available, a great deal of use was gained from sharing a single thing: the printed reference book. These tomes were costly and thus, not usually purchased by consumers, but useful and therefore perfect for collective access. However, the physical nature of the product and the subject matter involved acted as a perfect anchor. One person, in one place could read one volume at a time. (There were and are exceptions to this – inter-

library lending, for instance, but the single-format, single-location, single-user model ruled.)

Today content is distributed to libraries in a wide number of formats. Print continues to hang in there, but database and e-book distribution grow daily and in ways that are more dizzying than meets the eye, and getting dizzier. The idea of "re-purposing" content, of using it in a number of products, has become the norm. As a result, publishers routinely publish the same content in print, online in databases, and in e-book form. So, from a product-design standpoint, there are multiple packages for the same content.

Librarians are aware of this re-purposed content. They see the same material in print and electronic products, both database and e-book, and wonder at the array of prices and terms of access that shower from every publishing house. If fact, virtually every reference publisher has heard the complaint that all this diversity is merely a way to trick libraries into buying the same content twice. This writer isn't going to speak for the entire industry on this matter. However, the intent of most of us is to a) make our content available in whatever form libraries wish to purchase it, and b) try not to bet on any one horse (format, delivery method, discoverability strategy, etc.) because there is no telling how many of the steeds will actually finish the race, much less win it.

To further confound things, non-exclusive distribution rights to content often are licensed to multiple database aggregators. (Full disclosure: Salem Press, the writer's employer, is owned by EBSCO Publishing, a leading database aggregator.) Even more commonly, e-books are distributed either by the publisher directly to libraries or *via* e-book distributors such as NetLibrary, ebrary, Gale Virtual Reference Library, et cetera. This means that the several electronic versions of any given content are available in multiple formats from several sources.

So that you not think this complexity is solely the result of electronic publishing, there are distribution mazes for print, too. Libraries buy reference from catalogs, from salespeople and telemarketers, directly from publishers, and through wholesalers, online and off. The pricing, shipping, discounting, and general management of the printed things rivals the electronic ones for gnarly diversity.

SIMULTANEOUS USE

Electronic consumption of reference adds another dimension to the mix: simultaneous use. There was a time when "simultaneous use" of a book meant reading to the daughter in your lap. The physicality of the content metered – at least to some extent – the number of readers who could enjoy the thing. Reading books was a linear experience, one set of eyeballs at a time. So, like 33-1/3 record albums, the value of a single version of the product had a specific limit. Ultimately, the audience was limited by the clunkiness of an actual book. If you had a larger audience you needed to buy two books.

No more. Electronic distribution of content provides that content, if necessary, simultaneously to as many users as are authorized to view it. And there are, essentially, no significant additional costs associated with an additional simultaneous user. Nothing needs to be written, printed, or shipped to enable that additional user. From a purely technical standpoint, this is frictionless sharing.

Not surprisingly, librarians sometimes view the almost-free quality of one additional e-book or broader database access as reason to question various publishers' pricing models. The question appears to be intuitively obvious, but is in fact not so. Once again, reasonable people might conclude that the complexities of various subscription and perpetual access models are intended to obfuscate as much as recoup costs and fairly reward content developers. And, in some quarters that may be true. But pricing the ethereal is tricky, especially when identical content also exists in a 60-pound, 12-volume, library-bound, printed set. It's the same content. But its purchasers and users respond to its different forms, differently. It is perceived differently and used differently.

FAIR REWARD

Even if one puts aside the business imperative to maximize profits, establishing a price for a reference work remains a complex task for a publisher. Begin with a consideration of cost allocation. When reference was only printed, one could make a reasonable guess at how many of the printed things might be sold, calculate the editorial costs of creating the content, and do some long division to figure out what each book's editorial costs were. The same process worked for other costs such as printing, sales, rent, et cetera. But cost allocation in the new reference world is much more problematic.

To begin, there is a wide variety of pricing models for the various versions of any given content because the different distribution channels behave differently. A database aggregator has an entirely different sense of the value of any one reference work in a large database than does a print wholesaler or e-book distributor. All these channels charge their customers differently and so pay publishers differently for the content they license/purchase. Going into the details of the different pricing models might prove this point, but is way too tedious. Suffice it to say, access to a single printed book is priced differently from access to a database that provides unlimited simultaneous use to tens of thousands of students. Layer the confusion that finite simultaneous e-book access adds ("no more than three simultaneous users") and pricing gets weird.

The previous paragraph might easily be taken as sleight of hand, an effort to gloss over an issue that is near and dear to the hearts of librarians. For instance, the common pricing model, based on full time enrollment (FTE) irks lots of institutions, and it is far from a perfect method, but it isn't disconnected from the realities of the publishing and distribution world. Consider, for instance, a publisher of a popular scholarly journal whose business was built on the sale of print subscriptions. A great journal, with good sales to colleges and universities of reasonable size, this publisher is now faced with providing that journal electronically across all the campuses of a large university or in every branch of a big city library. Where once he might have sold several pricey subscriptions, he is now faced with potentially less revenue; at the same time he is delivering far greater access, discoverability and use. The FTE model was developed to address just this issue. Viewed from the challenging desk of a scholarly journal publisher one can imagine why this model was developed. There is, after all, a central fairness to it.

To re-state this in a slightly more blunt way, when librarians see multiple versions of the same thing they suspect skullduggery. When asked to pay based on an FTE model they wonder if the rate is fair, based on likely use. But when a publisher adds electronic access to his print product, he begins competing with himself (at least to some extent). Buyers of the electronic product almost never buy the print, too. These two viewpoints are both valid and tend to conflict with one another.

Think how you'd feel if you owned a large movie theatre. Your deal with a movie producer is to share in the revenue from each seat occupied. But movie-goers start to complain: projecting the movie on the screen costs the same whether the theatre has three people in it or is full. So why should everyone have to pay for their seat? Is the answer to this dilemma to build lots of very small theatres?

The nest of pricing models in the reference world, combined with uncertain access (and even more uncertain use) is important because it complicates publishers' financial analysis of their own products. Librarians should both know and care about that analysis because it greatly influences the price they pay for things. If a publisher has

some basic formula in mind for the reasonable and fair profitability of a reference work, the next chore is guessing at sales, licensing, access, and use *via* all the channels and all the formats of that content. Given the baffling number of product formats and equally complicating number of sales channels for those products, guessing at revenue, allocating costs, and then determining prices for all the different forms of the thing is a very difficult thing to do.

PRINTING IS CHEAP

By the way, many reference publishers spend a great deal of money developing their editorial content. Often, this process requires scores of contributors and several years. At the same time, employees, rent, phones, and keeping the lights turned on costs plenty. So, when at long last a reference product (book, database, and e-book version) is published, the printing of the thing is – proportionately – usually very small. In fact, it is often the smallest category of costs a publisher encounters. (A relatively small printing cost is one of the many counter-intuitive truisms of reference publishing.) Which is why, when pondering pricing for an apparently vaporous product (an e-book or database) publishers don't think much about the printing costs that are saved so much as they think about recouping the editorial costs of creating the content in the first place.

ROBBING PETER TO PAY PAUL

One final note on this conundrum. It will come as no surprise to anyone reading this that reference is in flux. The effect of the rapid changes in how content is delivered only adds to the uncertainty publishers face. There is no doubt, for instance, that database and e-book publishing is displacing some traditional print sales. It's likely that these electronic distribution methods are increasing use.

They are certainly increasing access. But it's not clear how the various pricing models will dovetail (during ever-changing distribution patterns) to result in fair and sustainable profitability levels.

Again, this really does matter to librarians. If prices are set too high (even for the best of reasons), things aren't sold and publishers go out of business. If prices are set too low, even if things are sold, publishers may go out of business. If publishers vanish, librarians end up with fewer choices.

ACCOUNTABILITY AND DISCOVERY

The steady migration from printed reference to electronic resources has had many repercussions. For the purposes of this chapter, the focus has been on content proliferation and the various business issues and models that impact libraries as a result of that proliferation. Underlying these issues is, of course, the discoverability of electronic content. It's ubiquitous distribution and availability is only marginally useful unless the content is discoverable. Not only does this go without saying, but this book is filled with a lot of saying about it. This writer's purpose is to put discoverability in a context of tumultuous change impacting publishers and so, per se, libraries. That is, what does discoverability mean to the relationship between publishers and libraries?

There are, of course, many, many answers to this question. Discovery services of all kinds are being created and made available so that search works across very broad and diverse collections. But, as you'll read elsewhere here, these services do their work in a wide variety of ways, providing very different experiences and search results. So librarians are paying very close attention to their functionality. That said, consider for a moment how a federated search or wide-ranging discovery service impacts publishers. Their influence is further reaching than immediately obvious.

Central to the issue is how databases keep track of the things they do. Whether an electronic resource is being "dished" as a database element or as an e-book, the server doing the dishing knows what it is distributing and to whom (more or less). So, electronic reference content that is being made available in libraries, and then is viewed by a student or patron, inherently includes in its use a record of that use. Unlike prior eras when librarians knew anecdotally what non-circulating reference was popular and used, they now know precisely what is popular and used.

It should be noted that these records don't always include good evidence of a user's satisfaction with the content they click through to, or even the relevance of the place they land. As everyone knows, searches lead us places that don't mean a thing. Still, they lead us there. So, usage reports aren't perfect. But they matter.

Most librarians now take for granted the database and e-book usage reports that are available to them. And many rely on these to guide their purchases and renewals. So publishers are interested in helping patrons, students, et cetera to find and use their content. Publishers are, all of a sudden, remarkably and precisely accountable for the use of their products. While this may not seem like a big change, it is. All of a sudden, what used to be non-circulating material (read "only vaguely accountable") is essentially a circulating product with absolute accountability.

DIRECT CONNECTIONS

Reference publishers are fond of saying they serve patrons. But they sell to librarians. So, traditionally, the connection between the user of the content and its acquisition relies on the interests, judgment, and awareness of librarians. Acquisitions traditionally have been made based on what patrons and students want and/or need and on the librarian's sense of what *should* be included in a collection. So, the collection development process, and its resulting purchase decisions, mostly went on between the ears of experienced librarians. With the advent of use-tracking software, combined with budget woes, purse string controllers are more and more interested in justifying purchases by demonstrating use. So, librarians are paying more and more attention to use and less attention to their personal sense of what constitutes a valuable addition to the reference desk.

To understand how this is so, consider the pharmaceutical industry. Not so very long ago, drug companies focused their sales and marketing efforts on physicians. The thinking was that educating doctors on the benefits of drugs would encourage them to prescribe them. (It should be noted that the effectiveness and absolute value of the prescription was not as important as the prescription itself.) Still, doctors were the marketing target. Today, the world is filled with advertising and marketing that is directed toward patients. Drug companies – to the extent they are allowed – now tout their cures directly to consumers. The interests, beliefs, and subsequent requests of patients now drive prescriptions. (In a sense, this is quite amazing.)

Librarians have traditionally acted as expert judges of quality and builders of balanced and appropriate collections for their communities. A great library had great things in it. But the patron-driven models that are emerging are shifting collection development influence and electronic use statistics are key in doing so. More and more, in libraries, use rules. On every level, and in ways we can't yet imagine, the use of content is now and will continue to be a very important part of the business of publishing reference. Great content, wonderful production values, terrific sales, and marketing are all important. But these things won't matter to publishers if the content is loved by librarians and not much used by students and patrons. The economics of librarianship will squeeze little-used content out of the mix in many libraries.

Librarians should be aware that this is happening to their world, which, interestingly, is in some ways good and in others, not so good. Publishers are keenly interested in partnering with libraries to promote the use of the content libraries have purchased or licensed from publishers and aggregators. Publishers want to work with librarians to get their content used so that the purchase of it makes sense and libraries will want to buy more of it. As mentioned before, this is an indirect form of patron-driven acquisition.

FRACTURED CONTENT

As a direct result of the accountability described above, librarians and publishers are progressively viewing their content in un-bundled, fractured ways. Whether or not librarians and publishers acknowledge as much, people actually using our content almost always did so one tidbit at a time. To cite an obvious and extreme example, who reads a dictionary? We read entries in them and move on. Progressively, we're all beginning to see that reference is used in this way, across the board. No one actually reads even a sizable fraction of the 12-volume classic, Salem Press' *Masterplots*. (This is a major, acclaimed, 60-year-old literary reference set now in its fourth edition.) They find what they need in the thing and use it. This was true in print and is even more so electronically.

Today, more often than not, *Masterplots* is not a single work of reference. It is, instead, a very large series of essays that live in a substantially larger database of similar essays. Users don't go to *Masterplots* for answers; they go to an online resource such as EBSCO's Literary Reference Center or Salem's online literature database where *Masterplots'* content is available, along with lots of other literary reference. Search results in this world may identify an article's source as *Masterplots*, but the chances that this will matter overmuch to a user are slim. Users are interested in material focused on their subject matter, the keyword in their search, and will value and use anything they find that expertly and coherently addresses their needs. (For the record, *Masterplots* is great at doing so.)

Still, it may well be that extended reference, such as any of Salem's multi-volume literary criticism, will find a lot of their use in searchable databases, useful only insofar as they are discovered, and valuable only to the extent they are used. Which leads, inevitably, to the question, "How should libraries pay for this content?" Current trends suggest that some form of patron-driven acquisition or pay-per-use might thrive. And the implication of this development would be that access (meaning availability) to information becomes secondary to its use.

We should all pause here. In a rather well-known essay in Wired, Robert Capps describes modern trends that increase use. The article's name is *The Good Enough Revolution*. The factors he posits lead to greater use: ease, low cost, and convenience. He makes a very strong argument that easy, quick, and good enough are all that's required, most of the time. Note that high quality is not among the factors he argues are important to most people. Libraries, of course, operate on different standards than the buyers of popular music or Flip video cameras. But, insofar as collections are influenced by use, the popular taste may well swamp the refined choice. Which is not a good thing. Expert selection, vetted collections, and quality matter. For those who don't think so, Wikipedia and Google have it all covered.

WALLED GARDENS

As is described elsewhere in this book, discovery services are enabling better and better searching of disparate, even competing databases and e-book collections. So the isolation that once existed for some databases is, happily, disappearing. Interestingly enough, this smoother and faster federated searching will make smaller, more vertical databases and e-book collections more useful and used, which is a good thing.

However, another not so distant trend is becoming clearer, further complicating the economics and discovery of content. That is the carefully controlled proprietary formats of Kindles, iPads, nooks, et cetera. This effort is clearly designed to maximize the sale of content through the device makers' storefronts. If you want to use a Kindle, buy from Amazon. All these devices support some open e-book standards, but they encourage their own formats. As e-readers extend their reach and libraries grapple with distributing content to them, the choices regarding acquisition and discoverability across these walled gardens will become more interesting.

DISCOVERY

All that said, the subject of this book, discovery, becomes critical to publishers and librarians as well as students and patrons. If use gains greater and greater sway over this marketplace and discovery drives use, then the discovery tools available and the guidance provided will control more and more of a library's collection. This will happen for sound scholarly and intellectual reasons. But, at the same time, the power of popularity may compromise the texture and coverage libraries offer. The economics of both reference publishing and librarianship will drive it in that direction. But, in helping to shape discovery processes, librarians should be aware that they are indirectly but substantially shaping their collections. More and more, what is used will flourish.

CODA

This last possibility, that use will overwhelm the value of quality selection and access to valuable content as the most important driving force in the world of reference, is disquieting. It implies that consumer-driven needs, both in content and proportion, may drive not just the use, price, and sale of content but also the development of content. This might mean we have lots of literary criticism of legal thrillers and much less of potential Pulitzer Prize winners. After all, legal thrillers sell like hotcakes.

Pause for a moment and consider what, exactly, it means when the precious, rare, and obscure becomes relatively worthless as a product. When the marketplace for elegant, little-known but wonderful content finds far less use than a recipe for the perfect scrambled egg? Has the value of a scrambled egg recipe suddenly grown far beyond the value of an essay explicating Rilke? We'll see.

Chapter 3
The Challenges of Discovering Online Research/ Reference Content:
An Introduction to the End User's Perspective

Anh Bui
HighWire Press, Stanford University, USA

ABSTRACT

"Discoverability" is the quality of being readily found by information seekers actively engaged in the search process. The path to discovery can vary based on a number of factors, including both external factors (such as accessibility issues) and ones specific to a particular user (such as the individual research habits of a given end user). However, the goal of finding efficiency within these discovery paths is universal. This chapter provides a broad outline of the problems of online research/reference content discoverability from the academic end-user perspective--in this case students in higher education and researchers. Starting with a look at common information seeking practices and the ways in which both "discovery failure" and "filter failure" can play a role, the primary challenges of new tools, content silos, accessibility, and loss of serendipity are reviewed within the context of end-user interviews, surveys, and studies conducted at Stanford University and elsewhere. The use of value signifiers—the signals that end-users look for to determine the relevance of found resources—is also discussed as an important part of the content evaluation and filtering process.

DOI: 10.4018/978-1-61350-308-9.ch003

INTRODUCTION

Publishers of academic reference content were early to recognize that by nature this content was inherently appropriate to digitize and distribute electronically. These works usually encompassed copious amounts of information that was ill-suited for the physical constraints of print, they were served well by frequent updates, they were used for quick lookups and strategic reading (rather than cover-to-cover reading), and they lent themselves well to organization as databases. Indeed online reference works abound, from collections such as Credo Reference, Gale Virtual Reference Library, Oxford Reference Online, SAGE Reference Online, and Springer Online Reference Works to stand-alone works such as the American Association of Pediatric's Red Book Online and the Oxford English Dictionary (OED).[1] It is not surprising then that users have shifted readily from print to online reference materials. "Many librarians have noticed a decline in use of print reference materials, with most patrons preferring the convenience and speed of online answers," Lindsey Schell notes (2011, p. 80) in advocating that librarians build their digital collections by looking at what users are already asking for online.

However, it is important to recognize that as information seekers become less interested in the container of information (a monograph vs. a traditional reference work vs. a review article) and focus instead on the currency and relevancy of the information contained, the term "reference content" has begun to evolve. It is now starting to include not just what we think of as traditional reference works (dictionaries, encyclopedias, medical handbooks) but also a fuller range of academic resource types and digital products that make information readily available to users in an organized fashion. It may be more fruitful to think less about reference works as containers than as just one target of the pursuit of reference information. It is this pursuit that is central to the user and, therefore, should be construed as the larger context in which to understand user behavior. For these reasons, the exploration of discoverability challenges in this chapter will focus on the broader construct of "research/reference content" and the way in which end users still face a host of barriers in finding relevant information. Further, bearing in mind that not all users seeking information are the same, this chapter will focus on students in higher education and researchers as a specific type of end user and key constituents for research and reference content.

Understanding users and their often heterogeneous workflows and information consumption habits is an important step toward understanding why discovering appropriate content can be difficult. It is possible to divide the problems encountered by digital research/reference content seekers into two broad categories. The first—"discovery failure"—is the failure to find any content. The second—Clay Shirky's "filter failure"—is the failure to find relevant or valuable content. This chapter provides a look into these failures more closely, examining the challenges users face that might contribute to them, within the context of the information practices currently in common use by information seekers in higher education, including undergraduates, graduate students, post-doctorates, and faculty. To do this, a number of important studies that have emerged recently examining the changing behaviors of students in using digital content in general are examined. Of particular note is the work done by JISC[2] and the Research Information Network[3] in the United Kingdom, as well as Project Information Literacy[4] out of the University of Washington's Information School. These groups have conducted longer term studies and broad surveys of student and researcher behavior to extract hard data about how users consume digital information. HighWire Press has also conducted a series of in-depth interviews of researchers from the Stanford University community, across multiple disciplines.[5] The findings corroborate the data gathered by other studies in this area, and this chapter draws on the insights they offer to provide illustrations of the discovery challenges users face.

THE DISCOVERY PROCESS AND WHERE IT FAILS

Common Discovery Practices

"Google is the universal access to almost everything." This comment came from a professor in chemistry who has been teaching for more than 30 years, and it illustrates just how pervasively discovery practices have boiled down to one type of tool: Web-scale search. Indeed, studies repeatedly show that large majorities of information seekers turn to Internet search engines for their academic information needs. In speaking with scholars, HighWire found researchers using Google not just to search for new information, but as a database of known information that they could mine as they would their personal libraries. One researcher even gave up the use of citation manager software in favor of using Google to maintain citation information. Head and Eisenberg of Project Information Literacy found in a 2010 survey of 8,353 college students that 92% use search engines for their course-related research (Head, 2010). A JISC review of a dozen surveys on information seeking behavior by students found that search, especially Google, is a dominant discovery tool (Connaway, 2010). Librarians surveyed by High-Wire in 2009 on e-book discovery behaviors also overwhelmingly listed Internet search engines as significant or very significant tools for discovery.[6] Additionally, a study in 2009 found that "when using freely available Internet resources, Google is top of the list, followed by Google Scholar, Wikipedia, and YouTube. Participants' decisions about which resources to use were based on their prior knowledge and experience with a resource and a belief that resources provided by Google and Google Scholar are reliable and relevant and most of all always return a list of results" (Connaway, 2010, p. 28).

The dominance of the Web-scale search engine, however, may be exaggerated. As Head and Eisenberg noted:

Notably, almost all students reported turning to course readings first—not to search engines such as Google, as assumed by some librarians and educators. In addition, students consulted Wikipedia to a lesser extent than they used instructors, scholarly research databases, search engines, and course readings when completing research for courses. (Head, 2010, p.8)

In other words, research is not confined to using large, Web-scale search engines. In some cases, talking with an instructor or browsing through a course list for resources is even more useful. These are forms of heightened filtering, providing limited scope and high value. It's important to mention these other methods to underscore how layered and heterogeneous the discovery process can be, and also to acknowledge that improving discovery by improving Web-scale search engines can only be part of the picture.

There is also evidence that habits strongly inform process. Head and Eisenberg also found that "the data provides strong evidence that students are driven by familiarity and habit, and that they use the same set of information resources in a very similar order of preference for course-related and everyday life research" (Head, 2010, p. 8). HighWire interviews with researchers bore this out: they tended to gravitate toward familiar databases and search engines even when they knew that the source they used was not comprehensive. For instance, one science researcher said that she knew books and reference material were excluded from her favorite abstract and indexing database, but she preferred to use it anyway. In other cases, users were simply unaware of the databases or discovery tools that were available specifically for their areas, leading to a double discovery deficit in cases where the database might be the only place that aggregated such information.

Almost universally, studies and interviews show that the process of discovery is also driven by the need for efficiency. In their 2010 study, Head and Eisenberg concluded that:

many of today's college students, no matter where they are enrolled and no matter what they are studying, adopt a strategic approach to their information-seeking research. Students use a strategy driven by efficiency and predictability in order to manage and control a staggering amount of information that is available to them in college settings. Moreover, students consciously manage their research tasks and activities within the constraints of the course-related research process (i.e., time, grades, professor's expectations). (Head, 2010, p. 35)

Similarly, the JISC review found that "speed and convenience are major factors" (Connaway, 2009, p.32) for users. Underscoring the broader context in which the discovery tasks are undertaken, one graduate student in English interviewed by HighWire noted: "It's really about efficiency because doing the literature review is only one step of the process." Another reason why efficiency is a premium is the sheer scope of the information that might be available. One post-doc in biology noted that research "takes less time but more time," pointing to the problem of being able to quickly find more information leading to having to spend more time culling or filtering through it.

Indeed the speed with which people find information can lead to two corollary behaviors: squirreling away discovered information without actually using it, and consuming discovered information in small chunks only. A number of the researchers interviewed by HighWire noted that they routinely gather information in the discovery process that they then do not read. One chemistry professor noted: "Of the things that I actually get to the point of downloading, I'll bet you I don't read more than one out of 50." Indeed, a CIBER 2008 study of academic journal content users similarly showed that "very little time is spent using content." Academic users will "squirrel away content in the form of downloads" (Connaway, 2010, p. 20). However, there is no evidence that all of these downloads are read beyond what it took to determine whether to download them.

In parallel, information seekers are consuming information in smaller chunks. It may be that the early advent of traditional online reference content has in turn inspired the desire and habit of consuming smaller bits of information across the board. (It certainly seems that research/reference content is well-suited to this atomization.) Alternatively, it may be that faced with so much information, users can only consume small pieces. Whatever the cause, "people dip and read, liking quick chunks of information. People make short visits and do power browsing" (Connaway, 2010, p.34). Moreover, "researchers from undergraduate student to professor share this characteristic" (Connaway, 2010, p. 20). HighWire's interview subjects corroborated these findings, with one historian commenting: "There's so much written these days, they say that Milton was perhaps the last person to have been able to read everything that was written at a given moment. We can no longer do that, even within the weird little subfields that we work on."

This leads to another key discovery practice: reference tracking. One of those "quick chunks of information" is the references section or bibliography of an academic or other reference work. Following the reference trail is an important method for both discovering and filtering content, for students and professors alike:

One of the most frequent routines students we interviewed used was going to Wikipedia as a starting point. Nearly half the students interviewed used Wikipedia for the hypertext-linked bibliography at the bottom of most entries for finding sources. Most described Wikipedia as a source to get them started, and they definitely continued with their research, often using library databases. (Head, 2010, p. 20)

Researchers interviewed by HighWire also overwhelmingly indicated that following citations was a critical part of their discovery process.

Unfortunately, all of these common discovery practices do not necessarily result in a successful outcome, and the result is that "discovery failure" and/or "filter failure" come into play.

Discovery Failure

In an age when "information overload" is a given, it is sometimes difficult to remember that the problem of failing to find information on a given topic is still a very real one. Missing something important in one's field is for some researchers (notably those conducting more advanced research) a much greater concern than the concern about having to weed through too many irrelevant results. A 2006 study by RIN found that "the main concern for most researchers is the fear that inadequacies in a particular discovery service or in their own expertise, or lack of time, might lead them to miss something significant for their research" (p. 8). Researchers in particular who are seeking very esoteric information in "those weird little subfields", for instance, still have difficulty finding what they think might be out there on that subject or at least ascertaining for certain that nothing is out there. Even with the advent and might of Google and other Web-scale search engines that allow a very wide body of information to be accessed at a user's fingertips, researchers can still be flummoxed, for instance, by the inadequacy of search terms to capture the nature of the information they are seeking, the inability to formulate the right search query, or the fact that the Web search engine may not index the needed source materials. Users might find that the results of their searches are not actually about the topic they thought they searched on. As one biology professor put it: "Some topics cannot be expressed in a series of keywords. Google is unsatisfactory for finding results on this kind of topic. One has to be broadly read in order to know where to start

to find literature on this kind of topic. Students don't understand the complexities of literature searching and they assume that if they can't find anything with a few keywords it doesn't exist."

Digital content, as ubiquitous as it may seem, is sometimes not discoverable by the tools that users have grown to rely upon for their research. Federated search is a source of confusion for student library users (Connaway, 2009), Google largely does not directly index content that is not free to access (as much reference content is not), and a lack of awareness about the availability of digital content can all get in the way of a fruitful search. Another researcher in statistics interviewed by HighWire noted that one of the problems with technology is that one can waste a lot of time trying different variations on a search that do not return anything new, and that often the scope of a particular database is unknown: "you don't know what is in the database, so you don't know when you've done a complete search. "

Filter Failure

As real as the problem of discovery failure may continue to be, focus in recent years has understandably shifted to the problem described in this way by one associate professor in statistics interviewed by HighWire: "Searching can take a lot of time, and Google and Google Scholar are quite good, and it is easy to find references on any topic, but it can be difficult to find the most useful references or the seminal work on a topic." It is increasingly rare (though certainly still possible) to conduct a search on a major search engine and come up completely empty-handed. The greater problem for many is to figure out if what was revealed in the discovery process actually yields any value, which is sometimes a tiresome and cumbersome exercise. For instance, one researcher interviewed by HighWire compared using Google to "crushing rock. You lose the delight of discovery in grinding through stuff."

It has become a truism that as the Web and its myriad sister technologies have become part of our every day existence, we are all plagued with information overload—that we are constantly bombarded by so much information, that we have trouble figuring out what is important. However, it has also become a truism ever since Clay Shirky declared it at a Web 2.0 conference in 2008 that "it's not information overload; it's filter failure." As he put it, "talking about information overload is a distraction—what has changed is that the filters that we've used for the past 500 years have broken. We need to rethink them." These two concepts—information overload and filter failure – are not mutually exclusive. Shirky's statement just reframes the problem as one of not having the right tools or skills. For users who feel as though they are drowning in too much information, the solution is not to get out of the water; it's to learn to swim.

To extend the metaphor, publishers and other purveyors of content have been quite interested in providing swimming lessons or even isolated life-rafts ("Come use our tools exclusively for your research needs!") over the years. The advantage for publishers is clear: if the exhausted or confused information seeker finds a haven in the publisher's academic resource, the publisher has gained a customer and habits form accordingly. In other words, if the information provided turns out to be the right fit—accurate enough, relevant enough, timely enough—then the reader is not only satisfied, he is likely to keep returning to that resource and that method. The challenge is to determine how to bring that reader and that resource together, or as Shirky might have it, the challenge is to find the right filter. The right filter can come from the end user (applying best practices, knowledge, and tools) or it can come from the purveyor of the content (also applying best practices and tools).

Another term that has been used to describe the problem is "discovery deficit" (coined by Cameron Neylon). This refers not to having too much information, not to having too much irrelevant information, but rather not having the right bit of information at the right time. As Neylon noted: "We don't need more filters or better filters in scholarly communications—we don't need to block publication at all. Ever. What we need are tools for curation and annotation and re-integration of what is published. And a framework that enables discovery of the right thing at the right time. And the data that will help us to build these. The more data, the more research published, the better. Which is actually what Shirky was saying all along…"

In the end, filter failure is a failure of efficiency. "Finding the data is easy," says another HighWire interviewee, a professor of medicine. "It's reading that takes a lot of time. Better search techniques would result in less wasted time."

Is it possible that this second problem—too much information to sort through—may also be feeding the inability to find information? One interesting phenomenon at least one broad survey has found is that "virtually all students intentionally make use of a small compass for traversing the ever-widening and complex information landscape they inhabit, whether they are finding information for course work or for use in their daily lives" (Head, 2010, p. 8). In other words, as noted earlier, they are forming habits around fewer trusted tools to seek information in what may be a conscious effort to reduce the amount they discover.

PRIMARY CHALLENGES TO DISCOVERY

Training and New Tools

As noted earlier, habits play a large role in how researchers seek information. Those habits can be formed within the context of academic research or within the broader context of general research for the questions that come up in daily life. As the lines between information containers and resources continue to blur (e.g., you might use Wikipedia to find an episode guide for your favorite TV show as well as to find some basic guidance on a topic for an academic term paper), it becomes increasingly important that discovery tools fit into the habits that are already forming. While some faculty and librarians may lament the perceived lack of information literacy embodied by younger digital researchers, others also recognize that formally training students to use discovery and research tools is both time-consuming and potentially unsuccessful. It is no wonder that for librarians surveyed by HighWire about e-book content, for instance, the ease of use and simplicity of an online book platform were keys to its success. At a recent HighWire Publisher's Meeting panel on e-books, one librarian noted about her purchasing behavior regarding platforms, "If you have to train them, you've lost the coin toss."

Increasingly, the training—or self-training—is being done in other non-research arenas of Web use. While some interviewees espoused skepticism for Google and Amazon, both these sites have also increasingly become content discovery tools that people trust as helpful filters and the discovery features of these sites (such as Google's one-box search) for everyday uses have become standards for scholarly use. For instance, one assistant professor in history interviewed by HighWire noted that she orders all her books through Amazon, and as she has ordered more and more books, she has noticed that Amazon has gotten more precise in its recommendations. While she didn't think its recommendations would have academic value, she now finds it very useful, commenting, "I didn't realize how smart that system could be."

Amazon's recommendation feature is part of a new breed of discovery tools that are less about discoverability in the classic sense (i.e., findability) than they are about visibility. In other words, these tools provide just-in-time information that emerges in the user's workflow even when she is not necessarily searching for specific information.

These include recommendation engines, content bundles, and collections driven by semantic tagging, and automated "see related content" links. While several HighWire interviewees mentioned being open to the idea of such features, again, the challenge these pose to users may be ones of unfamiliarity and hence ones of trust. "I think the kind of user generated pathways or recommendations could be quite useful, but you always have to take them with a grain of salt," one graduate student in English commented.

Content Silos

As mentioned above, one of the risks of forming discovery habits using a small number of resources is that users miss out on content that they might otherwise find. The problem is exacerbated by the fact that often research/reference information—and particularly traditional reference material—is siloed into separate resources so that each must be independently searched for the more granular level information. Neither traditional library catalogs nor federated search systems have been able to provide good, granular search into such resources, although the latest Web-scale discovery systems show promise in this area. It is understandably difficult, frustrating, and inefficient for users to separately visit independent silos of information. "I think the part that takes the most time is that I know there isn't one database that will give me all the information I need," said one biologist interviewed by HighWire. The 2006 RIN study found that

the plea for 'one stop shops' was made across a range of disciplines; some were for search engines covering quite a wide area e.g. 'physical sciences', while others were for developing fields such as cultural studies or for specific areas such as automotive engineering. Researchers working on the intersection of fields and those in very new fields also felt the difficulty of searching multiple overlapping sources (Research Information Network, 2006 p. 10).

Librarians, too, recognize the desire to break down barriers between resources. During one Library Journal webcast on reference content (attended by approximately 500 librarians), librarian and blogger Sue Polanka noted that "students often don't know that tools such as subject-area encyclopedias exist, especially if such content is in 'silos' that are inaccessible without a discovery layer tool." When webcast attendees were asked to respond to a poll on whether or not they'd like to search reference content on a single interface, nearly ninety-six percent responded yes." When asked, "Should reference content be indexed in journal databases?" nearly 70% responded yes (Ownes, 2010).

It is not surprising then that content integration that breaks down silos is on many wish lists from both researchers and librarians. However, that does not mean that all research information should be lumped into a single uber-portal—one size does not fit all. There is a valuable place for niche resources, so the trick is to find ways that help integrate content without disintegrating the tools that come along with them. Information seekers differ, and those differences can stem from their educational level to their field of research to their research (or other) goals. In particular, the target audience (or market) for reference content varies widely. A casual lay user may dip into a dictionary or encyclopedia occasionally to satisfy a momentary curiosity. A pediatrician may rely heavily on a pharmaceutical reference work on a daily basis to check dosages and counter-indications. A grade-school student may use encyclopedias to begin research for a report. A graduate student may use an abstract and indexing database to search for new relevant content in her field. A reference librarian may help patrons every day with a very wide variety of questions in every field imaginable. A journalist may need to check for the facts on a wide variety of topics. Each of these groups

will have different workflows and habits that will impact what tools will work best for the discovery process and what is considered relevant content. For some (the journalist, the physician), having up-to-the-minute information will be critical. For others (the grade-school student), having broad and easily comprehensible information that is also readily accessible will be key. As the JISC comparative survey report on digital information seekers found, one common finding amongst 12 studies was that "disciplinary differences do exist in researcher behaviours" (Connaway, 2010, p. 12). These differences may be subtle, such as the use of figures to evaluate content, or broader in scope, such as satisfaction with digital resources being greater amongst scientists than arts and humanities researchers.

Access and New Mobile Devices

Another important challenge to the discovery process is accessibility, which in this context refers to the user's ability to gain access to the content in question. The degree to which each of the groups mentioned above—the layperson, the pediatrician, the grade-school student, the librarian, the journalist—can access needed research/reference information is not the same. Google may be considered a great democratizer of information, but it still (mostly) indexes only free information, which is not necessarily the information that is required by all reference users.[7] Resources such as the Oxford English Dictionary, for example, are not available without a subscription, and their contents therefore are by design not normally indexed by search engines such as Google. Hence it is possible that users who consciously or unconsciously restrict themselves to searching freely accessible resources will miss relevant or important content.

However, accessibility is not just a matter of having the right permissions to read or use a piece of content; it is also about having the right devices. While most users may still prefer using their laptops for academic research, the current trend towards the use of new mobile device options (smartphones, tablets, e-readers) may change the landscape dramatically within only a few years. And just as there is some variation in behavior expected across user groups and academic disciplines, discoverability challenges can differ based on the device that users are using to access the content. Those favoring mobile devices may be at an accessibility disadvantage currently. While libraries are making strides in providing mobile discovery services, these are centered on the first part of discovery—"mobile websites, mobile catalogs, and SMS reference"—these services do not necessarily result in content that is then consumable on a mobile device. As Lisa Carlucci Thomas notes in a survey of librarians in 2010:

For example, reader interest in e-books has skyrocketed, yet libraries struggle to make them available via handheld devices owing to the limitations of digital rights management, restrictive (or nonexistent) lending rules, exclusive platforms, and noncompatible file types—all of which impede efforts to provide effective access to electronic collections. (Carlucci Thomas, 2010, para. 22)

In other words, even if they are able to find content geared for mobile devices, more confusion may arise when users in the discovery process are confronted with additional access limitations or multiple formats or, worse, the lack of a compatible format.

Even as librarians are trying to increase the content available on mobile devices, there still appears to be some reluctance among academic users to access research content via those devices. A 2009 study of library patrons at Cambridge University found that over 90% of respondents never read an e-book or journal article on their mobile device. This led the survey authors to conclude that "it is not worth libraries putting development resource into delivering content such as e-books and e-journals to mobile devices at present. E-books are already accessible via

some smartphones and other mobile devices, such as iPhones and Windows Mobile devices, and audio files such as podcasts and audio books can easily be played on many phones or portable media players. At present, however, most users are put off by the constraints of the technology, such as poor screen quality" (Mills, 2009, p, 9). Indeed a number of studies conducted by libraries on the use of mobile devices and e-readers have suggested that these devices are "not yet adequate for scholarly use" (Gielen, 2010, p. 6; Carlucci Thomas, 2010). Users appear to be put off by the reading experience provided by mobile devices, which is compounded by an unfavorable comparison to digital access via a full-featured Web browser with its attendant cross-integration of content and services

Of course, since the Cambridge study was released, Apple's iPad and other tablet and tablet-like devices have arrived on the scene, promising a greatly improved reading and research experience. Research/reference content purveyors are already making apps available: everything from medical reference to Audubon field guides to a multi-faceted reference of the periodic table of elements. However, navigating through the iPad or iPhone app store or the Android app store is not the same filtered experience as conducting a library search or asking a reference librarian. Users embracing mobile devices that provide their best experiences via apps are left largely on their own to develop and find new discovery and search filters and on their own to negotiate (i.e., buy) access to the content they might find. Perhaps even more importantly, the apps are by nature silos of their own, making it difficult for users to conduct a search across a broad, disparate swath of content. So what users may gain in content usability might be lost in efficient discoverability.

Loss of Serendipity

One of the most difficult challenges of the discovery process is that a critical part of a user's overall learning and growth process may be lost in the pursuit of efficient search techniques—that part is serendipity, stumbling across an unexpected source of ideas or inspiration. For academic endeavors in particular, finding information is not an end to itself. It is only part of a larger activity surrounding synthesizing information, forging new ideas, and inspiring critical thought. For some, the right information is not the specific answer, description, or background verification they were seeking; it is the piece that unexpectedly sparks a new creative idea. For these researchers, the challenge of discovery is the challenge of increasing or preserving fruitful serendipity. One researcher interviewed by HighWire noted wistfully, "The new process is efficient, but I have lost...serendipity. I can't browse online. Because of keyword search, I see only what I'm working on right now." Another researcher interviewed by HighWire noted that the physical act of flipping pages could allow something to catch his eye that he otherwise would never have seen. Yet another talked of visits to library shelves leading to unexpected discoveries. How one could empirically measure the loss of serendipity is, of course, debatable. And it may be that researchers do not lack serendipity at all, but rather they might be able to find it again in existing features that offer online browsing or in the myriad distractions that are inherent in online activities or in new tools developed to make new content visible to users when they are not looking. These visibility tools may foster a new, parallel form of serendipity that will emerge as powerful in the near future.

SECONDARY CHALLENGES TO DISCOVERY: FILTERING AND VALUE SIGNIFIERS

As already touched upon earlier, the next phase of the discovery process involves evaluation (filtering) of the information found and determining its relevance to the user.

Evaluation

Despite the prevalence of search as a discovery technique, content discovery does not end with a list of results on a screen. There is additional labor involved in further assessing those results to determine what is valuable and relevant to the task at hand. In their survey, Head and Eisenberg found that "filtering through irrelevant results was the third most difficult step in students' course-related research process." Students' frustration may be compounded by the feeling that they are not given enough mentorship or instruction regarding how to evaluate online content. As one engineering student interviewed by Head and Eisenberg put it:

None of the old-timers—the old professors—can really give us much advice on sorting through and evaluating resources. I think we're kind of one of the first generations to have too much information, as opposed to too little. We've never had instruction really on navigating the Internet and picking out good resources. We've kind of been tossed into this, and we've just learned through experience we have to go on a Web site and just raid it for information. So I would say despite all that's out there, it certainly is harder to find the right source and evaluate whether it's good, or not, because there is so much—you only have a little bit of time to spend on each source you find. (Head, 2010, p. 9)

But undergraduate students are not alone in their difficulty with filtering. In HighWire's interviews, we also found that professors and post-docs spent a lot of time downloading content without actually using it, suggesting that that they were still having difficulty with the filtering process. A researcher surveyed by Elsevier noted: "I've got 5,000 PDF files that I've downloaded on my computer, seriously." (Dunham, 2010, slide 3). This speaks to the fact that researchers are discovering plenty of content, but finding the relevant information in what they have already discovered or finding quality information (or both) requires a second layer of filtering that is still elusive.[8]

End-User Value Signifiers: Format, Access, Snippets, and Trust

In HighWire's interviews, it was found that users, in the constant battle for efficiency, have developed habits around value signifiers that allow them to assess whether found content is worth spending more time on. These signifiers allow them to take a list of search results and very quickly perform that second layer of discovery—filtering—that allows them to identify which subset of content may provide actual value. These signifiers are:

- **Format:** To many users, the format in which content is presented is (rightly or wrongly) an important factor in the evaluation process. Some users still persist in being suspicious of digital-only content. As a post-doc in rhetoric said in a HighWire interview: "We grew up with print copies. Therefore, when I see an e-book, this could be a little bit of an exaggeration, but I feel it's kind of a suspect. What is an e-book? Why should it be an e-book? Why shouldn't it be a print copy?" A preference for PDF over HTML by other users had its origin (in some cases) with a belief that the PDF was a better representation of authorial intention and therefore had more value. HTML was purely functional, for look ups or to follow links, but not for deep reading. One history professor described content as looking "so cheap in HTML, like the thought isn't as good." The discomfort that some readers have with digital content in general might dissuade them from engaging more vigorously with content. Although the rhetoric post-doc acknowledged that her thinking may be "old-fashioned," it did have an impact on how she conducted research. As online content formats continue to evolve—particularly with regard to mobile devices—it will be interesting to see if, over time, this value signifier becomes less or more important.

- **Access:** Access as a value signifier is not about whether something that is easy to access has more intrinsic value. Rather it is about weighing the time spent breaking through an access barrier vs. the time spent doing something else that has easier access. Barriers to access, while infrequent for the group of Stanford scholars HighWire interviewed, did cause headaches nonetheless. These barriers could be a lack of subscription or even just a lack of a digital copy at all. One researcher said if he had to physically go to the library to get a hard copy these days it feels like he's already being inefficient. Another person compared having to go to the library to physically pick up a copy to entering the "Stone Age."

- **Short Snippets:** Unsurprisingly, users relied on short snippets of content and metadata in order to assess quickly whether content was worth engaging with further. The list of snippets is fairly intuitive: title, abstract, figures, authors, affiliation, acknowledgements all go into the snap assessment of whether something is worth pursuing. What is surprising is how short these snippets could be. One statistics professor said that "the first three words of the title quite often is enough" to tell him whether or not to continue reading. Another professor skimmed just the first sentence of the legends on figures to tell him whether the content would be of value. Others found even glancing through a long table of contents too time consuming if it took more than few minutes. Also of interest is what bits of information were not mentioned here. Author-assigned key words were met with some skepticism, and citation lists, while considered very valuable for continuing the research trail, were not on the list of "short snippets" people used to quickly assess whether to continue reading.

- **Trusted brands:** Ultimately, the decision to continue reading a piece of content comes down to a matter of trust. The researcher is taking a leap of faith that the time spent delving deeper will be fruitful and lead to the discovery of information that is not only relevant but also reliable. Researchers interviewed by HighWire put their trust in known brands: publishers, authors, editors, institutions (including their libraries)[9], reviewers, URLs, sites, and tools. The challenge and opportunity both for users and information purveyors on the question of trust is that trust can grow and shift as the digital publishing landscape evolves. These findings pair well with Head and Eisenberg's studies, which looked at how undergraduates evaluated the credibility and reliability (as opposed to relevance) of Web content to figure out what to trust. These students also used these factors: currency, author's credentials, URL, interface design, external linkage, familiarity, "heard about site," chart quality, "author credits others," "different viewpoints acknowledged," bibliography included, and "mentioned by librarian."

Based on these observations, it is possible to conclude that users face additional challenges when their preferred signifiers are not available or are obscured. Metadata, which carry so many of these value signifiers, are important then not only for interchange and machine-discovery of information, but also to communicate these signifiers to readers for their own evaluation of the content. Obscuring the name of an illustrious scholar who has written an encyclopedia entry on the Web page for that entry is a disservice not just to the author but also to the reader.

CONCLUSION

This overview of the discovery challenges faced by information seekers in academia can only scratch the surface of the many nuanced questions that can and should be raised about the rapid evolution of digital content discovery. It would be useful to see more user-centered studies completed in the same rigorous vein as JISC and PIL, studies focused on broad survey and empirical data. More discipline-specific and task-specific studies, such as those being conducted by RIN, would also be welcome, to determine how specific activities such as a point-of-care look up vs. writing an undergraduate paper differ with regard to the specific barriers that a user might encounter. The other chapters in this section of the book will address the technology that publishers and librarians are bringing to bear on the question of discoverability, and it would be useful to pair those new product ideas with focus groups and behavior studies. Continued examinations of the steps users take to evaluate and filter content, as well as how they integrate that content into the greater task of scholarship and research communication, could provide publishers, librarians, and other information providers insights into what new tools and technologies would serve to make research and reference content more easily discovered and evaluated by end-user constituencies.

ACKNOWLEDGMENT

I am indebted to Michael Newman, Head Librarian of the Falconer Biology Library at Stanford University, for conducting the majority of the HighWire interviews referenced in this chapter. Thanks are also due to John Sack and Kristen Fisher Ratan for their insights into user behavior. Finally, special thanks must go to Helen Szigeti who offered her digital reference expertise, intelligent criticism, and keen editorial eye.

REFERENCES

Carlucci, T. L. (2010). Gone mobile? Mobile libraries survey 2010. *LibraryJournal.com*. Retrieved from http://www.libraryjournal.com/lj/ljinprintcurrentissue/886987-403/ gone_mobile_mobile_libraries_survey.html.csp

Connaway, L. S., & Dickey, T. J. (2010). *The digital information seeker: Report of findings from selected OCLC, RIN and JISC user behaviour projects*. Retrieved from http://www.jisc.ac.uk/media/documents/publications/ reports/2010/digitalinformationseekerreport.pdf

Dunham, J., & Neylon, C. (2010, September 8). *The future of search and discovery: Empowering researchers to accelerate science.* Presented at the Elsevier Webinar. Retrieved from http://mediazone.brighttalk.com/event/ReedElsevier/d7b76edf79-4207-intro

Gielen, N. (2010). *Handheld e-book readers and scholarship: Report and reader survey (White Paper No. 3)*. New York, NY: The American Council of Learned Societies. Retrieved from http://www.humanitiesebook.org/HEBWhitePaper3.pdf

Head, A. J., & Eisenberg, M. B. (2010). *Truth be told: How college students evaluate and use information in the digital age. Project Information literacy progress report.* Seattle, WA: The Information School, University of Washington. Retrieved from http://projectinfolit.org/pdfs/PIL_Fall2010_Survey_FullReport1.pdf

JISC. (2009). JISC national e-books observatory project: Key findings and recommendations. *JISC*. Retrieved from http://www.jiscebooksproject.org/wp-content/ JISC-e-books-observatory-final-report-Nov-09.pdf

Mills, K. (2009). M-Libraries: Information use on the move (A report from the Arcadia Programme). *Arcardia@Cambridge: Rethinking the role of the research library in a digital age.* University of Cambridge. Retrieved from http://arcadiaproject.lib.cam.ac.uk/docs/M-Libraries_report.pdf

Newman, M. (2010). *HighWire press 2009 librarian e-book survey.* Palo Alto, CA: HighWire Press, Stanford University. Retrieved from http://highwire.stanford.edu/PR/ HighWireEBookSurvey2010.pdf

Neylon, C. (2010 July). It's not information overload, nor is it filter failure: It's a discovery deficit. *Science in the Open Blog.* Retrieved November 22, 2010, from http://cameronneylon.net/blog/it%E2%80% 99s-not-information-overload-nor-is-it-filter-failure-it%E2%80%99s-a-discovery-deficit/

Ownes, D. (2010). Webcast report: Reference: The missing link in discovery. *LibraryJournal.com*. Retrieved November 22, 2010, from http://www.libraryjournal.com/article/CA6728783.html

Research Information Network. (2006). *Researchers and discovery services: Behavior, perceptions and needs.* Research Information Network. Retrieved from http://www.rin.ac.uk/system/files/attachments/ Researchers-discovery-services-report.pdf

Research Information Network and the British Library. (2009). *Patterns of information use and exchange: Case studies of researchers in the life sciences.* Retrieved from http://www.rin.ac.uk/system/files/attachments/ Patterns_information_use-REPORT_Nov09.pdf

Schell, L. (2011). The academic library e-book. In Polanka, S. (Ed.), *No shelf required: E-books in libraries* (pp. 75–93). Chicago, IL: The American Library Association.

Shirky, C. (2008, September). *It's not information overload. It's filter failure.* Presented at the Web 2.0 Expo, New York City, NY. Retrieved from http://www.youtube.com/watch?v=LabqeJEOQyI

Wikipedia. (2010, November 16). *About - Wikipedia, the free encyclopedia.* Retrieved November 23, 2010, from http://en.wikipedia.org/wiki/Wikipedia:About

ENDNOTES

[1] At this writing, these online reference products can be found at the following URLs: Credo Reference: http://www.credoreference.com/; Gale Virtual Reference Library: http://www.gale.cengage.com/servlet/GvrlMS?msg=ma; Oxford Reference Online: http://www.oxfordreference.com/; SAGE Reference Online: http://www.sage-ereference.com/; Springer Online Reference Works: http://www.springer.com/references; American Association of Pediatric's Red Book Online: aapredbook.aappublications.org/; Oxford English Dictionary: http://www.oed.com/

[2] JISC's ebook observatory program is only one of the many research and innovation initiatives that the group has undertaken as part of its mission to help UK colleges and universities use digital technologies effectively in their learning, teaching, and research. More information about JISC can be found on its website: http://www.jisc.ac.uk/.

[3] The Research Information Network (http://www.rin.ac.uk/) in the UK is also conducting some interesting studies on researcher behavior. They are currently examining the methods used by humanities researchers and researchers in the physical sciences. Reports for what promise to be very interesting studies were not yet available at this writing.

[4] Begun in 2008, Project Literacy at the University of Washington's Information School (http://projectinfolit.org/) is an ongoing study of the research habits of young adults across different types of higher education campuses, including community colleges, state colleges, and public and private universities across the U.S.

[5] As of this writing HighWire has conducted 38 one-hour interviews of Stanford graduate students, post-doctorates, and faculty in a broad range of disciplines who volunteered to be interviewed. The interviews were conducted largely by Michael Newman, Head Librarian at the Stanford Biology Library, as part of a general ongoing study of user information consumption in a digital age.

[6] HW surveyed 138 librarians, largely from academic institutions in fall 2009.

[7] Google Scholar notably makes exceptions to Google's general policy of indexing only freely available. Academic journal content and content available via Google Books may be fully indexed in Google Scholar even though access to full text may be restricted. The limitations on what is indexed in the various search engines does not appear to be widely known.

[8] A digital technologies facilitator at a major research university interviewed by HighWire told this story of how medical students in a problem-based learning situation recently went head to head on one of the key battles surrounding online research/reference literature: So a small group learning, six people. The students learn the material and teach each other largely and there's a facilitator in there.... Someone came in for their research portion that they were teaching everyone else and they had cited Wikipedia as one of the sources. They are supposed to list materials. An argument erupted, sort of a respectful argument erupted about the use of Wikipedia in scholarly work. The person's

argument was "Wikipedia is exactly like a peer review journal. It's peer reviewed by even more people." That argument seems a little extreme to me, but I think it is feasible to me nowadays to start at Wikipedia for a lot of topics. I think that that might be laughed at in certain circles. I'm not going to sit here and say, "Wikipedia is place to cite anything." If they want a quick answer to something like "What's in the atmosphere of Mercury or something like that?" Something very specific or some random question you want to answer, I think it's feasible. Regardless of what you might think of the legitimacy or illegitimacy of Wikipedia as an academic resource, the anecdote surfaces a number of key questions that publishers, librarians, and researchers are grappling with, particularly with traditional online reference. On the surface, the tension in this anecdote comes from the perceived illegitimacy of a wildly popular online resource. In one corner Wikipedia is an eminently useful but also eminently assailable resource—democratic in its principles as well as in its adoption rate. According to its own site, Wikipedia attracted nearly 78 million visitors a month in January 2010 and had more than 91,000 people actively contributing to the body of knowledge it holds ("Wikipedia," 2010). In the other corner is the established protocol of scholarly publishing—publisher-organized peer review and editorial processes, which have served academe and the research community well long before the web, let alone Wikipedia, was a twinkle in anyone's eye. However, just beneath the question of legitimacy is an equally interesting one about discoverability. How Wikipedia came

to be a cited reference in a medical school class bears some examination. The facilitator hints at something significant when he says "I think it is feasible to me nowadays to start at Wikipedia." Wikipedia is a good starting point not because it is comprehensive and unfailingly accurate, but because a) it provides a successful first-level filter for the novice in a given subject area, and b) it is so very, very easy to get to. It is so discoverable as to be is over-discoverable, meaning that not only is it too easy to access to be ignored as an information resource but it also ends up eclipsing other relevant sources. It is an enviable position to be in, but as the anecdote points out, not everyone is happy with Wikipedia. So, where it offers an answer, it also raises questions.

In the HighWire interviews, the library comes up again and again as a discovery resource especially for book content. In the High-Wire survey, the majority of librarians also indicated that they believed that the library catalog was a significant or very significant tool used to discover ebook content (Newman, 2010, p., 11). The use of the catalog, aside from providing assurance that access is available to discovered content, may also be motivated by trust that the library has already vetted content for its reliability. Head and Eisenberg also found that undergraduate "it is fair to assume that students think library sources require less evaluation than information posted by anyone on the open-source Web. Students may figure a less exhaustive evaluation is needed when they are conducting course-related research" (Head, 2010, p. 15).

Section 2
The Value of Information Literacy in Research

Chapter 4
An Overview of Trends in Undergraduate Research Practices

James Galbraith
DePaul University, USA

ABSTRACT

The resources undergraduates use for research have changed significantly over the past two decades as the Internet has become the predominant conduit for information. Access to academic resources has never been easier; undergraduate papers now include more citations, but more non-traditional, non-academic sources are being cited. Libraries' initial reactions to the ascendancy of the Internet ranged from mild concern to alarm, but soon libraries were themselves using the Internet as both an access point for academic resources and as a tool for information literacy. Studies also suggest that students' motivations and research methodology have remained consistent. The key to libraries' success is understanding the motivations that shape students' research practices and tying information literacy to the curriculum.

INTRODUCTION

"Since the mid-1990s, the academic library has lost its control as the sole information resource provider on the college campus, and now competes with a multiplicity of resources available over the Internet." (Davis, 2003, p. 40).

DOI: 10.4018/978-1-61350-308-9.ch004

Academic librarians are uniquely positioned to witness and appreciate cultural change. Every year we welcome a new class of freshman, add hundreds or thousands of new items to our collections, and update our technologies. We understand that successive generations have different cultural touchstones; we've come to grips with the notion that ours date us. The fact that undergraduates' research practices differ from those of a decade ago is not a shock. Our own research habits have changed: colleges and universities are full of faculty and librarians who turn to Wikipedia for reference assistance.

Even if change is understood, the rate of change is mind-boggling. When the phrase "Information literacy" was first coined in the early 1970s, few could have imagined the profound changes that would follow. In 2005, Thomas Mann was still explaining the idiosyncrasies of subject headings to researchers in his well-respected "Oxford Guide to Library Research."

One student, for example, became frustrated in looking for material under "Moonshining" because it is not entered under that heading. In a standard library catalog, works on this subject are filed under **Distilling, illicit**. *Another researcher wanted books on "Corporate philanthropy;" before asking for help she hadn't found anything because she was looking under "Philanthropy" rather than under the proper heading* **Corporations – Charitable contributions** *(Mann, 2005, p. 18-19).*

This kind of research process is meaningless to today's undergraduates.

No disrespect is meant to Mann, of course, or catalogers, or librarians who still teach the use of subject headings. Many of the techniques Mann describes are still relevant, even in a digital research environment, and the metadata librarians have created is powering new search technologies. Mann also argues persuasively for the physical library, pointing out that the information available for free on the Internet is necessarily limited by copyright and commercial restrictions. It is still true that "If you wish to be a good researcher you have to be aware of the trade-offs between virtual and real libraries" (Mann, 2005, p. xiii). As we shall see, being a good researcher is not high on most undergraduates' list of motivations.

Today's undergraduates and students at all levels have more information available to them, deliverable more quickly, than any students in history. The Internet, the preferred conduit for this information, is the largest user-customizable multimedia research tool ever created. Students can access library resources provided by their library, government sites, commercial sites, and myriad free resources 24 hours a day. Books, articles, videos, music, speeches, lectures, and scholarly discussions – all are retrievable, ideally, in a few clicks. The research potential of the Internet is profound. The Internet is the home of digital collections: libraries' digital collections, Google Books, the Haithi Trust, and the Internet Archive. Some of the best reference resources are freely available on the Internet: the Statistical Abstract of the United States, Wikipedia, the Internet Movie Database, AllMusic.com. Undergraduates may not be correct in believing that virtually everything is available through the Internet, but a great deal of it is, and certainly enough to write a 3-7 page paper. The Internet is a treasure trove of information, a natural research destination for a lifestyle that is always wired and thrives on constant communication.

This chapter is an overview of broader trends in undergraduate research practices, focusing on resources and methodology. Research practices and the larger topic of information literacy is a perennial hot topic. In 2009 alone, Johnson, Sproles, and Detmering listed 510 publications on library instruction and information literacy in their annual bibliography on information literacy. (Johnson, 2010, p.677) This chapter will focus on selected studies, primarily large-scale, from the past decade or so. Most focus on undergraduate behavior, but a few cover K-12 students: future undergraduates. After a review of undergraduate research trends, we will discuss how libraries are reacting to changing research practices.

BACKGROUND: A REVIEW
OF SELECTED STUDIES

The Internet took hold of the public's attention in the mid-1990s, with the emergence of graphic browsers such as Mosaic (1993), Netscape Navigator (1994) and Internet Explorer (1995). Search engines followed soon after, including Webcrawler (1994), Lycos (1994), AltaVista (1995), Excite (1995), Yahoo (1995), and HotBot (1996). Google, a late-comer, premiered in 1998. The browsers and search engines gave the public easy access to the World Wide Web, and the Internet was soon as ubiquitous as the telephone. Libraries recognized the Internet's potential, putting their catalogs and research tools online and in many cases discarding their card catalogs. The emergence of a new research paradigm was soon to follow.

The impact of the Internet's growth in the 1990s is documented in several early studies which are striking not only for their findings, but for their historical value. David Lubans' "How First-Year University Students Use and Regard Internet Resources," documents a Duke University Libraries survey conducted in the Fall of 1997. The surveyed found that 85% of students used the Internet several times a day to at least several times a week; 20% reported using it more than once a day. Even in this early stage of Internet adoption, half the students surveyed "claim a ratio of 20% Web use to 80% use of traditional library resources (including library databases). A not insignificant 26% say their ratio is at 50/50 between Web and print. And 14% use the Web 80% of the time to find resources and rely 20% of the time on traditional library resource." (Lubans, 2008). Lubans' conflicted feelings over the popularity of the Internet are familiar:

I admit to experiencing some dissonance when I contrast the standing-room only use at the Leavey Library against the frequent criticism about the questionable quality of Internet information and

the reputed inability of users to evaluate that information. There are other disparities. I observe much independent use of the Internet and yet I am told by librarians that Internet use is difficult and most successful when mediated by a librarian and, that student use is at an alarmingly un-informed level (Lubans, 2008).

One of the first studies to demonstrate that research practices were changing was conducted by Davis and Cohen at Cornell University (2001). Davis and Cohen performed a comparative bibliometric analysis of citations from a microeconomics projects submitted in 1996 and 1999 (67 and 69 papers from each year respectively). In 1996, 9% of citations were Web citations; by 1999, 21% of all citations were websites. The increase in Web citations was accompanied by a drop in the mean use of scholarly sources from 6.1 citations in 1996 to 4.6 in 1999. More disturbingly, perhaps, from a scholarly research perspective, only 55% of the Web citations actually went to the cited document; 16% could not be found at all (Davis and Cohen, p. 312). In concluding their article, they recommended "1) setting stricter guidelines for acceptable citations in course assignments; (2) creating and maintaining scholarly portals for authoritative Web sites with a commitment to long-term access; and (3) continuing to instruct students on how to critically evaluate resources" (Davis and Cohen, p. 313).

Davis updated the study in 2001. Davis found that while a number of academic citations remained consistent from 1999 to 2000, the median of non-academic citations rose from 3 in 1999 to 4 in 2000 (Davis, 2001, p. 57). This happened despite verbal communication from the microeconomics professor to his teaching assistants and the librarians that he wanted more academic content. Davis found that the verbal warning, though reinforced through library instruction, had little impact. Faced with this new data, Davis concluded:

A possible crisis in undergraduate scholarship is at hand, and there is no simple answer. What is clear is that librarians are not the entire solution. Professors, if they wish to see an improvement in the resources cited by students, will have to provide more clearly defined expectations in their assignments. Librarians have an opportunity to work with professors in developing research guidelines for student research assignments. This collaboration is necessary if librarians are to have any real impact on the education of students (Davis, p. 59).

Davis and Cohen's findings were supported, to some extent, by Leiding (2005) who studied citations from 101 undergraduate honors theses dating from 1993–2002. Leiding found that Web citations first began in 1997, peaked as a percentage of citations in 1999 at 16%, then decreased to around 10% over the following 2 years, eventually falling to 7.7% in 2002 (Leiding, 2005, p. 422). Unlike Davis and Cohen, Leiding did not attempt to measure the use of scholarly vs. non-scholarly resources. Leiding found that use of Web citations "does not appear to be a growing trend for advanced undergraduate research." On the contrary, Leiding found that undergraduates were still citing books and that the use of journals was increasing.

Leiding's study was one of several that found while students used the Internet, they were not citing free Web resources in academic work. David Mill analyzed 236 bibliographies from undergraduate papers written from 2004-2005 to determine if the use of traditional library resources had been usurped by user-generated open Web resources (Mill, 2008). Mill's answer was an unequivocal "no." He found books and journals were cited at a much higher rate than open Web resources "77.5% vs. 16.7% and 79.1% vs. 16.8% respectively" (Mill, p. 351). Unequivocal results aside, Mill reflects on Davis' warning about a crisis, suggests Davis may have overstated the threat, then has his own doubts: "Nevertheless, the fact that almost half of the sample bibliographies

derived, on average, just over one-third of their content from open Web resources indicates that there may indeed be legitimate cause for concern. Assessing the quality of these Web sites -a task that was beyond the scope of this project-would doubtless provide useful information for information literacy initiatives" (Mill, p. 354).

Analyses of bibliographies were indicating that the Internet's popularity was not translating into unrestrained citing of free Web resources and a disregard for academic. At the same time, large scale studies were revealing more details about students' use of the Internet.

In 1999, the Pew Center launched the Pew Internet and American Life Project to measure the impact of the Internet on society. In 2001, the American Life Project released "The Internet and Education," a survey of 754 students aged 12-17 and their parents regarding student use of the Internet in learning. Among the Project's key findings:

- 94% of students with Internet access use the Internet for research
- 71% of students used the Internet as the major source for their most recent project
- 58% of online teens reported using a web site set up specifically for their school or a class

Among the study's conclusions: "teens use the Internet as an essential study aid outside the classroom and that the Internet increasingly has a place inside the classroom" (Lenhart, 2001, p. 2).

The parent surveys were equally as revealing. 87% of online teens' parents indicated the Internet helps their children with schoolwork, 93% believed the Internet helps their children learn new things; 55% of the parents believed that learning how to use the Internet was essential to being successful (Lenhart, 2001, p. 2). Parents, like their children, embraced the Internet as an educational tool; they did not see it as cultural fluff.

The following year, the American Life Project released "The Internet Goes to College," (2002) a survey of 2,054 students from 27 colleges and universities. The goal of the study was learning "about the Internet's impact on college students' daily lives, and to determining the impact of that use on their academic and social routines." 79% of college students surveyed felt that Internet use has positively impacted their academic experience; 73% indicated they use the Internet more than the library; 80% indicated they use the library less than 3 hours per week (Jones p. 3). The researchers concluded: "the degree to which college students use the Internet as an information and reference source suggests that they will very likely continue to turn to the Internet for information in the future...In short, the Web has become an information cornerstone for them" (Jones, p. 19).

One the most noted studies of the 2000's was OCLC's "College Students' Perceptions of Libraries and Information Resources," (2005) a "companion piece" to a larger study "Perceptions of Libraries and Information Resources." The study focuses on the 396 college students who completed the comprehensive survey. "College Student's Perceptions" is widely known for documenting the influence of Google and other search engines. OCLC found that 89% of college students started their information search with a search engine (68% Google, 15% Yahoo, MSN 5%), 92% viewing search engines favorably or very favorably (DeRosa, p. 18). Asked which resources fit their lifestyles perfectly, 94% of college students indicated that search engines are a good to perfect lifestyle fit while only 63% of college students rate both online and physical libraries as having a good to perfect lifestyle fit (DeRosa, p. 3-20).

OCLC did offer some good news for librarians. 61% of the students surveyed reported they have used the library web site, and 85% viewed libraries favorably or very favorably (DeRosa p. 1-10).

More good news came in the American Life Project's "Information Searches That Solve Problems" (2007), a survey of 2,796 American adults about how people search for information and how they act on that information. Pew's researchers found that libraries were visited by more than half of those surveyed (53%) (Estabrook, 2007). In a surprising twist, members of Generation Y (ages 18-30), the generation researchers were identifying with the Internet, were also the most likely to use libraries: "it is young adults who are the most likely to say they will use libraries in the future when they encounter problems: 40% of Gen Y said they would do that, compared with 20% of those above age 30 who say they would go to a library" (Estabrook, 2007). Visiting a library for problem solving may be an indication of Gen Y's confidence in their information seeking behaviors.

By the mid 2000s, the majority of undergraduates were turning to the Internet for research, using search engines and free resources, but also accessing library resources for their assignments. Future undergraduates were clearly not going to behave any differently. This happened before the "Google"-ization of research (Google's initial IPO was in 2004 and "Google" became a verb on June 15, 2006). The shift also predated the Facebook phenomenon, arguably the most visible example of the Internet's role in our lives. Even so, citation studies did not show we were falling into a research "Wild West." On the contrary, students were using the Internet, finding more information, and continuing to cite academic materials over non-academic. Students were using the Internet as a portal to access information for class assignments. One reason why the research "Wild West" never happened was that students' motivations have not changed.

"Students have always procrastinated. This habit may never change, so perhaps there will always be those students who need information fast and are less concerned about the source of the information than with finding the required number of references" (Thompson, p. 267).

The question of motivation was asked directly by Thompson in his article aptly titled "Information Illiterate or Lazy: How College Students Use the Internet for Research" (2003). "Lazy" was not Thompson's opinion, but rather a reference to a prominent message the author was seeing in library literature at the time. After reviewing recent studies about student research, Thompson rejects the notion that students are lazy, arguing that studies to date were not extensive enough to make that determination. As Thompson points out, if students are just lazy, then libraries would necessarily be fighting a losing battle.

Indeed there is ample evidence that students are not one-dimensional in their research techniques, that research practices are motivated by very practical considerations.

In 2006, Heinstrom studied the information seeking behavior of 574 students grade 6–12 in New Jersey. It is a telling study, even if it isn't about undergraduate research behavior. Heinstrom conducted 4 different surveys at different stages of the research process; one survey was adopted from the Approaches and Study Skills Inventory for Students (ASSIST). A learning approach inventory designed for use in higher education, ASSIST provides information about students' motivation for education and their learning styles (Heinstrom, 2000). In using ASSIST, Heinstrom found that how middle and high school students approach their information searches depends on their motivation. Extrinsically motivated students often adopted a "surface" approach, going for resources that were easy to locate and use, a basic level of information literacy. Highly intrinsically motivated students took a "deep" approach, delving further into their work, analyzing and evaluating their resources. Strategic students took a more organizational approach, organizing and managing their work. Heinstrom stresses the importance of devising assignments that engage all three information-seeking styles (Heinstrom, 2006).

In 2004, Van Scoyoc and Cason noted the importance of motivation in their study of under-graduate research behavior in the University of Georgia's electronic library, the Student Learning Center. Van Scoyoc and Cason surveyed 884 undergraduates about their library visits, 75.7% indicated they used "other Web resources," 71.3% indicated they were using WebCT or class web sites, 19.6% electronic databases, and 16.1% the OPAC (Van Scoyoc, 2006, p. 52). The authors also found that juniors and seniors, who theoretically would have more research experience and library instruction, did not use library resources more frequently than freshmen and sophomores. The authors speculated that "research choices for research in the electronic library are driven by the students' desires to complete class projects, not explicitly to use the library-meaning library-funded research" (Van Scoyoc, 2006, p.53). They also felt that the novel library environment, which lacked visual cues such as a circulation desk, might have given students the impression that the area was for Internet use.

Van Scoyoc and Cason's observations about completing class assignments was echoed in Project Information Literacy's (PIL) "How College Students Evaluate and Use Information in the Digital Age" (2010). One aspect of this complex survey of 8,353 students from 25 community colleges and universities was to look into what motivated students to do research: 99% of students reported that passing the course was the most important factor, 97% finishing the assignment, and 78% indicated that doing comprehensive research and learning something new were also important (Head, p. 4). Students are motivated by practical considerations; happily, if this study is correct, they also want to do good research and learn.

Studies suggest that while the resources undergraduates use for research have changed, their motivations and research strategies have remained consistent. The copious amount of readily available information available over the Internet has made it easier for extrinsically motivated students to locate and utilize information that gets the job done. Similarly, the abundance of information has increased the reward for intrinsically motivated students.

WHERE DO WE STAND TODAY?

PIL's "How College Students Evaluate and Use Information in the Digital Age" provides an excellent snapshot of today research practices. PIL's researchers asked students which resources they used for scholarly research versus personal research. For scholarly research, students' top 5 resources were course readings (96%), search engines such as Google (92%), scholarly research databases (88%), instructors (83%), and Wikipedia (73%). For personal research, the top 5 were Search engines, including Google (95%), Wikipedia (84%), friends (87%), their personal collection (75%), and government web sites (63%) (Head, p. 7). The resources students select depend on their need. For scholarly research, course readings, scholarly research databases, and instructors are heavily utilized.

Other interesting findings include:

- 84% of the students responded that getting started was the most difficult step of the research process, with defining a topic (66%), narrowing it down (62%), filtering through irrelevant results (61%), and following and knowing if they had done a good job (46%).
- Students are "frequent evaluators" of information. They consider the source of the information, but they often take into account factors such as how well constructed the Web page is.
- Students often collaborate when evaluating resources: 61% of students turn to friends and family to help evaluate materials, 49% frequently ask instructors and 11% ask librarians for assistance.

LIBRARIES REACT

Librarians are proactively responding to changing research habits, leveraging the Internet and offering information at the point of need. Information Literacy programs in academic libraries are leading efforts to teach undergraduates how to conduct research and evaluate information. Undergraduates interact with librarians during orientation programs, in their classes, and through online tutorials. Libraries often offer credit classes in information science. Libraries have also developed virtual libraries, converted many of their print resources to digital, and developed the infrastructure to push content to students via the Internet. Some libraries have positioned themselves as the focal point for new technologies on campus, creating information commons, then virtual commons.

The important of teaching information literacy cannot be overstated. As we discussed, Davis (2003) was among the first researchers to warn about the use of non-academic materials in academic work. In the conclusion to his studies, Davis (2003) provides a solution to the problem. This time, the professor he was working with provided "explicit parameters for the students. A minimum number of citations was specified, along with a standard for electronic and nontraditional resources, followed by a warning, with consequences for those students who don't follow the guidelines" (Davis, 2003, p. 44). To support the students, the libraries offered workshops and an online pathfinder specifically for the assignment. As a result, students changed their behavior, citing more academic resources. Davis' solution is in keeping with everything studies tell us about students' motivation and, specifically, their reaction to the authority of their professors. This interaction is representative of thousands like it that take place every week in academic libraries.

Libraries collaborate with other campus units a number of ways to support research. The Library at the University of Wisconsin-Madison developed CLUE (Campus Library User Education). CLUE is a series of five online multimedia research tutorials that are part of a required information literacy module for the campus communications requirement courses. These modules are purposefully general, so they can also be used by anyone who wants to learn basic information-seeking skills and strategies.

North Carolina State developed the "Library Course Tools" application (previously known as Course Views), a system that "dynamically generates student-centric views of library resources and tools for all courses taught at NCSU" (http://www. lib.ncsu.edu/dli/projects/courseviews/). For their efforts, NCSU was recognized by the American Library Association (ALA) Office for Information Technology Policy (OITP).

Collaboration also comes in the form of cooperation with campus IT departments. "The Bridge" in the Z. Smith Reynolds Library at Wake Forest University is a collaborative effort of the library and the campus' Information Technology department. The Bridge features an array of services including equipment loans, a multimedia lab, maintenance services for the student's mandatory ThinkPads, and parts sales. In this case, the collaboration positions the Library as a point of service for technology needs. Not only is this a practical, useful service, it is an effective way of identifying the library as a technology center.

Some libraries have used popular culture to teach research skills. This could be simply by using popular magazines and web sites to illustrate points about academic vs. non-academic resources. Linda Behen discusses various approaches in "Using Popular Culture to Teach Information Literacy" (2006). Most notably, Behen describes how she channeled her love of reality TV into information literacy exercises based on Survivor and the Amazing Race, to the approval of her K-12 students at Saint Ursula Academy. A similar approach might not be useful for undergraduates who are, perhaps, more worldly and sophisticated. Still, Behen's success with sessions based on "Survivor chal-

lenges" demonstrates the principle that learning is easier when it is fun.

Games are also being tested as information literacy tools in higher education. Researchers at the University of Michigan developed the "Defense of Hidgeon," a game designed to teach students how to do research. Hidgeon was used in an Information Science course, with mixed results. Most students who participated did so just enough to meet the requirements for extra credit, others decided to "opt out" entirely. The researchers felt that for gaming to be successful, it cannot be done as an add-on, the game needs to be an integral part of the course, "pervasive and unobtrusive." As other researchers have noted, motivation is a key determination of success. In this case, students apparently saw a point of diminishing returns and participated up to that point.

One particularly interesting attempt to deliver point of need services through pop culture is the ongoing experimentation with creating immersive library experiences in Second Life, a virtual Internet world launched in 2003. A number of academic libraries have built virtual library presences in the Second Life, so even offering virtual library instruction. While some of the early fervor seems to have faded, efforts continue. A conference was held in October 2010 "Libraries in Second Life – Pathways to Virtual Treasure" in Second Life's Community Virtual Library (http:// infoisland.org/). The libraries' efforts are a noble experiment, which even if ultimately unsustainable, may well be the progenitors of future virtual libraries. Philosophically, one has to admire the goal of offering free library services in virtual worlds as well as the physical.

Less immersive projects include recent efforts to incorporate free Internet research tools such as Wikipedia into course curriculum. Wikimedia Foundation, the non-profit foundation that operates Wikipedia and its collaboratively edited brethren, recently launched a project designed to improve Wikipedia's coverage of topics related to U.S. Public Policy. The Foundation recruited nine professors from George Washington, Syracuse University, Georgetown, and Indiana University-Bloomington to incorporate Wikipedia in their courses. Professors are employing Wikipedia in different ways: One class will be writing detailed critiques of Wikipedia articles, submitting appropriate edits, then following the article to see how Wikipedia's future editors incorporate/respond to the changes. Another will be writing literature reviews and summaries of argumentative papers they plan to write, posting them to Wikipedia before they begin work on their papers. Future plans include boosting the number of professors involved and expanding the scope of the project to other subjects.

The project, which is still in its early stages, may signal a changing attitude toward Wikipedia, which has gained a following, albeit a relatively silent following, in academia. Libraries are warming up to Wikipedia, IMDB, and other popular reference tools. Students will continue to use them; a viable approach is to start utilizing free Internet resources more frequently, seeking to make them better resources in the process.

Technological solutions are also being employed; a notable example are the efforts to build an academic search platforms that replicate the functionality of the popular search engines (Google, basically). Hence the push to make all library resources accessible through a single search box that offers "one-stop-shopping" for library content.

The notion of single-search discovery platform was first applied to reference resources. Well-known reference publishers (Oxford University Press, SAGE, Wiley-Blackwell, and Gale) have all been consolidating their reference resources into a single database. Products such as Paratext's Reference Universe have taken this to another level by tying reference resources together.

More recently, we have the "single-search discovery platform" craze that has seen information providers racing to release the definitive search platform. Proquest has the aptly-named Sum-

mon, EBSCO the more blandly named "EBSCO Discovery Service," and OCLC (still engaged in their Sisyphean struggle to break their "World Cat <Noun(s)> naming convention) leapt into the fray with WorldCat Local." All of these search platforms seek to offer a unified search of a library's entire collection (or as much of it as possible). These platforms are "simple, yet powerful," "for end-users," "Google-like," and often "one-stop shops." Most are "Web-scale" and in "the Cloud." Meme de jour aside, the concepts are real, and the possibilities for building future research systems on these foundations are profound.

How this translates into making undergraduates better researchers with increased information literacy remains unknown. These platforms may address the student's desire for a single, Google-like, search. It is unclear if they will sate the student's desire for efficiency. OCLC recently announced that there are now more than 400 million articles, 170 million books, 10 million e-books and 1,100 databases accessible through the WorldCat Local service. Impressive numbers, but the real test of all these systems is how effectively students can isolate the 5-10 items they need for their 3-5 page paper. The next few years will be telling.

CONCLUSION

A review of studies from the past decade or so reveals several trends in how undergraduates do research:

- The Internet is now the predominant access tool for undergraduate research. Search engines such as Google, Yahoo, and Bing (but mostly Google) are key sources of information.
- Students are using the Internet for research, but they are still using scholarly resources, though it may be harder for them to determine a scholarly vs. non-scholarly resource.

- Most students are motivated by the practical goal of successfully completing their work, usually with the minimal effort required to either pass or get a good grade.
- Students respect and recognize the authority of their instructors; students will use course materials and scholarly tools for their coursework if instructed to do so, particularly if it will help them get a better grade.

While the resources undergraduates use may have changed, undergraduate research behaviors and their motivations for doing research have not. The Internet has not stopped undergraduates from wanting to find information as quickly as possible to complete and assignment; it has not curbed their natural inclination to procrastinate (it may have enhanced it), nor has it taken away their desire to get good grades.

The major change has been the emergence of a faster, more ubiquitous, more open method of information dissemination. Initially, the reaction ranged from "concerned" to "really concerned." Librarians were justly worried that easy access to free information would undermine the research process. Ultimately, that hasn't happened, in part because libraries responded proactively, harnessing the Internet and working with faculty who still maintained their bully pulpit.

Librarians need to continue advancing their understanding of how students are doing research, the nexus of learning, motivation, and technology. We need to keep an eye on Google, Facebook, and Wikipedia and use these resources appropriately. Now and then we should also reminder ourselves that today's undergraduates have more information available to them, deliverable more quickly, than any students in history. It is an amazing time to be an undergraduate or a librarian.

REFERENCES

Davis, P. M. (2002). The effect of the Web on undergraduate citation behavior: A 2000 update. *College & Research Libraries, 63*(1), 53.

Davis, P. M. (2003). Effect of the Web on undergraduate citation behavior: Guiding student scholarship in a networked age. *Libraries & the Academy, 3*(1), 43.

Davis, P. M., & Cohen, S. A. (2001). The effect of the Web on undergraduate citation behavior 1996-1999. *Journal of the American Society for Information Science and Technology, 52*(4), 309–314. doi:10.1002/1532-2890(2000)9999:9999<::AID-ASI1069>3.0.CO;2-P

DeRosa, C., Cantrell, J., Hawk, J., & Wilson, A. (2005). *College students' perceptions of libraries and information sources: A report to the OCLC membership.* Dublin, OH: OCLC.

Entwistle, N., McCune, V., & Scheja, M. (2006). Student learning in context: Understanding the phenomenon and the person. In Verschaffel, L., Dochy, F., Boekaerts, M., & Vosniadon, S. (Eds.), *Instructional psychology: Past, present and future trends.*

Estabrook, L., Witt, E., & Rainie, L. (2007). *Information searches that solve problems.* Washington, DC: Pew Internet and American Life Project. Retrieved on February 13, 2011, from http://www.pewinternet.org/Reports/2007/Information-Searches-That-Solve-Problems.aspx

Head, A., & Eisenberg, M. B. (2010). *How college students evaluate and use information in the digital age.* Seattle, WA: The Information School, University of Washington.

Heinstrom, J. (2000). The impact of personality and approaches to learning on information behaviour. *Information Research, 5*(3).

Heinström, J. (2006). Fast surfing for availability or deep diving into quality - Motivation and information seeking among middle and high school students. *Information Research, 11*(4), 265. Retrieved from http://InformationR.net/ir/11-4/paper265.html

Johnson, A., Sproles, C., & Detmering, R. (2010). Library instruction and information literacy 2009. *RSR. Reference Services Review, 38*(4), 676–768.. doi:10.1108/00907321011090809

Jones, S. (2002). *The Internet goes to college: How students are living in the future with today's technology.* Washington, DC: Pew Internet and American Life Project.

Krikelas, J. (1983). Information-seeking behavior-Patterns and concepts. *Drexel Library Quarterly, 19*(2), 5–20.

Leiding, R. (2005). Using citation checking of undergraduate honors thesis bibliographies to evaluate library collections. *College & Research Libraries, 66*(5), 417-429.

Lenhart, A., Simon, M., & Graziano, M. (2001). *The Internet and education: Findings of the Pew Internet & American Life Project.* Washington, DC: Pew Internet and American Life Project.

Lubans, D. (1998). *How first-year university students use and regard Internet resources.* Retrieved from http://www.lubans.org/docs/1styear/firstyear.html

Mann, T. (2005). *Oxford guide to library research.* Oxford, UK: Oxford University Press.

Mill, D. H. (2008). Undergraduate information resource choices. *College & Research Libraries, 69*(4), 342–355.

OCLC. (2010). *OCLC adds more content accessible through WorldCat Local.* Dublin, OH: OCLC. Retrieved on December 11, 2010, from http://www.oclc.org/us/en/news/releases/2010/201059.htm

Thompson, C. (2003). Information illiterate or lazy: How college students use the Web for research. *Libraries & the Academy, 3*(2), 259. doi:10.1353/pla.2003.0047

Van Scoyoc, A. M., & Cason, C. (2006). The electronic academic library: Undergraduate research behavior in a library without books. *Libraries and the Academy, 6*(1), 47–58. doi:10.1353/pla.2006.0012

Weiler, A. (2005). Information-seeking behavior in Generation Y students: Motivation, critical thinking, and learning theory. *Journal of Academic Librarianship, 31*(1), 46–53. doi:10.1016/j.acalib.2004.09.009

Zhang, Y. (2008). Undergraduate students' mental models of the Web as an information retrieval system. *Journal of the American Society for Information Science and Technology, 59*(13), 2087–2098. doi:10.1002/asi.20915

Chapter 5
The Research Habits of Graduate Students and Faculty:
Is There a Need for Reference Sources?

Miriam Matteson
Kent State University, USA

ABSTRACT

The work of faculty and graduate students is information intensive. These researchers make heavy use of particular types of resources to support their research, teaching, scholarly communication, and current awareness. They less frequently use traditional types of reference sources, however, raising questions of why that might be and what should be done about it. This chapter examines the research practices of graduate students and faculty to understand their information needs, their information seeking strategies and the information sources they use. It also looks more specifically at researchers' uneven use of reference sources and discusses reasons why these practices exist. An argument is made that changes must be made to the types of reference sources available to researchers, and that academic librarians must change the way they promote these resources to their constituents.

INTRODUCTION

This chapter explores whether and how traditional reference resources serve the needs of researchers, and what types of products researchers might want in the future. A reference source has been defined as: "A book designed to be consulted when authoritative information is needed, rather than read cover to cover. Reference books often consist of a series of signed or unsigned 'entries' listed alphabetically under headwords or headings, or in some other arrangement (classified, numeric, etc.)" (Reitz, 2004, p. 600).

DOI: 10.4018/978-1-61350-308-9.ch005

To explore how faculty and graduate students make use of reference materials now and in the future, we must first understand how they work, what information resources they use, how they identify those sources, how they search for information, and what they do with the information they find. Then we can begin to extrapolate how researchers use today's reference sources, which include a mix of traditional print resources, digitized print sources, and born digital sources. A better understanding of the research practices of graduate students and faculty will enable librarians, publishers, and content producers to develop new ideas about the design, discoverability, structure, and marketing of reference sources.

BACKGROUND

Both graduate students and faculty members are scholars in that they ingest, produce, and disseminate scholarship through research and teaching. Graduate students are often faculty members-in-training; thus these two user groups share many common characteristics in their information needs, seeking, and use. But there are also distinctions between the two user groups regarding their knowledge and expertise in their subject areas, and their familiarity with information sources in those areas. A direct comparison of the research habits of these two user groups is made somewhat difficult by the fact that researchers have not consistently asked the same research questions of each group, and that some research has focused exclusively on scholars in a particular academic discipline where other research has grouped sample populations across multiple disciplines. To be sure, differences exist across academic fields in terms of epistemology, scholarly communication patterns, and, to a lesser degree, the habits and preferences of the researchers. However, those differences are less relevant for the focus of this chapter; thus, the findings discussed here emphasize the similarities among researchers of different disciplines. A good amount of research about graduate students and faculty exists, and from that, we can begin to understand their research habits and their use of reference sources.

Information Needs

As a user group, graduate students undergo a transformation as they progress through their academic programs (Barrett, 2005; Chu & Law, 2008). Students early in a Master's program more closely resemble undergraduates in their need for information, their knowledge of resources, and their information seeking strategies. Generally speaking, they are taking courses and beginning to develop their own research paths. Their information needs at this point include materials needed for classes, and perhaps, if they have a teaching responsibility, materials to support their teaching. As they advance in their programs, their information needs change and begin to mirror the characteristics of faculty. Graduate students at this senior level express a need for information related to research, either their own research or faculty-sponsored research, information to support preparing presentations and publications, and information to support current awareness (Gabridge, Gaskell, & Stout, 2008).

Faculty information needs are inextricably linked to their work as scholars. Consistent over time and across disciplines, the primary information needs of faculty are: 1) to stay current in their fields, 2) to support their research production and scholarly communication, and 3) to support their teaching (Anderson, 2006; Bennett & Buhler, 2010; Borgman, Millwood, Finley, Champeny, Gilliland, & Leazer, 2005; Flaxbart, 2001; King, Tenopir, Choemprayong, & Wu, 2009). Even as Information Technology has changed dramatically, these fundamental areas of information need for faculty have largely stayed the same.

To meet these three categories of information needs, faculty browse current journals and web sites in their discipline (Beaubian & Buhler, 2010;

Borgman et al., 2005), participate in conferences (Hannah, 2005; Jamali & Nicholas, 2008), and communicate through personal networks with colleagues in their fields (Jamali & Nicholas, 2008; Rafiq & Ameen, 2009). They search library-supplied online journal collections and library catalogs for relevant journal and monographic literature (Westbrook, 2003). They use search engines to find scholarly materials available freely on the Web to support their research and teaching (Borgman et al., 2005; Mansourian & Madden, 2007). Finally, they also consult their own personal collections of information sources in print and electronic format (Mayfield & Thomas, 2005).

Graduate students differ from faculty in their "satisficing" behaviors - the decision-making process that guides a user in determining when they have good enough information to resolve their need. Students early in their graduate program report deciding to stop seeking information to resolve their needs when the requirements for the course assignment have been met, when they run out of time, when they have found accurate information, when the information is repetitive, and when they feel they have understood the concept (Prabha, Connaway, Olszewski, & Jenkins, 2007). Students further along in their graduate programs view their need for information as critical to their academic success. They are rigorous searchers who do not settle for good enough information, but continuously seek out relevant resources with comprehensive, reliable information (Carpenter, Wetheridge, Smith, Goodman, & Struijvé, 2010; Gabridge et al., 2008; Jamali & Nicholas, 2008).

Faculty members also assess whether the information they find is sufficient to satisfy their information needs, although they report several different factors that influence their decision to stop searching. For faculty, deadlines, exhausting all possible search combinations, finding current research, finding repetitive information, identifying an exhaustive collection of data, and meeting requirements were all named as factors in their stopping behavior (Prabha et al., 2007).

Information Seeking Strategies

There are several relevant models that represent scholarly information seeking strategies. Ellis (1989, 1993) and Ellis, Cox & Hall (1993) developed an information seeking model based on the behaviors of social scientists and scientists which includes eight behavioral components: starting, browsing, chaining, monitoring, differentiating, extracting, verifying, and ending. Subsequent findings from the literature show good support that these are frequently enacted scholarly information seeking strategies.

A more recent model from Palmer, Teffeau, & Pirmann (2009) represents scholarly activity using the concept of primitives – "basic functions common to scholarly activity across disciplines" (p. 7). Their framework of scholarly activity in the online environment includes five core activities, each with several primitive activities, shown in Table 1.

Table 1. Palmer et al. (2009) Scholarly activities and primitives

Core Activity	Primitive
Searching	Direct searching
	Chaining
	Browsing
	Probing
	Accessing
Collecting	Gathering
	Organizing
Reading	Scanning
	Assessing
	Rereading
Writing	Assembling
	Co-authoring
	Disseminating
Collaborating	Coordinating
	Networking
	Consulting

In contrast with the information seeking models of scholars described above, a recent study on the information seeking behaviors of Generation Y doctoral students shows the emergence of a preliminary typology of four types of students based on their research behaviors (Carpenter et al., 2010). *Multi-taskers* are students who are engaged in multiple research activities and who appreciate the overlapping of their information needs. *Uni-taskers* take a more linear approach to their research and are likely to follow a more orderly set of research strategies. The *Support-seekers* category describes those students who benefit from support from peers. They value and seek collaboration and spend time building networks. The *Go-it-aloners* tend to rely on their own methods and approaches for conducting research and will teach themselves a new skill if necessary. They spend time alone and consult only trusted resources. In this typology, students may belong in more than one category. They may change their preferences over time. Although faculty were not included in the research sample, these characteristics may be applicable to faculty researchers as well.

Both the Ellis (1989, 1993) and Palmer et al. (2009) models on researchers' information seeking behaviors are born out in the research. Numerous studies report that faculty members' strategies for seeking information include browsing, searching, citation tracking, reading, interacting with colleagues, and assessing or evaluating information (Borgman et al., 2005; Flaxbart, 2001; Jamali & Nicholas, 2008, King & Montgomery, 2002; Meho & Haas, 2001; Quigley, Peck, Rutter, & Williams, 2002). Graduate students practice many of the same strategies as faculty in their information seeking behavior. They browse for information in print and online journals, e-print archives, and in the physical stacks in the library (Barrett, 2005; Jamali & Nicholas, 2008). They search library-supplied resources including e-journal collections and databases, the library catalog, and special collections for known items, partially known items,

and topical information (Barrett, 2005, Brown, 2005; Gabridge et al., 2008; Kayongo & Helm, 2010). Both groups are regular users of web sites and frequently start their information seeking on the Internet using Google, Google Scholar, or other Internet search engines (Borgman et al., 2005; Carpenter et al., 2010; George et al., 2006; Hemminger, et al., 2007; Liao, Fin, & Lu, 2007).

Both graduate students and faculty make heavy use of citation tracking and pearl growing – using one relevant article to lead to others (Schlosser, Wendt, Bhavnani, & Nail-Chiwetalu, 2006). For graduate students, this may start with a recommended item from a faculty member or an item they discovered on their own, and then extend into a hunt for one relevant source after another. Faculty members often start with a recommendation from a colleague, or from a known article.

Graduate students and faculty track the scholarly output in their field to stay current and in the case of graduate students, to support building an extensive literature review for their dissertations (Barrett, 2005; Carpenter et al., 2010; Jamali & Nicholas, 2008). Finally, both user groups perform information seeking through attending conferences and meetings and interacting with student and faculty peers.

Information Sources

The information sources most important to faculty and graduate students are journal articles, both published and preprint, and to a somewhat lesser extent, monographs (Tenopir, King, Edwards, & Wu, 2009). Both groups also make heavy use of Web pages either identified through an Internet search, or from known URLs, particularly for preliminary information seeking (Carpenter et al., 2010; Gabridge et al., 2008). Rising in importance to faculty in particular are Web-based resources such as specialty resources in their disciplines, portals, and society or institute Web pages (Hemminger et al., 2007; Mansourian & Madden, 2007; Shen, 2007; Westbrook, 2003). Graduate students and faculty also make use of special collections (electronic and print) in their areas of research, such as museum artifacts, original manuscripts, or recordings in the humanities (Barrett, 2005), or specialized databases of bioinformatics data in biology (Brown, 2005).

Both groups place a high value on the speed and efficiency of information in electronic format. By discipline, faculty scientists are furthest towards full acceptance of electronic information, with social scientists close behind, and humanities scholars coming along. But data show that since 2003, the acceptance of e-journals in particular has risen in all three disciplines (Schonfeld & Housewright, 2010). Electronic resource usage data suggests graduate students underuse information sources that do not provide electronic access to full text (Earp, 2008, Finn & Johnston, 2004).

Graduate students' discovery of resources is heavily influenced by their faculty and advisors, fellow students, or other trusted personal sources (Brown, 2005; Gabridge et al., 2008; George et al., 2006). Graduate students learn the most appropriate and relevant sources in their area of research from the faculty with whom they work, and they will return again and again to a trusted or recommended resource (Brown, 2005, Brunton, 2005; George et al., 2006). However, one study (Earp, 2008) reported contradictory findings to this phenomenon, where 62.8% of the graduate students surveyed reported never or rarely seeking help from their faculty, and 51.4% reported rarely or never seeking help from other students.

Also inconsistent is graduate students' practice of consulting librarians for assistance. Kayongo and Helm (2010) reported 44% and 50% of students did not consult with reference librarians or subject librarians (respectively). Earp (2008) reported that 84.9% rarely or never consulted a librarian for help. George et al. (2006), however, found that the percentage of students who turned to librarians for help varied greatly by discipline, from as low as 15% with engineering students to as high as 72% in business and policy. Only 7%

of respondents reported getting assistance from a librarian as a reason for visiting the library.

Faculty consult a number of different discovery tools to locate information: library-supplied aggregator full text databases, library-supplied indexes and e-journal collections, library catalogs, Google Scholar, general Web search engines, subject-specific preprint archives, personal collections, and recommendations from colleagues (Bennett & Buhler, 2010; Hemminger et al., 2007). Over time, faculty are turning to electronic discovering tools such as a Web search engine or a specific electronic resource over the physical library or the library's catalog as a starting point for their research (Hemminger et al., 2007; Schonfeld & Housewright, 2010).

While it is a growing fact that scholars make frequent use of Internet search engines, we know less about what types of Web-based resources they consult to support their information needs. Mansourian & Madden (2007) explored this question in the biological sciences domain and found that in addition to library-supplied Web-based resources such as the e-journal collections, catalogs, and databases, scholars used the Web to consult specialized resources (in this case, an online gene database), other scientists' Web pages, biology research groups and institutes, and biology portals.

In summary, graduate students early in their programs have information needs related to courses and perhaps teaching responsibilities. More senior graduate students need information for their own research and/or research for faculty, for staying current in their field, and to support their scholarly communication. Faculty information needs relate to their research and scholarly communication, their teaching, and current awareness. Both groups make "satisficing" decisions regarding when they stop seeking information to meet their needs.

Graduate students and faculty seek information by browsing print and electronic collections of journals and monographs, and by searching for specific or topical materials. They look for new information using citation tracking (who cited the work) and pearl growing (who does the work cite, what are the relevant keywords or controlled vocabulary terms within). They scan and monitor favorite web sites and journals to stay current with developments in their fields, and they also seek information via contact with colleagues and by attending conferences.

Journal articles, preferably in electronic format, are the most important information source for most faculty and graduate students. Researchers also continue to consult books and print journals, but to a lesser extent. They consult information from specialized web sites in their fields of study, and they learn about valuable information sources from their faculty, their student peers, and faculty colleagues.

GRADUATE STUDENT AND FACULTY USE OF REFERENCE SOURCES

Very few studies have specifically explored graduate student and faculty use of traditional reference books. One of the few examples is Aked et al. (1998) who surveyed faculty use of the reference collection in their library and found that 76.5% of respondents reported using the collection, and that tenure track faculty used the collection more than tenured and non-tenure track faculty. They also found that 50% of the tenure and tenure-track faculty reported using the collection to support their research. Today these findings are difficult to put into perspective given that the data were collected prior to the boom of the Internet and Web-based information. More recently, Doraswamy (2009) found that engineering faculty respondents used reference books more frequently to support their research than to support their teaching, but did not compare respondents' use of reference books to other types of information, so again it is difficult to interpret the meaning of this finding.

The literature says very little about the use of reference sources such as encyclopedias, handbooks, maps, almanacs, or bibliographies. The types of sources reported in the literature most frequently include books, journals, databases, library catalogs, and Web pages, but the findings do not report one way or the other whether graduate students and faculty are making use of traditional reference sources. While we cannot conclude with certainty to what extent graduate students and faculty use traditional reference sources, the data from the general information seeking habits of these two user groups provide us with some insight.

Graduate Students and Faculty Make Extensive Use of Indexes

Of the major categories of reference sources, electronic indexes to journal articles are clearly the reference sources most frequently used by these two groups. The index has changed dramatically with technology. Gone are the days where the indexing and abstracting tool was a print-based item, only available in the library building, a single volume for each year, with only three access points (author, title, subject), which pointed to an article that one subsequently had to make note of and go off and hunt down in the library stacks. Now, as electronic delivery formats have developed, there is virtually no distance between the reference tool and the source. Most indexes and abstracts today (and here I am including aggregator databases and e-journal collections) include both the metadata about the articles and the full text, integrating the searching and retrieving step into one.

From the examination of the research habits of graduate students and faculty, we know that these groups make extensive use of electronic indexes for current awareness, in support of their research, and to support teaching. They perform known item, partial known item, topical searches, and browse tables of contents. Without a doubt, journal indexes, both those supplied by the library as well as the archives of preprints on the Web are indispensible to graduate student and faculty work.

The predominance of the index as the most used reference source type is because the currency both these user groups most value is the journal article. Newer features of index searching such as the capability to save searches and saving and emailing search results, formatted in the citation style of choice, only increase the value researchers place on this type of reference tool. Use of current awareness tools such as table of contents alert services through email or RSS feeds also increases these scholars' access to and use of periodical literature. Some disciplines rely extensively on preprint literature to disseminate information. Technology facilitates this practice as well with freely available online databases such as arXiv.org (www.arxig.org), Nature Precedings (precedings. nature.com), or CiteSeer[x] (citeseer.ist.psu.edu). Simply put, because indexes point to the type of resource most valued by these two populations, they are naturally heavily used.

There is some debate, however, about how efficiently and effectively researchers make use of indexes. For instance, data show that graduate students report feeling less successful and less efficient when searching for partially known items or topical searching compared with known items (Gabridge et al., 2008). In another study, 42% of graduate student respondents reported that a lack of knowledge of the appropriate databases, and having trouble using those databases were barriers to their information searching and use (George et al., 2006). In the area of biology, graduate students were found to consult a single well-known biology-related database significantly more often than other biology databases, even though the other databases contained more molecular biology articles from the journals the students reported reading the most (Brown, 2005). Faculty members also show some skepticism regarding how effectively they think they find relevant information in electronic databases. Hemminger et al., (2007) reported that only 10% of the faculty respondent reported be-

ing very confident they were finding everything they should on their topics, and collectively 40% answered they were neutral or not very confident they were finding everything.

Thus, we know that graduate students and faculty make extensive use of at least one type of reference source – journal indexes – because they provide access to a highly valued form of scholarly output. With more and more full text linked to the indexes, and developments in the design and functionality of the indexes, there is every reason to believe faculty and graduate students will continue to view such tools as essential to their work.

Internet Search Engines

What is a Web search engine, if not a reference source? Google, or any search engine, points to definite pieces of information and is not intended to be read all the way through. Search engines veer from the classic definition of a reference source in that the results from a search engine – the information that they point to – may have considerably less established authority than other reference sources that have been authored, compiled, or otherwise vetted by experts or professionals. Depending on the specific online search tool, no human reasoning (direct or indirect) was involved in deciding the results returned for a given search from a quality, authenticity, or authority position. However, Google has been touted as an effective reference tool for discovering background or introductory information on an unfamiliar topic, particularly where there may be the need to learn new vocabulary terms, or for topics with no controlled vocabulary (Thelwall, 2005). The prevalence with which graduate students and faculty turn to the Internet at the beginning of a research endeavor suggests that they are making use of the reference features of Internet search engines.

Research tells us that graduate students and faculty place tremendous value on information sources that can be located quickly and efficiently, which is almost always equated with materials in electronic format. The difficulties in locating information quickly and efficiently have been well-resolved with the development of high quality Web-based content and powerful Internet search engines to find it. The fact that not all information available on the Internet is accurate, complete, authoritative, current, or of high quality may not necessarily be seen as a problem by researchers. Professionally they are budding or established experts in their research areas, and are thus positioned to evaluate the authority or authenticity of the information acquired from non-referred sites (Quigley et al., 2002). Because staying current is viewed as an essential task for researchers, they make it a point to know who are the emerging scholars, the recent trends in their research areas, and the latest scientific developments (Palmer et al., 2009). With this level of immersion in a field, scholars are presumably confident in their ability to discern the wheat from the chaff when locating Web-based information.

To the extent that searching the Internet is an instance of using a reference source, we know that graduate students and faculty are doing so with great frequency, because they prefer information in online formats due to the speed and efficiency that format affords. More data is needed however, to understand the kinds of information researchers seek from the Internet, whether or not they find the information they need, and how effectively or efficiently they are able to do so.

Print Reference Sources

What little research there is shows that traditional print reference sources are not frequently consulted. This point is made most strongly by the absence of reference materials, other than indexes, as a category that emerges from any of the studies reported above as frequently used types of materials by graduate students and faculty. This is also corroborated by data that show that graduate students and faculty do not visit the physical library very frequently, and when they do, their reasons for visiting include picking up or dropping off a book, reading current journals, making photocopies, and finding quiet study space (Hemminger et al., 2007; Kayongo & Helm, 2010).

One reason that graduate students and faculty infrequently use print reference sources is likely because they are infrequent users of the physical library and infrequently interact with library staff. As summarized earlier, students and faculty do not tend to consult librarians in their information seeking. Other research shows that the faculty perceptions of their dependence on the library for research are decreasing. Across humanities, social sciences, and sciences, data show that faculty members' perception of the library as the starting point for locating information for their research has declined in the last seven years from approximately 80% to 65% in the humanities, 70% to 58% in the social sciences, and 65% to 43% in the sciences (Schonfeld & Housewright, 2009). Even if that perception is slightly erroneous because faculty may not be aware they are using library-supplied tools when they consult a database or e-journal, that perception may translate into faculty being less and less aware of reference sources in any format that might be useful to their work. For both user groups, the discovery of a particular resource comes frequently from the recommendation of a personal contact. If graduate students and faculty have less contact with library staff and a lowered perception of the library as a gateway to research, the opportunity for a librarian to introduce a reference source is significantly reduced. That results in reference sources staying undiscovered and unused.

Another factor that explains infrequent use of reference sources is that traditional reference sources are secondary sources that provide background information, report facts, or provide discrete pieces of information. For researchers, information such as this would be used only as a small part of a larger scholarly endeavor. Further, many of types of traditional reference sources are most useful to someone new to a particular domain who needs to be oriented to a topic (i.e., encyclopedias, bibliographies, or manuals). Graduate students and faculty are usually completely immersed in their area of research and are well beyond the need for general resources, unless they are engaging in a new line of research. Because of their expert status, scholars are more likely to benefit from reference sources that are specific, advanced, and comprehensive in their areas of interest.

Given what we know about the information seeking behaviors of graduate students and faculty members in general, and their use and non-use of reference sources more specifically, academic librarians might naturally ask, should those researchers use library vetted reference sources? Here librarians must not lose sight of the essential purpose of a reference collection and reference service – to help users "identify sources of information in response to a particular question, interest, assignment, or problem" (Cassell & Hiremath, 2009, p. 5). Librarians naturally would like graduate students and faculty to make use of the reference materials the library provides. That requires making informed, careful choices about the resources purchased or licensed by the library. But ultimately, academic librarians should be committed to assisting these users with their information needs, whether or not that involves consulting library-supplied traditional print sources or electronic tools, or reference sources freely available over the Internet. The library must strive to provide access to the highest quality, most useful reference sources available in all the disciplines served, but librarians should resist any thinking that falsely pits library-supplied reference sources against information found on the Internet. In the minds of graduate students and faculty, the lines are already blurred as to whether a Web-based resource is from the library or not. Rather than lamenting a lack of use of more traditional refer-

ence sources, librarians need to both continue to select appropriate sources for the library to offer, as well as teach and remind users about evaluating the quality authority, accuracy, comprehensiveness, and currency of the information they find, especially for Web-based information, but across all sources, too.

Realistically libraries will need to provide access to many reference sources in all formats if for no other reason than the cost of many such materials is impossibly expensive for a single scholar to bear. Faculty and graduate students are not interested in paying for scholarly resources; therefore, the role of the library as a provider of reference sources will continue to be important (Guthrie & Housewright, 2008). Reference materials can be more expensive than other materials purchased or subscribed to by libraries because they contain complex information that has been gathered, organized, and presented by many people. As the complexity of the reference source increases, so does its cost. To the extent that faculty and graduate students place a high value on these reference sources, they will demand them from their libraries, because they cannot afford to purchase them for their own use.

To answer the question posed in the title of the chapter, yes, graduate students and faculty need access to current, authoritative reference information in their areas of research and teaching. Although how scholars search for and retrieve information has changed as a result of developments in Information Technology, the fundamental work of producing research and scholarly communication has not changed (Guthrie & Housewright, 2008). Librarians must keep sight of their role in supporting those endeavors – making available relevant, high quality, useful reference sources to graduate students and faculty, promoting those resources, and training users to locate and search them effectively.

SOLUTIONS AND RECOMMENDATIONS

To the extent that there is a growing perception of scholars' decreasing dependence on the library, that graduate students and faculty may not be successfully getting their information needs met, that researchers want information in electronic format, and that reference sources are underutilized, librarians should embrace these concerns as an opportunity to respond to this situation with innovative solutions. If we see the information needs and information seeking habits of scholars as relatively enduring (and as long as the tenure system continues in its present form, we have no reason to think differently), then this is a population who would benefit from innovation both the kinds of resources consulted to support their long established research habits, and in the discoverability of those resources. Solutions exist for both the reference sources and for how academic librarians provide reference services to researchers.

Continuous Improvement of Traditional Reference Sources

E-reference sources – reference sources in electronic formats that incorporate enhanced design features available only with digital content – are growing rapidly, and this trend should continue. Researchers are comfortable in the electronic environment and have even come to consider the availability of print-only resources as a barrier to their work (Tenopir et al., 2009). Content producers should continue to create high quality reference materials that are more than just a digital version of a print source, such as enabling full text searching capability and adding hypertext links within the text. Librarians should continue to improve access to these information sources with appropriate metadata and cataloging, and promotion to the user community.

One of the most powerful facets of electronic material compared with print is the freedom to chunk the content in new ways, since no longer are there limitations based on page layout. This enables the user to more quickly find and retrieve information nuggets across the larger work. Further, the capability to link content within a work or across works brings greater utility to an otherwise flat reference source. As more and more reference sources are born digital, these and other features are standard. But they should also be applied to materials converted from print.

Design and Build New Kinds of Reference Sources

Digital technology affords content providers new ways to envision reference content. Features not available in two dimensional print can now be accomplished with digital technology: automated rotating DNA strands, jet propulsion videos, audio files of symphonic motifs linked with composer biographical data, embedded links to datasets in scholarly articles, researcher-maintained wiki sites. Technological advancement affords each discipline and sub-discipline possibilities for producing new kinds of reference sources that perhaps do not yet even exist.

A first step on this path is to learn more about the information needs and information behaviors of researchers by discipline. To that end, research should look at how scholars within a discipline use Web-based resources. This will reveal what sources they consult as opposed to read through, and what they value about those sources. It will also shed light on disciplines where few Web-based sources exist but could be developed, as well as disciplines where resources do exist, but graduate students and faculty are not aware of them. Ultimately, the findings from this line of research should inform the design of resources and tools.

Librarian practitioners and researchers should be active participants in the design of new reference tools. By virtue of the research they conduct, and their knowledge of the principles of information structure, storage, retrieval, and use, they bring tremendous value to the process. They also have the potential to work closely with scholars and thus be aware of their information needs and behaviors. Librarians should work hand-in-hand with product designers and content experts "to lead the migration to more evolved digital artifacts" (Flaxbart, 2001, p. 24).

Another consideration for the design of new reference sources is how to maximize their discovery, a topic covered in other sections of this book. With so much digital content available to researchers, it cannot be assumed that users will even know of the existence of many quality reference sources. One way to confront this problem is to embed digital reference tools within other electronic resources so that users discover and make use of them in a just-in-time manner. Although when using the Internet, one is never "far" from many reference sources, the virtual distance can be so great that users never encounter what would be useful resources unless they know of them in advance. An example of a product that does this quite well is EBSCO's Literary Reference Center, an electronic tool that combines information on authors and their works with literary criticism, a dictionary, a literary encyclopedia, bibliographies, timelines, and citation help. Though this particular product is pitched to undergraduate level work, the structure of the product proves the concept.

Rethinking How to Promote the Reference Collection

Librarians can make reference tools more discoverable with more effective selection, promotion, and recommendation of reference tools. In traditional service models, librarians spent time building and maintaining a print collection of reference sources. Now, librarians must continue to manage a print collection, because although it may be shrinking, as more sources become available online, print collections will probably not go away entirely. But librarians must also build and maintain collections of electronic resources, both library-supplied sources and free Web content. Librarians increase their value to the researchers they serve when they discover and recommend high quality, useful digital resources, and when they make them easily accessible through commonly used Internet platforms. Information overload is a very real phenomenon for researchers (Baldwin, 1998). Librarians can make a major contribution in reducing the effects of information overload by filtering out the best information sources in a given area from the mass of less credible or less useful information. Also, researchers depend rather significantly on recommendations of resources from personal contacts, and are repeat users of trusted sources. The more librarians can position themselves in the social networks of the researchers to promote reference tools, the more likely it is that researchers will try out those tools. Facebook pages and Twitter feeds may be effective mechanisms for spreading the word, akin to current awareness tools.

Academic libraries already do a good job of grouping reference resources by broad subject area on their web sites, but a more nuanced approach may increase the awareness of reference sources. Operating at a deeper level of specificity would enable librarians to point to fewer, but more focused resources. Examples of this can be found in information literacy instruction Web pages created for specific academic departments or even particular courses. The difference comes in the type of resources selected for inclusion. Because most library instruction occurs at the undergraduate level, the resources included in these kinds of compilations are necessarily broad. The same model, however, could be adapted to create finding tools for more advanced researchers within a particular subspecialty. Creating such a tool using wiki technology enables the intended users to add their comments or suggestions about the resources, potentially increasing the impact of the resource on colleagues because of the personal recommendation of peers.

CONCLUSION

Graduate students and faculty have strong needs for information to support their teaching, research, and current awareness. They make extensive use of indexes to periodical literature and Internet search engines for nearly all their information seeking. They value personal recommendations for sources to use, but do not very often consult with a librarian and underutilize other reference sources. Rather than lament what might be perceived by some as an over reliance on Google and Wikipedia, librarians can be innovative in their response to this situation by exploring new ways to contribute to the design and promotion of new references sources. To that end, e-reference tools should

- Be more than digitized versions of their print-based precursors
- Make use of the many powerful features afforded by digital technology
- Be embedded in the technologies and platforms scholars use daily

In serving the information needs of their scholar constituents, librarians should

- Cultivate personal relationships with the researchers they serve
- Participate in the background research, the design, and the creation of new forms of reference sources
- Regularly identify and evaluate new reference tools, both library-provided resources and freely available Web-based products
- Promote these resources to researchers by sharing compilations of highly relevant, high quality resources in narrow topical areas

This chapter makes the case that indeed researchers have a strong and enduring need for reference sources. To maximize researchers' use of reference sources, opportunities exist for creating new kinds of tools and for increasing their discoverability and use. Academic librarians are well positioned to lead the way in these endeavors.

REFERENCES

Aked, M. J., Phillips, J. C., Reiman-Sendi, K., Risner, K., Voigt, K. J., & Wiesler, J. (1998). Faculty use of an academic library reference collection. *Collection Building, 17*(2), 56–64. doi:10.1108/01604959810212444

Anderson, T. D. (2006). Uncertainty in action: Observing information seeking within the creative processes of scholarly research. *Information Research, 12*(1). Retrieved September 14, 2010, from http://infomrationr.net/ir/12-1/paper283.html

Baldwin, R. G. (1998). Technology's impact on faculty life and work. *New Directions for Teaching and Learning, 76*, 7–21. doi:10.1002/tl.7601

Barrett, A. (2005). The information-seeking habits of graduate student researchers in the humanities. *Journal of Academic Librarianship, 31*(4), 324–331. doi:10.1016/j.acalib.2005.04.005

Bennett, D. B., & Buhler, A. G. (2010). Browsing of e-journals by engineering faculty. *Issues in Science and Technology Librarianship, 61*. Retrieved September 14, 2010, from http://www.istl.org/10-spring/refereed2.html

Borgman, C. L., Smart, L. J., Millwood, K. A., Finley, J. R., Champeny, L., Gilliland, A. J., & Leazer, G. H. (2005). Comparing faculty information seeking in teaching and research: Implications for the design of digital libraries. *Journal of the American Society for Information Science and Technology, 56*(6), 636–657. doi:10.1002/asi.20154

Brown, C. (2005). Where do molecular biology graduate students find information? *Science & Technology Libraries, 25*(3), 89–104. doi:10.1300/J122v25n03_06

Brunton, C. (2005). The effects of library user-education programmes on the information-seeking behavior of Brisbane College of Theology students: An Australian case study. *Journal of Religious & Theological Information, 7*(2), 55–73. doi:10.1300/J112v07n02_05

Carpenter, J., Wetheridge, L., Smith, N., Goodman, M., & Struijvé, O. (2010). Researchers of tomorrow: A three year (BL/JISC) study tracking the research behaviour of "Generation Y" doctoral students. Retrieved September 14, 2010, from http://explorationforchange.net/index.php/rot-home.html

Cassell, K. A., & Hiremath, U. (2009). *Reference and information services in the 21ˢᵗ century: An introduction* (2nd ed.). New York, NY: Neal-Schuman.

Chu, S. K., & Law, N. (2008). The development of information search expertise of research students. *Journal of Librarianship and Information Science, 40*(3), 165–177. doi:10.1177/0961000608092552

Doraswamy, M. (2009, June). The relationship of academic role and information use by engineering faculty. *Library Philosophy and Practice, 11*(1), 1–9.

Earp, V. J. (2008). Information source preference of education graduate students. *Behavioral & Social Sciences Librarian, 27*(2), 73–91. doi:10.1080/01639260802194974

Ellis, D. (1989). A behavioural approach to information retrieval system design. *The Journal of Documentation, 45*(2), 171–212. doi:10.1108/eb026843

Ellis, D. (1993). Modeling the information-seeking patterns of academic researchers: A grounded theory approach. *The Library Quarterly, 63*(4), 469–486. doi:10.1086/602622

Ellis, D., Cox, D., & Hall, K. (1993). A comparison of the information seeking patterns of researchers in the physical and social sciences. *The Journal of Documentation, 49*(4), 356–369. doi:10.1108/eb026919

Flaxbart, D. (2001). Conversations with chemists: Information-seeking behavior of chemistry faculty in the electronic age. *Science & Technology Libraries, 21*(3/4), 5–26. doi:10.1300/J122v21n03_02

Gabridge, T., Gaskell, M., & Stout, A. (2008). Information seeking through students' eyes: The MIT photo diary study. *College & Research Libraries, 69*(6), 510–522.

George, C., Bright, A., Hurlbert, T., Linke, E. C., St. Clair, G., & Stein, J. (2006). Scholarly use of information: Graduate students' information seeking behavior. *Information Research, 11*(4). Retrieved September 14, 2010, from http://informationr.net/ir/11-4/paper272.html

Guthrie, K., & Housewright, R. (2008). Attitudes and behaviors in the field of economics: Anomaly or leading indicator. *Journal of Library Administration, 48*(2), 173–193. doi:10.1080/01930820802231369

Hemminger, B., Lu, D., Vaughan, K. T. L., & Adams, S. J. (2007). Information seeking behavior of academic scientists. *Journal of the American Society for Information Science and Technology, 58*(15), 2205–2225. doi:10.1002/asi.20686

Jamali, H. R., & Nicholas, D. (2008). Information-seeking behavior of physicists and astronomers. *Aslib Proceedings: New Information Perspectives, 60*(5), 444–462.

Kayongo, J., & Helm, C. (2010). Graduate students and the library: A survey of research practices and library use at the University of Notre Dame. *Reference and User Services Quarterly*, *49*(4), 341–349.

King, D. W., & Montgomery, C. H. (2002). After migration to an electronic journal collection: Impact on faculty and doctoral students. *D-Lib Magazine*, *8*(12). doi:10.1045/december2002-king

King, D. W., Tenopir, C., Choemprayong, S., & Wu, L. (2009). Scholarly journal information-seeking and reading patterns of faculty at five U. S. universities. *Learned Publishing*, *22*, 126–144. doi:10.1087/2009208

Liao, Y., Finn, M., & Lu, J. (2007). Information-seeking behavior of international graduate students vs. American graduate students: A user study at Virginia Tech 2005. *College & Research Libraries*, *68*(1), 5–25.

Mansourian, Y., & Madden, A. D. (2007). Perceptions of the Web as a research tool amongst researchers in biological sciences. *New Library World*, *108*(9/10), 407–423. doi:10.1108/03074800710823944

Mayfield, T., & Thomas, J. (2005). A tale of two departments: A comparison of faculty information-seeking practices. *Behavioral & Social Sciences Librarian*, *23*(2), 47–66. doi:10.1300/J103v23n02_03

Meho, L. I., & Hass, S. W. (2001). Information-seeking behavior and use of social science faculty studying stateless nations: A case study. *Library & Information Science Research*, *23*, 5–25. doi:10.1016/S0740-8188(00)00065-7

Palmer, C. L., Teffeau, L. C., & Pirmann, C. M. (2009). *Scholarly information practices in the online environment: Themes from the literature and implications for library services development*. Report commissioned by OCLC Research. Retrieved September 14, 2010, from http://www.oclc.org/programs/publications/reports/2009-02.pdf

Prabha, C., Connaway, L. S., Olszewski, L., & Jenkins, L. R. (2007). What is enough? Satisficing information needs. *The Journal of Documentation*, *63*(1), 74–89. doi:10.1108/00220410710723894

Quigley, J., Peck, D. R., Rutter, S., & Williams, E. M. (2002). Making choices: Factors in the selection of information resources among science faculty at the University of Michigan. *Issues in Science and Technology Librarianship, 34*, Spring. Retrieved September 14, 2010, from http://www.istl.org/02-spring/refereed.html

Rafiq, M., & Ameen, K. (2009). Information-seeking behavior and user satisfaction of university instructors: A case study. *Library Philosophy and Practice*, *11*(1), 1–9.

Reitz, J. M. (2004). *Dictionary for library and information science*. Westport, CT: Libraries Unlimited.

Schlosser, R. W., Wendt, O., Bhavnani, S., & Nail-Chiwetalu, B. (2006). Use of information-seeking strategies for developing systematic reviews and engaging in evidence-based practice: The application of traditional and comprehensive Pearl Growing- A review. *International Journal of Language & Communication Disorders*, *41*(5), 567–582..doi:10.1080/13682820600742190

Schonfeld, R. C., & Housewright, R. (2010). *Faculty survey 2009: Key strategic insights for libraries, publishers, and societies*. Retrieved November 5, 2010 from http://www.ithaka.org/ithaka-s-r/ research/faculty-surveys-2000-2009

Shen, Y. (2007). Information seeking in academic research: A study of the sociology faculty at the University of Wisconsin-Madison. *Information Technology and Libraries, 26*(1), 4–13.

Tenopir, C., King, D. W., Edwards, D., & Wu, L. (2009). Electronic journals and changes in scholarly article seeking and reading patterns. *Aslib Proceedings: New Information Perspectives, 61*(1), 5–32.

Thelwall, M. (2005). Directing students to new information types: A new role for Google in literature searchers? *Internet Reference Services Quarterly, 10*(3/4), 159–166.

Wastawy, S. F., Uth, C. W., & Stewart, C. (2004). Learning communities: An investigative study into their impact on library services. *Science & Technology Libraries, 24*(3/4), 327–374. doi:10.1300/J122v24n03_07

Westbrook, L. (2003). Information needs and experiences of scholars in women's studies: Problems and solutions. *College & Research Libraries, 64*(3), 192–209.

Chapter 6
Hidden Greenlands:
Learning, Libraries, and Literacy in the Information Age

Frank Menchaca
Cengage Learning, USA

ABSTRACT

This chapter considers the role of libraries and educational publishers in the information age. Studies show that, for most college and university students, the trigger for research remains the classroom assignment. Tasks associated with specific learning objectives—writing a paper, preparing an interpretive reading, engaging in historical or statistical analysis—still motivate students to engage in research. What has changed is the fact that students no longer rely on librarians, libraries, or traditional publishers for information resources. They go directly to search engines. Today's learners are, however, quickly overwhelmed and, despite being "digital natives," struggle to evaluate information and organize it to build ideas. The ability of publishers, librarians, and libraries to address this issue will determine their relevancy in the 21st century and, perhaps, the success of students themselves in the information age. This chapter reviews a wide variety of literature and experiential data on information literacy, findability, metadata, and use of library resources and proposes how all players can re-think their roles.

DOI: 10.4018/978-1-61350-308-9.ch006

INTRODUCTION

Recently, during what is usually one of the duller stretches of a transatlantic flight—when passengers obliterate the hours with sleep, read, or escape tedium watching movies on postcard-sized screens—the captain addressed the cabin and alerted us we were in for something unusual: Greenland, typically hidden under a misty shell of clouds, was fully visible.

Maybe it is axiomatic in post-September 11ᵗʰ times that warning of anything out of the ordinary, particularly from a pilot mid-flight, grabs our attention. In any case, within moments, passengers clustered around the tiny, oval windows, straining to take in the event.

And an event it was: soaring mountain peaks and precipitous slopes. Between them, giant, grooved fjords stretched down to scraps of land: brown, with a little green at the fringes.

I remembered an article describing the expansion of Greenland's arable land, a consequence of shorter winters, higher temperatures, and other effects of global warming (Trautfetter, 2006). And now, here it was as part of a scene of colliding histories: ice dating back to prehistory, next to 21ˢᵗ century agriculture, itself a result of industrialization begun in the 1800s.

The incident revealed something paradoxical.

I realized how little I knew about the place, and, how little *reliable* knowledge I had about climate change. I should, I decided, start keeping tabs on Greenland.

More than a year of search engine alerts and Really Simple Syndication (RSS) feeds later, my inquiry seemed well-timed: Greenland had risen from obscurity to topicality in much the way it appeared out of the mist on that transatlantic flight.

On November 13, 2010, for example, *The New York Times* reported that Greenland had become no less than a locus of major global warming study. Scientists take the temperature of the surrounding ocean to gauge the rate of melting in glaciers. Their

conclusions are stunning in their implications as well in their *inconclusiveness:*

...researchers have recently been startled to see big changes unfold in both Greenland and Antarctica.

As a result of recent calculations that take the changes into account, many scientists now say that sea level is likely to rise perhaps three feet by 2100 — an increase that, should it come to pass, would pose a threat to coastal regions the world over.

And the calculations suggest that the rise could conceivably exceed six feet, which would put thousands of square miles of the American coastline under water and would probably displace tens of millions of people in Asia (Gillis, 2010).

One degree of temperature change or several? Three feet of water level increase, or six? The implications of the numerical differences, in a human context, are tiny: whether to take a sweater or not; wading in up to the knees or swimming. In a global context, over time, the impact is enormous.

The indeterminacy of the data, the range of their potential consequences, should make us ask: which other unknown uncertainties are out there influencing our future? How many hidden Greenlands do we pass over unthinkingly until to notice them is to be shocked by our own ignorance of their impact? How do we interpret information in shifting contexts? And how do we convey the urgency of these issues to learners in the 21ˢᵗ century?

I. TRUTH 2.0

As consumers and producers of educational publications, such questions ought to preoccupy us. The answers go straight to how human beings will learn and flourish in the information age.

We live in a world where communications technology makes information instantaneously accessible. The sheer volume and availability have had, on the one hand, a revolutionary and democratizing effect. The collections of some of the world's most elite libraries now yield their treasures in a simple, online search. Any user can monitor scientific research—that may have profound future implications—as it unfolds in the laboratory or field through Open Access websites. Even an organization like WikiLeaks, with its controversial (some would say irresponsible) online distribution of sensitive diplomatic documents, can be seen as a safeguard against foundation of the Minitrue ("Ministry of Truth")—what George Orwell called the government agency charged with disseminating the one, "official" version of the truth in his novel, *1984.* In the digital age, then, we are poised to be more informed, less easily manipulated, and more autonomous.

Aren't we?

More than 60 years after Orwell published his dystopian vision of society, information authoritarianism —a single, centrally distributed version of the truth— hardly appears to be our threat. We seem to be at risk, rather, from Truth 1.0, 1.2, 2.0—multiple versions of facts, endless iterations of information, the data slipstream from which it feels increasingly difficult to fix verifiable knowledge. Instead of conferring power, a surfeit of information seems to leave us powerless. Writes poet Hoagland (2010, p. 40), "…the swamp of excess information in which we each day swim, and our paradoxical lack of influence on that world—they make us ill. We have communication sickness."

II. PROJECT INFORMATION LITERACY

What effect does this have on education? Two University of Washington researchers, Alison J. Head, and Michael B. Eisenberg, have been engaged in an ongoing, comprehensive study—Project Information Literary (PIL)—of the ways in which college students find, evaluate, and use digital information to perform assignments and to learn.

"[A] risk-averse strategy based on efficiency and predictability in order to manage and control the information…." (Head, 2010, p.3) is how PIL describes students' approach to research in the November 2010 report, "'Truth Be Told': How College Students Evaluate and Use Information in the Digital Age." The ironies should be immediate: in the digital age, students narrow, not expand their inquiry; at a time when new data overthrows old in hours, even minutes, students seek continuity, predictability.

Think of the narratives, tapped out covertly on Twitter, of crackdown during the 2009 Iranian elections; the photos of Abu Ghraib prisoner abuse; the index to climate change waiting to be read in Greenland's ice. Information does not play it safe or straight with us; yet students want to play it straight and safe with information. Why?

The result of 8,353 college students' responses to surveys on 25 U.S. campuses, PIL's report provides insights—by turns disheartening, encouraging, and surprising—on where librarians and information publishers fall short in enabling knowledge creation—and how we can transform it—in the information age.

PIL shows that today's students begin information-seeking primarily with classroom materials, well ahead of the library, and, interestingly, the immersive Web 2.0 worlds many associate—perhaps falsely—as natural to "digital natives." (Ibid., p.3) That course readings are the first stop in research is unremarkable. Notable, however, are the next steps students take, as this chart (Ibid., p. 7)—a comparison between 2009 and 2010 survey data—demonstrates. (See Figure 1)

The dual points of departure in investigation—course readings and search engines-including Google—are predictable: they are the most readily accessible and familiar. Other points were

Figure 1. Project Information Literacy Progress Report, 2010. Used with permission.

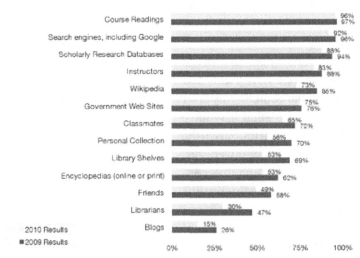

news: scholarly research databases are more often go-to options than Wikipedia. Print or electronic encyclopedias receive priority over blogs.

For a publisher of reference materials for libraries, the data ring bells in alarm as much as celebration. Students distinguish between value-added resources publishers produce--which libraries evaluate and purchase--and the unmediated, open community constructions of Wikipedia. And they seek the guidance of their instructors in answering research questions. Troubling is that librarians—who should be the source of information expertise on campus—rank just above the anything-goes world of blogs in students' research hierarchy.

PIL data suggest multiple factors contribute to this situation. Students demonstrate a clear, if underdeveloped, appreciation for information literacy: the ability to differentiate and weigh the value of diverse types of information to create new ideas.

Students in the sample took little at face value and reported they were frequent evaluators of information culled from the Web and to a lesser extent, the campus library. More often than anything else, respondents considered whether information was up-to-date and current when evaluating Web content (77%) and library materials (67%) for course work (Ibid., p. 3).

Students take critical reading of information seriously and identify currency as an indicator of relevancy; but in the 24-hour news cycle, currency is hardly a proxy for information integrity or value. Yet on these counts as well, students seem cognizant of other important factors, per Figure 2. (Ibid., p. 11).

Students consider author credentials and source (URL) in assessing information. Interestingly, interface design closely follows these. It would be misleading, however, to assume that students mean they favor only attractive websites. Good, user-centered information design—particularly what Edward Tufte calls the visual display of quantitative information (Tufte, 2001) --may be a key indicator of information's value to today's visually-oriented learners. Consider these criteria (Head and Eisenberg, 2010, pg. 15) reported applying to library resources. (See Figure 3)

Figure 2. Project Information Literacy Progress Report, 2010. Used with permission.

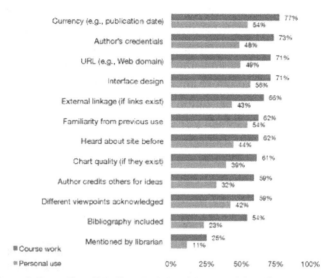

Chart quality ranks just below currency in importance. The *look* of information signifies its worth and utility to students. Note: To the placement of "different viewpoints acknowledged" in a closely-linked chain of currency and chart quality.

III. FROM DEFINING AND FINDING TO DESIGN AND INTENT

The findings urge questions on publishers and librarians: does the emphasis we place on visual representation of information—content design—match the priority students assign to it in evalua-

Figure 3. Project Information Literacy Progress Report, 2010. Used with permission.

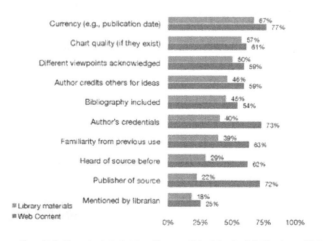

tion? And how effective are we in helping students understand the *tendencies* of online content?

Libraries and publishers do show an increasing awareness of the importance of information design and user experience (UX). Cengage Learning, the company I work for, employs several UX teams and integrates users in product conceptualization early on, through usability testing of design prototypes. It is not unique in this regard. Libraries engage similar processes.

For many years, moreover, Cengage's Gale imprint has published products like *Opposing Viewpoints in Context* and *Global Issues in Context*, online databases predicated on explicitly describing and helping users compare and contrast the positions taken by various information sources.

The PIL results, however, say that students, to become better researchers and learners, need publishers and librarians to go further in design and, for lack of a better term, *information intent*. We need to see these not as extensions, but rather as parts of a new nucleus of our mission. This may require a fundamental change in our self-conceptions.

The PIL report distinguishes between lower- and higher-order thinking skills. It associates the former with "procedural, memorized routines, techniques, and rules for conducting research and finding information" (lbid., p.37)—in other words, searching and retrieving. "[I]nterpreting, synthesizing, and creatively manipulating abstract concepts to generate new constructs, meanings, interpretations, and knowledge," (lbid., p.37) constitute higher-order competencies. It concludes:

The survey findings suggest that the students in our sample considered themselves fairly adept at lower-ordering thinking skills for research: checking the publication date of an article for evaluative purposes, finding citations for other sources in a bibliography at the bottom of a Wikipedia entry, writing a paper from an outline, coming up with search terms, and so forth.

At the same time, the findings suggest that the students in our sample considered themselves to be at a great disadvantage when asked to apply some of the higher-order thinking skills for information seeking and research, especially starting, defining and narrowing a research inquiry so it framed their entire research process. (lbid., p. 37)

Publishers and librarians have, for much of our histories, tended to focus on servicing these lower-order duties. We create, provision, organize, collect, and store information. We understand how faculty and students want to use that information, but we have limited our role to guiding them to it, then leaving them to *find* answers. Less familiar to them are we as collaborators in formulating *questions*.

As a reference publisher, for example, Cengage's Gale imprint, even with its emphasis on viewpoints, has largely adhered to the traditional view of content that the originating theorists of the modern encyclopedia—Denis Diderot and other figures of the French Enlightenment—articulated: knowledge could be fixed, summarized, and systematized. Encyclopedia articles, therefore, <u>defined</u> a topic. They communicated verified knowledge and an understanding of its place in a hierarchy, eschewing perspectives for reportage. Those would come from other sources readers encountered as they ascended a hierarchy and moved from a broad base of facts to more refined opinions and primary sources.

On the one hand, this editorial policy has allowed reference publishers like Gale to aspire to goals of accuracy, balance, and authority. And these qualities warrant preservation, particularly in the increasingly axe-grinding, partisan world of media—satirized well by comedian-commentator Stephen Colbert's term "'truthiness': truth that comes from gut, not from books" (Merriam-Webster Online Dictionary. http://www.merriam-webster.com/info/06words.htm), in other words: *what I want you to believe*, supported through conviction, not substantiation.

On the other hand, it must be acknowledged that every piece of content—no matter how much it strives for neutrality—has a design upon the user, and an intent to influence. This has always been so. The *encyclopédistes'* systemization of knowledge, though beautiful in its pursuit of programmatic inquiry based on rationality and tolerance, also reflected a set of culturally, politically, and personally-determined beliefs and preconceptions. Today, the sheer volume of available information means we are inundated in obvious and subtle calls to action, persuasions to what to think, say, and do. To become better informed citizens with greater chances for success in the world are among those calls, no question. Consider, however, this statement--"In 2008, the advertising on Google's search engine was responsible for 98 percent of the company's $22 billion in revenue" (Petersen, 2010, p. 60) —as a context even for tools like Google Books, Google Scholar, YouTube, and Google Earth. These are all inarguably useful; they also exist in a matrix predicated, overwhelmingly, on selling you something. Publishers and libraries are just as compelled by commercial interests. Success in their educational missions is also not divisible from commercial success. Reference products that do not transmit knowledge fail; textbooks that cannot support student achievement will not sell; unused libraries become unfunded ones. Both publishers and librarians might have greater chances at commercial and educational success in actively identifying the interpretations and objectives nested within the information ocean around our users.

We may define new relevancy for ourselves in doing so. And we may be among those most capable of doing the job. Identifying information intent is something that the massively-popular, socially-constructed Wikipedia *cannot* do, for example. In relying on amalgamation vs. authorship, a Wikipedia article necessarily distributes—even atomizes—intent. This is why Wikipedia is reliable and useful for quick look up but not preferable as a source for building ideas. Indeed, the success

of Wikipedia has opened the door for reference publishers and libraries to create and engage users with higher-order informational content that overtly questions itself, as well as other content, teaching literacy. In this sense, Jimmy Wales's revolutionary, online encyclopedia has raised, not lowered, the bar on reference publishing. For their part, librarians can constitute a qualitative alternative to search engines—often preferred by students over library resources—by helping students *use* information, to articulate the questions they want to ask, ahead of guiding them to answers.

The benefits of this are well documented. The British Library, in cooperation with the Joint Information Sharing Committee (JISC) issued a report in 2008, "The Information Behaviour of the Researcher of the Future." The report is based upon comprehensive study of literature on research in the digital age, as well as on mining of usage logs from both institutions. Their conclusions link directly improved student outcomes with active engagement by educators—librarians, teachers, and parents—in research.

There are two particularly powerful messages emerging from recent research. When the top and bottom quartiles of students – as defined by their information literacy skills - are compared, it emerges that the top quartile report a much higher incidence of exposure to basic library skills from their parents, in the school library, classroom or public library in their earlier years. It seems that a new divide is opening up in the US, with the better-equipped students taking the prizes of better grades. At the lower end of the information skills spectrum, the research finds that intervention at university age is too late: these students have already developed an ingrained coping behaviour: they have learned to 'get by' with Google (The Information Behaviour of the Researcher of the Future, 2008, pg. 23).

Students who are trained in higher-order information skills receive better grades than those who deal only with information in lower-order, search and find modes represented by search engines. Yet in PIL's findings, one of the key stakeholders poised to support student achievement—the librarian—has the lowest mind-share among students. Why is this so and how can the situation be addressed?

IV. FINDABILITY AND BEYOND

In 2008, the not-for-profit research organization, Ithaka, issued "2006 Studies of Key Stakeholders in the Digital Transformation in Higher Education" (Schonfeld, 2006). The culmination of 2000, 2003, and 2006 academic faculty surveys, the 2006 investigation also included librarians. That year, a total of 4100 faculty and 350 librarians responded. One specific objective was to test faculty perceptions of libraries.

Among the report's findings was that faculty's perception that the library, as a "gateway to information," was declining in importance.

The declining importance assigned to the gateway role is cause for concern in general, and especially when considered by discipline. The importance to faculty of this role has decreased across all disciplines since 2003, most significantly among scientists. While almost 80% of humanists rate this role as very important, barely over 50% of scientists do so. Beyond the differences between these general disciplinary groups, there also exist substantial variations by individual discipline, as demonstrated by the perceptions of economists. Between 2003 and 2006, the percentage of economists indicating they found the library's gateway role to be very important dropped almost fifteen percentage points. In 2006, the percentage of economists who believed this gateway role to be very important was actually below the average level of scientists, falling to 48%.

The decreasing importance of this gateway role to faculty is logical, given the increasing prominence of non-library discovery tools such as Google in the last several years. Since 2003, the number of scholars across disciplines who report starting their research at non-library discovery tools, either a general purpose search engine or a specific electronic resource, has increased, and the number who report starting in directly library-related venues, either the library building or the library OPAC, has decreased. Despite the rising popularity of tools like Google, overall, general purpose search engines still slightly trail the OPAC as a starting point for research, and are well behind specific electronic research resources. This overall picture, however, hides a number of variations by discipline; scientists typically prefer non-library resources, while humanists are more enthusiastic users of the library (Ibid., p. 6).

The Ithaka results echoed OCLC's 2005 report, "Perceptions of Libraries and Information Resources." (OCLC, 2005) The academic library was gradually being dis-intermediated by search engines as the primary portal for research and information. Search engines and their affiliated services, such as Google Scholar, Google Books, et cetera seemed to be more effective in connecting researchers—students and faculty—to the information they needed. They library's problem was, therefore, one of findability within those search engines.

In 2010, this statement still seems true. Libraries need to become more visible to students and researchers where they perform their work. The PIL results also support this. To help address this problem, Cengage's Gale imprint has, for its part, produced applications (apps) for mobile devices such as the i-Phone, i-Pad, and others, under the banner of Access My Library (AML). The AML apps locate a device's user and connect her with Gale resources at the local school, public, and academic library. In the instance of public libraries, authentication is removed, and anyone can access and use Gale online resources. We also began to explore making Gale library resources available to students and instructors via Learning Management Systems (LMS), such as Blackboard (Dunn and Menchaca, 2009).

Today, however, none of those initiatives seems adequate, and the assumption that search engines and their services can be effective as alternatives to libraries, only by being more convenient, rings hollow. Looked at in the context of the PIL findings, findability of library resources on the Web is only one step, and a first one at that, in addressing the issues around information gathering and learning in the 21st century. While critically important, making library resources findable is, fundamentally, another form of "storefronting:" placing information in front of learners without the skills and context to enable them to turn it into new concepts.

Information findability without literacy will make students neither smarter nor more successful. The British Library-JISC study, in fact, points to little change among digital natives' capacities to interpret and make use of information—readily accessible though it is in Google—when compared to learners in earlier, non-digital generations. When the study applied a set of statements to a myth or reality test, based on research, it reported the following assumption and response:

They [Google generation users] are expert searchers***

Our verdict: This is a dangerous myth. Digital literacies and information literacies do not go hand in hand. A careful look at the literature over the past 25 years finds no improvement (or deterioration) in young people's information skills (Information Behaviour, 2008, pg. 20).

Digitally-enabled is not knowledge-enabled. And the digital library may be just one more corpus of information users must learn to underutilize in the name of predictability and avoidance of risk.

Though a noble concept, the online public library that Harvard University's Robert Darnton and others have called for may be of limited consequence to actual learning (Darnton, 2010).

Librarians and publishers, performing in expanded and new roles, are required to help make a qualitative difference in research and learning.

V. TOWARD AN INTEGRATED LITERACY

In 1987, years before the terms "World Wide Web" or "Internet" entered the vernacular, writing teacher Michael Kleine envisioned the library, on the eve of an assignment due date, as a place where students performed a kind of rough transplant operation: "lifting and transporting textual substance from one location, the library, to another, their teachers' briefcases" (Bowles-Terry, Davis, Holliday, 2009, p. 226). They hunted quotations, excised those that sounded correct, and installed them in papers. They were not analyzing, evaluating, interpreting, or speculating; in short, they were not thinking or learning. A generation later, the night library is no longer a physical place; it is students' Web browsers. As the British Library-JISC research shows, their information-seeking behavior has changed little, despite the fact that they live in an age predicated in every way, down to its name, on information. Seen in this context, the question writer Nicholas Carr asked rather famously in *The Atlantic*—"Is Google Making Us Stupid" (Carr, 2008)—seems to miss a bigger question: *Why hasn't Google made us smarter?*

Writing in *Reference & User Services Quarterly*, three librarian/writing instructors, Melissa Bowles-Terry, Erin Davis, and Wendy Holliday examine reasons why students' information skills are deficient, and what can be done to improve them. The authors indicate that the shortcomings in information literacy (IL) may have less to do with media (print or digital distribution) and more to do with how librarians themselves are trained and how writing is taught:

Many writing instructors and librarians still conceive of and practice IL from a behavioralist framework. Behavioral theories of education, dominant in the 1950s and 60s, assume learning is based on precise, well-defined, and measurable behaviors and rules. For IL, behaviorism focuses on information sources and procedures. Librarians teach the 'correct' sources and the 'correct' order in which to search those sources while discouraging 'wrong' approaches, much like the avoidance of 'text errors' in writing instruction (Bowles, 2009).

This step 1-2-3 approach, straight out of the industrial age—think of Henry Ford's assembly line—seems particularly anachronistic in a digital environment, where information is networked, and knowledge creation involves engaging multiple, simultaneous sources, all varied in their purpose and viewpoints. Searching for the correct answers, moreover, becomes increasingly pointless in an environment where information is both unmanageable and highly manipulable. To apply the vocabulary of the PIL study, students fail at higher-order thinking skills because they operate in lower-order paradigms, themselves reinforced in outmoded educational practices. At a time when information is as pervasive, plastic, and powerful as our own, this failure can be particularly deleterious to students' success at learning and in daily life.

Instead, the authors call for a new kind of information instruction that emphasizes the communities and contexts in which information is constructed, received, and used. They describe this sociocultural approach as follows:

In this view, learning happens in a community of practice where novices learn to become practitioners and experts mediate the information environment, guiding them toward information that the

social community values. Learning is conceived not as a mastery of formal and generic skills, but as expanded participation in a community of practice or activity system. (Ibid., p. 226)

The authors cite case studies at Utah State University (USU), where librarians put this theory into practice, in partnership with writing instructors, with groups of students in specific classes.

Playing the role of "expert mediators", the librarian-instructors started by establishing learning objectives associated with the classes. Based on those, they created a series of problem-based lesson plans, involving the actual questions students were asked to research and upon which they would write papers.

Instead of pointing the students toward information sources where they could find the "right" answers, the librarian-instructors worked with them to examine the qualities of the questions themselves.

- What *position* did the questions imply?
- How did that position change, depending on context?
- Why might that position be held in one context, not in another?
- How is that position communicated?

For an English 2010 (Intermediate Writing) course, the procedure went as follows:

...the class had to decide whether fast food restaurants should be held accountable for contributing to obesity in America. Students approached the question from various angles: the medical consequences of eating fast food, the economics of the fast food business, and marketing—particularly advertising aimed at children. This provided a concrete focus exploring how different discourse communities operate, including the questions they ask, the information and knowledge they value, and where and how they communicate within their communities and the general public. (Ibid., p. 227)

Librarian-instructors and students conducted brainstorming sessions. The group considered various viewpoints, and motivations for holding them, before ever searching for any information. The focus was not on finding answers, but rather on accumulating sets of questions about questions, or hypotheses. The process was dialogic, and real time.

The USU results were tellingly mixed. Some students reported being uncomfortable with the less routinized approach. How would they know if they were finding the "right" answers? At the same time, they appeared to grow more aware of the *uncertainty* of the information they encountered. In some cases, this spurred students on to deeper, more original research and thinking:

In their final projects, it became clear that some students were engaged in a more authentic research practice than simply reporting on existing wisdom. A few students, for example, went beyond textual sources by observing customers in a fast food restaurant. These students focused on making connections between what they had personally observed and what they found in literature. Other students, however, were simply building bibliographies and made fewer connections (Ibid., p. 227).

While its effects on student behavior were equivocal, the USU program hints at a new role for librarians—as "expert mediators" of information, fully integrated in student learning—that publishers can support and enhance. This implies new forms of partnership, new uses of technology, and new ways of doing business.

VI. "FACTS FOR WHATEVER"

Notable in the USU cases was that the librarian/instructors interacted with students on a wholly personal level. This is highly engaging, but difficult to scale. On a multi-campus, state university system, for example, an army of IL specialists would be required—along with the funding—to reach the student population.

How can students learn and utilize higher-order information skills on a mass scale? This seems an excellent problem for publishers to help solve. Currently, one of the more scalable resources for distributing library materials to students is the learning management system (LMS). LMSs permit librarians to disseminate course-related readings and bibliographies. Some librarians even hold LMS "office hours" when they are available to consult on research via chat. A large university, however, can operate several systems at once, and LMSs do not provide a space for a dialogic, qualitative exchange between librarians and students that the USU approach utilized, albeit in physical mode. The opportunity exists, then, for library and classroom publishers to produce a user experience that enables, via software, the higher-order thought processes identified in the PIL study, in a large-scale manner.

The timing seems propitious. IPad, Kindle, Nook, Android system-enabled slates: a growing number of hardware tools are being used in learning and research. Meanwhile, Apple and others have encouraged the development of apps to assist in an increasing number of discrete learning activities in innovative ways. What is missing is software that integrates these apps with high quality research and learning materials, interoperates with the LMS, and is delivered across a variety of hardware: traditional personal computers (PCs) as well as newer mobile devices and tablets.

Meeting this challenge requires software design and more. It means that publishers and librarians must directly link research materials with learning content. If the impact of this link is to drive qualitative vs. quantitative value—in other words, to amount to more than just more *stuff*—we need to think about metadata more expansively, as a form of content design. In the USU case studies, librarians and instructors, posing questions, were engaged, essentially, in an information architecture activity. They were making information about information: defining details about perspectives and positions, closely examining sources, and identifying qualitative differences among pieces of information. Our metadata currently is not robust enough to capture these nuances. Dublin core records provide for descriptive metadata. Yet even Dublin core records enhanced through the Gateway to Educational Materials (GEM) initiative get at only some of these qualities (Adamich, 2010). Librarian Tom Adamich writes:

[A] useful addition to this GEM cataloging example is the inclusion of the mediator, beneficiary, and essential resources sections. The mediator describes educators who would provide instruction or work together in instructional teams. A beneficiary would be the educational population who would benefit from this instruction. Essential resources lists [sic] useful tools that would supplement this lesson (Adamich, 2010).

Librarians and publishers can, together, begin to see metadata as a form of content design, a medium for identifying intent, source, usage, and other characteristics that reflect higher-order thought activities. Another option is to allow students and faculty to contribute these aspects in a form of social construction: information users providing usage information.

It is one thing to create software and information programs. It is another to acquire them. Integration of learning with research content also prompts consideration of new business models. Today, libraries purchase and provide research content for the entire campus. Students are responsible for buying learning materials at the instructor's recommendation. Economic pressures weigh on both activities. Libraries more often need to demonstrate return on investment through usage. And students increasingly seek lower-cost alternatives to learning materials. Is it possible to construct a business model where an institution extends the library's buying model to classroom

materials, particularly if they are integrated? If so, libraries would be, in effect, subsidizing learning content. Would their budgets change to accommodate this? Would there be a charge-back to the student? Would the institution make a centralized purchase? Should pedagogical and research information be purchased the way institutions purchase, say, electricity—as an ongoing part of the infrastructure, to be used when, where, and how it is needed?

These are large questions. They require publishers, librarians, provosts, and university CFOs to engage in a dialog. Today, these factions largely do not deal with each other. Meanwhile, economic pressures on both the library and the student prompt decisions and work-arounds that, if silo-ed, risk being ineffective, or worse, harmful to everyone's shared mission—education. One large theme emerging from the PIL data is that we may well be sending students out into an information age under-equipped to succeed. A knowledge economy depends on workers who can quickly and critically evaluate information and synthesize often highly-changeable data into sustainable, executable ideas, products, and services in all kinds of businesses. "Satisficing" with what search engines point to will surely not do.

In addition to enabling workers in a new economy, publishers and librarians have a role in contributing to an information literate citizenry. Many sources of information were used to support the Bush administration's decision to invade Iraq and eradicate weapons of mass destruction, for example. Arguably missing was the application of *judgment* to those sources: were they accurate? Could they be trusted? What motivations did they support? At a time when there are, to borrow a phrase from Radiohead's Thom Yorke, "facts for whatever," a population adept at critiquing information is less likely to fall for *whatever*.

The research discussed throughout this chapter indicates that in nearly every aspect of education—libraries, publishers, research, learning—change *from without* is already underway. Change *from within* is needed. Doing anything less would be treat the future as a "hidden Greenland"—something which we traverse blindly.

REFERENCES

Brown, J. S., & Duguid, P. (2000). *The social life of information*. Cambridge, MA: Harvard Business School Press.

Carr, N. (2010). *The shallows: What the Internet is doing to our brains*. New York, NY: Norton.

Gorz, A. (2010). *The immaterial*. Ithaca, NY: Seagull Books.

Head, A. J., & Eisenberg, M. B. (2010). *Project Information Literacy progress report: "Truth be told": How college students evaluate and use information in the digital age*. The Information School, University of Washington. November 1, 2010.

Lanier, J. (2010). *You are not a gadget*. New York, NY: Knopf.

MacNeely, I. F., & Wolverton, L. (2010). *Reinventing knowledge: From Alexandria to the Internet*. New York, NY: Norton.

Trautfetter, G. (2006, August 30). Arctic harvest: Global warming a boon for Greenland's farmers. *Der Spigel Online International*. Retrieved from http://www.spiegel.de/international/ spiegel/0,1518,434356,00.html

Wright, A. (2008). *Glut: Mastering information through the ages*. Ithaca, NY: Cornell University Press.

Chapter 7
Online Research without E-Reference:
What is Missing from Digital Libraries?

Jackie Zanghi-LaPlaca
Credo Reference, USA

ABSTRACT

With so many e-resources in the library, and so many avenues to it, what tools point users to the information relevant to their research? Investing in an electronic library without a strong online reference service leaves resources undiscovered, unapproachable, and underutilized. This chapter will discuss the important and welcoming function of reference services in order to increase the value and use of an institution's e-resources collection, especially resulting with increased information literacy for students.

INTRODUCTION

Librarians were among the first to adopt new educational and information technology. The creation of online library catalogs and the automation of circulation and technical services began in some libraries in the 1970s. By the mid-1980s, reference services were adopting online tools, and by the 1990s, they were moving from mediated to unmediated services.

DOI: 10.4018/978-1-61350-308-9.ch007

Virtual reference was introduced well over a decade ago. One of the best known of the early efforts was the Internet Public Library (www.ipl.org), a service launched in 1995 by the University of Michigan's School of Information and Library Studies. Initially a case study, it is now a well established service that is a collaborative effort among four schools of library and information science. Beginning in 2007, the service host for the program changed to the Drexel University College of Information Science and Technology. The Internet Public Library (IPL) provides a variety of online resources arranged in broad subject areas, a number of pathfinders, an extensive FAQ section, and an online form for asking reference questions. IPL has a staff of volunteers that answers questions, usually in no more than three days, and the service can be accessed directly or through a link on a library's website. Despite its name, many academic libraries link to IPL.

The one holdout—and the focus of this chapter—is the area of collection development. In particular, the development of e-reference materials was clearly the last to be affected by the new digital technology (Branin et al., 2000). But as scholarly materials moved beyond reference databases and catalogs into full-text journals and e-books in the mid- to late 1990s, there was no escaping the significant changes underway. Print, which held sway in reference collection development, was still the dominant format in many disciplinary fields in 2000, but digital formats could not be ignored and were quickly being adopted by students, faculty, and librarians. The University of Washington Libraries (2002), in one of many research studies on this subject, found through a survey of their faculty and graduate students that between 1998 and 2001, visits to the reference desk in the physical library were declining while use of networked computers increased in offices and homes. Access to information was growing across all reference needs and disciplines.

This chapter will build on that research. Rather than discussing the well-documented need for services such as online chat, it will instead focus on the collection development aspect of online reference. As more libraries continue the transition from print to online, how can we help online reference services and their content meet the extent of librarian knowledge? In other words, what services will point students and faculty to the information truly worth using? This is especially crucial in today's world with online teaching and learning; students often use library services from places other than the physical library. Information provided in this chapter will demonstrate

innovative collection development choices that combine content acquisition with information literacy services.

BACKGROUND

Millennial Generation students, those born after 1990, clearly perceive the Open Web as their information universe. This is in opposition to the view of many librarians and faculty, who perceive the library as the center of resources relevant to academic work. Students usually approach their research without regard to the library's structure or the way that the library segments different resources into different areas of its website. Library websites often reflect an organizational view of the library (for example, how to access the reference department or search in the institution's online catalog); they do not do a particularly good job of aggregating content on a particular subject area or more importantly teaching students when to use a particular database or resource (information and digital literacy). It is clear that faculty should also have a role to play in teaching subject-specific information literacy. Some examples of successful bridging of library resources, information literacy, and faculty teaching involve scaffolding and similar projects, but this collaboration in many institutions is not significant (Connaway, 2008).

Undergraduate and graduate students usually prefer the quick search of Google to more sophisticated, but more time-consuming search options provided by the library. In libraries without federated search, students must make separate searches of the online catalog and every database of potential interest, after first identifying which databases might be relevant. Conversely, in libraries with federated search, students are often overwhelmed with thousands of results, many which are not relevant to their work. In addition, not all searches of library catalogs or databases yield full-text materials, and Millennial Generation students want not just speedy answers, but full gratification of their information requests on the spot, if possible. Faculty members have the research skills and information literacy to thrive in federated search environments and sometimes do not take students through the process of using library resources for an assignment, often due to an assumption that the students will visit the library for assistance (Weiner, 2010).

Recent surveys exploring university student use of Open Web versus the library confirm the commonly held perception of faculty and librarians that students' primary sources of information for coursework are resources found on the Open Web and that most students use a search engine such as Google as their first point of entry to information rather than searching the library website or library catalog (Online Computer Library Center, c2006). Several campus studies also examined where students gather information for a paper or an assignment. One study at Colorado State University yielded information that over 58 percent of freshmen used Google, Yahoo, or a comparable search engine first, while only 23 percent started with a database or index. Other studies have shown that less than 5 percent of students start their research with library resources (Kaminski, Seel, and Cullen, 2003).

As stated in the research done by Alison Head and Michael Eisenberg of the Information School at the University of Washington in 2009 (and sponsored by ProQuest), "research seems to be far more difficult to conduct in the digital age than it did in previous times" (Head and Eisenberg, 2009, p.2). There are no easy answers for those who have been studying online research behavior. There is a wealth of electronic information resources, produced by a wide range of publishers, using different structures and vocabularies; providing simplified searching of these resources is part of the need, but how does information literacy fit in? Students may perceive that librarians have developed systems that are complex and make sense to information professionals, but are too difficult to use for non-experts (Connaway, 2008). However,

as new generations of information products are developed, producers and system developers should try to address the information-seeking habits of Millennial Generation students.

Libraries and the global service provider OCLC have been working with Google so that information from peer-reviewed journals, books, theses, and other academic resources can be accessed through the Google Scholar search service. This is a step in the right direction, taking library resources to where students want to find them—under their noses. But more needs to be done to integrate multimedia resources (videos, images, audio, etc.) into their searchable content; this type of digital content is becoming increasingly important to Millennial Generation students, who may wish to study an audio recording of political speeches and incorporate segments into a term project as well as access books and journals on the topic. However, libraries typically incorporate information objects into their catalogs only when those resources are owned or licensed by the library, which leads to the question: Is this still a relevant strategy in a world of global access to information via the Open Web?

ONLINE REFERENCE SERVICE

This chapter is not an argument that library-leased databases are better than Google databases, since Google databases may be more precise. Both the Open Web and library databases have benefits, and both should be used for the benefits they provide.

Google Scholar can often find more results than a database search and assist with citations. Google Books can find topic pertinent information within a book that one would never suspect to be there or would never find without access to this tool. But faculty and libraries are more likely to perform complex searching in comparison to undergraduate students.

Therefore, what can library-leased databases do that Google cannot? They can be extensions of the librarians' knowledge of the students, their institution's resources, and the information literacy needs. The abilities to do advanced searches, to use proximity operators not limited to exact phrases, and to limit search statements to specific fields like title or subject headings, among other features, allow users of bibliographic databases to do far more precise searching. This can save huge amounts of time in wading through source citations to find a few that are on target, as can often happen in Google search results with its limited one-step and out-search interface.

Time is also a reason that Wikipedia has become a go-to resource for many students. Wikipedia's pages are a one-stop route to information, each page centering on a single topic. The community of writers understands that Wikipedia's broad audience appeal depends on its ability to explain concepts in the most basic ways, be it by simple vocabulary, crosslinks, audio files, or images. Bibliographical databases can be overwhelming for undergraduates, with hundreds of databases to choose from and thousands of pages of potentially overlapping information to look through (Lim, 2009); as many students have not been properly taught how to use these databases, they run a higher risk of hitting a dead-end, either unable to find any adequate resources or failing to fully comprehend the ones they do believe are suitable. Wikipedia, on the other hand, is far less intimidating to them – A single database with a wide variety of articles, each with its own unique topic and heading, is much more inviting.

Of course, Wikipedia's most obvious downfall is in its production itself: Though the website does have a system of checks to maintain some level of the site's reliability, the fact remains that literally anyone with an Internet connection can alter the website. Because of this, most teachers and professors still refuse to accept it as a credible and citable source (Rand, 2010). While it is wonderful that Wikipedia has incited an interest in learning, it has also forced us to acknowledge the void in many students' education: the existence of a resource that is at once quick, extremely filterable, and easy to understand for the general population of students. How do we solve this?

Library resources have not in recent years been marketed to students and scholars as effectively as they should have been. As a result, the content of those resources has remained largely undiscoverable. But librarians are not the only ones to take responsibility for this. Producers of the services that libraries purchase—publishers, database providers, and library vendors—all need to be a strong source of this kind of public service promotion of libraries and their materials. To encourage libraries to thrive, there needs to be a real partnership between libraries and their vendors/publishers. There are not always enough examples of true collaborative projects, but some include: MERLOT (www.merlot.org), Libraries Thriving (www.librariesthriving.org), and 2CUL (www.2cul.org), which formed a unique partnership between the libraries, technology departments, and learning centers at Cornell and Columbia with the goal of transformative learning.

Much is on the line if this partnership does not take place. Unless changes to current practices are made, the market for database and other publication products may shrink significantly if libraries are not there to provide access to these products (Gibbons and Reeb, 2004). Lobbying state governments to provide public and K-12 libraries with access to databases for general information needs will facilitate some learning of these tools if taught before students get to college.

K-12 instruction in database searching technique and information/digital literacy is another area in which database and databank providers should be proactive. A major part of the battle to teach students how to do research is lost if students come to college with none of these database-searching skills in their background. At least some knowledge of the value of using library resources and information literacy is crucial for a successful learning and research experience to develop. Millennial Generation students are very digitally literate, but without information literacy, their digital literacy falls short of its potential; it becomes less valuable.

In a nutshell, both free online sites and library databases have strengths and weaknesses. However, one has grown while the other has faltered. Statistically, free resources have made significant improvement during the past several years, primarily due to data availability posted by publishers on the Open Web, and also due to improved capability of covering publishers' data by free search services. In that same time period, library databases have not made significant improvement. The library and library vendor communities have attempted to tackle the issue of low usage by applying relatively small fixes like social media tools, which is not making a dent in the larger issues. We have now gotten to the point where some library databases are no longer worth the costs of steep subscription, maintenance, and instruction, partly because many free products can do the same, similar, or better jobs without the costs of subscription, maintenance, and instruction. Budget challenges at almost all public and academic libraries may force us to develop important new approaches.

At Credo Reference, an online reference service with a multi-publisher platform, there are set standards for these new approaches with the definition of an online reference service as providing both content (e-reference books) and service (technology):

- **Discovery:** Visibility of the library, its resources, and access to librarian expertise
- **Context:** Deliver overview, summary, and vocabulary on a topic from multiple perspectives
- **Connection:** Seamless integration with relevant resources chosen by the library
- **Innovation:** Smart use of technology and partnerships

The four points above are all crucial to working towards information literacy in partnership with a library. Credo defines discovery as the visibility of a library on the open Web with Topic Pages, customized discovery of institutional resources through related resources, and meeting users where they are through partnerships with educational and related online services. Credo Reference Topic Pages are an all-in-one starting point for students to begin their research process. The unique structure of Topic Pages combines quality research, images, and additional library resources such as databases and the library catalog to promote information literacy and improve research effectiveness. The next point is context, which is the content acquisitions process completed with a librarian partner. And similarly, connection is demonstrating that e-reference material is more than a traditional e-book, such as seamless integration with all library resources and services—print and electronic. Using Topic Pages provides subject-specific paths to pre-searched results of relevant resources, and enhanced XML (non-PDF) content presentation provides connections facilitating discovery. The fourth item on the list, innovation, is an on-going process of developing the best learning methods for users with technology.

SOLUTIONS AND RECOMMENDATIONS

The latest Project Information Literacy report sees gaps in information literacy as part of a larger problem: Colleges and universities may be failing their students at a time when research skills and collaborative learning are becoming more important than ever (http://projectinfolit.org/pdfs/ PIL_Fall2010_Survey_FullReport1.pdf). Upon leaving the university, students need to face an information-driven workplace, where they spend much of their time formulating questions, finding relevant information, and drawing conclusions, often working in virtual teams scattered across the globe. Although it would seem that Millennial Generation college students are among the savviest users of Web 2.0. who can easily take on this challenge after graduation, they often are not ready for this type of workplace. New research points to plenty of evidence that students use social networks, like Facebook and Twitter, to find information in their everyday lives, but few are using other Web 2.0 tools, such as blogs or wikis, to manage or collaborate on course research assignments. This trend is likely to continue.

According to a study conducted by Eisenberg and Head (2010), which is the largest scholarly analysis of information literacy among college students, students continue to fumble research assignments. Although many consider themselves fairly adept at finding and evaluating information, especially from the Open Web, 84 percent were often stymied at the outset of a research assignment. Nearly half of students in the study, 49 percent, sought professors for help with course research. Almost two-thirds, 61 percent, reported checking personal research with friends and/or family members. Very few students turned to campus librarians.

The time has come to try significantly different methods for improving information literacy. A survey by OCLC (Connaway & Dickey, 2010) found that one of students' top suggestions for libraries on how to increase usage of e-resources was to offer interactive maps, study tips, and guides. An example of this type of environment is a website developed by the British Museum as a "student's room" for an exhibit of Mughal, India, an ancient civilization. Students see an office-style room that they can explore by clicking on components such as a globe, file cabinets, bookshelves, and so forth. They are then led to museum resources including an atlas and primary resources from the museum's collections on the Mughal period, such as weapons and art. Some clickable items lead to learning games that are simple enough for a child to understand, but complex enough to entertain (and teach) older users, as well. This type of model could be used for a library reference room and its resources and certainly providing a strong "welcoming" function.

Libraries could also add value to key pages of their websites by including interactive tutorials on how to find information or how to judge quality information resources. They could use part of their home page to highlight a "resource of the week" to better publicize information content that could likely assist students in their assignments. Or customized mouse pads could advertise URLs for selected information resources. Libraries also need to think about new services using mobile technology such as cell phones. They might allow students to reserve group study rooms and be alerted to availability via their cell phones, send simple text-message queries to library catalogs or databases, or check library hours via text messaging. Such services might be particularly valuable for students who live off campus.

In this process of needed change, librarians, publishers, and library vendors should collaboratively consult with students in the design phase of all services and incorporate students on teams that make decisions about the implementation of those services. Making use of the imagination, creativity, technical skills, and perspectives of Millennial Generation students is the best way to ensure that new services will be responsive to both their needs and their lifestyle.

FUTURE RESEARCH DIRECTIONS

The creation of online reference services serving Millennial Generation students will value student input while designing new services and Web environments, integrate services into course management systems, and explore services for mobile devices. Librarians will also continue expanding the library's virtual presence through involvement in course management systems and online social networking sites, the creation of online tutorials and other instruction aids, and more vibrant and interactive websites. Conveying the value of the complementary nature of the physical and online services to support the teaching and instruction mission of the university to campus administrators presents an ongoing challenge, but the benefits of investing in the "welcoming" function of an online reference service always outweigh the obstacles.

Investment in developing online reference services will only be accomplished in a collaborative atmosphere between libraries, publishers, and library vendors. With the common goal of promoting information literacy, libraries and library vendors should research the following areas:

Learners

- Give users a compelling place to start research on a new topic, providing both "big picture context" and subject-specific vocabulary needed to continue the research process
- Less time spent searching for answers, and more time spent actually finding them
- Access to trustworthy content
- Tools to quickly build their bibliography
- Connection to other trusted resources
- Brainstorming and discovery made easy

Libraries

- Bringing libraries to learners
- Allowing libraries to invest in high-quality, specialized subscription and perpetual purchase reference collections to meet the needs of their end-users
- Increasing value from e-resources—features that allow librarians to customize the research experience for their end-users
- Promoting greater usage: Discoverability and compelling research experiences can lead to higher usage

CONCLUSION

Everyone who has a stake in the education of students—be it a faculty member or a librarian in collection management, reference, or technical services—must take on new roles as information literacy providers.

In this new role, libraries, library vendors, and developers of content will be:

- *Information literacy developers*, working more closely with faculty, students, and library vendors to design, organize, and maintain a broader range of digital assets;
- *Information literacy integrators,* having a more active role in the educational and research mission of university, integrating information resources and services in course and research projects;
- *Information literacy educators*, teaching and training students and faculty information literacy and how to organize, preserve, and share their own information resources;
- *Information literacy researchers*, applying library and information science and new digital technology to create new organizational (metadata), retrieval, and storage (preservation) options.

With this focused innovation for online reference services, the current lack of information literacy can be changed in a new world of opportunity for libraries, e-reference materials, and all e-resources.

REFERENCES

Branin, J. (2000). The changing nature of collection management in research libraries. *Library Resources & Technical Services, 44,* 23–32.

Campbell, J. (2006). Changing a cultural icon: The academic library as a virtual destination. *EDUCAUSE Quarterly, 41*(1), 16–31. Retrieved October 17, 2010, from http://www.educause.edu/apps/eq/eqm01/eqm014.asp

Connaway, L. S. (2008). *Expectations of the Screenager Generation* [PDF document]. Retrieved from http://www.oclc.org/programs/events/2008-11-05c.pdf

Connaway, L. S., & Dickey, T. J. (2010). *The digital information seeker: Report of the findings from selected OCLC, RIN, and JISC user behavior projects* [PDF document]. Retrieved from http://www.jisc.ac.uk/media/documents/publications/reports/2010/digitalinformationseekerreport.pdf

Cullen, K., Kaminski, K., & Seel, P. (2003). Technology literate students? Results from a survey. *EDUCAUSE Quarterly, 26*(3), 34-40. Retrieved August 1, 2010, from http://www.educause.edu/ir/library/pdf/eqm0336.pdf

Daly, J. (2004). George Lucas: Life on the screen. *EDUTOPIA, 1*, 34–40. Retrieved June 14, 2010, from http://www.glef.org/magazine/ ed1article.php?id=art_1160&issue=sept_04

Dempsey, L. (2009). Always on: Libraries in a world of permanent connectivity. *First Monday, 14*(1). Retrieved September 5, 2010, from http://firstmonday.org/htbin/cgiwrap/ bin/ojs/index.php/fm/article/view/2291/2070

Eisenberg, M. B., & Head, A. J. (2009). *What today's college students say about conducting research in the digital age. Project Information Literacy progress report.* Retrieved July 15, 2010, from http://projectinfolit.org/pdfs/PIL_Progress-Report_2_2009.pdf

Eisenberg, M. B., & Head, A. J. (2010). *How college students evaluate and use information in the digital age. Project Information Literacy progress report.* Retrieved September 10, 2010, from http://projectinfolit.org/pdfs/PIL_Fall 2010_Survey_FullReport1.pdf

Foley, M. (2002). Instant Messaging reference in an academic library: A case study. *College & Research Libraries, 63*(1), 36–45.

Gibbons, S., & Reeb, B. (2004). Students, librarians, and subject guides: Improving a poor rate of return. *Portal: Libraries and the Academy, 4*(1), 123–130. Retrieved October 2, 2010, from http://muse.jhu.edu/journals/portal_libraries _and_the_academy/toc/pla4.1.html

Lim, S. (2009). How and why do college students use Wikipedia? *Journal of the American Society for Information Science and Technology, 60*(11), 2189–2202. doi:10.1002/asi.21142

Lippincott, S., & Kyrillidou, M. (2004). How ARL university communities access information: Highlights from LIBQUAL+. *ARL: A Bimonthly Report, 236*, 7-8. Retrieved October 10, 2010, from http://www.arl.org/newsltr/236/lqaccess.html

Massy, W. F., & Zemsky, R. (2004). *Thwarted innovation: What happened to e-learning and why.* West Chester, PA: The Learning Alliance at the University of Pennsylvania. Retrieved July 4, 2010, from http://www.thelearningalliance.info/Docs/Jun2004/ThwartedInnovation.pdf

McEuen, S. F. (2001). How fluent with Information Technology are our students? *EDUCAUSE Quarterly, 24*(4), 8–17. Retrieved October 17, 2010, from http://www.educause.edu/apps/eq/eqm01/eqm014.asp

Online Computer Library Center. (c2006). *College students' perceptions of libraries and information resources: A report to the OCLC membership.* Dublin, OH: OCLC.

Online Computer Library Center (OCLC). (2002). How academic librarians can influence students' Web-based information choices. Retrieved June 15, 2010, from http://www5.oclc.org/downloads/community/informationhabits.pdf

Pyatt, E., & Snavely, L. (2004). *No longer missing: Tools for connecting the library with the course management system.* Retrieved October 21, 2010, from http://www.syllabus.com/print. asp?ID=9094

Rand, A. D. (2010). Mediating at the student-Wikipedia intersection. *Journal of Library Administration*, *50*(7/8), 923–932. doi:10.1080/01 930826.2010.488994

Rogers, S. A. (2003). Developing an institutional knowledge bank at Ohio State University: From concept to action plan. *Portal: Libraries and the Academy*, *3*(1), 125–136. doi:10.1353/ pla.2003.0018

University of Washington Libraries. (2002). *Newsletter*. Seattle, WA: University of Washington Libraries.

Weiner, S. A. (2010). Information literacy: A neglected core competency. *EDUCAUSE Quarterly*, *33*(1), 8.

ADDITIONALREADING

CIBER report (n.d.). Retrieved from http://www. ucl.ac.uk/infostudies/research/ciber/

Janes, J. (2003). *Introduction to Reference Work in the Digital Age.* New York, NY: Neal-Schuman Publishers.

Mellon Library/Faculty Fellowship for Undergraduate Research. (n.d.). UC Berkeley. Retrieved October 21, 2010, from http://www.lib.berkeley. edu/mellon/

Visible Knowledge Project. (n.d.). Retrieved October 21, 2010, from http://gallery.carnegiefoundation.org/collections/exhibits/vkp/index.htm

Visible Knowledge Project. (n.d.). Retrieved from http://crossroads.georgetown.edu/vkp/index.htm

KEY TERMS AND DEFINITIONS

Database: A collection of data; information stored, typically in electronic format.

E-Resources: Term used to describe all of the information products that a library provides through a computer network. This includes electronic books and journals, bibliographic databases, and library website pages.

Federated Search: Refers to an ability to search across multiple archives, data collections or multiple content aggregator services.

Index: An alphabetical listing of names and topics along with page numbers where they are discussed.

Information Literacy: Skill in locating and evaluating information.

Millennial Generation: Generation Y, also known as the Millennial Generation or Generation Next or Net Generation, describes the demographic cohort following Generation X.

Online Reference Service: A service that provides reference content, as well as discoverability, connection and innovation for all library resources.

Perpetual Purchase: Lasting forever, or for an indefinitely long time. In the case of a library, it is a one-time purchase of an item, such as an e-book.

Subscription: A payment for consecutive issues of a database or library service for a given period of time.

Chapter 8
Undergraduate Information Seeking Behavior, E–Reference and Information Literacy in the Social Sciences

Jason B. Phillips
New York University, USA

ABSTRACT

As we consider the potential impact of e-reference, librarians should keep in mind another important concern that has received much attention in recent years, namely information literacy. The composition and differential usage of specialized indexes in the social sciences – resources that are not necessarily designed for undergraduate research – and of aggregated interdisciplinary databases present challenges to achieving information literacy. Users have e-reference tools at their disposal to help them navigate information found in such resources, but it is a classic problem of reference and now e-reference that these resources are underutilized. Interviews conducted with twelve undergraduates at New York University form the basis for a case study which is used to illuminate the issues discussed herein.

DOI: 10.4018/978-1-61350-308-9.ch008

INFORMATION LITERACY AND THE SOCIAL SCIENCES

In the social sciences, one key outcome for undergraduate students is that they have the ability to think critically about important issues through the lens of their chosen discipline. This often means acquiring the ability to distinguish social, cultural, historical, economic, or anthropological arguments from arguments that originate outside of the social sciences in fields such as the natural sciences, medicine, or technology. For instance, in sociology there is consensus around the idea that students should be able to "show the relevance and reality of structural factors in social life" (Persell 2010) and understand sociological manners of inquiry (McKinney et. al. 2004). In economics, some scholars emphasize the importance of liberal education and the ability to comprehend and apply economic arguments (Salemi 2009). If students who choose to undertake coursework in social science disciplines do not learn the skills which are crucial to social and cultural understanding in their chosen disciplines, it is fair to ask if they have learned much at all of importance.

While teaching is the province of the members of the teaching faculty at academic institutions, librarians, too, have an important role to play in promoting good outcomes by helping undergraduates navigate the information landscape. In our emphasis on information literacy, librarians have also increasingly recognized the importance of disciplinary boundaries and approaches (Grafstein 2002, Instruction and Information Literacy Committee 2008). There are modes of thought that are specific to each discipline, and reference librarians, in particular, must provide reference services with those modes of thought in their minds in order to best serve the students in their institutions.

We know, however, that one of the classic problems of reference is that undergraduates do not utilize the services of reference librarians with either the frequency or efficiency that librarians would hope they would. This phenomenon makes it that much more difficult to promote good learning outcomes. The reasons are myriad and may include the notion that students do not perceive librarians as helpful assistants in their work (Ismail 2010), the notion that the library is primarily a physical place for study and not necessarily for reference services (Whitmire 2001), or the affinity that undergraduates have for electronic resources (Kriebel and Lapham 2008). Undergraduates are also sensitive to strategies that they perceive as saving them time (Weiler 2005).

Regardless of the cause, the problem caused by undergraduates' lack of reliance on reference services is borne out by studies that indicate difficulties in assimilating and evaluating information gathered during the research process, in understanding how information is organized, and in identifying appropriate or useful resources for finding information (Maughan 2001). Literature indicates that undergraduates in the social sciences preferred the use of journals and normally followed citations as opposed to using indexes and abstracts (Whitmire 2002). Furthermore, students do not normally consult librarians as a matter of habit (Burns and Harper 2007).

SPECIALIZED INDEXES AND AGGREGATED INTERDISCIPLINARY DATABASES

Teaching faculty want their students to use library resources. They are also likely to want their students to use many of the same resources that they utilize in their own research. Depending on how particular researchers go about their work, that can sometimes lead to the myopic use of library resources. Among databases with scholarly content, resources such as JSTOR and Project Muse are most widely known (Harley et. al. 2006). Although JSTOR was not originally intended to be used as a source of information for undergraduate instruction and research (Guthrie, Kirchhoff and Tapp 2003), its utility to a wide range of users in many types of institutions became clear over the course of its development (Schonfeld 2003, 2005).

I see evidence of its ubiquity as teaching faculty sometimes request that I demonstrate its use for their students to the exclusion of specialized disciplinary indexes. Students also often come to the library having already been informed about JSTOR but asking for further help from librarians when they run into that database's moving wall. Of course this unfamiliarity with other useful resources aside from JSTOR speaks most to the need for academic librarians to ensure that their constituents are informed about and guided through the constantly changing array of library resources available for teaching and for research.

Another important problem is identified by Fister, Gilbert, and Fry (2008). They noted that over time, undergraduates were increasingly frustrated by the results of searches from aggregated interdisciplinary databases – especially by "the inclusion of highly specialized science, technology, and medical (STM) articles." This phenomenon was partly driven by vendors' desire to market larger databases in order to compete with Google. This argument can be extended to suggest that the same phenomenon is now increasingly an issue with some specialized social science indexes.

Not only is this phenomenon likely driven by the same market issues, but it is driven by the increasingly interdisciplinary nature of some social science research and is related to scientific challenges to the social sciences themselves (Duster 2006, Shreeves 2000). It should be noted, as it often is when discussing undergraduate information-seeking behavior, that these indexes are not primarily developed with undergraduate researchers in mind. Nonetheless, librarians do recommend them to undergraduates, and teaching faculty expect undergraduates to use them in their work. Graduate students and faculty members can distinguish materials that do not utilize social and cultural arguments even if they discover those materials in social science indexes. However, given their novice status, one might expect some

undergraduate researchers to assume that any article they find in a social science index views its stated problem from a social science perspective.

UNDERGRADUATE INFORMATION-SEEKING BEHAVIOR

To provide an empirical context for this chapter, twelve interviews were conducted with undergraduate students in the social sciences at New York University. These interviews were structured in a manner which was designed to determine respondents' use of library resources, their academic histories, and their knowledge of electronic resources that might be of utility to students in the social sciences. Four respondents were sophomores at the time of the interview. Of the upperclassmen, two were juniors and six were seniors. A balance was sought in the hopes that it might also reveal patterns in the knowledge or opinions of students as they progressed through their programs.

And indeed, students reported a mix of library contact based on the length of time they had been enrolled at NYU. For instance, none of the sophomores had any exposure to the library's bibliographic instruction program – either those associated with social science courses they had taken or free-standing offerings provided by the library. Upperclassmen noted much more contact with the library's robust offerings of bibliographic instructions sessions. Half of respondents had participated in the bibliographic instruction program in one form or another. However, all students reported little contact with reference services and a reluctance to enlist librarians in support of their research as might be expected given the earlier discussion of the literature concerning undergraduates' information-seeking behavior. Only one of the twelve respondents would normally consider consulting a librarian to get assistance in researching an assignment for a social science course. All would consult library databases and the

Internet. Four of the twelve respondents indicated that they would consult an encyclopedia or other reference work.

These patterns emphasize how important early instructional contact might be with respect to student outcomes and should prompt librarians to consider the importance of that instructional contact (Martin and Park 2010) and use it to its maximum potential as a platform for promoting the tools and mechanisms of subject specific e-reference resources. Introducing undergraduates to subject-specific information resources can help them to better order and structure literature searches and provide the disciplinary context that is crucial to critical thinking, and ultimately, to information literacy. The problem is awareness. If users do not approach or are not brought to librarians, they are unlikely to learn about these resources.

During the conversations with undergraduates, it was discovered that they were generally not familiar with these particular types of e-reference resources such as Annual Reviews, Elsevier's *International Encyclopedia of the Social and Behavioral Sciences,* Paratext's Reference Universe, or Credo Reference. However, they were familiar with the aggregated interdisciplinary databases provided by ProQuest, Gale, and EBSCO and products like Project Muse and JSTOR and could claim familiarity with more than two of these databases on average. As it concerns the specialized disciplinary indexes and e-reference resources, one could not draw the conclusion that experience and coursework led to further knowledge about either type of resource.

Students were also asked to contemplate a hypothetical situation in which they were writing a paper for a course that had them explore the social and cultural reasons that teenagers start smoking. They were then asked to evaluate and suggest whether they would or would not use the papers represented by three abstracts taken from a major sociology index. One of the abstracts was for a peer-reviewed article that examined the role

of environmental and genetic factors in tobacco use among adolescents taken from the EBSCO's specialized disciplinary resource SocINDEX.

There was no clear consensus as to whether students would use this particular article. Five students suggested that they were unlikely to use the article. Four students indicated that they would possibly use the article and three students indicated they would certainly use the article for this hypothetical paper.

One student – a senior – noted that the paper did not address the problem from a social or cultural standpoint. That student indicated a willingness to use the article but would take care to note the fact that the paper used a method that was not social or cultural. This instance, where the methodology of the abstract goes largely unnoticed by respondents, is one in which undergraduate researchers could benefit both from the perspective of carefully chosen or recommended e-reference materials and the insight that librarians have on specialized disciplinary indexes like CSA's Sociological Abstracts, EconLit, SocINDEX, or Anthropology Plus.

CONCLUSION

Despite the changes and trends that present a challenge to undergraduate learning and instruction, librarians do have insights and tools available that can improve learning outcomes for undergraduates. Electronic resources can help undergraduate students of the social sciences better understand social and cultural phenomena in a format that they want; if only there was greater awareness of the library's resources and the students' willingness to use them. Librarians can also save users time by alerting them to important scholarship in a manner and in the electronic format that undergraduate users prefer.

In order to raise awareness and promote the value of these resources, librarians need to mind information literacy concepts and their practical disciplinary implications at each possible service point. For instance, outreach, with respect to instructional programming, is important as that is sometimes the earliest and most substantial contact that underclassmen have with the library and the librarian (Johnson, McCord and Walter 2003). This instructional contact represents an opportunity to emphasize the growing challenges of using specialized indexes in the social sciences as well as aggregated interdisciplinary indexes. It represents an opportunity to demonstrate the value of e-reference materials and their potential positive impact on learning outcomes. And, in some respect, the harder we work to emphasize the importance and rigor of social and cultural arguments, the more likely it is that these arguments will form the basis of strong academic inquiry in the future as some of these undergraduates become graduate students and finally, scholars in their own right.

REFERENCES

Burns, V., & Harper, K. (2007). Asking students about their research. In Foster, N. F., & Gibbons, S. (Eds.), *Studying students: The undergraduate research project at the University of Rochester* (pp. 7–15). Chicago, IL: Association of College and Research Libraries.

Duster, T. (2006). Comparative perspectives and competing explanations: Taking on the newly configured reductionist challenge to sociology. *American Sociological Review, 71*(1), 1–15. doi:10.1177/000312240607100101

Fister, B., Gilbert, J., & Fry, A. R. (2008). Aggregated interdisciplinary databases and the needs of undergraduate researchers. *portal. Libraries and the Academy, 8*(3), 273–292. doi:10.1353/pla.0.0003

Grafstein, A. (2002). A discipline-based approach to information literacy. *Journal of Academic Librarianship, 28*(4), 197–204. doi:10.1016/S0099-1333(02)00283-5

Guthrie, K., Kirchoff, A., & Tapp, W. N. (2003). The JSTOR solution, six years later. In Hodges, P., & Lougee, W. P. (Eds.), *Digital libraries: A vision for the 21st century* (pp. 100–121). Ann Arbor, MI: Scholarly Publishing Office, The University of Michigan University Library.

Harley, D., et al. (2006). *Use and users of digital resources: A focus on undergraduate education in the humanities and social sciences.* Berkeley, CA: Center for Studies in Higher Education, University of California Berkeley. Retrieved December 30, 2010, from http://cshe.berkeley.edu/research/digitalresourcestudy/report/

Instruction and Information Literacy Committee Task Force on Information Literacy Standards. (2008). *Information literacy standards for anthropology and sociology students.* Chicago, IL: Association of College and Research Libraries. Retrieved December 30, 2010, from http://www.ala.org/ala/mgrps/divs/acrl/ standards/anthro_soc_standards.cfm

Ismail, L. (2010). What net generation students really want: Determining library help-seeking preferences of undergraduates. *RSR. Reference Services Review, 38*(1), 10–27. doi:10.1108/00907321011020699

Johnson, C., McCord, S. K., & Walter, S. (2003). Instruction outreach across the curriculum: Enhancing the liaison role at a research university. In Kelsey, P., & Kelsey, S. (Eds.), *Outreach services in academic and special libraries* (pp. 19–38). Binghamton, NY: Haworth Press.

Kriebel, L., & Lapham, L. (2008). Transition to electronic resources in undergraduate social science research: A study of honors theses bibliographies, 1999-2005. *College & Research Libraries, 69*(3), 268–284.

Martin, P. N., & Park, L. (2010). Reference desk consultation assignment: An exploratory study of students' perceptions of reference service. *Reference and User Services Quarterly, 49*(4), 333–340.

Maughan, P. D. (2001). Assessing information literacy among undergraduates: A discussion of the literature and the university of California-Berkeley assessment experience. *College & Research Libraries, 62*(1), 71–85.

McKinney, K., Howery, C. B., Strand, K. J., Kain, E. L., & Berheide, C. W. (2004). *Liberal learning and the sociology major updated: Meeting the challenge of teaching sociology in the twenty-first century.* Washington, DC: American Sociological Association. Retrieved December 30, 2010, from http://www.asanet.org/images/teaching/ docs/pdf/ Lib_Learning_FINAL.pdf

Persell, C. H. (2010). How sociological leaders rank learning goals for introductory sociology. *Teaching Sociology, 38*(4), 330–339. doi:10.1177/0092055X10378822

Salemi, M. K. (2009). Economics and liberal education: Why, where, and how. In Colander, D., & McGoldrick, M. (Eds.), *Education economists: The Teagle discussion on re-evaluating the undergraduate economics major* (pp. 99–106). Northhampton, MA: Edward Elgar.

Schonfeld, R. C. (2003). *JSTOR: A history*. Princeton, NJ: Princeton University Press.

Schonfeld, R. C. (2005). JSTOR: A case study in the recent history of scholarly communications. *Program, 39*(4), 337–334.

Shreeves, E. (2000). The acquisitions culture wars. *Library Trends, 48*(4), 877–890.

Weiler, A. (2005). Information-seeking behavior in generation Y students: Motivation, critical thinking, and learning theory. *Journal of Academic Librarianship, 31*(1), 46–53. doi:10.1016/j. acalib.2004.09.009

Whitmire, E. (2001). A longitudinal study of undergraduates' academic library experiences. *Journal of Academic Librarianship, 27*(5), 379–385. doi:10.1016/S0099-1333(01)00223-3

Whitmire, E. (2002). Disciplinary differences and undergraduates' information seeking behavior. *Journal of the American Society for Information Science and Technology, 53*(8), 631–638. doi:10.1002/asi.10123

Section 3
Design and Delivery of Reference Content

Chapter 9

Interactive Reference:
Online Features to Enrich Content and Improve the User Experience

Tom Beyer
iFactory, USA

ABSTRACT

This is a survey of the current state of online reference products and the variety of interactive features that can help make the next generation of these products more functional and their content more discoverable. Topics examined include: addition of multi-media content to text; interfaces for comparing texts; timelines and maps for browsing; taxonomy and ontology; improvements to search functions and search results; inter-linking of products; issues around saving data, personalization, and creation of custom publications; and mobile devices.

INTRODUCTION

What is the definition of "interactive reference?" The word "reference" refers to the product that aims to answer our questions in a way that is authoritative, accurate, and comprehensible. The "interactive" part refers to the product interacting with the user to do that job better. So what is the

end goal for the ultimate interactive reference product?

In order to get a sense of this, let's first focus on the reference products provided online and accessed through libraries. We are currently in the midst of the same sort of transition as when movies were first being made or TV first came online. The initial attempts/products mimicked an older medium (theater for film, radio for TV), but eventually the medium matured and developed its own aesthetic sensibility. In the same fashion,

DOI: 10.4018/978-1-61350-308-9.ch009

the initial online reference products were derived from their print counterparts. Beyond providing search and some cross-linking capabilities, they were very similar to their print interfaces. There were few if any online features, with little or no hyperlinking and indexes that didn't link to the text. Many even preserved the page boundaries and numbering from the print work; many still do. The majority of early online reference products were just e-book versions of the print titles bundled together into an online platform. In contrast, other products were dubbed databases, and the content was extracted from its original print context to provide a subject or topic-based collection of content.

Over time, online products slowly started to develop interfaces and navigation and interactivity separate and different from the original books. Database products started this by separating the content from the original print container and presenting it in a new way in an online environment. Navigation is an area that diverged early on because in the book world there is a strong one-dimensional ordering that is placed on the contents of the book—entries have to be ordered front to back, often in an A-Z fashion. On the Web, the page has a stronger focus because interaction is mediated through a single screen. From the entry that the user is looking at, there are many different possible next places to visit, of which the next entry in the print order is only one such possibility and not even usually the best. For instance, if the user got to the entry by doing a search, it is potentially much more useful to give the user access to the next entry in the search results, or to other similar entries related through subject keywords. These different kinds of links provide different entry orderings, and no one ordering has the same overwhelming presence as page ordering has in a book.

Another aspect that is pushing change is the plethora of devices that people use to access these products. In addition to your standard computer monitor, users are increasingly using laptop and note-book computers, tablets, and smartphones all with different screen size, connection speed, and technology constraints. At a minimum, each device is capable of presenting text and images, usually in color. Sound can often be generated as well as animation and video. Input can be taken in the form of text, sometimes speech, and increasingly, location. With the advent of smartphones and other mobile devices, multi-touch sensors are standard, and increasingly, the devices know what time it is and where the user is located.

When thinking about interactivity of reference products, it may be useful to think along two different axes. The first is the content. The questions to ask here include: What kinds of interfaces and interactivity are best suited for different kinds of content? And how can different interfaces improve the way that the information is conveyed? Is it possible to unpack information hidden within the content or that was compiled during the production of the content but had no easy outlet in the print product? The second axe is the user, who comes to these products trying to answer particular questions for different reasons and with different goals. If the online reference product can anticipate the task that the user is trying to accomplish, it can provide tools to the user to help him/her accomplish that task. The main goal of this chapter is to examine interfaces through these two lenses and to look at features that try to enrich the meaning of the content as well as those that try to help users accomplish their goals. The industry is just starting down this path and where it will end up is anybody's guess, but there is no question that the reference products of the future are going to look increasingly less like their print companions.

CONTENT-CENTERED INTERACTIVITY

In this section we examine the interactive features that help increase the number of ways in which the content is conveyed in order to make it more understandable for the user. In other words, the more interactive the content, the more improved the comprehension. This involves conveying the same information through different kinds of media, including images, audio, video, even simulations where applicable.

In addition to the text, there is a second kind of data that is provided in reference products. This is data about the text itself, which is called metadata. The metadata allows the system to know what order to display the content in, how the different pieces relate to each other, and a host of other information about the content that is not embedded in the actual text. Metadata is important for driving many of the features that make these interactive products compelling. It can provide extra context around the original content as well as different ways for the user to get from one piece of content to another. It can even allow users to see patterns and relationships in the entire set of content that is otherwise not possible just from reading the text.

Enriching Text

Using images, sound, and video are all obvious ways to enrich the text. From the beginning, when reference products first came online, images were used to enhance understanding of the subject matter. For instance, in the Berg Fashion Library (http://www.bergfashionlibrary.com), in addition to the encyclopedia data and the many books that make up the content, there is also a large library of images. These images are treated as entries in the product in their own right—a search of the library returns both textual and image results. Of course, simply providing images is only the first most obvious step. Depending on the kind of content, there are a number of ways of enhancing the image presentation to make it more useful to users. For instance, in situations where the images are showing works of art or archival materials, the ability to zoom into the image to see the item at

the highest possible resolution could significantly increase the utility of the images. Another example is to allow users to create their own collection of images and to provide a slide show mode. This could be very useful for teachers preparing for classes. One example of this functionality is the Harvard Art Museum site (http://www.harvardart-museum.org), which allows saved images to be downloaded as a custom PowerPoint slide show.

Another way of increasing comprehension is to simply present the text differently. Many products are now providing audio of the text; and for many user populations, this is invaluable in increasing comprehension. Columbia Granger's World of Poetry (www.columbiagrangers.org) includes audio for selected poems, while the Gale Virtual Reference Library (http://www.gale.cengage.com/servlet/GvrlMS?msg=ma) provides audio for all articles. The audio is an automatic machine translation and is provided both as an audio stream and as an MP3 download (for educational use only).

Another increasingly popular supplement to the original text is automatic language translation. Examples of this include Gale's Virtual Reference Library and Rosen Publishing's Teen Health and Wellness Database (http://www.teen-healthandwellness.com). Both of these products include a button that translates every entry into the desired language. Since Rosen's product is aimed at teenagers and educators, this feature is especially important; not only do teenagers expect these kinds of bells and whistles as digital natives, but given the nature of the content (health and wellness information that is often difficult for them to talk about with their parents), it is important to help convey the information to kids for whom English may not be their native language. It should be noted that as these translations are generated automatically by the computer, they are certainly not idiomatic and may be only borderline comprehensible, but they are generally good enough to help get the gist of the text across to someone whose native language is not the language in which the text is written.

Video and animation are also an obvious possible supplement to text. With the ubiquity of YouTube and news sources providing video everywhere, online users increasingly expect video to be an alternate or even a primary content source. Alexander Street Press has been a pioneer with video, providing a wide-ranging series of products. Audio and video can add significantly to a user's comprehension of an issue or event: seeing and hearing Martin Luther King at a rally or on a march, or Hitler at the height of his power, and seeing the reaction of the crowd provide a level of detail and context that is impossible to get from the text of their speeches alone. Other examples of online reference products that include video are some new products from SAGE Publications: SAGE Research Methods Online (http://srmo.sagepub.com) and for their SAGE Reference Online platform of reference encyclopedia's, SAGE is introducing a multi-media encyclopedia (The Multimedia Encyclopedia of Women in Today's World) in 2011.

Then there's the added benefit of simulations. There are many examples where simulation can provide real value in aiding comprehension of a subject, especially in the sciences and math. It's one thing to say that a sea shell is made of a simple mathematical equation and another to allow users to manipulate the parameters of the equation and see the different shells that result from it. Predator prey models are much easier to understand if you can see them visualized: (http://demonstrations.wolfram.com/PredatorPreyEcosystemAReal-TimeAgentBasedSimulation/). Schools have access to sophisticated math packages. There is no reason that reference products that include math couldn't be integrated with these math packages to provide simulations right from within the product.

Of course adding significant amounts of multi-media content to reference products does not come without its own set of problems. What must not be overlooked when in the process of adding this new content to plain text is that these additions need to be of the same level of quality as the text itself. Publishers need to put the processes in place to produce, edit, and vet this content just as they have always done with text. For instance, it is critically important that mathematical equations and simulations are tested and approved by mathematicians with the appropriate expertise. In addition, publishers need to be able to produce, commission, or license audio and video that is at the same level of sophistication as the core text—this is something that is new and difficult for most of them. They have spent years putting together the workflows, processes, and people necessary to develop high quality text content. They are now asked to provide the same for the kind of content that they simply do not have the expertise and processes in place to handle. This puts significant stress on publishers' internal infrastructure and on their business models. They need new staff in place, new workflows, and new relationships with different external suppliers, to name just a few challenges. On the other hand, not doing this will increasingly render publishers obsolete for large parts of the market.

Comparing Documents

So far we have discussed augmenting the content itself. What about showing the connections between different pieces of content? This is an area where the digital interface excels over what is possible with a bound book. For some types of content, the ability to closely compare two pieces of related content is very useful. For instance, Oxford University Press's Oxford Biblical Studies Online includes a side-by-side document comparison interface (http://oxfordbiblicalstudies.com). The user is free to switch from a view showing a single Bible to one with the Bible and its associated commentary or to compare two different translations of the Bible. Or even to relate concordance terms with these views. Imagine trying to do this with print resources. Document comparison interfaces of this sort are useful anytime it is important to compare multiple documents at once. Another example is Columbia's Granger's World of Poetry (http://www.columbiagrangers.org), where poems can be examined side by side. In a situation where poems are often written in response to other poems, or are parodies or translations of a given poem, being able to quickly and easily put the poems side by side for close examination is very useful for researchers.

One interesting technical note is that citing work done in such an interface can be difficult if the product doesn't explicitly provide support for it. One can imagine that a researcher would want to cite the exact state of the screen after carefully lining up different documents to support an argument. In this case, the citation needs to take into account multiple documents and their exact state on the screen. As interfaces increase in intricacy, it becomes imperative for academic products to explicitly provide citation support for the more dynamic and interactive aspects of the product so that users can return to the exact state of a dynamic interface.

Browse Interfaces

A-Z is the default arbitrary organization of reference works. This has always been necessary with the printed book because of the need for a single, one-dimensional ordering scheme. The Web de-emphasizes this, allows for many other orderings, and allows the editor of the work to weigh those other orderings as they see fit in the product design and through the multiple browse orderings that can be provided. For the most part, each ordering needs a set of metadata to control the relationship among the different items of content.

Browse interfaces are important because they allow users to get a feel for the overall nature of the content collected in the product. They provide a mechanism for the user who doesn't know exactly what they are looking for to see different ways in which the content is collected and get a sense for amount, complexity, and breadth of the content. By being able to organize the content in a variety

of different ways, the online product is much more flexible than its printed counterpart in providing users different avenues into the content.

Timelines & Maps

Depending on the content, there may be a natural wealth of metadata about the content that can be used to drive different grouping interfaces. There are two kinds of metadata that are applicable to content: date/time data and location data. These are typically surfaced in an interface as timelines or maps or a combination of both. Grouping the data provided in a reference product through the timelines and maps can provide a context that is hard to provide simply from data within an article. Relationships between items can become quickly evident. An excellent example of a combined timeline/map interface with building simulations, courtesy of Google Earth, is Digital Karnak from the Encyclopedia of Egyptology (http://dlib.etc. ucla.edu/projects/Karnak/timemap).

Time/date and location data are useful across a broad swath of content and are seen in an increasing number of products. What is especially interesting about this is that these timelines and map interfaces interact with the user to show just the information that the user is interested in. The new version of the Oxford English Dictionary (OED) now provides a totally integrated timeline view of the words in the dictionary (http://www. oed.com). In addition to providing a way to browse the dictionary through a timeline, the results of any search done in the dictionary can be seen in both the standard A-Z format and in a timeline format. Suddenly it is possible to see trends for particular types or classes of words with just the click of a button. The Berg Fashion Library is another example of a product that offers both a timeline view and a map view of the content.

One thing that we have to be careful about with time and location data is that they don't convey information that is an artifact of the underlying set of content. We once looked at a dataset that appeared to have really interesting information that was conveyed by a timeline view of the information. But in fact what was really showing up was the bias of collection—we were seeing trends imposed by the way that the content was collected, not information inherent in the content itself. This can often be a problem with reference collections, because there is less control over exactly what is or isn't included in the collection than in the scholarship of each content item. As interfaces that show the relationships of the content items across the entire reference product improve, publishers are going to need to worry about the overall scope and depth of the collection more than they ever had to with print collections.

Taxonomies & Ontologies

For any particular set of data there may be a variety of possible subject-based groupings for organizing the content. Each of these may be linear or hierarchical (i.e., they may be a simple list or they may be composed of A heads, B heads, etc). The individual content entries may be associated with a single item in any particular hierarchy or multiple items. Different content entries may be related to a taxonomy item in different ways. Different kinds of items can be linked together to provide rich and complex ontologies. For instance, in SAGE Publications' Research Methods Online there is an ontology that brings together a graph of subject nodes with key authors and content items. These taxonomies and ontologies can provide useful metadata within reference products for enriching search, providing subject-based browse interfaces, and providing cross-linking between content items.

There are lots of considerations that need to be thought through when constructing an interface to show the taxonomy or ontology included with a product. For instance, if there are multiple taxonomies, is it useful to combine ways of linking articles into a single browse page, or should they each be presented separately? What sort of

interface is required to handle the specifics of the taxonomy in question: hierarchical tree views, visual graph views, something else? The number of nodes in the taxonomies and interconnections with the content can vary greatly, which will have a huge effect on what the appropriate interface for navigating the taxonomy should be. The needs of the content will dictate these choices, but there doesn't seem to be any question that ways to organize and break down large sets of content prove useful in the long run.

Are these groupings used just to suggest related content or should the user actually be able to navigate them? It seems that we are still in the infancy in terms of what the best practices are for representing this information for navigating the content. Most online reference products currently use some combination of lists, or tree-views for browse pages.

Another interface choice has been some sort of graph representation. The visual thesaurus (http://www.visualthesaurus.com/) was an early exponent of the ball and spoke visualization. The question that always needs to be asked is: What are we trying to convey through a particular visualization and how is it helping the user? We need to understand what we are really trying to do with the visualization. Does it provide an overview of the subject of the collection? Does it provide the user with another way to get from one place to another in the collection? In what way does it help increase their comprehension of the material? One would hope that there are obvious and good answers to these questions for any particular visualization.

Furthermore, these interfaces they provide an opportunity to combine different types of objects in a single view. Nodes can be different kinds of things: subject-based concepts, people, documents, et cetera. In addition, the links can show the strength of the relationship as well as different kinds of relationships. Collexis has created an interesting interface as part of the UniPHY site (www.aipuniphy.org), showing the relationships among authors of journal papers. The interface shows an author and all of her co-authors in the first ring. In the second outer ring it shows co-authors of the co-authors. Using the slider bars and a list of authors on the right, the user can explore the strength of the relationships among this network of people. Using this kind of interface to explore a variety of relationships embodied in our reference collections could provide all kinds of insight at a level that isn't currently possible.

Another example is SAGE Publications' Research Methods Online (www.srmo.sagepub.com) and its Methods Map interface. This ontology has around 2000 subject terms linked together in parent, child, related, and contrasting relationships. Each node in the map is also associated with content from the collection and with key authors. The methods map is tightly integrated with the search feature so that every search shows the most relevant Methods Map node and it is always possible to search the content when traversing the Methods Map. The Methods Map ontology is important data for the product in its own right: it provides users with an overview of the research methods field and how different parts of the field are linked together.

An important point to consider about interfaces that show connections between pieces of content is that they are fed with metadata (content about the content in the product). This means that we now need to ensure that the quality of the metadata is as good and as complete as the content itself. Are publishers prepared to become taxonomy/ ontology developers? Do the taxonomies and ontologies provide real value to the users in and of themselves or are they primarily navigation systems leading users from one piece of content to the next? What happens when the "correct" taxonomy doesn't actually map to the content collection very well? Is this a problem with the taxonomy or is it a problem with the reference collection? Should the publisher scale down the taxonomy, which may give the user an incomplete view of the overall field of research, or should they commission more content to round out the

collection? These are the kinds of issues that reference publishers now need to grapple with as they forge ahead with these innovations.

USER-CENTERED INTERACTIVITY

Things get even more interesting with the topic of interactivity when we consider the user on the "other side" of the screen. With a book, there is only one kind of interaction: users scan and read the content. They may choose to do it in a different order than anticipated and they may take notes, but the book itself does not provide any tools to help users with the task that they are trying to accomplish. Users come to the reference work to gain knowledge for a reason. With the advent of the online resource, things get much more complicated. Users can ask questions, provide data, and respond to what the application does. The application can try to anticipate what they want, save information for them, and respond to their actions. Essentially, in an online environment, a dialog ensues between the user and the application.

The first things that publishers need to ask when developing a new online product are: Who are the users for the product? How are they going to use the product and what do they want to get out of the experience? As a designer of online products, iFactory (http://www.ifactory.com) uses personas to try to get at this information. Personas try to distill certain kinds of users that will come to a product and are used to embody not just how they will interact with the product but also some general characteristics of their overall personality. In the world of reference products, a persona for a typical undergraduate is often a given (one client dubbed this persona the "slovenly student"). For many if not most reference products aimed at the higher education market, students come to these products because they need information to write their papers. And typically, they are in a hurry, so they want to get the information as painlessly as possible. Unfortunately, as designers of these products, we are precluded from building in any kind of "Write My Paper" function.

Students need to write papers as quickly as possible. Librarians are trying to help, giving pointers about how to find what they are looking for, and educating them along the way that not all information is created equal. Unfortunately, students avail themselves of librarians relatively infrequently. Consequently, publishers need to anticipate this and start designing products that can help students get to the information they need. This means providing as much context as possible to point the student in the right direction. It is not enough to just provide a large collection of content around a certain subject. It is increasingly necessary to give the student context around the content. The following questions must be addressed: How in-depth is this content? What is and isn't included? Where to go if this isn't the right content for the user? And once the user has found the content they, what tools can publishers provide to help them accomplish the user's task?

Before we dive into the kinds of interactive features that can help in this endeavor, let's look at the conceptual model that different people have in their heads about what it is that they are doing when they are looking for reference information online. From a publisher's perspective, the world of reference is divided into many separate applications: products each with their own content and their own unique interface. There is a sea of different reference products on the market, all with substantially similar interfaces that are essentially individual islands. Each product has its own URL, its own homepage, its own navigational structure, and for the most part, the different products do not interact with each other. The main point here is that it's easier for the publisher to provide features for a particular product than to provide features that work between products. The reason for this is that publishers have control over the interface and content of their product while they need to collaborate with other publishers or product vendors to provide features that integrate products together. This is not to say that products aren't being integrated; it is simply slower and harder to integrate separate products than it is to add new features to the product itself.

Examples to alleviate these communication issues between reference products include federated search (which has mostly failed), discovery services, the library OPAC, OpenURL linking, et cetera. These efforts have worked to a varying degree, but all are an indication that a universal interface across all reference content does not yet exist.

Publishers clearly have an interest in linking their products together. If they are big enough, they may have a variety of products that link together naturally. But, of course, none of them produce all the content that a library needs. No library is ever going to buy just one publisher's product line. Publishers know this, and consequently, they work hard to conform to standards such as federated search and COUNTER, but there is also an obvious and natural tendency to make their own products interoperate better. And because publishers can control the technology of their products, it is easier to connect their products than to connect with those of their competitors. And even so, publishers are increasingly moving to consolidate their products into fewer technology platforms, because providing good interoperability across different platforms is difficult.

Librarians are invested in providing a common and coherent interface across all the products in their holdings. These are inevitably from different publishers and have different interfaces suitable to the differing needs of their underlying content. Librarians buy the products that make sense for their user population and budget. They know that the different products are substantially similar and often wonder why they can't have a single-search interface to access all this content. They cannot buy access to all the content available because their budgets preclude it. Consequently, most librarians would prefer that links to content and products outside of what the library has purchased are not shown to users because this may cause more confusion. When users click on such a link and cannot access the content, it is not always clear why that is the case. They may ask if the link is broken in some way. Or, they may be aware that the library hasn't bought access to the content they need, but will still remain frustrated about it.

This model of a unified interface across all library holdings with a clear demarcation between what the library holds and what it does not makes a lot of intuitive sense and is easily explained, since it matches our ideas of the physical world. But as previously mentioned, it's actually hard to pull off because it doesn't match the realities of the electronic products and/or what publishers ideally want. The first obstacle working against a unified interface is that different content collections need different interfaces and different ways of searching, browsing, and presenting the content. A unified interface is, by necessity, a lowest common denominator interface that can work across all content. All of the interactivity and specialized interfaces described early works against a common search interface. The second obstacle is the technical problem of actually trying to integrate products and platforms. This integration is hard to pull off technically (often the underlying technologies do not match very well) and is rarely a top priority for the publishers who are most interested in promoting use of their products.

And finally, there are the users. Users are familiar with tools that have global span such as Google and Wikipedia. The Web implicitly pushes this worldview. It may be possible to get them to understand why searching a single library holdings might be better than searching in Google, but that is the extent of it. Most users go to Google first when they are searching for reference content. In fact, in so far as there is a universal search interface for reference content, as far as the user is concerned, it is and in all likelihood will remain Google. Consequently, publishers and librarians are scrambling to get their content searchable by Google. This is difficult for publishers because the content is not freely available, and Google is not interested in providing links to content that users cannot access.

What all of this means is that many interactive features are problematic if they can't conform to librarian or user needs. Features that only work within the confines of a particular product don't make sense to the user unless that product is comprehensive enough that the user is likely to start and finish his or her task within it.

The Search Function

The single most important feature that all reference products have is the Search function. The ability to "query" the product is powerful and the main reason why all reference content has migrated online quickly. Any user that comes to a reference product is interested in only a very small subset of the content provided and Search provides the easiest and most natural mechanism to find that content. Even if users initially arrive at the product through a Google search or by using a library's discovery service, once in the product it is very important to provide a search function simply because the majority of time the user will not land on the correct content item the first time.

When reference products first appeared online, publishers often spent a great deal of time augmenting the quick search box with increasingly complicated and sometimes numerous advanced search forms. Unfortunately, as usage statistics were compiled, it was discovered that people hardly ever used those forms. Most users' needs are satisfied through a simple quick search interface.

Consequently, publishers are now spending much more time trying to make quick search better. Much of this work is largely invisible to the user and involves making better use of the metadata to improve the search results. In addition, there has been a great deal of effort put into making the search results better by faceting those results and providing a host of refinement options in the results screen. Nevertheless, Web application designers still have a long way to go with this. What is the best way to present search results to the user? For instance, as mentioned previously, the OED now presents search results in both a standard list view and in a timeline chart. Showing search results on a map makes a great deal of sense in certain contexts. Essentially, search results try to prioritize the results to show the most relevant results to the user first, and we are just at the beginning of exploring different possible interfaces.

In addition, getting the search results right is often not a technical problem but an editorial one. Depending on the kind of content, different technically correct results are appropriate. In certain cases, it makes sense to return a small number of highly relevant results, while in other cases, returning more, less relevant results is more useful. This is the difference between precision and breadth. In general, the more advanced the user, the more likely providing fewer, more precise results is better. Consequently, it may even make sense to vary results according to the skill level of the user.

In an effort to provide more context for the researcher, applications often include special pages that provide more context about a particular topic. One example of this is the BBC web site (www. bbc.co.uk/search/iraq). Another is the Credo Reference Topic Page (http://www.credoreference. com) functionality that was introduced in 2010. For certain key terms, a special page is produced that provides a host of different links related to the topic with some editorial organization to allow the user to navigate the topic better. In Credo's case, these are links to both internal Credo content, other products within the library and external public content. The tension here is between the amount of editorial work needed to create a good topic page and the essentially unlimited number of queries that users will want to perform. In another example, the Oxford African American Studies Center (http://www.oxfordaasc.com) provides "At a Glance" pages that provide the user with context

for the available materials in the collection about specific individuals and topics.

A simple but useful feature for these products is the search widget, which is easily embedded in Web pages. The search widget is a piece of HTML code that can be pasted into the page of any site. This allows the librarian to incorporate the product's search box into a library page outside of the product itself. It also allows the library to describe different online products right on its web site and to provide a convenient way for users to immediately search those products. This helps to solve one of the major problems for libraries: it is challenging to organize online reference works and to make them easily discoverable for users.

Another search-related piece of functionality that is increasingly seen is the ability for users to set search alerts. These alerts are triggered anytime new content is added to the collection that matches a particular search that a user has saved. This functionality was originally implemented in journal platforms but is seen more and more across the breadth of academic platforms. It is useful with any database of content that is regularly updated as it allows researchers to keep up with changes and additions to the content they are particularly interested in. This is a case where interactivity allows the product to reach out to the user instead of simply being material for the user to reference.

Links

When the user searches and then selects a result that looks promising, it is important to consider that this is rarely going to be the only result they are going to want to see. And if it isn't quite the right result, we need to give them the tools to navigate to other content. Is the current result too advanced? Too general? Is it possible to point the user to content that is at the right level for them? Have they found everything relevant within a particular product and if so, what other products are available to them? Ideally, the product should provide a set of possible links to related content based not only on relationships within the content but also on the user's actions.

This kind of cross-linking is something that needs to happen within the products at the level of search results and especially on the entry pages. Given that increasingly users are coming into these products from an external search, either from Google or from a library discovery service, it is critical that the entry itself provides links to other related content. Providing truly relevant linking of content within the product is difficult enough, but ultimately what is really necessary is linking across products, which is even more difficult because it involves understanding how the product is situated within the larger library context, and ultimately, within the world of scholarship.

This is an area of enormous potential for these products. It is not very sexy, but it would go a long way in reconciling the world views of users with the technical realities. Of course, technically it is going to be tricky to get it right. The taxonomies for different products will not match, and how they interpret search queries can be quite different. This means that the same search query in two different products can produce results that are significantly less related than one would expect them to be.

Publishers clearly have an interest in providing these answers/links in a way that promotes their own content, while librarians are interested in customizing these links so that they are specific to their collections. Credo's Topic pages are clearly a step in the right direction, because they provide links to content outside of the Credo Reference product and because librarians can customize the set of products that are integrated into the Topic pages, but this is still only a beginning. It will be interesting to see how effective cross-linking progresses over time.

Bibliography Linking

A related set of linking issues comes from bibliographies and citations. Ideally, bibliography entries would be linked to their digital instantia-

tion whenever possible. Digital Object Identifiers (DOIs) were created to help solve this problem. They are used to provide a mechanism for linking to the digital reference. DOIs provide a mechanism where the publisher registers the DOIs with an organization (CrossRef: http://www.crossref.org) that provides a link database that translates the DOIs into a link to the item wherever it may be. OpenURL is a similar standard that attempts to enable finding a referenced item within the library holdings using a standard query definition and a link resolver database. Links to global databases such as WorldCat and Google Books are also increasingly popular.

In addition, showing the Web of relationships among content that can be created by following citation links is a potentially very useful feature for users. To be able to see what content references the content that the user is currently looking at and to follow those links both allows the user to see the relevance of the content within the academic discourse and to see how that discourse has progressed over time. DOIs are increasingly important for this, and publishers are starting to populate CrossRef's bibliography database with the link information that will allow this linking to be far more comprehensive that it has been up until now. One interesting aspect of this functionality is that these forward links will increase over time, which in and of itself provides valuable feedback to the user on the relative importance of different pieces of content.

Paying Attention to Users

Another way of improving searching is to pay attention to what previous users have done. In the commercial world, many applications use recommendation engines that match what the user is searching for against what other people using the same queries have ended up purchasing. Amazon is the obvious example. For reference products, a modification of this functionality would monitor what users end up reading, saving, downloading, et cetera after initially landing on a piece of content.

Another aspect of leveraging users' actions is in relation to taxonomies. Why not let users tag content? User tagging can provide another means of linking content together. This doesn't have to replace editorially-governed taxonomies and ontologies, but it could augment them. It's not clear that users will be willing to tag the reference content, but in certain contexts, it may be a viable and useful feature. A similar feature is provided by SAGE Research Methods Online, which allows users to create related lists of content and to make them public. These lists are then available to other users of the product.

Finally, some commercial products query their users to try to get as good an understanding of them as possible to improve recommendations and search results. Netflix is one example of this, where they ask for the types of movies that the user likes as well as asking them to rate movies that they have seen. For certain academic and reference products, especially ones heavily used by graduate students and faculty, publishers would benefit from understanding their users at this level. Having the ability to query and get feedback from directly within a reference product could lead to significant improvements of reference online products over time. This level of interaction with and monitoring of their own users has never been part of publishing culture, but it has proved to be the lifeblood of most successful online applications.

Saving Information

Reference products need to allow users to save information—any one user is interested in only a small portion of what the product entails. Products have allowed users to print, e-mail, and show how to cite content for a long time. Citations support has gotten more sophisticated as more styles are supported and the link to different citation products has improved. At the same time, keep-

ing products up to date with the latest changes in citation formats is a challenge.

Saving searches and bookmarking content can be provided for an individual session without having to make the user register, but if we are going to save information between sessions, the user will need to register with the product. For a long time reference publishers were resistant to features that required users to register a personal account. That seems to be changing now. Many products now allow users to register and save searches and selected content. Some allow these to be grouped, annotated, and made public. This is roughly equivalent to playlists on iTunes. This feature can be useful for a wide variety of users, from the student collating information for a paper to a teacher putting together a course pack.

PubFactory (http://www.pubfactory.net), an online publishing platform that iFactory developed for the publishing industry, has extended this idea: saved content can be organized into groups, and these groups can then be packaged into a custom e-book for the user. The user can create a cover page, reorder the content as they see fit, and decide to produce the e-book as a PDF or an ePub file. If the publisher allows it, these custom e-books can be downloaded and read on any e-book reader that supports PDF and ePub files.

Of course, one problem with saving information is that users need to create individual accounts within all the reference products that they use. And if they need access to several different products for a single project, that saved information is going to be spread across all those different reference products. Again, this is an example where the current technical realities come up against what the user really wants to–to have a single place to store all the content that they are putting together for their research that seamlessly integrates with all the different reference products being used. One possible solution to this problem is a browser plugin from Zotero (http://www.zotero.org), which allows bookmarks and citations to be saved. One caveat: this only works with one particular browser and does not work if the user accesses the product from different computers or their mobile device.

Mobile Support and the Future

With the explosion of smartphones, e-readers, and tablets, it will become increasingly important for online reference products to support these devices. This means supporting a variety of screen sizes, multi-touch interfaces, and, depending on the device, some additional technical constraints such as the use of Flash on Apple devices. At the same time, all major devices now support browsers based on WebKit, which includes support for HTML5 and has a wealth of features that can help support even more advanced interactive interfaces.

Where to look for the future of reference interfaces? In a word: mobile apps. These apps and the mobile devices on which they run are a radical transformation in our relationship to the still young Internet—with a mobile device the Internet is always there and always with us. In addition, the applications that are becoming available on these devices are pointing the way toward the full use of communication beyond the traditional search box: location, audio, pictures, et cetera. Perhaps it's safe to say that the best, most innovative reference applications are on the iPhone/iPad:

- iBird is an application that points the way to what a reference field guide should be. In addition to photos and drawings of the birds, it knows where you are and is able to limit the set of possible birds to the ones that live in your current vicinity. It also has bird songs for all birds in the database so if you are having trouble getting a good look at the bird but you can hear it, you can use the audio to distinguish the birds. The quality of the audio is so good that it comes with a warning that using the bird calls to draw the birds in is against the bird watchers' code of ethics.
- Shazam still feels like magic. Point your phone at the source of some music and it will tell you what it is.
- Word Lens – Point your iPhone at a piece of text in Spanish and it will automatically translate the text into English, replacing the Spanish text with English—in the camera viewfinder in real time. This is clearly the ultimate app for hungry tourists on vacation.
- Yelp – it augments buildings with information about what is inside them. It does this to help you find the nearest restaurant, but there is no reason that this couldn't be used to help tourist figure out what they are looking at – imagine Digital Karnak updated to respond to the precise location of people visiting the ruins to provide answers on the spot.

CyberTracker (http://www.cybertracker.co.za), not itself a reference application, is creating a datastore that is providing incredibly valuable information. It is a handheld computer that allows users to put in animal tracking data. All data is tagged with time/date and location information and stored centrally. The aggregate information can then be viewed and graphed. It turns out that elephants passing a village in the night don't poop until they are well beyond it. An odd area in a forest that was surprisingly free of deer turned out to indicate the presence of a mountain lion where no one thought they existed. Although this isn't strictly a reference application, it is indicative of the closing gap between creating data and using it.

CONCLUSION

The bottom line in all this is that as online products progress they will only get more interactive. The kinds of content that are provided are increasing.

The interfaces to handle that proliferation of content by necessity must increase as well. Interfaces for exploring the relationships across entire reference collections are now possible, and that raises a whole new set of interface and interactivity issues. Products need to try to help their users accomplish the tasks that are the ultimate reason for bringing those users to the product. As users come to these products, their actions provide a significant amount of information that can be used to help subsequent users and can improve the products themselves. The products can reach out and alert users to new data and new connections that add and change over time. And of course, the way in which users come to the products is changing as mobile devices proliferate and diversify.

This is an exciting time for reference products: both the technical landscape and user expectations are changing quickly. In the past, the most important thing for publishers has been their content. In the online world, content will still be important, but so increasingly will be the interactivity provided and the relationship between the user and the product. The history of the Web has shown that the products and ultimately the publishers that are most successful at managing this increased complexity and listen to and manage their users most effectively will ultimately be the ones that succeed.

NOTE

Adapted with permission of Against the Grain Press, Charleston, S.C.

Charleston Conference Proceedings, 2009. Edited by Beth Bernhardt and Leah Hinds. Series Editor: Katina Strauch. Charleston, SC: Against the Grain Press, 2010, p. 496-511.

Chapter 10

Theory and Practice:
Designing for Effective Mobile Content (Service) Delivery

Alix Vance
Architrave Consulting, USA

David Wojick
U.S. Department of Energy, USA

ABSTRACT

Design of mobile applications to deliver reference content and services is a new grand challenge. We present a template of design considerations, ranging from the general theory of content restructuring to strategic planning and tactical execution.

INTRODUCTION

Conventional reference materials such as sprawling Web pages and large documents do not work on the tiny screens of mobile devices. A new design approach, which frees facts from these busy, large scale formats, then hyperlinks them into a coherent mobile structure, is described below. Key theoretical features are new modes of selection, clustering, and compression of factual reference content. New approaches to structure and navigation are also discussed.

Following this scene setting, the conversation shifts from mobile design theory to business practice, zeroing in on strategic planning considerations and following with steps and tips governing tactical execution. Questions are raised and responded to, which include: What makes mobile content delivery fundamentally different? What are the key considerations for content providers to review before embarking on a mobile development project? Tactics and implementation steps are examined from service, content, business, and development perspectives. A concise summary ties theory and practice together

DOI: 10.4018/978-1-61350-308-9.ch010

The objective of this chapter is to provide reference content providers with step-by-step issues that must be addressed in any mobile application project.

BACKGROUND

Web-like applications for the smartphone and other portable devices are a new medium of reference communication that has arrived. Often called simply "apps," this medium is an alternative to the familiar Web page, but with very different design requirements. The reference community has myriad projects going to explore and develop apps that will provide access to its many resources and collections. It won't be easy and it won't be quick, but it is happening.

Apps have taken off with the phenomenal growth of smartphones and similar hand held computers. Apple alone has hundreds of thousands of apps for its iPhone; some are free, but many are for sale. App development is now a major industry, and several federal government agencies, such as NASA, have fielded popular apps.

There are really two very different kinds of apps, although they may look and feel the same. The standalone or native app is one that runs on the mobile device, as a piece of native software. Common examples include games, a scheduler, a dictionary, or other reference works, photo albums, et cetera. No outside connection is required to use these apps, although they are typically acquired by downloading from the Web. The content of these apps is typically static, except for user inputs.

Then there is the Web app, which is really a Web site designed for the tiny screen of the mobile device. The Web app is viewed using the device's Web browser, so no special software is required. As with any Web site, the Web app requires the user to be online when it is used. And as with many Web pages, Web apps can have dynamic content. Common examples are similar to Web uses, such as news, weather, or search engines.

However, there is also a hybrid kind of app, which runs in standalone mode, but which is updated via the Web.

It is estimated that the volume of mobile access to the Web is now greater than desktop computer access. However, the vast bulk of Web pages are still designed for large format desktop and laptop computer screens. Thus, the vast bulk of accessible reference material is still not designed for mobile access. It is this challenge that we address below.

THEORY: GOING FROM FORMAT TO STRUCTURE

Restructuring Reference Content for Mobile Applications

Our objective here is to present a systematic design method for restructuring reference content, to make this content work well when presented on mobile devices. The rapid rise of mobile devices presents reference content providers with a grand challenge. Traditional content designs, especially Web pages, simply do not work on the tiny screens of mobile devices. The typical computer screen is 50 or more times larger than the typical mobile device screen, from 200 to 300 square inches for the computer, compared to just four to six square inches for the mobile machine. As a result, traditional Web based content designs are virtually unreadable on the tiny mobile screen. The solution is to radically restructure content, presenting it in a way that works.

What is needed is to break content down into tiny pieces, freeing the facts from the format, then organize and hyperlink it for effective presentation to the user. But the organization will not be on the screen as format, as it typically is with Web pages. Instead, the key to effective presentation of factual material will be in the linkages among the tiny pages, of which a great many will be required. We call this principle of design "going from format to structure."

Interestingly, content design based on freeing facts from format harkens back to the early days of hypertext. Before the advent of the World Wide Web, with its large format, magazine-style pages, many hypertext systems featured small pages. Apple's HyperCard software is a good example, where pages were the size of filing cards. This card-like interface required careful design of individual, small pieces of content. These many small pieces were bound together by a coherent, carefully structured navigation system of links. Mobile device content systems require just such a careful, well structured design method.

While our design methods will be quite general, we give special attention to restructuring existing reference Web pages and Web sites for mobile applications. This is because great sums of money have already been invested in content development for the Web. It is estimated that there are already one trillion Web pages, many of which are of a factual, reference nature (Alpert, 2008). For example, most scientific and technical communication today occurs via the Web, with new content added constantly, as science and technology proceed.

There are three types of reference Web content: home, hit, and text pages.

Our content restructuring considerations focus on the three basic types of Web pages typically found in reference Websites.

Home (or menu) Pages: The home page is typically a large menu, providing a combination of information about and access to the interior pages of the Web site. Such pages often provide between 50 and 100 separate links to other pages within the site, together with textual link annotations that provide information about where the links go. Restructuring this much information for the tiny mobile screen and linking it all together into a coherent front end menu system is a formidable challenge.

Note that in addition to the true Home page, a reference Web site may have numerous internal menu pages to provide navigation, especially if it includes browse features. Thus, the home or menu page is a type of page, of which there may be many in a given reference Web site.

Hit (or list) Pages: Reference information is often found via a Web site specific search engine. This is in part because reference materials are typically voluminous, and modern search technologies can be quite accurate in finding content related to specific concepts and/or topics. Searches generate hit pages that list relevant items selected by the search engine. These hit pages provide menu-like lists the user can choose from to select and access specific documents.

As with the home page, a hit page is basically a large, annotated menu of links to other pages, but it is much more dynamic. The content of hit pages is essentially unpredictable. Restructuring these dynamic hit pages for the tiny mobile screen is a challenge that is quite different from that of restructuring the home page.

For one thing, the amount of information provided for each hit is often enough to fill the mobile screen. This may include a title, an abstract, authors, and numerous links to additional data. All of this secondary information needs to be separated and provided separately to make room for the basic hit list. In fact, it may take a whole system of hyperlinked mobile pages to provide this information for each hit.

Text Pages: Behind the home page and hit pages of most large reference Web sites there lays a number of Web pages of textual material. In many cases there is a vast amount of documentary material. This is the actual reference information, the purpose of the site. These pages of text (including graphics, pictures, etc.) must also be restructured for viewing on the tiny mobile screen, to the extent possible. Because of the internal coherence of writing, this may be the most challenging restructuring of all.

In addition, the ability to restructure these pages for mobile use often depends on how and where the content is created. For example, documents imported from outside can only be changed in certain limited ways. But documents created for the mobile application can be radically different from ordinary large format documents. Even for fixed documents it may be possible, for example, to take the user to specific sentences, based on their search criteria.

TECHNICAL APPROACH

Our technical approach is based on our prior work analyzing the structure of technical information. There are, implicit in any body of information, a number of distinct structures (Wojick, 2010). Some of these are obvious on inspection, other much less so. The basic approach must be to identify the underlying structures in a way that guides the design of mobile applications. What this means is to identify those structures that can be restructured to fit the tiny screen.

Information is lumpy, especially on Web pages. The magazine format means that there are typically several columns of content, as well as banners, footers, et cetera. These distinct format features are in fact distinct lumps of information. This sounds abstract, but in practice, it is quite specific. For example, many home-type pages include what might be called "boilerplate," that is, sets of links that appear on every page. In fact it is common to have a boilerplate banner, a boilerplate side menu, plus standard links along the bottom of every page. These all need to be removed and provided separately, in mobile screen sized pieces.

By the same token, many hit pages provide multiple, standardized links to additional information for each hit on the list. These can be relocated to only appear once a hit is selected.

Many other forms of content restructuring are possible, and many will be needed to break today's large format Web pages down into mobile screen sized pieces. However, an equally challenging task is to then reassemble all these pieces into a coherently linked whole, a hypertext system. This

will require designing many new menus. We call this the transition from layout to linking.

The size of the mobile application system is itself a significant design issue. Typically it will be a constraint, sometimes a severe one. It is clear that in transitioning from large format, information laden Web pages to a host of small, hyperlinked mobile pages, the number of potential pages grows dramatically. Smaller units require more organization.

For example, if a single Web page translates into 30 to 50 mobile pages, then a 100 page Web site might translate into a 3,000 to 5,000 page mobile application. If the Web site is large, the mobile application it translates into might easily become enormous, far too big to be useful, or even feasible. In such cases it may be necessary to drop a significant amount of information.

The need to eliminate some information means deciding what is most important and what can be dispensed with, perhaps via a form of triage. The same is true when it comes to linking information on different pages. Too much linking creates confusion, such as getting lost in the navigation. Mobile applications call for simplicity as well as parsimony. This kind of intellectual discipline has seldom been necessary in Web design.

Thus in addition to looking for strategies for breaking down Web content into distinct structural components and the restructuring these components into new hypertext systems, one needs design principles for eliminating the less important content. In many cases this will mean refocusing on the core function of the enterprise, which is delivering reference content in an efficient manner.

DESIGNING FOR THE TINY SCREEN

Some crucial design issues arise no matter whether the reference content comes from a Web site or is newly created. Paramount among these is what we call the mobile page size. Mobile page size is measured in terms of what we call "screens." A screen is what appears on a mobile device, without any scrolling, zooming or other dynamic alteration.

The idea of a screen as an amount of content is somewhat fluid. Different mobile devices have different sized screens, they may display different amounts of content on the same sized screen, and even for a given device, what is displayed can be changed. However, for design purposes it is necessary to pick a paradigm screen. This can be done by specifying a specific device and the settings on it.

One the paradigm or "design screen" is set, the design question becomes how to constrain the mobile pages. For example, are pages allowed to be greater than one screen in area, so that scrolling will be needed? Keeping all pages to one screen in area is a very severe constraint.

If pages can be larger than one screen in area, how much larger can they be? Then too, in what shapes can they be larger? For example, pages that are one screen wide but several screens long do not require horizontal scrolling. This may be best for text pages, because horizontal scrolling is unpleasant when reading text. On the other hand, scrolling through a horizontal row of pictures each one screen wide is quite common. Maps, on the other hand, often benefit from both horizontal and vertical scrolling.

So, for example, one might adopt a standard page layout that has a column of text one screen wide and three high, with a three screen wide row of pictures at the bottom. Obviously there are a myriad of such formats, all different. Deciding how big each mobile page can be, and in what shapes they can come, fundamentally constrains the design of the mobile content. This design determines how much information can be presented on each page of the app.

Note too that a lot of reference material is textual in nature. We are quite used to finding text in widths of seven inches or more on Web pages and in print. If this text has to be wrapped into a 2 or 3 inch screen width, to avoid scrolling, then one or two sentences can quickly fill a screen. What appear on a Web page to be small blocks of text, such as abstracts, can quickly turn into long scrolls many screens in length. Short articles become many feet long and long articles hundreds of feet long. None of this is desirable, making how text is handled the greatest challenge of all in the new mobile medium.

The severe constraint of having text columns just a few inches wide leads to many issues of composition. Interestingly it is similar to the constraint that newspaper writers have long faced. This in turn leads to a major design issue, namely can the textual content be written for the mobile application, or is it developed independently?

Configuring and/or designing text for mobile apps is a major design issue. It makes a tremendous difference whether the text used in an app can be designed for that purpose, or whether it is conventional text brought in from outside sources. What we can call "app text" can be designed for the tiny screen. This means implementing design strategies such as using short titles, short sentences, and small, self contained paragraphs.

Textual content that is not designed for app use is unlikely to have these features. For example, the abstracts of journal articles are not likely to fit into a single screen area. By the same token, Web-based text in general is unlikely to fit the needs of apps. When using text that has not been app designed, there are a variety of "workarounds" that might be used. In fact this is a complex topic all in its own, because ordinary text and the app screen are simply not compatible.

It should be clear by now that there are a host of difficult design choices to be made in developing a good app for reference type material. Moreover, there is an intrinsic progression to these choices, such that making one constrains many others. Good app design means identifying these choices and following their logical progression, for the standard types of pages.

Solutions and Recommendations

If endeavoring to create a content application, how can an organization help to ensure its success? Moving from an academic and theoretical view of application development to one that is more business minded – i.e., translating theory to practice – begins with identification of five critical components: i) a service need to support, ii) a well-understood target audience, iii) relevant content stream(s), iv) tools that add value and will support repeat use, and v) an enduring business case.

The process does not originate with content identification but with service identification. This is where the mobile delivery vehicle places a higher premium. Information transmitted by mobile device delivers in-the-moment utility in a way that a book on a shelf cannot. The promise of mobile reference is that it provides users with quick grabs of content *in context*, which helps the user respond to questions or solve problems in situ.

Another essential aspect is brevity. As described in the preceding section, the mobile screen is many times smaller than the standard computer screen. Engagement must be quick and focused, without extraneous navigation.

DEFINING SERVICE PARAMETERS

To narrow the scope of services your app will support, identify one or more potential audiences for the product. Success will hinge on the accuracy of your team's understanding of customer use needs and behaviors, which include their "pain points" and routine problem-solving behaviors. Your concept should be oriented to service requirements that your application will meet. Applications that correctly identify and respond to a recurring service need will thrive, while those that miss the target will quickly lose their attraction.

Because the mobile application environment for content/service delivery is necessarily more targeted, successful outcomes hinge on having accurate knowledge of audience needs. Holding other commercial factors equal, it pays to test market prospective solutions and make development choices that evaluate audience demand and incorporate detailed feedback during the conceptualization, design, and deployment process.

For each audience under consideration, be prepared to describe its size, classification, demographics, and activities. Note which devices and operating systems it uses and where it uses them. Asking (and answering) questions, such as those listed below, can help narrow the concept scope and will help define service and product characteristics.

Questions: Service Definition

- What is your audience?
- What needs are you seeking to meet?
- How are these currently being met?
- How does your app propose to better service user demand?
- Will mobility or mobile app features add unique value? If so, how?
- What defines a successful user engagement?
- Will users return? Are you supporting a repetitive or time-sensitive behavior?
- What device types and operating systems will you need to support?
- Are you passively providing information? What are you seeking to have users do next?
- What will make your app necessary and engaging?

Having worked through this process, you will be better equipped to identify whether: i) your concept is a good fit for mobile service delivery, ii) you have a solid understanding of your target audience, iii) your service will meet a need or serve a valuable function, and iv) what you envision will have a distinct and repeatable value. You will also know whether additional research is needed. Once your concept passes this stress test, you may have the beginning of a viable app concept.

CONTENT SELECTION

Because this process began by evaluating service considerations, step two will be to make content selections. Oftentimes, Web sites become catchalls for anything a publisher wants to post. However, in a mobile environment, targeting and selectivity are essential. The choices made on the front end will ultimately dictate whether your app is used and can accomplish its intended goals.

When making content decisions, it can be useful to create a matrix that cross references content options with user needs and mobile deliver options. Your aim will be to identify content that will best fit specific user needs in a mobile content, to determine how well content streams will operate together, and to evaluate relevance and demand. Usage statistics will be helpful in evaluating demand for content across a variety of situational cases. Non-high use content may become high use content if it is transformed by in situ delivery, but this is the exception and not the rule.

In addition to thinking practically about service niches and content applicability, the conceptual design phase provides an opportunity to review recent advances in mobile capabilities and to generate blue sky solutions. Mobile delivery capabilities can open doors to new ways of thinking about content selection and delivery. They can give content owners opportunities to experiment with new models and content service combinations. They can also add value by virtue of their mobility to content streams that may not have been as useful in another context.

Applications are not only vehicles for pushing information to end users. Handhelds are also increasingly used to capture and transmit inbound information. Multitouch screens, sensors, in-built cameras, and geo-locating capabilities enable two-way communication and are effective at gathering data from users about their activities or surroundings. Not only can they transmit information, with permission, about users' geographic locations and the context of their activities, they can also provide an opportunity for users to upload images, upload audio and video input, and answer questions. For researchers, apps can be developed to function as data gathering devices for participants in clinical studies.

Questions: Content Selection

- How does your content compare when seeking to answer a mobile need?
- Will mobile delivery and tools enhance perceived content value and drive repeat use?
- Is need for the content timing-dependent? Will it update frequently?
- Does it present well independently of other content (can it be chunked)?
- Can the content service be delivered in a shallow environment, without the need for multiple click-throughs or extensive scrolling?
- Can the impact of your content be boosted by combining it with content from other sources?
- Will your approach (via proprietary materials, tools, or partnerships) create a unique market advantage for your content?

BUSINESS CONSIDERATIONS

In addition to strong conceptual design, having a defensible business plan that demonstrates an application's chances for success is also essential. There are innumerable reasons to publish an application, which may include traffic generation, monetization, marketing/branding, and the desire to create inroads into adjacent markets.

Project objectives will be driven by the mission and project goals that the business owner has defined for the project—their definition of success. Regardless of motive, the decision to create an application should be carefully considered. The concept should be described in a launch document with market research and feedback and recommendations from prospective customers. Financial implications should be modeled in a multi-year profit and loss statement that demonstrates: i) timing of investments, ii) projected revenue streams, iii) anticipated break even, iv) unit sales requirements, and v) internal rate of return (IRR) of the project.

Competitive advantage is another critical ingredient in the conceptual design process. There are numerous ways to create barriers to entry based on proprietary content. Some include combining public and proprietary data in unusual, innovative ways, licensing information from a specialized, high-value source, or repurposing archival materials that have already been developed and catalogued. If your value is hard to mimic, your chances for commercial success will be greater.

The business model for an application will also be dictated by market expectations (e.g., pricing and terms), the intended audience, anticipated demand, and uniqueness of the value proposition. In addition to projecting audience uptake and revenue streams, by year, be sure to model all up-front costs for content acquisition, royalties, technology design and development, marketing, ongoing maintenance, and user-driven improvements. Depending on the intended business purpose, the business plan should articulate expected gains and should provide a measurable definition of success, which is likely to be expressed in terms of dollars, traffic, and/or community uptake or input.

For example: Assuming a three year investment of $10,890, reflecting start up costs and ongoing maintenance, the application publisher will break even with 11,000 paid installations at 99 cents per *download. 11,000 users represent 2% of a target market of 550,000 users. The publisher currently sells products to 3% of the total market.*

Alternatively: The publisher will make the application freely available but will measure success by unique user downloads, usage statistics, and viral marketing impact. A three-year investment of $10,890 will be offset by savings in the traditional marketing budget.

In addition to the costs of developing the application, there will be additional costs associated with ongoing marketing, maintenance, and upgrades. A launch plan and financial modeling should include all of these phased considerations:

- Pre-launch market assessment
- Proof of concept, including testing and feedback
- Marketing and promotions plan that extends beyond live release and drives future adoptions
- Launch documents and financial modeling that anticipate ongoing investment

An expectation should be set that improvements will be made at intervals in order to reinforce the utility of the application to its existing and prospective customers. Many conceive of an application being a one-off, "set it and forget it" offering. This is unwise. An application publisher should expect a successful application to require ongoing cultivation, enhancement, and market reinforcement.

THE VENDOR PROCESS

With a launch document and financial modeling in hand (including concept, audience definition, scope of financial and human resources available, timeframe for implementation, and definition of success), an application publisher will be prepared to draft a request-for-proposal (RFP) from prospective technology vendors. The application publisher will pave the way for a productive and efficient vendor relationship by thinking through concept and business plan requirements in advance and having the ability to articulate project specifics. The benefit of this process is that time (and money) will not be wasted in the development process by re-examining premises and filling in the blanks.

Individual vendor partners will have their own working styles and strengths—some are stronger in process management and others may have a unique flair for design. Think in advance about the strengths sought from a vendor partner. Regardless of their particular attributes, any vendor should help guide an application publisher through their development choices by providing wireframes that represent the proposed content and service delivery in multiple device environments. Consider whether what looks good on an iPhone looks equally good in an Android, Blackberry, or iPad environment, and develop for all operating systems rather than for one.

The best way to ensure a successful development outcome is to think around the corners and be prepared. Far after beta release and into alpha, expect to make changes and adjustments based on market feedback and incorporate upgrades and enhancements into your vendor agreement and financial/project plan. Although application development may seem like a limited undertaking, at relatively little expense compared to a Web site build, this does not mean that there are fewer outcomes to consider. In fact, there may actually be less flexibility in the application environment because, unlike a Web site, an application is not intended to provide all things to all people. The process of making choices forces a series of commitments that define outcome.

Figure 1. iPhone landing page for the Annals of Internal Medicine application

Guidelines

- Keep it simple. Remember that, in a mobile framework, less is easily more.
- Sit in the user's seat: develop from the user's perspective, not the deliverer's perspective.
- Make your product as scalable and extensible as possible – suited for multiple device types and operating environments.
- Know what your business objectives are and what a successful outcome entails and looks like.
- Test, test, and re-test. Don't consider your application complete upon release. Prepare to incorporate feedback at each step along the way.
- Anticipate different outcomes.

Examples

Figures 1 and 2 provide examples from a mobile application recently released for *Annals of Internal Medicine*, an academic medical journal published by the American College of Physicians (ACP). Figure 1 depicts the journal's landing page as presented on an iPhone. Figure 2 includes a

Figure 2. Screenshots and menu options for the Annals of Internal Medicine application

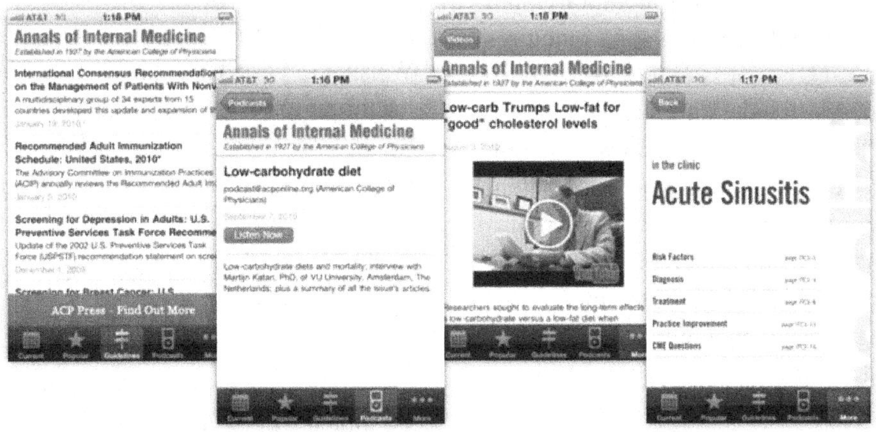

montage of screenshots and navigation options available to users within the mobile application.

FUTURE RESEARCH DIRECTIONS

It is reasonable to expect that opportunities for research, discovery, and reporting in this area will be expansive because devices, technologies, and legislation governing their use, are subject to continual transformation. Emerging topics for discussion include (but are in no way limited to):

privacy; security; e-commerce; two-way data collection; sensor use; multichannel communication; multisensory input; scalability; and globalization

Acknowledging the rapid pace of change, the theory and practice framework of this discussion is designed to provide a scalable structure that will accommodate the examination of conceptual and practical implications of new innovations as they are released. From both a theoretical and practical standpoint, assuming that technology increasingly supports scalability across device types, a paradigm shift will occur when there are sufficient varieties of portable wireless devices in use, such that non-mobile use no longer considered a standard for comparison. As this comes to pass, it may be expected that alternatives for

content capture, dissemination, and sharing will be distinguished by technology speeds, display sizes, and user interface navigation capabilities, rather than distinctions in mobility.

CONCLUSION

From a theoretical standpoint, the discussion in this chapter has focused on "freeing facts from format." To summarize, traditional content designs, especially Web pages, do not work on the tiny screens of mobile devices. That being said, given substantial investments in textual Web pages, a practical method is advocated for systematically triaging less relevant content and contextually displaying and delivering "facts" (less text-intensive knowledge structures) via mobile device, free of extraneous text. The chapter has described strategies for breaking down Web content into distinct structural components and restructuring these components into new hypertext systems that favor "linking" versus "layout." The chapter also begins to investigate the trade-offs inherent in designing for a screen that is limited in size.

Having laid the theoretical groundwork, the chapter focuses, from a systematic perspective, on the steps and choices that will give one mobile content application a greater change for business and/or commercial success than another. This section outlines the steps, considerations, and questions involved at decision-making junctures during the editorial, business modeling, and development process. Readers are presented with a generalized "how to" guide, which walks them through the process of creating a mobile content application from inception to delivery and maintenance, emphasizing the importance of: service orientation; informed business decisions; scalability; and organizational simplicity.

Acknowledging the topic's scope and the rapid pace of technological innovation in the mobile technology, the chapter does not seek to define next research steps in a restrictive manger, but raises questions for future examination and identifies topics that will have increasing relevance for mobile development theory and practice.

The chapter advocates for systematic examination of fundamental shifts in content delivery, which have theoretical and practical implications. Examples include the increasing relevance of data and facts and linking in a mobile environment and requisite shift away from reliance on long-form narrative. The authors furthermore suggest that application creators adopt a service-centric approach to development that adopts a more business-focused, versus strictly editorial, set of strategies and tactics.

REFERENCES

Alpert, J., & Hajaj, N. (2008). We knew the Web was big…. *The Official Google Blog*, Retrieved February 5, 2011, from http://googleblog.blogspot.com/2008/ 07/we-knew-web-was-big.html

Wojick, D. (2010). Untangling the web of technical knowledge: A model of information content and structure. *Information Bridge*. Retrieved December 12, 2010, from http://www.osti.gov/bridge/product.biblio.jsp?query_id=0&page=0&osti_id=991543&Row=0

ADDITIONAL READING

Brown, Q., Bonsignore, E., Hatley, L., Druin, A., Walsh, G., Foss, E., et al. (2010). Clear Panels: a technique to design mobile application interactivity. In *Proceedings of the 8th ACM Conference on Designing interactive Systems* (pp. 360-363). New York: ACM.NY, 360-363.

Charsky, C., & Raisinghani, M. (2009) Mobile Devices and Mobile Applications: Key Future Trends. In B. Unhelkar (Ed.), Handbook of Research in Mobile Business, Second Edition: Technical, Methodological and Social Perspectives (pp. 200-205). Hershey, PA: IGI Global.

Girardello, A., & Michahelles, F. (2010). AppAware: which mobile applications are hot? In *MobileHCI '10: Proceedings of the 12th International Conference on Human Computer Interaction with Mobile Devices and Services* (pp. 431-434). New York: ACM.

Gonçalves, V., & Ballon, P. (2011). Adding value to the network: Mobile operators' experiments with Software-as-a-Service and Platform-as-a-Service models. *Telematics and Informatics, 28*(1), 12–21. doi:10.1016/j.tele.2010.05.005

Holzer, A., & Ondrus, J. (2009). Trends in Mobile Application Development. *Lecture Notes of the Institute for Computer Sciences, Social Informatics, and Telecommunications Engineering, 12*(1), 55–64. doi:10.1007/978-3-642-03569-2_6

Holzer, A., & Ondrus, J. (2011). Mobile application market: A developer's perspective. *Telematics and Informatics, 28*(1), 22–31. doi:10.1016/j.tele.2010.05.006

Jones, C. M., & Willis, M. (2009). Edutainment in the field using mobile location based services. In *Proceedings of the 21st Annual Conference of the Australian Computer-Human interaction Special interest Group: Design: Open 24/7* (PP. 385-388) New York: ACM.

Jones, N. (2010). Ten Mobile Technologies to Watch in 2010 and 2011. Gartner Research. Retrieved October 30, 2010, from http://www.gartner.com/DisplayDocument? ref=clientFriendlyUrl&id=1311324

Li, Z., Bhowmik, A. K., & Bos, P. J. (2008). Introduction to Mobile Displays. In Bhowmik, A. K., Li, Z., & Bos, P. J. (Eds.), *Mobile Displays: Technology and Applications*. Chichester, UK: John Wiley & Sons, Ltd. doi:10.1002/9780470994641.ch1

Raisinghani, M. (2009). Current Impact and Future Trends of Mobile Devices and Mobile Applications. In Pagani, M. (Ed.), *Encyclopedia of Multimedia Technology and Networking* (2nd ed., pp. 312–317). Hershey, PA: IGI Global.

Saroiu, S., & Wolman, A. (2010). I am a sensor, and I approve this message. In *Proceedings of the Eleventh Workshop on Mobile Computing Systems & Applications* (pp. 37-42). New York: ACM.

Vogel, B., Spikol, D., Kurti, A., & Milrad, M. (2010). Integrating mobile, web and sensory technologies to support inquiry-based science learning. In *6th IEEE International Conference on Wireless, Mobile, and Ubiquitous Technologies in Education* (pp. 65-72). New York: IEEE.

Wojick, D. (2010). Untangling the Web of Technical Knowledge: A Model of Information Content and Structure. Retrieved November 18, 2010, from http://www.osti.gov/bridge/product.biblio.jsp?query_id=0&page=0&osti_id=991543

KEY TERMS AND DEFINITIONS

Android: Android is a mobile operating system developed by Android Inc. and purchased by Google in 2005. Android is a participant in the Open Handset Alliance.

API: An "API" is an application programming interface that enables communication across and between software programs.

Geolocation: The identification of real-world physical location of a person or object, transmitted by internet-connected device.

iPhone: A line of multimedia-enabled smartphones designed and released by Apple Inc. in 2007.

Internal Rate of Return: Used in capital budgeting to measure and compare the profitability of investments.

Metrics: Quantitative measures of performance.

Mobile Application: Computer software programs designed to operate on smaller, low-power devices, which may include handheld devices or mobile phones.

Multitouch: References the capacity of a device having a touch sensor-enabled screen to simultaneously register three or more inputs.

P/L: Profit and loss statement, used for business evaluation purposes.

Smartphone: Handheld devices that include telephone capabilities as well as running complete operating systems/software platforms.

Sensors: Derived from "wireless sensor network", which refers to a network of spatially distributed nodes that collaboratively monitor physical or environmental inputs.

Chapter 11
Medical E-Reference:
A Benchmark for E-Reference Publishing in Other Disciplines

Terese DeSimio
Wright State University, USA

Ximena Chrisagis
Wright State University, USA

ABSTRACT

Electronic medical information retrieval systems and reference sources were some of the first discipline-specific e-resources to be developed, due to physicians' need to access the most current and relevant clinical information as quickly as possible. Many medical publishers and information aggregators have been incorporating the features their users demand for years. Thus, medical e-reference publishing could serve as a benchmark for e-reference publishing in other fields. Yet medical e-reference is not without its challenges. Today's physicians and medical students expect immediate and user-friendly electronic access to media rich and value added clinical references, particularly via their mobile devices. Publishers, librarians, and network administrators will need to ensure that mobile information sources users demand are discoverable and easy to access and use, even in healthcare environments where increased data security is necessary.

INTRODUCTION

Medical publishers and aggregators were among the first to begin developing electronic desktop and mobile publications, due to the obvious need of physicians and medical students to access authori-

tative reference sources quickly and conveniently, but with the current increasing adoption of mobile devices and smart phones among the general population as well as the physician population, user expectations for anytime, anywhere access to enhanced content is increasing as well. Therefore, medical publishers, aggregators, and access providers (like librarians and network analysts)

DOI: 10.4018/978-1-61350-308-9.ch011

must continue to meet these expectations as much as possible. Medical librarians and publishers take for granted that authoritative reference sources are critical for quality patient care, but today's physicians and medical students also expect a flexible and media rich experience, that is still quick and easy to discover and to access, even on a secured network. For decades, the medical field has been at the forefront of discovery of and access to scholarly resources. One reason for this may be because of the influence of the National Library of Medicine (NLM), which has long been a leader in Information Technology.

BACKGROUND

The NLM published the first volume of *Index Medicus: A Monthly Classified Record of the Current Medical Literature of the World* in 1879. This index included books, medical articles, reports, and other literature (Miles & National Library of Medicine, 1982). NLM set high standards for information retrieval systems and vocabulary control in 1964 when it developed MEDLARS (Medical Literature Analysis and Retrieval System), which was based on *Index Medicus*. This database was too large for the remote access by computer systems in 1970 (McCarn, 1970), but by 1971, NLM had developed the first available online IRS, MEDLARS ON-LINE or MEDLINE, by using existing U.S. Department of Defense computer programs. DIALOG, the first well known, multidiscipline, and searchable database, was developed after MEDLINE in 1972 (Palmer, 1987). The NLM's impact can even be seen in current copyright practices. The 1976 Fair Use sections of the copyright law developed as a result of lengthy litigation between NLM and publishers who objected to NLM's photocopying practices (Miles & National Library of Medicine, 1982). During the 1980s, the NLM benefitted by having a director who was simultaneously the director of NLM and the National Coordination Office for

High Performance Computing and Communications (Groen, 2007). Under this director's leadership, NLM developed a computer program called Grateful Med, which was the precursor to PubMed (Hersh, 2003). PubMed became freely available on the Internet in 1997 and currently includes the full text to over 100 medical e-books (U.S. National Library of Medicine and the National Center for Biotechnology Information, 2010).

Very early medical e-reference books published include the Physician's Desk Reference and the Merck Manual (Hersh, 2003). STAT!Ref was a very early medical e-book aggregator, with its first version published in the early 1990s (Heyd, 2010). Another early medical e-book aggregator is Unbound Medicine which now partners with many e-book publishers: American Academy of Pediatrics, The American Public Health Association, The American Society of Health-System Pharmacists (ASHP), BMJ Group, Consumers Union and ConsumerReportsHealth.org, F. A. Davis, McGraw-Hill Professional, Merck & Co., Inc., Oxford University Press, Wiley-Blackwell, and Wolters Kluwer Health (Unbound Medicine Inc., 2011). Many medical e-books are available through these platforms: STAT!Ref and American College of Physicians (ACP), McGraw-Hill's Access products (including AccessMedicine, AccessSurgery, and AccessEmergencyMedicine), Elsevier's MD Consult, NetLibrary, Books@Ovid, and R2 Digital Library. Because of their relatively early development compared with those of publishers in non-medical disciplines, current medical e-reference book interfaces are very robust when compared to their general academic counterparts. Most medical e-book aggregators have allowed the functions that current e-books users complain are lacking in many other subject area e-book offerings: the options to download (to computers or to mobile devices), print, and email sections or whole chapters (*e.g.* Access Medicine, MD Consult, and Psychiatry Online); the ability to personalize the experience with bookmarks, saved information, and annotations; the inclusion of hyperlinks to more information and to multimedia; and the availability of interactive tools and continuing education opportunities (Lorbeer & Mitchell, 2008), (PRNewswire, 2009), (Newman, 2010). In late 2009, the American Medical Association (AMA) announced that it had launched an e-book portal in order to provide more frequent updates to their published content without the expense of reprinting. The publisher that the AMA chose, Impelsys.com, provides the user-desired features previously described (PRNewswire, 2009).

IMPACT OF CURRENT MEDICAL E-REFERENCE USE

An important concept to remember is that most medical books and almost all medical textbooks can be considered reference books based on the usual criteria for reference books. Users of medical books do not typically read the material in a "linear fashion" but are "typically searching for an answer" (White, 2008). This is also true of the way that medical e-books are used (Lorbeer & Mitchell, 2008). Several studies have shown that medical e-book use far surpasses the print version of the same title, and that medical e-books are often the most accessed e-books within library collections (Heyd, 2010), (Raynor & Iggulden, 2008), (Ugaz & Resnick, 2008), (Prgomet, Georgiou, & & Westbrook, 2009), (Fischer, Barton, Wright, & Clatanoff, 2010).

Electronic Access Correlates to More Use and Improved Patient Care

The medical use of e-books is so high compared to that of other disciplines because medical students, residents, and faculty need remote access to information, since they are likely to be in several clinical locations in a single day and they are limited in the paper resources they can carry on their person (Ugaz & Resnick, 2008). A systematic review of the literature has shown that physicians

much prefer mobile electronic access to reference resources and consult them more often than if they had to use the print version of the same resource (Prgomet et al., 2009). Physicians were the early adopters of portable data assistants when they were introduced in the 1990s (Prgomet et al., 2009), and this is possibly due to the convenience of carrying just one device to manage their schedules, communicate, and access clinical decision support systems like medical e-reference books, drug reference sources, and medical calculators (Ugaz & Resnick, 2008). Estimates of physician use of mobile devices in clinical settings are high. In Feb 2010, one market research firm found that 94% of physicians were using smartphones for personal and professional use (Dolan, 2010b). As of July 2010, Pew Research Center reports that 82% of American adults own a device that "is also a cell phone" (Smith, 2010).

The combination of increased mobile device use and preference for e-reference has been shown to improve patient care in several statistically significant ways, especially when time is a critical factor: faster physician response times, fewer prescription drug errors, and fewer medical documentation errors. Patients whose doctors use a mobile device get more prompt treatment, have decreased antibiotic use, and have decreased length of stay in hospitals (Prgomet et al., 2009). Physicians are already able to view radiology scans on their smartphones screens with the same diagnostic accuracy as they achieve on full-sized work stations (Dolan, 2009). More improvements may come as continuous patient monitoring (like real time EKG) by mobile device becomes more widespread and patient electronic medical records (EMRs) become accessible by mobile devices (Prgomet et al., 2009).

E-Resource Use Trends in Medical Education

Just as physicians provide faster and more accurate care to the patient when they combine the use of mobile devices with medical e-reference resources, so do medical students (Kho, Henderson, Dressler, & Kripalani, 2006). Wright State University's Boonshoft School of Medicine might be viewed as a single case study example of medical students' mirroring the physicians' trend of adopting mobile devices and electronic reference sources. For the first two years, all of the students' class materials are made available through course management software. It is standard practice in medical education to use course management software. Even in 2006, 97% of medical schools used course management software to augment classroom instruction (Kamin et al., 2006). These materials can include lecture notes, lecture videos and audio recordings, journal articles, and e-book content. According to an Academic Technology Analyst in the Medical Education Technology Group at WSU's BSOM in an interview on October 25, 2010, medical students at WSU all download e-books for medical board test preparation and a free drug e-reference called ePocrates Rx. (A more comprehensive version of ePocrates is available for purchase from http://www.epocrates.com/). By their third year clerkships, all students also download a program called Diagnasaurus, a full text differential diagnosis tool made available through the WSU Libraries' subscription to McGraw Hill's AccessMedicine. An informal poll of WSU BSOM students in October and November 2010 revealed these e-reference sources as favorites: USMLE question books, ePocrates, Diagnasaurus, Medscape (http://www.medscape.com/, a free product intended for medical professionals and produced by WebMD LLC, the company that also produces the consumer health website called WebMD at http://www.webmd.com/), and UpToDate. UpToDate (http://www.uptodate.com/) is a subscription medical e-reference produced by Wolters Kluwer Health, a well-known health sciences publisher. UpToDate is supported by a number of medical specialty professional associations and is "recommended" by the American Academy of Family Physicians

(Wolters Kluwer Health, 2010). The information included is constantly updated and summarized by physicians who are considered experts in their area of specialty. The quality of a one stop place to go for all current medical reference makes this product very appealing to medical students and physicians. Another reason this product may be so popular is that it allows users to earn Continuing Medical Education (CME) credits automatically by simply searching UpToDate. According to the American Medical Association, "Physicians may be required to demonstrate that they have obtained CME credit by state licensing boards, medical specialty societies, ABMS specialty boards, hospital medical staffs, the Joint Commission, insurance groups, and others" (American Medical Association, 2011). The UpToDate CME program keeps track of and reports CME progress without any additional effort on the part of the user.

Mobile Applications in Medical Education

While most medical students and faculty seem to carry a smartphone voluntarily for its multipurpose qualities, some medical schools are requiring all students to purchase or are issuing to them mobile devices, smartphones, or tablet PCs (Bhanoo & Post, 2009), (Boudreau, 2010), (Feeman & Wilson, 2010). Medical professionals prefer not to carry more than one device (Bhanoo & Post, 2009), and so they seem to prefer devices that serve more than one purpose. Tablet PCs may provide an easier user experience for physicians when they consult medical e-reference sources, since not all e-reference material is optimized for small screens like those on smartphones. It is too early to tell how many medical schools are or will be integrating iPads or similar devices into their curriculum, but some are predicting that this will soon become standard practice for all medical schools (Vasich, 2010), (Thomas & Sun-Times, 2010). WSU BSOM seems to be considering integrating the use of iPads into medical education in the future, as it hosted a public presentation called "Apple Seminar: iPad in Health Science Education" on November 12, 2010 (Feeman & Wilson, 2010). A number of faculty members brought along their new iPads to the presentation, and the presenters, an Apple account specialist and a system engineer, discussed bulk purchase discounts. Free or inexpensive medical e-reference applications available from iTunes the presenters described included:

- Pages allows anyone to e-publish and store material on Apple's servers
- Papers can search PubMed, and download and organize articles
- "Goodreader," a way to annotate articles using your finger or a stylus to write on the touch screen
- "Instapaper" has a "read later" button than downloads a mobile optimized version of articles for reading later
- "Inkling" allows social reading, see free Biology version at http://www.inkling.com/mh_raven_biology/
- iMeds XL (drug reference)
- modalityBODY, (interactive anatomy and medical imaging)
- Blausen Human Atlas HD (3D animated atlas)
- Medical Spanish (with audio) by Batoul Apps (canned Spanish medical phrases and questions)
- ePocrates
- Medscape
- Airstrip OB ("delivers vital patient waveform data — including fetal heartbeat and maternal contraction patterns — in virtual real-time")
- Netter's Anatomy
- Allscripts Remote (access to a medical practice's patient health records)
- STAT ICD-9 (diagnostic code reference)
- Dragon Dictation (records dictations and transcribes them into text)

An added benefit to iPad use is that they can be made accessible with Braille readers and keyboards, simplified touch screen menu for those with limited hand motion, text readers, and low visibility screen viewing options (Feeman & Wilson, 2010). With all of these features, it is no wonder that more than 50% of physicians are now considering purchasing a tablet PC (Dolan, 2010a). Even physicians who used only print medical reference sources during their own education seem to be enthusiastic about the shift from print to electronic reference. When asked what he thought of this shift, a WSU BSOM faculty member who used only print resources during his medical education replied that electronic resources are "more convenient and up to date. I only use books or paper versions when I can't get what I want electronically. In the past, I bought e-books for use on a PDA or PC, but I mostly use Internet based versions now." This faculty member also said these habits are typical for his students and colleagues as well.

CHALLENGES TO MOBILE AND E-REFERENCE USE IN HEALTHCARE

Balancing Access and Security

Despite the appeal and ever-increasing prevalence of mobile devices, both inside and outside the medical arena, balancing security with ease of use and appropriate levels of access continues to be the most obvious challenge. Traditionally, hospital IT departments have made demands of physicians to accommodate hospital IT resources and policies, but physician demand for mobile access to medical resources is beginning to reverse these traditional roles (Gamble, 2010), (Dolan, 2010b). Nevertheless, some current hospital security policies interfere with the convenience of using mobile technologies (Dolan, 2010b). In 2008, Pharow and Blobel stated:

Quite often, especially in the mobile domain, proprietary solutions, outdated approaches, and traditional principles are still in routine use for communicating sensitive information. The awareness level of principals is not significantly high, so real and potential threats and risks are often not addressed. (p. 699)

As it stands currently, the security issues surrounding access to EMR systems via mobile devices prevent about two-thirds of mobile-device-using-physicians from connecting to these systems (Dolan, 2010)

There is definitely a lack of consistency in the data access and security measures at healthcare institutions. Medical librarian blogger Michelle Kraft has bemoaned the fact that her hospital system's IT department will not allow iPads on the hospital network because they are "consumer device[s]" rather than "medical device[s]" while other esteemed healthcare institutions, such as Beth Israel Medical Center, have managed to integrate the device into their daily activities (Kraft, 2010c). It also seems that the hospitals and medical centers affiliated with WSU are quite liberal concerning physician use of mobile devices. When asked if he has ever experienced any IT issues like firewalls or restrictive hospital policies, the same faculty member mentioned above responded that the only problems he has encountered while accessing electronic resources are "some dead spots in hospitals and other medical buildings for mobile devices, but no firewall issues. Occasionally I have to get 'permission' to visit a blocked site." Information Security Officer for the Albany Medical Center Kristopher P. Kusche, in describing his academic medical center's implementation of a mobile encryption suite, acknowledges the challenges in balancing academic freedom and the need to protect confidential information (such as patient records):

Special considerations for implementing encryption in a blended healthcare and academic environment include the regulatory requirements for each component of the organization, the need to maintain sufficient flexibility in functionality and performance of the mobile device for sometimes divergent clinical, research, and educational purposes, and the need to balance desired security with an anticipated and fostered level of business and academic freedom (2009, p. 25).

Lack of Interoperability/Cross Platform Searching and Discovery

Another ongoing challenge to the use of e-reference sources is that in general, there are no tools that allow quick easy searching across multiple platforms. As previously stated, one reason Up to Date is such a popular e-resource among physicians and medical students is its appeal as a "one-stop shop" for reference, CE, and CE tracking. This desire to use one platform to meet a variety of needs underscores the need to have easy to use discovery tools that search across platforms. Medical e-reference aggregators (*e.g.,* MD Consult and Access Medicine) allow users to search and access full text across their entire platform, yet, due to proprietary content and interfaces, they are not generally interoperable, unless the subscribing institution has developed its own federated search system to search across these silos of information, as is the case with the Health Sciences Library System at the University of Pittsburgh (Medical Library Association, 2010). Many librarians would likely agree with Michelle Kraft's observation that "we need a federated e-book search system" because "patrons do not use the catalog"(2010), and also because catalog records are limited in what they retrieve because they are missing chapter headings and full text, even if they do include the tables of contents (Kraft, 2010b).

Overcoming the Barriers: Everyone's Responsibility

Network administrators and IT professionals have an obvious responsibility to resolve these security and access issues, but the responsibility is not solely theirs. All parties must be involved in overcoming these barriers. Indeed, some hospital CIOs are already working with their network vendors to make hospital network access "device-neutral" (Gardner, 2011). IT professionals also need to keep current on standards and best practices in order to implement networks with the most secure yet flexible access available within their "regulatory requirements," HIPAA and Payment Card Industry Data Security Standard (PCI DSS), for example (Krusche, 2009). However, public services librarians and end users of mobile and e-reference need to continue to insist upon secure access to networked sources that is still quick and easy to use. Librarians should be broadly aware of IT research directions and trends and should harness that knowledge to use and encourage patron use of platform and device-agnostic reference sources and mobile applications. Finally, third party developers, publishers, and aggregators must find ways to de-emphasize platform dependent-content in favor of interoperability in order to allow easy discovery of their unique content through a platform neutral single search that goes beyond the basic catalog record. An ideal level of access for physicians may be through links within the appropriate context of their patients' electronic medical records. Indeed, ePocrates is developing an electronic medical record system that will do just that (When your carpet calls your doctor, 2010).

FUTURE RESEARCH DIRECTIONS

Toninelli et al. indicate that because today's healthcare consumers and professionals expect "anywhere anytime mobile healthcare," the service discovery/discoverability tools currently being developed should ensure both flexible and personalized access, and user-specific visibility and retrieval, including on mobile devices. In other words, not only would the material be accessible only to authorized users, but services would only be discoverable by people with the appropriate authorization. They have developed and tested a "secure discovery framework" for patient discovery of available healthcare services. (Toninelli et al., 2009). Although their framework emphasizes appropriate credentials for accessing patient records and physician availability data, this type of framework also has obvious implications for flexible, "on the go" discovery of subscription e-reference sources. Such a system could allow appropriately authorized users to access the reference sources seamlessly.

CONCLUSION

As the earliest type of electronic reference content to be developed and widely used, medical e-reference publications and user adoption could serve as a benchmark for e-reference publishing in other academic areas. Nevertheless, if medical e-reference sources are to be the best they can be in terms discoverability, ease of access, and ease of use, all parties concerned have a role. The need for security must consistently be balanced with the need for quick and easy use. In order to achieve this balance, librarians and end users of mobile and e-reference should continue to insist upon easy access, search functionality, and interoperability of secure networks and platforms. Furthermore, IT professionals should implement the most user-friendly and most flexible network access possible while complying with the security standards required for their type of institution. Last but not least, content producers and providers need to optimize interoperability and/or cross platform discoverability of their content. No one disputes the value of medical e-reference sources.

As says Meredith Ressi with Manhattan Research (a health-care market research firm that studies doctors' use of technology): "You've got a whole medical library right in the palm of your hand" (Boudreau, 2010). Imagine how much more efficient it would be if all the content in that library were easily accessed through an EMR system or a single search tool, regardless of the EMR, publishers', or mobile device's platforms.

REFERENCES

American Medical Association. (2011). *Continuing medical education.* Retrieved January 27, 2011, from http://www.ama-assn.org/ama/pub/education-careers/continuing-medical-education/frequently-asked-questions.shtml

Bhanoo, S. N., & Post, S. T. W. (2009, May 19). New tool in the MD's bag: A smartphone. *The Washington Post,* pp. HE01.

Boudreau, J. (2010, September 26). Doctors rely on iPhones to guide treatment: "We want the data right at our fingertips." *Times-Picayune (New Orleans),* pp. B 12.

Dolan, P. L. (2009, December 21). Smartphones becoming clinical tools. *American Medical News.* Retrieved November 17, 2010, from http://www.ama-assn.org/amednews/2009/ 12/21/bica1221.htm

Dolan, P. L. (2010a, February 22). iPad stoking doctor interest in tablet computers. *American Medical News.* Retrieved November 17, 2010, from http://www.ama-assn.org/amednews/2010/ 02/22/bica0222.htm

Dolan, P. L. (2010b, August 23). Physician smartphone popularity shifts health IT focus to mobile use. *American Medical News.* Retrieved November 17, 2010, from http://www.ama-assn.org/amednews/ 2010/08/23/bil10823.htm

Dolan, P. L. (2010c, October 4). Doctors, patients use smartphones, but can't make mobile connection. *American Medical News.* Retrieved November 17, 2010, from http://www.ama-assn.org/amednews/ 2010/10/04/bil21004.htm

Feeman, M., & Wilson, J. (2010). *Apple seminar: IPad in health science education.* Unpublished manuscript.

Fischer, K. S., Barton, H., Wright, M., & Clatanoff, K. (2010). *Give 'em what they want: Patron-driven collection development.* Paper presented at the Charleston Conference, Charleston, South Carolina. Retrieved November 18, 2010, from http://ir.uiowa.edu/lib_pubs/61/

Gamble, K. H. (2010). Wireless tech trends 2010. Trend: Smartphones. *Healthcare Informatics: The Business Magazine for Information and Communication Systems, 27*(2), 24, 26-7.

Gardner, E. (2011, January). Moving target: New mobile devices offer opportunities and headaches for healthcare CIOs. *Health Data Management,* 62.

Groen, F. K. (2007). *Access to medical knowledge: Libraries, digitization, and the public good.* Lanham, MD: Scarecrow Press.

Hersh, W. R. (2003). *Information retrieval: A health and biomedical perspective* (2nd ed.). New York, NY: Springer.

Heyd, M. (2010). Three e-book aggregators for medical libraries: NetLibrary, Rittenhouse R2 Digital Library, and STAT!Ref. *Journal of Electronic Resources in Medical Libraries, 7*(1), 13–41..doi:10.1080/15424060903585693

Kamin, C., Souza, K. H., Heestand, D., Moses, A., & O'Sullivan, P. (2006). Educational technology infrastructure and services in North American medical schools. *Academic Medicine: Journal of the Association of American Medical Colleges, 81*(7), 632–637. doi:.doi:10.1097/01.ACM.0000232413.43142.8b

Kho, A., Henderson, L. E., Dressler, D. D., & Kripalani, S. (2006). Use of handheld computers in medical education. *Journal of General Internal Medicine, 21*(5), 531–537. doi:10.1111/j.1525-1497.2006.00444.x

Kraft, M. A. (2010, November 17, 2010). E-books: The library catalog and federated searching, part 1. *The Krafty Librarian: Every librarian needs a bag of tricks*. Retrieved December 7, 2010, from http://kraftylibrarian.com/?p=834

Kraft, M. A. (2010b, November 18). E-books: The library catalog and federated searching, part 2. *The Krafty Librarian: Every librarian needs a bag of tricks*. Retrieved December 7, 2010, from http://kraftylibrarian.com/?p=839

Kraft, M. A. (2010c, June 16). iPad use in the hospital and IT departments. *The Krafty Librarian: Every librarian needs a bag of tricks*. Retrieved January 17, 2011, from http://kraftylibrarian.com/?p=633

Kusche, K. (2009). Lessons learned: Mobile device encryption in the academic medical center. *Journal of Healthcare Information Management, 23*(2), 22–25.

Lorbeer, E. R., & Mitchell, N. (2008). E-books in academic health sciences libraries. *Against the Grain, 20*(5), 30-34.

McCarn, D. B. (1970). Planning for online bibliographic access by the Lister Hill National Center for Biomedical Communications. *Bulletin of the Medical Library Association, 58*(3), 303–310.

Medical Library Association. (2010). *ABCs of e-books: Strategies for the medical library* (MLA webcast).

Miles, W. D., & National Library of Medicine. (1982). *A history of the National Library of Medicine: The nation's treasury of medical knowledge*. Bethesda, MD & Washington, DC: U.S. Dept. of Health and Human Services, Public Health Service, National Institutes of Health, National Library of Medicine.

Newman, M. L. (2010). Collections strategies for electronic books. *Information Outlook, 14*(4), 10–12.

Palmer, R. C. (1987). *Online reference and information retrieval* (2nd ed.). Littleton, CO: Libraries Unlimited.

Pharow, P., & Blobel, B. (2008). Mobile health requires mobile security: Challenges, solutions, and standardization. *Studies in Health Technology and Informatics, 136*, 697–702.

Prgomet, M., Georgiou, A., & Westbrook, J. I. (2009). The impact of mobile handheld technology on hospital physicians' work practices and patient care: A systematic review. *Journal of the American Medical Informatics Association, 16*(6), 792..doi:10.1197/jamia.M3215

PRNewswire. (2009, August 25). American Medical Association launches e-book strategy with iPublishCentral from impelsys; AMA inaugurates e-book offerings with bestselling clinical title. *PR Newswire.*

Raynor, M., & Iggulden, H. (2008). Online anatomy and physiology: Piloting the use of an anatomy and physiology e-book–VLE hybrid in pre-registration and post-qualifying nursing programmes at the University of Salford. *Health Information and Libraries Journal, 25*(2), 98–105.. doi:10.1111/j.1471-1842.2007.00748.x

Smith, A. (2011). *Mobile access 2010*. Retrieved January 25, 2011, from http://www.pewinternet.org/Reports/2010/ Mobile-Access-2010/Summary-of-Findings.aspx

Thomas, M., & Sun-Times, T. C. (2010, October 19). iPad functionality just what doctor ordered: Ultra-portable tablet becoming hospital fixture. *Chicago Sun Times,* pp. 14.

Toninelli, A., Montanari, R., & Corradi, A. (2009). Enabling secure service discovery in mobile healthcare enterprise networks. *IEEE Wireless Communications, 16*(3), 24–32..doi:10.1109/ MWC.2009.5109461

Ugaz, A. G., & Resnick, T. (2008). Assessing print and electronic use of reference/core medical textbooks. *Journal of the Medical Library Association, 96*(2), 145–147..doi:10.3163/1536-5050.96.2.145

Unbound Medicine Inc. (2011). *Unbound Medicine: About us.* Retrieved January 24, 2011, from http://www.unboundmedicine.com/company

U.S. National Library of Medicine and the National Center for Biotechnology Information. (2010). *NCBI bookshelf.* Retrieved November 18, 2010, from http://www.ncbi.nlm.nih.gov.ezproxy.libraries.wright.edu:2048/books

Vasich, T. (2010). *Medicine's new wave.* Retrieved January 25, 2011, from http://www.zotzine.uci.edu/2010_11/imed.php

When your carpet calls your doctor. (2010, April 10). *The Economist, 395*(8677), 65-66.

White, M. (2008). E-books in health sciences circa 2008-What have we got for our journey now? *Against the Grain, 20*(5), 26-30.

Wolters Kluwer Health. (2010). *UpToDate Inc.* Retrieved November 20, 2010, from http://www.uptodate.com/

Chapter 12

INFOhio Transforms Content Delivery for PreK–12 Students:
From Physical Classrooms to Virtual SchoolRooms

Theresa M. Fredericka
INFOhio- The Information Network for Ohio Schools, USA

Jennifer Schwelik
INFOhio- The Information Network for Ohio Schools, USA

ABSTRACT

This chapter presents a case study of how INFOhio, Ohio's library and information network for PreK-12 schools, transformed content delivery through partnerships and collaborations to benefit today's digital learners. It chronicles the formation of a unique relationship between INFOhio and library software vendor SirsiDynix, a partnership that was shaped by the common vision of creating a virtual classroom of reference, research, and discovery material to support student curricular needs. Discussion covers the creation and implementation of the Discovery Portal for student research and inquiry, which brings together Internet content, electronic resources, and physical library materials under one, online interface for Ohio students. Significant traditional and non-traditional partnerships have enabled INFOhio to become one of the largest school library Information Technology projects in the country.

DOI: 10.4018/978-1-61350-308-9.ch012

21ST CENTURY LEARNERS

The transformation of knowledge tools has shifted the manner in which students and teachers approach research and learning. This transformation from accessing information to creating and transmitting new discoveries in an open networked world changes the role of school libraries. Just as teachers and textbooks are no longer the sole classroom expert, school librarians and school libraries are no longer the sole information source.

Today's students access and analyze information often without ever visiting a library or consulting with a librarian. They retrieve information through Google's search box 24x7. They believe the Internet provides substantially more material and is easier to use than the library, and it does not require a librarian to act as intermediary because they can independently access the information.

Transformations in technology and expectations in the late 20th century directly influenced the role of school libraries as information provider. Student research shifted from asking a teacher or a librarian a question to being able to ask the world for a response; from watching and listening to interactive learning. Today's learners expect remote access 24x7, with instant information retrieval and virtual assistance.

Language use reflects these changes: reference to e-reference, searching to discovering, learning to active learning, looking-up something to inquiry-based learning, books to e-books, indexes to databases, knowledge to proficiency (test), and so on.

Generational attitudes and expectations reflect these changes: Baby Boom-generation teachers are working with Generation X teachers who are teaching the Generation Z children of Generation Y parents. Children have changed; parents have changed; teachers have changed.

All of these changes have altered the way today's student learns.

This chapter is a case study of how INFOhio, Ohio's library and information network for PreK-12 schools, has embraced these changes and developed a virtual student research and inquiry content portal for all Ohio students.

THE 21ST CENTURY ENVIRONMENT

For the first time in our history, various pieces of legislation, most notably the *No Child Left Behind Act*, mandate specific instructional and learning standards for evaluating students and educators (No Child Left Behind Act, 2002). To meet these standards and the goal of creating 21st century learners, teachers and librarians must have the tools necessary to permit students to assume responsibility for their own learning and become active knowledge seekers.

In 2007, the American Association of School Librarians (AASL), a division of the American Library Association (ALA), adopted new standards for the "21st -Century Learner." These standards provide a vision of school librarians as leaders, instructional partners, information specialists, teachers, and program administrators who collaborate with other education professionals to shape the learning of students in schools through school libraries. However, to accomplish this vision, access to appropriate educational and instructional content must be available for both students and educators.

This is where INFOhio comes in.

INFOHIO: A CASE STUDY

The Vision

In November 1989, a group of school librarians in northeast Ohio proposed a statewide plan to automate school libraries. The first two libraries, Austintown Fitch and Boardman high schools, were automated in 1994. Now, a little more than twenty years later (as of January 2011), 2,447 individual school libraries, serving more than 1.1

million students, are automated and networked together by INFOhio with library automation software from SirsiDynix.

In addition to this very successful effort that created interconnected virtual catalogs among these school libraries, INFOhio realized that every student needed access to a robust virtual reference environment. INFOhio quickly expanded beyond a library automation project to include providing electronic and digital resources, resource sharing, professional development, information literacy instruction, and support for teachers and parents. The mission statement of INFOhio accurately reflects that it "supports and enriches teaching and learning by providing equitable access to quality resources for Ohio's PreK-12 community of students, educators, and parents" (*About INFOhio*, 2009).

Partnerships to Benefit Learning

INFOhio began as a grassroots effort that depended on a wide variety of partnerships and collaborations to meet student needs. This was due in part to the management style of its founders and the need to secure adequate funding. INFOhio is only partially funded by the state, while local school districts and regional Information Technology Centers (ITCs) support the costs of automating their libraries. Consequently, there is a strong partnership among the schools, ITCs, and INFOhio.

Committed to providing excellent reference service to every child in every school across the state, INFOhio knew they could not accomplish their mission alone. To provide equitable statewide access to licensed databases and online information appropriate for K-12 students and teachers, INFOhio worked with the State Library of Ohio, the public library network (OPLIN) and the academic library network (OhioLINK) to form Libraries Connect Ohio (LCO). LCO partners work together to provide database and e-reference services to the all Ohio residents (*Libraries Connect Ohio*, n.d.).

INFOhio has always been very open to exploring or proposing partnerships with traditional and non-traditional agencies, institutions, networks, or vendors. This openness is driven by the recognition that INFOhio is not in the business of making libraries better just for the sake of making better libraries. Rather, INFOhio is in the business of helping students learn and teachers teach more effectively and efficiently. Educating Ohio students is and must be the first priority.

Meeting 21st Century Reference Challenges

Once the PreK-12 INFOhio virtual reference environment was in place, school librarians observed that the licensed databases alone were not meeting the reference and informational needs of students. School librarians realized that students were first turning to Google, Wikipedia, Google Scholar, and a myriad of other Web resources as part of their information seeking patterns when completing assignments or conducting research for papers. To address this issue, INFOhio developed the *DIALOGUE Model*, which has recently been revised to embrace 21st century skills and the inquiry and knowledge building process. Additionally, INFOhio provided over fifty workshops addressing information literacy instruction for more than 1,000 Ohio librarians and educators (*DIALOGUE Model for Information*, 2010).

In 2003 OCLC released the study *Environmental Scan: Pattern Recognition*, which outlined three major information consumer characteristics: (1) Self-Service: Moving to Self-Sufficiency; (2) Satisfaction; and (3) Seamlessness. The study found that well over half of those surveyed regarded open Web information as meeting their information needs and found "nothing is missing" (De Rosa, Dempsey, & Wilson, 2004, p. 7). This study supported the need for school librarians to become more directly involved in information literacy instruction.

In addition, there were serious issues with both the content retrieved and the tools the students were using to obtain information. As early as the 2004-2005 school year, INFOhio recognized the need to rethink how it made informational resources available to students and how it could guarantee that the information retrieved was not only accurate and credible, but was also aligned with the state's content standards. One thing was also very clear: students wanted, in fact were demanding, an information portal that used a simple Google-like search box.

The lack of single-search capability, which allows students to simultaneously search the school library catalog, the local public library catalog, the available electronic databases, as well as good Web-based resources with a single click, became a fascinating challenge.

The Evolution of SchoolRooms: Virtual Reference Need

As educators observed students seeking information from the new digital resources, it became apparent that new types of search and retrieval tools were required. INFOhio ventured into a contractual partnership with a vendor to develop a new innovative learning portal that included content aligned with state standards.

INFOhio knew what needed to be done, but certainly did not have the research and development dollars to pursue a new generation of software that included an integrated search capability to seamlessly link the card catalog, subscription based electronic resource databases, and relevant websites. However, a confluence of events occurred in 2005 that resulted in a breakthrough that would help shape learning in the 21st century for Ohio students and educators.

At the American Library Association Midwinter Conference in Boston, the INFOhio Executive Director and her colleagues were invited to a reception to launch a new product for SirsiDynix called "Rooms." Rooms was a new portal

platform, which offered the capability to create "virtual rooms" that were organized much like a physical library. The presenters proposed that a public library might build electronic "rooms" on popular topics such as cooking, travel, parenting, or home improvement. At that time, SirsiDynix had not considered developing a Rooms product for schools, but rather intended to market it only to academic and public libraries. But to INFOhio, Rooms seemed to be the perfect marriage between software product and real world application.

INFOhio wanted to aggregate its subscription databases under one search box, and the Rooms portal offered a federated search. INFOhio saw the need to differentiate additional content by age-appropriateness. The Rooms product offered "rooms" or containers where different audiences could find content specific to their need.

Finally, INFOhio wanted to promote information literacy and research skill instruction. INFOhio identified the need to involve teachers, other educators, and parents. The Rooms software had the potential to integrate all of the resources of the 21st century school library, including its books, resources, and reference assistance. Rooms provided a vehicle for school librarians to assist students in developing essential 21st century learning skills.

The first step in the process, however, was building bridges – not developing software.

When SirsiDynix first heard INFOhio's concept of a K-12 product based on Rooms, they were intrigued, but not ready to act. It took persistence on the part of INFOhio, which eventually led to a strategic meeting between SirsiDynix and INFOhio.

During the meeting, SirsiDynix expressed real interest and recognized the potential, but were concerned about developing the product in a quick and cost-efficient manner. They also were concerned because the Rooms portal was developed for use by adults. They knew children, who would be using the proposed SchoolRooms, searched differently. In addition, they knew content for the K-12 population, aligned to state or national standards, would need to be developed.

INFOhio had all the right answers, and School-Rooms was born.

SchoolRooms Developed

Along with the automated school library catalogs and the electronic databases currently available, INFOhio had already recognized that young researchers needed a portal that provided a single-search of databases, the library catalog, and selected open Web content. INFOhio also knew that K-12 students needed Web-based content that was curriculum relevant, age appropriate, and a lot of it. INFOhio understood that students needed a range of content -- enough to satisfy both a third-grader inquiring about dinosaurs and a high school senior researching the Holocaust. They realized they had to create a "young learners" environment that was safe and filtered from "noise" - (referred to within INFOhio as "the Internet on training wheels") as well as a robust experience for independent learners. Finally, they needed to create grade level specific information literacy research and teaching tools.

INFOhio turned to the experts for help. INFOhio hand-selected Ohio school librarians recognized as leaders in the school library field. Each school librarian chose a teacher partner with equally high credentials. The teams were each assigned a curricular topic for a specific grade level (i.e., elementary, middle, or high school). Ultimately, these outstanding professional educators delivered content for nine topic areas for a beta test in one school district in the fall of 2005.

Concurrently, SirsiDynix developed a "kid-friendly" Room interface. To test this new interface, SirsiDynix contracted with ScanPath™, a commercial usability testing service run by the Kent State School of Library and Information Science (KSU SLIS), to conduct a formal usability study. ScanPath™ observed students utilizing

SchoolRooms to complete actual lessons and assignments.

The study was conducted in the Shaker Heights (OH) Schools from January 30 to February 17, 2006. The participants included students from second through tenth grade, more than twenty teachers in forty different classes, plus parents and teacher/librarian focus groups. The evaluation used eye-tracking software, tasked searches, individual and group observation, questionnaires, interviews, screen and audio capture, think-aloud, and Web cams to track responses (Holmes, Robins, Zhang, Salaba, & Byerly, 2006).

This study found that the interactive elements were a success, and that teacher/librarian teams were essential in content development. The study also revealed that young students focus on the center section of a webpage while older students focus on the upper left corner. See "Eye-tracking Results" [Figure 1]. These findings were noted for future interface improvements. The vast majority of the students said that they would use the interface again for their homework needs.

The data was enough to convince SirsiDynix to proceed with the full product. In fact, once they made the commitment in March 2006, SirsiDynix announced that SchoolRooms would be available for the school year beginning in September – leaving just six months to create all of the K-12 content.

SchoolRooms Grows

INFOhio stepped up its game. INFOhio again selected school library leaders and highly qualified content-specialist teachers to develop the new rooms. INFOhio continued to partner with KSU SLIS and arranged for 140 Ohio educators to come to the KSU campus for 2½ days of training on how to find the type of content needed to develop the remaining sixty-two rooms. Some "Teacher/Librarian Teams at Kent State" can be seen [Figure 2]. SirsiDynix and KSU SLIS faculty worked with educators to ensure the websites would be

Figure 1. "Eye-tracking Results." (© 2006, Kent State School of Library and Information Science. Use with permission.)

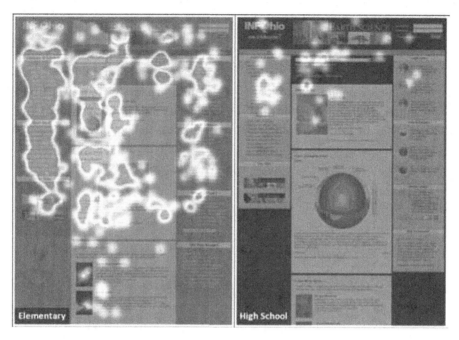

kid-friendly and attractive. Ohio Department of Education content specialists assisted the teams to make sure that topics were curriculum related.

After completing the training, the two-person teams had six weeks to find, select, annotate and align the content to the standards for their specific subject and grade level (e.g., websites for 4th grade social studies or high school history). Their efforts resulted in the creation of seventy-one new rooms (nine more than planned) with more than 1,700 Web page views and links to more than 22,000 educator-selected web sites.

At this point, SirsiDynix had a tested portal for children and young adults and the K-12 standards-aligned content needed to turn Rooms into SchoolRooms.

The remaining challenge: to devise a way to refresh the safe and secure content.

Again, INFOhio and SirsiDynix put on their collaborative thinking caps and found a solution. They selected an advisory group of teachers and librarians from the initial 140 educators. The ad-

Figure 2. "Teacher/LibrarianTeams at Kent State." (© 2006, Kent State School of Library and Information Science. Used with permission.)

visory team developed content- and audience-specific editorial calendars, which outlined frequent updates to visible seasonal content and decided that deeper content would be updated annually.

In September 2006, INFOhio introduced SchoolRooms Basic to all Ohio schools. Due to INFOhio's size and complex nature, the rollout was phased. The initial offering included the educator-selected content. In fall 2007, single-search capability for the electronic database subscriptions, and each of the 600 individual school district catalogs was incorporated. In 2008, search options limiting the library catalog

search to individual buildings became available. For full timeline please see "INFOhio Timeline: Significant Events" [Figure 3].

After its full release in September 2008, students and teachers immediately embraced School-Rooms across Ohio. In the first year, more than 1.4 million pages were viewed. INFOhio's agreement with SirsiDynix provided Ohio schools with free access to SchoolRooms, for that first year—an excellent introductory offer. (*INFOhio and SchoolRooms*, 2009).

Figure 3. "INFOhio Timeline: Significant Events." (© 2011, INFOhio. Used with permission.)

		INFOhio Timeline: Significant Events
1994	Beginnings	Austintown Fitch and Boardman High Schools, Mahoning County, are first two schools automated through ACCESS ITC, Ohio Education Computer Network.
1996		Theresa M. Fredericka becomes Executive Director of newly formed INFOhio project.
1998	Building critical mass	First statewide online resource, 126 ProQuest titles branded as *INFOhio's Electronic Resources for Social Studies*, is launched.
2004		Number of Ohio school libraries automated by INFOhio surpasses 2,000.
2005		INFOhio provides *Core Collection of Electronic Resources* in partnership with State Library of Ohio, OhioLINK, and OPLIN which offers 14 electronic resources to schools statewide, including 22 databases from EBSCO Publishing with more than 6,000 titles.
		SirsiDynix introduces *Rooms* at ALA conference; partners with INFOhio to create nine *School*Rooms.
2006		Positive usability study spurs SirsiDynix to give "green light" to expanding *Rooms* for full curriculum.
		SchoolRooms built and introduced at two pilot schools in the fall.
2007	Staying Relevant	INFOhio provides *SchoolRooms* content to all Ohio schools.
2008		INFOhio adds selected *Core Collection* electronic resources to *SchoolRooms*.
		School catalogs are added to *SchoolRooms* by fall.
2009		Number of INFOhio automated school exceeds 2,400.
2010		With *SchoolRooms* no longer a commercial priority of SirsiDynix, it is reinvented as the *INFOhio Discovery Portal* – becoming the innovative learning portal that INFOhio has sought since 2004.

SchoolRooms Transforms to Discovery Portal

Unfortunately, in 2008 the United States experienced an economic downturn and plummeted into a recession. The subsequent reduction in the tax-base forced unplanned budget reductions in libraries across the nation, including Ohio. Realizing future funding was uncertain; INFOhio began working with schools and vendor-partners to devise ways to maintain information tools for teachers and students.

SirsiDynix also worked with INFOhio to provide SchoolRooms at minimal cost to school districts. INFOhio collected funds from districts and provided SchoolRooms to those districts with the ability to pay. Throughout the 2009-2010 school year school, INFOhio continued to try to determine ways to bring SchoolRooms back to every teacher and student in Ohio.

With no additional funding forthcoming from the state and local districts already forced to cut other student services, INFOhio again turned to its partner in good faith. SirsiDynix and INFOhio worked diligently to continue expanding School-Rooms in a time of economic difficulty. The concept of a "portal" for K-12 students continued to evolve at a very fast pace, and thus, some of the highly desired enhancements to SchoolRooms could be implemented.

The jointly developed solution morphed SchoolRooms into a new, state-of-the-art learning portal, now known as the INFOhio Discovery Portal. The INFOhio Discovery Portal incorporates revisions suggested by the SchoolRooms Advisory Council based on students input and gave INFOhio staff additional control of the content and design of the overall portal. An example page from the "INFOhio Discovery Portal" is shown [Figure 4].

Figure 4. "INFOhio Discovery Portal." (Adapted from SirsiDynix Enterprise™ © 2010, SirsiDynix.)

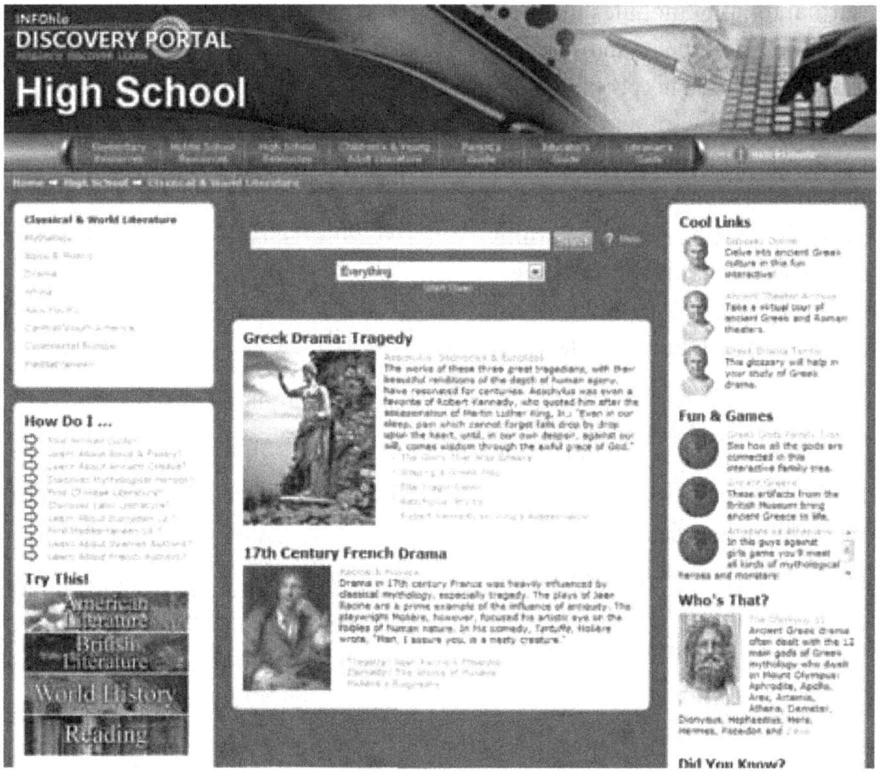

Working with SirsiDynix, INFOhio knew that even with the difficult financial environment, it was important to provide the Discovery Portal to *all* of the 2,447 individual school libraries and the more than 1.1 million students, automated and networked together by INFOhio – without any additional local expense for the 2010-2011 school year. The partners found a solution by moving the Discovery Portal maintenance from the SirsiDynix staff to the INFOhio team. As a result, the Discovery Portal launched to all networked libraries in October 2010 (NOACSC & Banks, 2010).

Next Steps in PreK-12 Virtual Content Delivery

In this changing environment, no project is ever "done." While its partnership with SirsiDynix continues and the Discovery Portal use grows, INFOhio continues to develop virtual reference and learning portals for PreK-12 students and teachers. In 2010 INFOhio launched a teacher portal that includes an introduction to 21st century education initiatives and virtual training modules that help teachers apply library e-reference and learning tools in instructional settings. This portal, known as the INFOhio 21st century Learning Commons, is free and open to all. It has provided training for nearly 2,000 educators during its first year.

In 2011, INFOhio expanded the Learning Commons to include a community portal that encourages the sharing of ideas among educators on the application of virtual reference and e-learning tools in the PreK-12 classroom.

INFOhio will always be looking for opportunities to collaborate with new people, organizations, and vendors who share the same vision for student learning, who are willing to create new learning environments, and who genuinely believe that equitable access to quality content and innovative reference services are critical to student success.

INFOhio is a grassroots effort that has taken a dream and turned it into a reality. It is based on the needs of students, the beliefs of professional educators, and the willingness of unlikely partners to collaborate to make the impossible happen. INFOhio is simply what libraries and librarians are all about.

REFERENCES

De Rosa, C., Dempsey, L., & Wilson, A. (2004). *The 2003 OCLC environmental scan: Pattern recognition - Social landscape* (A. Wilson, Ed.). Retrieved from http://www.oclc.org.htm

Holmes, J., Robins, D., Zhang, Y., Salaba, A., & Byerly, G. (2006, May 22). *Report on the usability and effectiveness of SirsiDynix SchoolRooms for K-12 students.* Retrieved from http://www.schoolrooms.net_KentState.pdf

INFOhio. (2009, August 14). *About INFOhio.* Retrieved February 2, 2011, from http://www.infohio.org//.html

INFOhio. (2010, August 30). *DIALOGUE model for information 21st century skills - inquiry and the knowledge building process.* Retrieved February 9, 2011, from http://www.infohio.org.html

INFOhio. (2011). *Website.* Retrieved February 9, 2011, from http://www.infohio.org

INFOhio. (n.d.). *INFOhio & 21st century learning skills.* Retrieved February 9, 2011, from http://learningcommons.infohio.org

INFOhio and SchoolRooms. (2009, June 29). Retrieved February 10, 2011, from http://www.infohio.org.html

Kenney, B. (2006, July 1). Keeping up with the Googles [Editorial]. *School Library Journal, 52*(7), 11. Retrieved from http://www.library-journal.com-427/_up_with_the_googles.html.csp

Libraries Connect Ohio. (n.d.). Retrieved February 7, 2011, from http://www.librariesconnectohio.org/

No child left behind act, 20 USC U.S.C. § 6301 (2002).

NOACSC, & Banks, J. (2010, August 13). *Introducing INFOhio Discovery Portal*. PowerPoint presented at INFOhio Technical Support, Lima, OH.

SirsiDynix. (n.d.). Retrieved February 9, 2011, from http://www.sirsidynix.com

Section 4
Solutions for E–Reference Discovery

Chapter 13
Discovering Authoritative Reference Material:
It's all about "Location. Location. Location."

Lettie Y. Conrad
SAGE Inc., USA

ABSTRACT

For reference publishing, recent revolutions in digital communications undermine the success of traditional methods of information delivery and retrieval. The need to present online reference material for easy discoverability presents challenges and opportunities for technological advancement – for data management and website design. Equally, reference discoverability demands that we foster a greater understanding of what today's researchers need, and incorporate that knowledge into modern publishing tactics.

INTRODUCTION

The attraction of any property and the success of many businesses can be summarized in three words: "Location. Location. Location." The last decade's disruptions to publishing have produced both danger and opportunity for reference pub-

lishers, inspiring us to reconsider the position of our publications within the scholarly landscape. Advances in the Web and other digital communication tools have given rise to new methods for conducting and circulating research. Traditional print-based publishing practices for disseminating reference materials are challenged by growing demands for digital delivery, as today's students, faculty, and other users conduct their research

DOI: 10.4018/978-1-61350-308-9.ch013

almost entirely online. Free, social reference media, such as Wikipedia, inspire publishers to find innovative new ways to direct readers to authoritative, citable scholarly content. New tactics must be developed so that today's students and researchers can find trustworthy reference content when it is needed most. When one click of a mouse can either direct or detour a search, we need to be mindful that, on the information superhighway, the signpost *is* the location.

Despite recent revolutions in communication and scholarship, the driving missions of academic publishing and librarianship have not changed. Students of all stripes continue to thirst for knowledge, search for answers to questions, and seek definitions to new terms – and these needs must be met with first-rate, authoritative content. We must therefore incorporate quality reference publications into the new online communication tools employed by today's users. As we continue to move our products online, publishers must both cultivate and comply with techniques for ensuring that our products are findable on the open Web and within library systems. These new demands pose a challenge for publishers, but also open up potential for publishers to reinvent the value they offer academia.

"Discoverability" has become a charged buzzword in publishing circles. Despite the buzz, we must not forget our duty – the successful dissemination and retrieval of information by our readers. The measure of how successfully our content is discovered is not found exclusively in usage statistics or rankings of search engine optimization (SEO). Our true success metrics are relative only to meeting the needs of scholars, in various disciplines, at various stages of their careers, around the world.

For reference publishing, our collective success rates are much lower than is sustainable – either to meet our underlying mission or for successful business practices. Dictionary.com and Wikipedia are standard open-Web fare for online reference queries and may be excellent products for quick

answers or to begin one's research. However, authoritative reference works more fully meet the requirements of scholarly research, for valid citations and other standard practices, as scholars at all levels advance our academic discourse. Publishers must therefore compete with the usability and accessibility of many mainstream online information tools.

In three parts, this chapter will define the primary obstacles and opportunities of online discoverability for reference publishers. The first two sections articulate common burdens and benefits in meeting new demands for achieving product visibility, both on the open Web and within library services. The third outlines topics not typically raised in the context of discoverability – important aspects for students, faculty, and other end users successfully finding the authoritative reference content they need – topics that go beyond optimizing technical functions of online search. The objective of this chapter is to summarize real experiences of publishers in achieving successful online discoverability and draw some conclusions about our next steps.

1. FINDING AUTHORITATIVE REFERENCE CONTENT ON THE OPEN WEB

Historically, instructors and librarians acted as the primary signposts, guiding students to academic content appropriate for their research needs and training young scholars how to judge the authoritative nature of reference publications. Today's students still seek out these resources, but far less frequently than in years past. Mainstream search and information tools on the open Web are the primary starting points for a great majority of students who make up the prime target audience for reference publications. Project Information Literacy reports that 84% of students encounter the most difficulty starting their research, but only 11% look to librarians for assistance. Instead of drawing on library advisors, which regularly point to the type of primary research found in reference publications, most students sift through Google search results for the material they need for their studies (Head & Eisenberg, 2010).

Rather than deny these facts, we must make sure scholarly works are accessible and visible within these search engines. And, as advocated at the 2010 Ithaka Sustainable Scholarship Conference, publishers, librarians, and instructors should collaborate on new ways to assure students are armed with adequate information literacy to vet the materials they find online (Asher, 2010). To achieve discovery of reference products on the open Web, publishers are pressed to remove traditional barriers to content. This poses challenges both in the technical expertise required for search engine optimization (SEO) and disruptions to traditional business models.

Search Engine Optimization

The root goal of SEO is improving the visibility of a website within search engines. Ultimately, SEO provides many roadmaps on the Internet to help readers find locate the information they need. Although this is not the sole determiner of discoverability, publishers have rightly integrated SEO techniques for our products into our business infrastructure. While this is a relatively new skill within the toolkit of traditional publishing, it is quickly becoming a standard element of our editorial and operational divisions. Publisher staff must grow and maintain actionable knowledge of SEO techniques, which fluctuates regularly as advances are made in online technologies and the businesses that offer them. Publishers must continually monitor the successful discovery of our material from products, such as Google and Bing, and make rapid modifications to our platforms to keep pace with the changeable landscape of online search.

For reference publishing, additional challenges are faced by the broad queries and generic topic areas involved in primary research. For instance, searches for "Arizona law" will likely find news reports of recent controversies or websites for law schools before discovering encyclopedia entries or legislative history on the topic. Mathematical algorithms and rankings based on links or Web traffic do not always serve the best results to scholars beginning their academic work. As librarians have known for many years, automated indexing does not provide the level of service and accuracy often required for scholarly research. However, the human resource required for extensive manual indexing is not practical in large volume, especially given the wide range of broad topics covered by reference works. Publishers must find a workable balance between automated routines and editorial contributions to our products.

The online reference technique showing the greatest success thus far is when publishers host public pages with product summaries. For example, each encyclopedia entry or handbook chapter would have associated pages with abstracts and product metadata. Accessing the full product is then based upon subscription or purchase authentication. This technique has proven a successful SEO tactic for reference publishing, but it also demands additional editorial resources to prepare these pages, which can reach into the tens of thousands for some organizations. Some publishers have tried automated techniques where extracts of the first 100-200 words of a work are visible outside the firewall. However, this is not considered significant enough for many open-Web search engines to index and does not provide the publishers with the level of discoverability the library market finds necessary.

Libraries and publishers together can leverage open Web tools to expose authoritative academic material to the readers that need them. For instance, as demonstrated in chapter 15, Credo's topic pages successfully integrate authoritative reference materials on key subjects that are found both on the open Web and within library catalogs.

Our focus on the open Web now must include adding signposts within the mobile Web, as we see increasing numbers of librarians and scholars conducting quick reference searches from their smartphones in the course of their work. The need to make certain authoritative reference material is findable via the numerous handheld devices and mobile platforms on the market, with new products released each quarter, is another new skill now expected from publishers. The expectations from the market for mobile research are as yet undefined. Complex issues of managing access and tracking usage via mobile research tools, not to mention guaranteeing adequate user experiences, are unknown territories to many in our field. The techniques required for mobile Web discoverability vary when it comes to demands for device-agnostic websites and application development.

Some success has been found in the use of controlled vocabularies to enhance the visibility of online reference products. Publishers know they must move beyond the static delivery of our material on the Web and can no longer simply replicate print products online. Ten years ago, we mastered HTML – the basic mark-up language required for online display of text and images. Today, we are developing expertise in more advanced mark-up techniques that deliver both formatting and meaning through digital publications. Semantic indexing technologies are a complex and powerful new opportunity for publishers to expose the richness of our material via both proprietary and mainstream search engines, and enable unique, efficient browse and discovery options for users. More information on semantic indexing can be found in chapter 17.

Freeing Traditional Business Models

A majority of students report using Wikipedia to quickly answer questions, locate definitions, and begin their research projects (Head, et al., 2010).

Therefore, as publishers and librarians, we have little choice but to provide the market with innovative solutions for the visibility of authoritative reference publications. The premise of free online content challenges the basic tenets of traditional for-profit publishing.

Barriers to access are in place to safeguard paid content typically available only with purchase, subscription, or institutional membership. The debate about how, when, and if these barriers should be removed is ongoing among various factions of our industry. Access walls that require authentication are also obstacles for online discoverability, as most mainstream search engines necessitate both easy access to our platforms for automated indexing and demand that a percentage of material is free to their users as a matter of policy.

Our library customers, who pay for access to our online platforms via traditional models, however, are not pleased to see publishers open up those products to unauthenticated users. The more expansive the content hosted on these products, however, the less concern we see from the library market. As the livelihoods of publishers and libraries are challenged by free online products, the greater the wish to collaborate on alternatives that both meet the needs of researchers and support the survival of our industry.

Lifting those traditional access barriers also risks undermining the publisher brand and perpetuating online piracy. If our material is easily transported to other platforms, we are unable to validate its quality and authority. The free proliferation of our products, outside of our control or ability to monetize, is a direct threat to our success.

There are several new approaches to open access publishing underway as experiments in various segments of our industry, primarily for journals, such as *PLoS One* and, more recently, *SAGE Open*. Without typical online access controls, these publications are much more easily indexed by search engines. However, they have not been fully proven successful enough to replace traditional models and their extension to book and reference products is as yet unclear. For now, reference publishers are primarily working to balance the amount of open content required for online discoverability with the access controls required for the standard models of paid subscription and purchase by libraries.

Some publishers are finding creative ways of leveraging free, open-Web tools to drive traffic to paid products, which they expose just enough to be findable. For example, as demonstrated by Casper Grathwohl, Vice President and Online and Reference Publisher for Oxford University Press (OUP), recruiting authors to draft and edit Wikipedia entries in their specialty topic areas can prove a successful discoverability measure for both publisher and author. Wikipedia contributions by OUP authors of reference works on Islamic studies, for example, increased traffic with links to related OUP products by 82% (Grathwohl, 2010). This is a proven technique for increasing the findability of authoritative reference material and expands the marketing of expert contributors. It also provides publishers an opportunity to contribute to information literacy training, by directing users to authoritative resources within the publishers' brands when they conduct searches within Wikipedia.

Advertising-supported open access publishing is a potential alternative, which has worked for some media, such as newspapers and academic journals. However, for scholarly reference publishers, this model risks quality control and brand authority. If the values of advertisers are perceived to be at odds with academic publishing values, we have defeated one of our primary purposes. There are also fewer interested advertising parties for reference products.

It is in this context that Kevin Kelly's inventory of the eight aspects of online content that are "Better than Free" must be heeded by publishers (Kelly, 2008). Today, we are successfully addressing many of these features, such as interpretation, authenticity, and accessibility. However, findabil-

ity – through good, clean, user-centered design – is the last item in this famous list and is an area with which many reference publishers are still struggling. Shifting our focus away from saving our historically profitable business practices and toward providing researchers with the information they need, when they need it, could pave the way for new online business models.

2. FINDING AUTHORITATIVE REFERENCE CONTENT IN THE LIBRARY

While a majority of students gravitate toward Google and Wikipedia for academic queries, many also make use of scholarly research databases in the course of their research. While slightly lower than 2009 figures, Project Information Literacy's 2010 survey reveals that 84% of respondents utilize library-purchased materials for their work. When searching library databases, students typically rely on those with which they are familiar or have formed habits (Head, et al., 2010). Most institutions subscribe to hundreds of publisher platforms and database products, in addition to their print collections. The information overload is a struggle for students of all ages, and competition for their attention is a challenge for reference publishers.

As with the open Web, library discoverability is not exclusively a matter of SEO. Ensuring findability and usability within library systems demands new technical initiatives of publishers, whose online product development must also be well informed by a strong and ongoing focus on the needs and habits of today's researchers. However, unlike the open-Web, library discoverability provides many new opportunities for libraries and publishers to work more closely together. Collaboration on information literacy, for instance, could greatly benefit beginning students and undergraduates who have not yet formed research skills.

Optimizing Library Search

As reference products compete for visibility on the open Web, publishers are equally concerned with confirming our products are mapped effectively for use within library services. This landscape is as diverse as the open Web, if not more. There are wide varieties of cataloging (OPAC) systems, library website interfaces, and uneven degrees of technical support and network capabilities within institutions around the world. The primary demand of publishers, to guarantee their products are visible within libraries, is data management – for governance of electronic product records, online hosting support, user registrations, standardized institutional identifiers, and more. These are essentially new skills for publishers.

In order to fulfill these new requirements of our business, publishers are drawn to offer services that qualify more as indexing and filtering, not the traditional editorial functions expected of publishers. Libraries expect publishers to provide free bibliographic data at the point of sale for cataloging purposes. Yet, publishers cannot be assured that libraries will use this data in uniform ways, if at all. Attempts by publishers to enrich these services by providing with additional metadata to improve discovery, such as expanded machine-readable catalog (MARC) records with readers guides or abstracts, are not always well received. While metadata standards exist for bibliographic records like MARC, each library catalog has set individual standards for the use of this data within their organizations. Institutions with more than one library have multiple cataloging staff and, thereby, varying rules for such data. Some libraries choose to contract with dedicated bibliographic data services, bypassing publisher-controlled catalog data entirely.

Library customers also contract with electronic resource management (ERM) vendors, who provide technical services, such as Open URL. These vendors expect publishers to provide both metadata and easy access to platforms for indexing. These requirements are as unique as each individual vendor, with little opportunity for publishers to warrant the data is used in ways that allow our products to be delivered to readers when and where they are needed. Some ERM requirements call for technologies not yet available by a given publisher, such as application programming interface (API) appliances, which allow easier automated indexing and can provide the basis for other library signposts.

While, in theory, many of these tools are accessible to anyone with an Internet connection, technological skills in both libraries and publishing houses are still uneven and data standards for some functions are not yet universally accepted. Publishers are challenged to provide as many options as possible, pulling resources and product strategies in many directions. For example, as more libraries adopt widget-based website services, such as LibGuides, publishers are challenged with the opportunity to provide new tools for searching our products. Creating functional, branded widgets for libraries to place within their online systems requires both a new level of skill and a leap of faith for publishers. Since we can neither be sure these bits of portable code are used by either librarians or researchers, some publishers choose not to invest in this potential opportunity.

A much sought-after service that requires new technical resource by both publishers and libraries is federated searching. Over the years, we've found that achieving smooth, accurate unified searching is not as simple as it sounds. Aggregated indexing services, such as EBSCO Discovery Service and ProQuest's Summon, have begun addressing this need to tackle library information overload. These tools are understandably focused on centralizing metadata and streamlining the search experience for researchers. Publishers who partner with these services stand to benefit by improved library SEO, thus driving usage and visibility of our products. We take a slight gamble, however, when we deliver full-text data, en masse, for indexing, with the faith that contracts will be upheld and potential pirates will not interfere. More importantly perhaps, we risk a loss of branding identification. Once product data is surrendered to a meta-search company, publishers cannot easily verify that it is used accurately or completely within shared library customers' systems.

The resource demands for meeting these library indexing and cataloging requirements are not just in staff knowledge and time, but in systems and equipment. Many functions noted here can be managed manually via spreadsheets or delivered with a full-text PDF of a publication. However, for these operations to be scalable, efficient, and sustainable, new automated systems using more advanced XML technologies are required. Our investment in such systems is becoming a standard infrastructural addition to publishing houses, as these advancements are required for production, as well as delivery and maintenance, of our products.

Innovative library discovery systems, such as unified searching tools, demand close collaboration between libraries, publishers, and electronic indexing experts. We share a driving goal of making the products and services within the library highly usable and findable by the users in need – therefore, we have a prime opportunity to cooperate in the ongoing refinement of library search. Together, we can drive new standards for product metadata, be sure usage reporting keeps up with user behavior, allow one another a better view into the end products, and readily share user feedback and market research.

Your Patron is My Patron

In the throes of all these changes, it may be easy to overlook the primary focus of our mission: researchers. Their successful retrieval and application of scholarly information is the core driver for both publishers and librarians. Meeting this goal and serving students well requires achieving many technical functions outlined thus far in this chapter. However, the more difficult aspect of successful discoverability is not technical – the key

to fluid reference research within the library rests in understanding users' behavior and modifying our practices to fit well within their workflow.

Undergraduate library patrons are the primary audience for reference products, and therefore, their habits and needs are central to our success. Fewer and fewer seek out librarian assistance in their studies (Hargittai, Fullerton, Mancen-Trevino & Yates Thomas, 2010). Beginning students report that, at times, they do not bother to scroll through a long alphabetical list of library collections and holdings, opting instead to make the most of whatever they can find in a database beginning with "A" or a product with which they're most familiar. This is only one of countless examples that demonstrate how critical usability is to discoverability. In our profession, understanding the young library patron is an important new proficiency.

Tactics to achieve smooth findability of reference material must become a number-one priority of libraries and publishers alike. Just as we prioritize the development of new technological skills to manage and standardize reference metadata, we must also build into our infrastructure new resources to regularly monitor the study habits and research needs of our shared patrons. We regularly share platform usage statistics, but they do not reveal knowledge about research workflows and scholars' behavior. Promoting the advancement of standard reports on Web analytics and end-user testing could provide greater insights into discoverability tactics than traditional usage metrics, such as the amount of full-text downloads.

These tactics should not be the singular responsibility of any one element of the scholarly community. Instead, collaboration between libraries and publishers is critical. For instance, creative approaches to information literacy training could revitalize the brand of reference publishing in general, as the key resources for students to begin their research. If publishers and librarians work together to standardize the use of terminology – for instance, "primary research" instead of "reference" – we stand a better chance of shaping the habits of young researchers. Perhaps routines for delivering research training materials should be as standardized as cataloging metadata for each release of a new publication.

3. DISCOVERABILITY IS MORE THAN SEO

As outlined earlier in this chapter, the scientific practice of search engine optimization (SEO) is focused on the technologies of an individual platform. In order to meet the new demands of reference scholarship, publishers are rightly investing in these techniques, such as sophisticated website encoding and content mark-up. These are important factors in making reference materials findable and usable online. However, the greatest challenge in providing scholars clear pathways to discover the publications they need is not technical. The mechanics of online discovery are important, but truly successful discovery of reference publications should be equally measured by and focused on human behavior.

The lessons publishers must draw from competition on the open-Web, such as Wikipedia, is that usability is key to discoverability. As Kevin Kelly outlined in *Better than free*, utility is worth paying for, and readers will be drawn time and again to resources that are easily accessible and visible (Kelly, 2008). Getting the right information to the right person at the right time requires a studied understanding of researcher habits via market research and usability analysis. It also requires new partnerships with libraries to certify adequate filtering tools are applied to reference material.

User-Centered Design

For decades, publishers could rest assured that scholars had fairly uniform needs for research tools – such as encyclopedias, directories, dictionaries, and handbooks. Libraries had a near monopoly on the indexing and collection of these materials, which provided reliable methods for indexing and discovery. The locations were predefined and roadmaps highly functional.

Today, research habits and methods of scholarly communication are in flux, so publishers and libraries must reexamine how they meet the needs of global academic communities. This requires, to a large degree, going back to the drawing board and asking basic market research questions of students, faculty, and other members of our industry. To successfully serve today's students, product design processes now include careful examination of the changing modes of research, with regular consultation by library advisory, student focus groups, and end-user testing sessions. Ensuring this feedback regularly informs the conceptual and technical development of new tools is vital to achieving our purposes. Publishers are motivated to integrate such market research practices into staff and budgetary infrastructure.

Recent studies, such as work by Project Information Literacy (Head, et al., 2010) and by scholars at Northwestern University (Hargittai, et al., 2010), have demonstrated the need to both evaluate those needs articulated by researchers in the course of interviews and focus groups, as well as habits and behaviors observed within observational studies. Squaring what users say they do with what they actually do is sometimes a challenge. If we look at the whole process involved in online research, opportunities arise for improvements to the online research pathways provided by publishers and libraries.

Application of agile research and design practices are new skills for many in our industry. Being willing to experiment, to risk the abandonment of a new database technique or a new marketing tool in the course of development is not typically comfortable for some publishing companies. Here, the dangers and the opportunities are more pronounced – fraught with the greatest risk of failure and the highest potential for success.

Publishers as Filters

In the opening chapter of *Reference Renaissance*, David W. Lewis pronounces the current state of publishing to be the result of our third revolution – with the first being the invention of the printing press, the second the industrialization of the press, and today's upheaval brought about by digital publishing (Radford & Lankes, 2010). It is clear that traditional tactics of reference publishing are not successful in this third wave of change. For instance, production systems must be revised to support the automated delivery of publications to a variety of online platforms. And, while the Dewey Decimal system successfully classifies physical publications, it is not adequate for indexing those printed on the Internet. Although there have been many admirable attempts to apply print-based methods to the organization and distribution of online publications, the plain reality is that many of our traditional approaches to academic discovery must be either reviewed and reworked, or retired and reinvented.

In order to fulfill our goal of placing authoritative reference materials where they are needed most, publishers are compelled to act as the guides within the research workflow, the creators of signposts. To do this, we must expand our influence beyond the traditional roles of editorial, marketing, and fulfillment. Making our online products visible and functional for today's readers, we must move into tasks that are best characterized as filtering, which have long been the function of libraries. Our past practices successfully relied upon instructors and librarians to steer scholars to the publications they need. In that schema, publishers were expected to provide tables of contents, readers guides, and / or alphabetical indices within products to aid in their use. Abstracting and indexing vendors also produced valuable additional print discovery tools.

Today, publishers must also deliver products with library catalog metadata, in varying standards for diverse systems. For online products, publishers must perfect electronic indexing, for successful SEO via mainstream search engines as well as library tools. We work to address quickly changing requirements to satisfy a wide variety of global search providers. These new demands for expanded filtering techniques are required to both guarantee discoverability via open-Web and mobile Web search tools and the worldwide library cataloging systems as well.

New expectations – such as delivery of bibliographic records to libraries at the point of sale and competition with free, mainstream reference products – drive publishers to become experts in areas such as data indexing and information literacy education. These require the support of additional budgetary and staff resources. In fulfilling these new expectations, publishers have the opportunity to add value to published products by partnering with libraries to enrich the metadata assigned to our publications, developing links between our products and other online tools, and expanding the discovery of our content via new channels.

Social Media for Scholars

At our core, we are social beings, and we likely all have stories about discovering a new book or publisher upon the recommendation from someone else. This same basic exchange carries on within scholarly communities, now often with the aid of online tools. A majority of today's scholars are using at least one form of mainstream social tool in the course of their research (Nicholas, Rowlands, & Wamae, 2010). Researchers today benefit from conducting their research within a more social setting than generations before them. Recent studies show reliance on crowd-sourced sites, such as Wikipedia, and resources such as friends and classmates, especially for vetting the authority of publications (Hargittai, et al., 2010). This trend provides publishers and librarians new opportunities for connecting with researchers and providing platforms for academic communities.

Publishers are challenged now to determine how to best utilize existing social media to connect readers with the primary research they need to conduct their studies. Scholars likely will neither be looking for encyclopedias on Facebook nor "friending" a publisher. Publishers cannot market whole products via Wikipedia. However, when targeted to a specific subject area or research goal in demand by researchers, social media can be leveraged successfully. Regular posts on Twitter drive increased visibility and the use of hashtags has proven an effective tool for engaging users and publishers. Recruiting authors to contribute to Wikipedia can vastly increase traffic to published products, where entries include links to online encyclopedias (see examples from Oxford University Press in section 2).

The community aspects of publishing must not be lost in the flurry of social change inspired by new online communication tools. In fact, publishers have a chance to enhance the discovery of products by moving our skills in generating and supporting these communities to online forums. For instance, Methodspace is a community site sponsored by SAGE to promote discourse among scholars of research methodology. Here, scholars at all levels can gather to solicit advice on how to approach a new research project, exchange examples of various methods, or discuss how to blend methods within their disciplines. SAGE launched this site over a year before launching *SAGE Research Methods Online*, a new research tool to query hundreds of publications using a custom taxonomy, intended for subscription or sale to libraries. The interest in and visibility of this new product among researchers is partly due to the popularity of Methodspace, which currently supports a community of more than 8,000 scholars.

Demands to fit research into new socially driven academic workflows represent another opportunity for publishers and librarians to address the reinvention of our industry to meet the needs of researchers. In order to reach our goals and sustain scholarship within these new communication tools, we must reshape our products and services to fit the lives of today's scholars.

CONCLUSION

Recent research cited in this chapter points to an ever-urgent need for findable, usable, authoritative reference products. Despite being savvy users of online tools and new technologies, a majority of undergraduate students report that the beginning steps of research are the most difficult. (Hargittai, et al., 2010; Head, et al., 2010) It is at these early stages that easily accessible reference materials are most in need. As research habits change for scholars of all types, publishers and librarians must find new, creative methods for directing readers to appropriate, authoritative reference material.

As we face competition by free, crowd-sourced online reference websites, such as Wikipedia and Dictionary.com, producers and distributors of authoritative scholarly works cannot rely solely on traditional tactics of the publishing business. Once new staff resource is applied to focus on online products, publishers have an opportunity to engage with open-Web services at low costs and develop strategies for engaging in new ways with researchers online. Some modification to existing editorial positions is required to ensure that content acquisition and generation is geared toward discoverable and well-designed online publications. Equally importantly, publishers must invest in systems and related expertise to produce quality, agile digital content – this is often the most difficult and expensive task at hand. There are no silver bullets in meeting these new challenges, yet each publisher must carefully consider their primary value to their scholarly readers and develop new strategies that both meet their needs and are economically sustainable.

For these known facets of ensuring findability, and new challenges that lie ahead, we have an opportunity to develop more flexible and proactive skills in publishing. In many ways, we must redefine reference publishing. We must continually review, renew, and reposition our signposts along the information superhighway, both to ensure we meet the current needs of today's scholars and guarantee the survival of reference publishing as a profession in general.

REFERENCES

Asher, A. (2010, November). *The changing role of libraries in discovery.* Presented at the Ithaka Sustainable Scholarship Conference, New York, NY.

Grathwohl, C. (2010, November). *The tower and the open Web.* Presented at the Charleston Conference, Charleston, SC.

Hargittai, E., Fullerton, L., Mancen-Trevino, E., & Yates Thomas, K. (2010). Trust online: Young adults' evaluation of Web content. *International Journal of Communication, 4,* 468-494. Retrieved November 20, 2010, from http://ijoc.org/ojs/index.php/ijoc/article/view/636/423

Head, A., & Eisenberg, M. (2010). *Truth be told: How college students evaluate and use information in the digital age. Project Information Literary progress report.* Retrieved November 1, 2010, from http://projectinfolit.org/pdfs/PIL_Fall2010_Survey_FullReport1.pdf

Kelly, K. (2008). Better than free. *The Technicum.* Retrieved October 24, 2010, from http://www.kk.org/thetechnium/archives/2008/01/better_than_fre.php

Nicolas, D., Rowlands, I., & Wamae, D. (2010, November). *Are social media impacting on research?* Presented at the Charleston Conference, Charleston, SC.

Radford, M. L., & Lankes, R. D. (Eds.). (2010). *Reference renaissance: Current and future trends.* New York, NY: Neal-Schuman Publishers, Inc.

ADDITIONAL READING

Krug, P. (2005). *Don't make me think: A common sense approach to web usability* (2nd ed.). Berkeley, CA: New Riders Press.

Shirky, C. (2008). *Here comes everybody: The power of organizing without organizations.* New York, NY: Penguin Press.

Chapter 14
Indexing Scholarly Reference:
Helping Researchers do Less

Eric Calaluca
Paratext, USA

ABSTRACT

The diminished interaction between novice or non-specialist researcher and trained librarian has its root case as much in increased financial pressures on libraries as it does with the simultaneous promotion of single search discovery systems being developed for academic and public libraries systems. Nevertheless, the historical context of the role of specialist finding aids in research, and additionally, the renewed appreciation for the value of specialized subject encyclopedias to facilitate solid research, can provide needed context. The application of new technologies to unlock and apply the content of specialized encyclopedias offers a familiar, yet newly-configured approach to discovery and scholarly search. Rather than exposing the novice to an increasing amount of materials they may not be ready to absorb, a renewed attention to this genre within libraries holds the promise of allowing researchers to actually achieve more by researching less.

INTRODUCTION

"But it is not the offensiveness to us indexers of such a suggestion that I would make most prominent or ask your space to point out. It is rather the fact that it voices one of the rankest literary heresies of the age—namely, the idea that anybody can make an index if he only knows the alphabet."[1] *(Fletcher, 1883, p.73)*

The quotation above is taken from correspondence between scholars, librarians and "men of letters" played out in the pages of *The Nation* in 1883. The episode which fostered this discussion was the publication of Dr. William Frederick Poole's ground-breaking *Index to Periodical Literature*.

DOI: 10.4018/978-1-61350-308-9.ch014

The value of Poole's *Index* was a matter of intense debate among scholar-librarians at the time, but it was immediately popular among working librarians. Its publication triggered the production of subsequent finding aids, including William Thomas Stead's *Index to Periodicals* in 1901 (which introduced the first 'subject headings' to periodicals citations) and, soon thereafter, the first iteration of the *Reader's Guide to Periodical Literature.*

The intense discussions regarding the value of the ground-breaking activity of Poole, Stead, and others presages contemporary discussions of the role of finding aids within library information architecture. The issues addressed in the present volume might be said to be traceable as far back as the invention of indexes themselves within the monastic scriptoria of Western Europe during the Middle Ages.

It offers clues as to the path forward, and insight into contemporary activities among information providers seeking to maximize the opportunities now presented through the massive digitization of scholarly materials. It further reveals that parties active the present information industry participate in a continuum of discussion concerning appropriate mechanisms for access to research materials, particularly those mechanisms appropriate for the novice or non-specialist researcher. Guiding the novice or non-specialist has historically been handled through the application of specialized reference works, and now in new clothing, e-reference.

What can be offered technologically to bridge the space between the traditional practice of introductory reference and the advance of vast aggregation systems linking to terabytes of full text documents? What can technology do to incorporate the accumulated wisdom of more traditional research methodologies, while still make the most of the speed and scope of Web-based queries?

As the quotation above suggests, a thread which echoes the scholarly debate of years past with those of the present is, at least in part, the re-evaluation of the role of *scholarly indexing*. This issue is set in relief with the advent of full-text "string" searching. Put differently, the issue revolves around the role of *mediation* within the library setting. Can library staff responsible leave a researcher in a library without the assistance of a librarian or easy access to authoritative introductory material, and expect the researcher to leave with a satisfactory research experience? Can new information systems replace the traditional function of the authoritative reference work, or the reference librarian themselves?

E-reference anticipates a research landscape in which library users may have no need to set foot in a library at all, even less working directly with a trained librarian. In some quarters of public and academic library administration, this is viewed as *a fait accompli*, based not simply (though substantially) on library budget constraints, but also upon the growing evangelism for single search software solutions. The goal of these single search systems is to recast library resources in a manner similar to searching the Web itself, and, it is hoped, encourage the Web-savvy novice researcher to explore the special or unique contents of the library, rather than searching only outside the realm of a library's collection.

With this some historical context established, our goal now is to explore some options. We will narrow our focus now to the way in which e-reference in general, and scholarly reference in particular, serves to *prepare* the novice for more serious research. We will focus on one vital type of publication found in abundance in every serious library. As in the past, this one genre of materials is constructed specifically to aid the researcher to getting started confidently with new research.

This genre remains immensely valuable to librarian, scholar, novice researcher, or non-specialist. It is vastly underused. It is inherently multi-disciplinary. Indeed, in the absence of the mediation of a reference specialist, its use can reliably assist the non-specialist in moving through the riches of a library more quickly and more effectively than any other method.

The publications referred to here are the library's carefully selected collection of *specialized* or *subject encyclopedias*. Vast troves of specialized reference works, focused on specific disciplines or areas of study, designed solely to give the research a solid grounding in a topic before engaging in more detailed research. We will discuss recent efforts to encourage and improve access to these resources. More than this, it will be argued here that more extensive use these subject encyclopedias will not simply help researchers make the most of their library's resources, but will, in fact, allow them to do so in *less time* and with *less effort*.

Walking in Another Researcher's Shoes

"The best way to start many inquiries is to see if someone has already written an overview article outlining the most important facts on the subject and providing a concise list of recommended readings. This precisely what a good encyclopedia article does." (Mann, 2005, p. 1)

It is worth noting that the statement above serves as the *first sentence* of Thomas Mann's remarkable *Oxford Guide to Library Research.*

What Mann refers to here are *subject encyclopedias—The Encyclopedia of Philosophy; The Encyclopedia of Food and Nutrition; the Encyclopedias of Space Sciences*, to name a few. In many cases, these are multi-volume sets, some as large as 20 volumes with a cumulative index volume as well. Since roughly 2001, many of these titles can now be accessed in electronic form. However, in whatever format they are acquired, they remain among the most expensive individual works any library acquires.

Major publishers in this realm include Oxford University Press; Cambridge University Press; McGraw-Hill; Cengage/Gale; Blackwell; Wiley; Springer: Routledge (Taylor and Francis); SAGE;

and many more. In some cases, the publishers host electronic editions through their own proprietary platforms. In other cases, smaller reference publishing organizations license their publications to larger platforms, and some do both. This will be discussed later in more detail.

Subject encyclopedias represent a very small percentage of contemporary scholarly publications. Because of their considerable editorial and production costs, subject encyclopedias and similar works (scholarly compendia and handbooks) constitute approximately 3% of the entire scholarly academic monographic output based on statistics tracked since 1997.[2] (Hysell, 2010)

This is in no small measure due to the substantial costs for editorial and data acquisition on the part of the publisher. For those readers not familiar with the process of scholarly publications, it may come as news that publication of a scholarly work in electronic format does not necessarily mean lower costs to the publisher. It many cases, the costs are actually increased.

While the same amount of editorial preparation and gathering of experts is required, along with rights clearances, editorial oversight, and gathering specialists to write the articles, there are additional costs. Reference publishers, if they publish their own electronic data, must also provide a search and retrieval platform to use the works, as well as extensive customer service modules or personnel to handle technical questions. Paper copies have no such requirements.

Conversely, for libraries themselves, subject encyclopedias—in print or electronic form—are among the most expensive single title items a library acquires.[3] Therefore, given the remarkable research value of subject encyclopedias for research, the substantial investment by the publisher, and the substantial cost to the libraries, it would be reasonable to assume that these subject encyclopedias would constitute a core element of the contemporary library's mission to improve research. Returning to Mann for a moment, the opening lines of his important work articulate a solid position within the discipline of library science, yet also represent a truth which remains unknown to most researchers, and unappreciated as well by many librarians who might reasonably be expected to know better.

Mann's recommendation suggests a course of action which, upon consideration, seems glaringly obvious. To accomplish solid research, begin with a primer on the core issues. Find out what an expert thinks about a topic before you go any further. This is what a trained librarian would traditionally have done to help the novice—or themselves—become acquainted with the basic points of a topic.

It is the unique quality of these publications that have encouraged libraries to acquire them consistently for over one-hundred years. They are solid research tools to help anyone make better use of the riches of a library.

Subject encyclopedias assist in three, fundamental ways. First, they are designed to *introduce* a topic to an unfamiliar researcher, in a manner and tone that does not require previous technical knowledge of the subject. Second, they focus on *major themes* and major terms in the ongoing discussion of the topic, rather than diving into advocating for any one side of a topic. Third, these articles provide a solid, reliable, "state of affairs" view of a topic, seeking to articulate the *"settled argument."*

"Encyclopedias by their very nature seek to summarize knowledge that is more or less "established" and not subject to rapid change." (Mann, 2005, p. 2) This may be in itself the most vital benefit of using subject encyclopedias, and their value is anticipated through the very method of publication by the publishers themselves. After all, among the principal activities in the preparation of a subject encyclopedia is the recruitment of noted specialists in the field.

Why does this matter to the researcher? Because it is exceedingly helpful for any researcher to know with some confidence that the author is presenting all sides of an issues, or at least, all

sides that merit serious consideration. It is worth noting that, insofar as any specialist and/or scholars is recruited to contribute an article for a subject encyclopedia, there is "vetting process" already at work. Beyond the editorial oversight of the book's general editor, it is unlikely that a specialist will advance an article in a subject encyclopedia that posits ideas or positions suspect to colleagues in the field. Indeed, a good many of the colleagues in question may well be contributors to the same book.

Thus, this process provides a sense of security in the information being presented in a scholarly overview article, the work having, gone through the process of peer-evaluation and editorial oversight. It should be noted that the same may not necessarily be said for a scholarly monograph, which is often designed to advance *new* or *unprecedented* views of a topic—in other words, a *thesis*.

This built-in vetting process gives a further level of credibility and authority to the article. More important, it offers the novice researcher or non-specialist confidence related to the topic being researched. These introductory articles provide the novice or non-specialist with the *a priori* knowledge required for both effective and efficient subsequent research in scholarly monographs or journals.

However, high-quality subject encyclopedias articles do much more. Specifically, they serve as a guide to further research. The best-produced subject encyclopedias conclude with bibliographies or *further readings*. In such a case, the specialist has mapped out the territory for the researcher who wants to move on from an introduction to deeper knowledge. This encourages the novice researcher to go further with confidence, having thus identified the scholarly books or journal articles in the field the authors finds uniquely helpful or relevant.

Conversely, and of equal importance, is what the article's author can convey regarding subsequent research paths that are unnecessary or will prove fruitless. Put differently, a well-written encyclopedia article is, in many ways, written to *obviate* research. A single example from a very well-constructed subject encyclopedia will make the point.

In volume I of *Medieval Italy: An Encyclopedia* we find an article on the medieval hill-town of Assisi. The article is well-written, concise, and provides context for the novice. However, it does more than this. Near the end of the article we find the following. *"There are no books in English that provide a straightforward history of Assisi, but most books about the lives of Saint Francis and Saint Claire contain some historical setting."* (Kleinhenz, 2004, p. 72)

This seemingly passing comment bears scrutiny. What is the author telling the reader here? What the author is doing is *educating* the reader not only on the topic, but on *researching the topic.* One might say the author is teaching. This example illustrates the remarkable benefit imparted in this instance by the writer to the researcher. It is imparted not by encouraging further readings, but by *discouraging fruitless exploration.* It allows the researcher to do less.

Not even the most qualified reference librarian could be expected to convey this kind of specific research experience to a library user—experience available only to the specialist in this focused area of study, who has no doubt spent many hours within library stacks and searched online databases looking for the very same book. Expertly-written articles in subject encyclopedias assist the researcher by telling them what not to bother looking for.

To summarize, we've shown that, authoritative introductory articles within subject encyclopedias impart to the reader what they need to know, as well as, in many cases, what they *do not* need to know, or bother looking for. This is core value authoritative subject encyclopedias supports the history of such publications within library collection development activities, and why well-trained librarians have worked diligently to see these subject encyclopedias receive high levels of use.

In light of the important function role these works to assist library users, it would be safe to assume that professional information science programs would require familiarity with the scope and research value of subject encyclopedias. One might imagine it would be among the very first parts of a core curriculum for training librarians. In reality, this is not the case.

Trends in information science curricula suggest that it is no longer required within graduate library program to possess a familiarity with subject encyclopedias. Even though Mann convincingly posits the preeminent role that specialized encyclopedias should have both librarian and novice researcher, the teaching of reference services generally—and serious familiarity with the role of specialized encyclopedias in research specifically—is on the wane.

In fact, "reference" itself, is an elective within many programs. Is the use of subject encyclopedias a lost art? Not really lost, but it is proving to be a familiarity increasingly hard to find, measured by the competencies of recent information science graduates.

I find that for students who grew up never even seeing a print index, they don't get it. They don't get it when they look at it online what an index is as opposed to a bibliography. That to me is the biggest challenge...getting them to understand the underlying structure of reference materials and what they are.[4] (Agosto, 2010)

Do libraries still acquire subject encyclopedias? Yes, they do, but they are largely focused on electronic editions, with little or no attention given to the enormous cache of previously published encyclopedias already in their possession. What does appear true is that, in some libraries, the subject encyclopedia collection is becoming a *legacy* issue.

Moreover, the introduction of new, single-search solutions, referenced earlier, is overwhelming any consideration of *context* and *process* within

Figure 1.

> **Medieval Italy: an encyclopedia** *Christopher Kleinhenz, editor.*
> p.cm. –(The Routledge encyclopedias of the Middle Ages) Includes bibliographic references and index.
> ISBN 0-415-93929 -1 (set) – ISBN 0-415-93930-5 (vol. 1) –ISBN 0-415-9391-3 (vol. 2)
>   1.   *Italy --Civilizations—476-1268 Encyclopedias*
>   *Italy—Civilization—1268-1559 Encyclopedias.*
>   **DG443.**M43 2003
>   945 '.03'03—dc21

research. How is the researcher best prepared? How do they make sense of all the data a single search solution can return? As a result, a substantial (and expansive) component of a library's overall reference collection is increasingly becoming relegated to a rarely employed part of the library's collection.

But isn't this what the library's online public access catalog (OPAC) is for, to lead the researcher to the appropriate material? In the absence of guidance from a trained librarian, the vast majority of all researchers do begin their research of library's holdings through the catalog. Unfortunately, the evolution of machine-readable cataloguing did not fully account for the breadth of content within the typical, multi-volume subject encyclopedia.

I Know We Own it, Why Can't I Find It?

There is a reasonable expectation among novice library users that what the library owns will be present in the online catalog, in such a way to make it readily apparent to a researcher. With that in mind, the sole means of discovering the existence of a specialized subject encyclopedia has, until recently, been catalog entry itself.

There are, however, limited points of access for subject encyclopedias as they are widely represented within most library OPACs. Efforts to enhance catalog records with table of contents data are limited, both in terms of works covered, as well as by the limitations inherent in the size of any one record within a catalog.

Fundamentally, in nearly all cases, the information in an OPAC about any particular subject encyclopedias is limited to title, basic publication data, and in most cases two or three Library of Congress Subject Headings. Using our example from earlier, Figure 1 shows the record for the work, as it appears in virtually every library catalog that owns it.

Bear in mind, *Medieval Italy: An Encyclopedia,* contains 841 articles and nearly 13,000 index terms. Unless the user queries "Medieval and/or Italy and/or Civilizations," this will appear. But it will appear along with hundreds if not thousands of other works bearing the same subject headings.

Not only is the breadth of content in no way apparent from the catalog record, the *role* or *function* of the work is also not made apparent. How would the novice understand that this work is more appropriate for an introductory article on the Medici family than a 400-page monograph which also appeared in the same results set? Once again, the catalog does not provide any *mediation* for the research, nor context, nor the role of any one type of work in the continuum of research. Put differently, the catalog entries cannot make up for an absence of basic bibliographic instruction on which works to use at what stage of the research process.

In light of this, it seems highly unlikely that the novice, non-specialist would find this work through a library catalog. In fact, it is furthermore unlikely that even a trained reference librarian will be able to recall quickly any single subject encyclopedia title during a reference interview, particularly if it involves an uncommon research topic.

This represents a serious shortcoming for the researcher who may not have access to talk to a trained specialist prior to research. It represents a further weakness if current and future librarians are not being trained in understanding the value of subject encyclopedias to library users and themselves. If reference and public services librarians cannot recall the best introductory material on a moment's notice, what possibilities does the novice library user have when using a catalog that essentially obscures that library's most authoritative introductory texts?

Such a circumstance not only fails to assist the researcher when they are beginning research, it may actually prove to make their research more *time-consuming* and *more difficult*. By leaving the unmediated user to decipher works as they appear within a library catalog, or any other library-specific discovery system, often encourages the researcher to read scholarly journal articles or even entire scholarly monographs without knowing the basic state of affairs for the topic in question.

In summary, it has been posited that subject encyclopedias should be the first works consulted by students and researchers when beginning research on an unfamiliar topic. It has further been posited that knowledge of the role and value of subject encyclopedias appears to be on the wane within professional library and information programs.

Finally, it has been shown that the paucity of even the most basic access points for a subject encyclopedia in library catalogs makes them virtually invisible to the user, and as a consequence, has the effect of making the library user's work potentially far more difficult and time-consuming. We will now turn to an initiative designed to produce a comprehensive finding aid specifically for subject encyclopedias, its history, development, and potential applications in the future as new Information Systems continue to develop.

Finding and Using Subject Encyclopedias

The landscape of information retrieval for academic and other libraries in the first years of this century was mutating in a way far greater than the animated discussion following the publication of Poole's great *Index*. Now, as in Poole's day, librarians and library administrators understand the potential of newly-developed finding aids to unlock the content of an expanding knowledge-base of information. At the same time, researchers familiar with traditional methodologies voice concerns about the impact such new finding aids would have on the quality of research itself.

Prior to the advent of the World Wide Web in the mid 1990's, library directors, collection development specialists, and library technical specialists had embraced the potential of new forms of search and retrieval—as well as the physical space reduction potential—represented by the expansion of CD-ROM storage and delivery.

At roughly this same time, the information company Paratext began to explore the development of a unique Web-based finding aid that would seek to merge traditional methods of reference research with the speed and comprehensiveness of Web-based database search and retrieval. My business partner Bob Asleson and I revisited earlier project development discussions inside the company on enhancing access to subject encyclopedias and scholarly compendia.

Prior to this, Bob had introduced me to a small but important reference book, *First Stop: The Master Index to Subject Encyclopedias edited* by Joe Ryan (Oryx Press, 1989). It became clear that an entirely new kind of finding aid for libraries could be developed building on the impulse of Ryan's work. Several noteworthy and valuable works designed to assist both advanced and novice librarians to expand use of subject encyclopedias preceded Ryan's work. However, Ryan's was the first to attempt any manner of a deeper finding aid for these works.

First Stop *was conceived when three revelations struck me one frustrating day while I was working in my position as a reference librarian: (1) There was an amazing demand for background information from library users, both novice and advanced: (2) The sources of background information form a surprisingly large, though underutilized, part of our reference collection; and (3) I was getting pretty tired of recalling, after a user had left the service desk, a better source of background information that the one I had recommended. (Ryan, 1989, Introduction)*

Ryan's work was influenced by two main publications, *Best Encyclopedias: A Guide to General and Specialized Encyclopedias*, Kenneth F. Kister, ed. (Kister, 1986) and the *ARBA: Guide to Subject Encyclopedias and Dictionaries* (Wynar, 1986). Ryan's familiarity with extant finding aids for subject encyclopedias, as well as his own frustrations at the reference desk, led to the publication of *First Stop,* "A keyword and broad subject index to 430 specialized encyclopedias." (Ryan, 1989, Introduction).

First Stop was, however, restricted to works which were still in print; readily available; were "authoritative, analytical and of some length (250 words or more)"[5] and finally, inclusive of bibliographies. *(Ryan, 1989, Introduction)* Ten years later, in 1999, Allan N. Mirwis produced *Subject Encyclopedias: User Guide, Review Citations and Keyword Index* (Mirwis, 1999) as an expansion of *First Stop.* Mirwis' work lists 1,129 encyclopedias and indexes articles from the 98 titles ranked highest according to the author's own ranking system.

With this as a prelude, Paratext began discussing the possible value of an expanded database of analytical materials to subject encyclopedias with library administrators and reference librarians. The discussions were designed to elicit opinion on the possible need for such a database. Encouraged by these initial discussions, we began to build a bibliography and online prototype. As we

learned, there was no *comprehensive* bibliography of English-language subject encyclopedias, insofar as Kistler, Wynar, Ryan, and Mirwis were required to be selective of works to be included in their own finding aids compendia

Upon consultation with librarians and bookselling organizations, it was decided that the project would base our o base our bibliography upon works published in English from 1980 to present, and would be called *Reference Universe.*

The inclusion of such a substantial back-file of titles was suggested by librarians who noted that many libraries lacked the acquisitions budget to replace their extensive subject encyclopedias collections with e-book equivalents as they were being made available. In many cases, however, the older titles were note converted to electronic form at all.

A bibliographic boundary having been established, it was clear that adding search and retrieval functionality would need to be deployed if *Reference Universe* were to prove useful in the age of online research. Simply expanding the work of Kistler and Ryan in e-form would not be enough, by failing to take advantage of contemporary data processing possibilities.

Beyond simply identifying appropriate works from 1980 forward, it was also concluded that additional, more granular bits of information about the subject encyclopedias would have to be included to make the project more useful than Ryan's keyword and broad subject index. Additionally, whereas Ryan's work was by necessity limited to covering approximately 300 titles, and limited only to those titles published at time of *First Stop*'s printing, this new initiative would have the potential to be remain up to date, as well as embrace older print titles.

It was decided that that *Reference Universe* would, wherever possible, include not only a list of all article titles within the encyclopedias, but complete *back-of-the-book index* to each encyclopedias as well. This was a substantial enhancement for libraries that could not find or afford e-book equivalents of older, expensive subject encyclopedias in their collections. Additionally, and perhaps obviously, it was determined that the service would also emphasize the growing number of electronic encyclopedia editions, which began to be available to libraries in the early 2000s.

Indexing and Subject Encyclopedias

The inclusion of back-of-the-book indexes to subject encyclopedias was a decision made subsequent to discussions not only with working reference librarians, but also with reference publishers themselves. The publisher made it clear to us that the indexing reference works was vital to making the most of their use, and constituted a very expensive part of the publication process.

Reference publishers invest substantial amounts of money to commission indexing professionals to index their subject encyclopedias. This level of indexing is considerably more involved than what is required for a standard scholarly monograph. It is in many cases a major scholarly undertaking itself.

Sylvia Miller, former head of reference publishing at Routledge (Taylor and Francis), provides a vitally important example of the value of indexing within encyclopedias, which were designed to *"reflect the tone of the text but at the same time provide multiple levels of access." (Miller, 2008, p. 3)* Miller continues with an example on the role of indexing for users of a subject encyclopedia.

"For example, if there is an entire article in the encyclopedia focused on the state of Massachusetts, the page references for the article might appear in boldface. Following that, there might be a number of subheadings summarizing the aspects of Massachusetts that are discussed on the various pages listed, such as "Massachusetts, economy" and "Massachusetts, foodways."

It is important to note that the exact words "economy" and "foodways" <u>may not appear on the referenced pages.</u> *Such categories are often the summation devised by the indexer, who anticipates what sort of information the reader might seek. "[emphasis mine] (Miller, 2008, p. 4)*

These last two sentences quoted are worthy of serious consideration for those exploring the role of new technologies within scholarly research. *No full text search of an electronic edition of this encyclopedia would be sufficient to guide the user to this page, because the words are simply not present on the page.*

Only through the careful work of a professional indexer is the user lead to a potentially useful section of the article. Miller's comments remind us of the quotation with which we began this chapter, decrying *"one of the rankest literary heresies of the age—namely, the idea that anybody can make an index if he only knows the alphabet."* One might say that this level of professional indexing provides the user of the print edition with multiple levels of access.

It is this *semantic* indexing that often proves most valuable to library users, particularly the novice. It is this *a priori* knowledge that so many current iterations of electronic search systems presume, and sole reliance on which can lead many researchers to unsatisfactory results.

Therefore, confident in the vital research importance of indexes to subject encyclopedias satisfactorily established for us, Paratext set about to build the *Reference Universe* database. Many further technological obstacles were overcome to also deploy a system that would simultaneously match user queries to the library's own encyclopedia collection. Put differently, the goal for *Reference Universe* was to offer libraries a service with the depth of a cumulative index, along with the speed and customization of a local catalog.

In 2003 *Reference Universe* was formally launched. As of April 2011, the service contains more than 35 million index-level and article-level citations to approximately 50,000 English-language e-book and print encyclopedias and similar works.

Additional Platforms for Accessing and Using Subject Encyclopedias

While Reference Universe is the only resource which addresses the subject encyclopedias in their totality, many electronic platforms emerged to provide access to selected electronic reference titles.

Some were offered through the exclusive electronic platforms of reference publishers themselves, e.g., Oxford University Press' *Digital Reference Shelf* or *AccessScience* from McGraw-Hill. These have the benefit of being controlled entirely by the publisher themselves, who can update them on a continuing basis, offering new contents to the user in a regular way.

Additionally, some electronic subject encyclopedias can be accessed via the search platforms of larger reference publishing houses, integrated into their proprietary search and retrieval systems along with those of smaller publishers, e.g., *Gale Virtual Reference Library*. This is a popular approach, because it exposes the library to a wider variety of titles, and also offers the smaller publisher a contemporary online presence without absorbing the substantial development and deployment cost such databases entail.

Another avenue is accessing selected reference titles through the platform of *non-publishing* aggregation packages (e.g. *NetLibrary, Credo Reference.*) These have had the benefit of deploying innovative and engaging interfaces to help make a variety of titles accessible, regardless of the publishing source.

Finally, some reference publishers have chosen to license the full text of their encyclopedia material to the recently announced discovery layers currently being promoted to libraries. These materials are re-indexed within these large systems. The objective here is to deliver as much electronic content to the user as possible—both journal and monographic—through a very simplified search structure (e.g., *Primo* from Ex Libris, *EDS* from EBSCO). These have obvious benefits of being single search approaches, but, as of this writing, they have not been installed for a sufficient period to gauge their effect on overall quality of research reliably. Additionally, none of these approaches deal with more detailed access to the library's legacy titles, but only focus on works held in electronic form.

As can be seen, emphasis of these new systems are focused largely upon the *format* of the work, and not necessarily the function or s *role* of any particularly work within the research process. This is the piece of the puzzle *Reference Universe* was designed to fill—to bring forward subject encyclopedias *wherever* they exist in a library's collection—in online collections or on library's own shelves. In 2011, additional technologies have been deployed to allow the full breath of data contained in Reference Universe database to be made visible through larger library discovery services.

Wikipedia

Prior to addressing additional technological issues related to the integration of subject encyclopedias data into larger library technical services architecture, it seems obvious here to make mention of the most obvious alternative to using a library's encyclopedia collection for introductory information, viz., *Wikipedia*. Growing dramatically since it first launched, Wikipedia has proven to be a remarkable and easy to use resource for background information.

However, the method in which Wikipedia articles are created should produce caution when used by the serious researcher. Put differently, the very energies which have produced so vast a repository of data so quickly carry within them the roots of its limitations, with limited fact-checking or oversight, as one would expect in a professionally-produced subject encyclopedia.

This is not to say *Wikipedia* is full of errors—it may be or not, but it is the lack of confidence and scholarly consensus, addressed earlier, which poses such problems for the novice. Indeed, the founder of Wikipedia himself acknowledges the limitations of employing the service for *academic use*. "It is pretty good, but you have to be careful with it," he said. "It's good enough knowledge, depending on what your purpose is." (Young, 2006) "Good enough knowledge" is precisely why *Wikipedia* is so valuable for general, non-specialist use, and why it is inherently unreliable as an authoritative introduction to the serious research.

Nevertheless, Wikipedia's vast popularity on the Web indicates that there currently exists a substantial need among general Web users for introductory material. It may also be the case that mechanisms to foster a more deliberate editorial underpinning for Wikipedia may be established. But given the nearly endless possible articles which can and are being written, and a dizzying pace, this seems unlikely. Editorial oversight and fact checking is, as any reference publisher knows, a costly enterprise. In the meantime, the safest path for an introduction to any topic when conducting serious research to lies in using professionally-edited subject encyclopedias.

DOIs, OpenURL and Reference Discovery

We have outlined the many ways in which library users can access electronic subject encyclopedias and similar reference works. At this point, the issue of multi-platforms raises a question. Why aren't e-books accessible via citation services in the same way that journal articles are accessible via journal citation services? Why can't I simply start with a library catalog and move to a platform through a common interchange? The answer lies in the different development paths which were undertaking by journal publishers and reference publishers, respectively, since the mid-1990's.

By the late 1990s, journal publishers and library administrators had already realized the tremendous benefit to be gained by the deployment of a common linking protocol to help libraries manage and control the linking of information—specifically as it relates to *scholarly journals*. To that end, the *OpenURL protocol* was embraced quickly by journal publishers as well as librarians as a clear-headed approach to linking of journal literature with journal citations services. OpenURL provides a framework in which libraries would have greater control and flexibility in moving users from journal citations to the electronic document cited, as well as restricting the duplication of a library's journal acquisitions.

At roughly the same time, efforts were made to establish a similar—though not identical—protocol for identifying and linking to the content of eBook publications. In 1997, at the Frankfurt Book Fair, the Digital Object Identified (DOI) Initiative was launched by the Enabling Technologies Committee of the Association of American Publishers. The committee defined the DOI as a unique, persistent "identifier of intellectual property in the digital environment.*"*

According to Norman Paskin in the *Encyclopedia of Library and Information Science* (another subject encyclopedia) the DOI is a *"managed system for persistent identification of content on digital networks. It can be used to identify physical, digital, or abstract entities. The identifiers (DOI names) resolve to data specified by the registrant, and use an extensible metadata model to associate descriptive and other elements of data with the DOI name."* Publishers have been able to register with the Foundation since October of 1998, and by late 2009, more than forty million DOI names had been assigned by DOI System Registration Agencies in North America, Europe, and Australia. (Paskin, 2010, p. 1586)

However, this number does not approach the needed level of granularity of access which would facilitate greater access to electronic subject encyclopedias articles. Eric Hellman, founder of Openly Informatics, a library technology application company founded in 1998, has written that DOIs were promoted as a *"solution to two problems, broken URLs and rights management"* (Hellman, 2010).

However, as Hellman points out *"the fact that fifteen years later broken URLs are still a problem and digital rights are a quagmire suggests that the DOI has had limited impact in these areas. Did something go wrong?"* (Hellman, 2010) Essentially, DOI was not accepted among scholarly e-book publishers in the way that OpenURL was embraced by those in the scholarly journal publishing communities.

Despite wider adoption by individual publishers, the exception to this has been the development of *CrossRef,* the official DOI link registration agency for scholarly and professional publications. Hellman notes that *"CrossRef added some useful machinery onto the DOI and turned it into an absolutely essential service for publishers of e-journals other types of content that need to embed persistent links."* (Hellman, 2010)

DOI is still gaining ground, and there is reason for optimism. However, based on Paratext's own work in maintaining a bibliography of English-language scholarly reference works, it has been found that only a small percentage of scholarly reference publishers are deploying persistent DOIs for their electronic editions. In fact, some that had even initially embraced DOIs are no longer supporting them. The reasons for this are not clear, but the absence of widespread adoption of article-level DOIs-for scholarly reference works inhibits wider use of detailed information about the contents of the works.

Hellman sums up the scenario in this way,

Things have changed in 15 years. The World Wide Web turned out to be not so interested in digital objects with complex management systems and rights regimes. Instead, the World Wide Web turned out to be an unthinkably large number of web pages with negligible rights management indexed by search engines. Persistence of links turned out to be less important than the 'findability' of content in search engines. (Hellman, 2010)

Persistent links means more services could find any e-book in question, with greater flexibility and availability to a wide array of information systems. It is hoped that as CrossRef continues to expand, this limitation will be overcome, particularly as it relates to article-level DOIs.

Nevertheless, despite the lack of wide spread adoptions of the DOI protocol currently found within the world of scholarly reference e-books, there are still significant benefits to be gained within library information architecture through a more widespread and consistent application of *OpenURL* e-book metadata. This is the link in the chain before the user even gets to the DOI, if it exists.

Why aren't library OpenURL resolvers populated with e-book metadata with the breadth and urgency with which they cover journal literature? If they were, e-books could be discovered and used with the same speed and comprehensiveness in which journals are now accessed: in many cases, directly from a library's existing technological infrastructure, the OPAC. What is holding up this development? The reasons are both economic as well as technological.

There was no consensus among e-book publishers on the role or value of DOI, as there had been among journal publishers for the widespread adoption of the OpenURL protocol, although OpenURL applications enjoy widespread support from librarians and technologists who had incentive to maximize access to their scholarly journals. However, even with the support of library technologist, there is continued resistance among scholarly book publishers to deploy yet another layer of 'findability' for their works. The most recent severe cutbacks in library acquisitions budgets means that, the incentive for book publishers to add to existing production costs is further diminished.

Additionally, not all libraries even *have* OpenURL resolvers. They are expensive to acquire, and require ongoing technical support from both inside the library and from the resolver vendor. This also explains, in part, the absence of article-level DOIs in most e-reference books. However, virtually all libraries do provide Web access, so aggregating reference e-books within proprietary or third-party platforms still provides an avenue of access for users, despite the absence of common linking mechanisms.

Nevertheless, it seems an opportunity has been missed. It can be argued that had more consideration been given by reference publishers to the application of persistent DOIs as well as encouraging the most consistent deployment of e-book metadata, the issue of the discoverability of e-reference might be largely settled by now. CrossRef holds promise in this area, but there remains a great deal of ground left to be covered.

We will never know how E-reference would look now had the issues of persistent links and metadata been widely adopted earlier. It is possible that smaller reference publishers would now be better able to compete by hosting their own electronic editions, confident that the means of finding and linking to that data were well-established within a majority of their library customers. This may have, in turn, allowed publishers to invest more in new publications, instead of being preoccupied with divining the technological trends within libraries.

Future Prospects for Disseminating Reference Content

With hindsight as a guide, the future for reinvigorating e-reference and scholarly reference specifically is nevertheless optimistic. We have addressed here the unique bibliography and cache of index-level data now compiled and deployed for libraries within the *Reference Universe* service. However, this compilation of data is not, by

necessity, bound to any single proprietary search system.

On the contrary, through the use of APIs (Application Programming Interfaces) this kind of information can be exposed to a variety of library Information Systems. This is in addition to the more established mode of accessing the service through employing a federated search system (z39.50 protocol), which is already available for the service, and active within many of the new discovery systems listed above.

Put simply, library systems can use the *Reference Universe* dataset without using the full service itself. This means that libraries will have a greater flexibility in how they choose to display and use very detailed bits of information about their own subject encyclopedia collection. This flexibility extends to seeing detailed reference data within LibGuides, library catalogs, single-search platforms, and knowledge management systems. It offers the possibility of moving subject encyclopedias from a largely underutilized part of the reference collection to a more firmly established entry point for library users.

Finally, and of equal importance, search results returned from this these merging of technology can be configured to give equal attention to *print* subject encyclopedias, if the library chooses. Libraries still possess vastly more *print* subject encyclopedias than e-reference titles, though this is clearly evolving toward e-reference[5]. Nevertheless, as library's logically move to substantial investments in works in electronic form, it is logical to assume that many library administrators will chose to continue to encourage use of the unique print resources they have in their possession, whatever the format. This is especially true for the novice researcher, who may believe that anything and everything of value is already online.

Better Research through Doing Less

"The student turned loose in a huge library finds the librarian an incarnate index, an ever avail-

able guide, philosopher, and friend" (Stead, 1901, preface).

We began by asking what can be offered to bridge the space between the traditional practice of introductory reference and the advance of vast aggregation systems linking to terabytes of full text documents. Put differently, are the recent deployments of new library Information Systems, which are designed to largely *disintermediate* the interaction between librarian and researcher, producing better research?

It is suggested by some librarians that deploying large-scale, single search discovery services more closely meets the expectations of today's Web-savvy novice researcher or student. This may prove to be true, especially for those libraries which support large undergraduate populations. However, while impressive in scope and speed, there is not enough information available yet on how (or if) they will improve research.

In the same way as an OPAC can identify nearly all the works a library possess, an even larger discovery service can show even more data to a user. But the question remains, will bringing even more of the library's holdings to the attention of a library user put the user in a position to really *understand* what is being presented to them? Do they systems truly obviate basic bibliographic awareness regarding the *process* of good research, let alone obviate the librarian?

This is relevant because what is often lost in discussions of library technology is the experience of the novice researcher—the untrained researcher or the trained researcher encountering a new area of study for the first time. We have discussed the many ways in which the use of subject encyclopedias assists the novice research or non-specialist. They provide the basic terms and themes of a topic. They present the *established* or *vetted* positions on a topic. They provide a pathway toward continued research beyond the article itself, and, in the best of cases, spare the

user time spent searching fruitless for something that doesn't exist.

History repeats itself, and we see, as Stead suggests, that the researcher is, once again "let loose in a huge library." Today the notion of a library extends far beyond the walls of physical library itself to technology interchanges designed to offer access to vast amounts of data. In this environment, what are the research success prospects for a researcher exposed to *terabytes* of scholarly information *without* a librarian to assist?

It is at this point that the argument for the wider use and application of the rich introductory material of subject encyclopedias, written by specialists, offers the contemporary researcher the most hope. Instead of offering the researcher more data, scholarly introductions offer the prospect of *less*. Less data, but fully vetted by specialists, which in terms saves the researcher time.

They winnow the field, highlight a few quality works for continued research, and warn against fruitless queries. They nearly do what a trained librarian would do, gently guide the novice down a path to a successful project, thesis or something more. By aggregating and disseminating the contents of a library's subject encyclopedia collection, through the various technologies discussed here, the prospects for even better research in the digital age are much improved.

REFERENCES

Agosto, D. E., Rozaklis, L., MacDonald, C., & Abels, E. (2010). Barriers and challenges to teaching reference in today's electronic information environment. *Journal of Education for Library and Information Science, 51*(3), 177–186.

Cook, W. R. (2004). Assisi. In Kleinhenz, C. (Ed.), *Medieval Italy: An encyclopedia*. New York, NY: Routledge.

CrossRef. (2011). DOI Resolver. Retrieved May 18, 2011, from http://www.crossref.org.

Fletcher, W.I., Hartford Connecticut. (1883). Letters. *Library Journal, 8,* 73–74.

Hellman, E. (2010, May 30). Book expo, digital book 2010, and e-book messes. Retrieved from http://go-to-hellman.blogspot.com/2010_05_01_archive.html

Hysell, S. (2010, November 16). Telephone interview.

Kister, K. F. (Ed.). (1986). *Best Encyclopedias: A guide to general and specialized encyclopedias.* Phoenix, AZ: Oryx Press.

Mann, T. (2005). *Oxford guide to library research.* Oxford, UK: Oxford University Press.

Miller, S. (2008). *Encyclopedia Indexes in the digital age.* Unpublished Manuscript.

Mirwis, A. N. (1999). *Subject encyclopedias: User guide, review citations and keyword index.* Phoenix, AZ: Oryx Press.

Paskin, N. (2010). Digital object identifier (DOI®) system. In Bates, M., & Maack, M. N. (Eds.), *Encyclopedia of library and information sciences* (3rd ed.). Boca Raton, FL: CRC Press.

Ryan, J. (Ed.). (1989). *First stop: The master index to subject encyclopedias.* Phoenix, AZ: Oryx Press.

Stead, W. T. (Ed.). (1901). *Review of Reviews: index to the periodicals of 1901.* London, NY: Review of Reviews.

Wynar, B. S. (Ed.). (1986). *ARBA: Guide to subject encyclopedias and dictionaries.* Littleton, CO: Libraries Unlimited.

Young, J. (2006, June 12). Wikipedia founder discourages academic use of his creation. *The Chronicle of Higher Education.* Retrieved from http://chronicle.com/blogs/wiredcampus/wikipedia-founder-discourages-academic-use-of-his-creation/2305

ENDNOTES

[1] *The Nation*; April 1883. Reprinted in *Library Journal,* May, 1883. The full quote is here *"No more can we, who have made indexing the field for the exercise of our best energies, and find in it ample scope for all our powers and all possible culture and scholarship, consider inoffensive the suggestion that it is mere hackwork, drudgery, convict labor. But it is not the offensiveness to us indexers of such a suggestion that I would make most prominent or ask your space to point out. It is rather the fact that it voices one of the rankest literary heresies of the age—namely, the idea that anybody can make an index if he only knows the alphabet."* These quotations are taken from a war of words played out within the Letters section of *The Nation.* They were initiated by a librarian (later discovered to be William Hand Browne, the librarian at Johns Hopkins University) commenting on the recent publication by Dr. William Frederick Poole's *Index to Periodical Literature.* The skirmish was later reprinted in *Library Journal.* Dr. Poole, who's seminal *Index* was only then becoming prominent among librarians and other 'men of letters, raised the discussion of increasing access to periodical and other literature, as a valuable aid to scholarship and research. Browne was apparently having some fun with Poole. He further wrote, *"let all convicts who can read and write, be set, under competent supervision, to <u>indexing books</u>; and let those who cannot, receive the necessary instruction as soon as may be. That kind of labor proposed is peculiarly suited to the reformatory idea, being incomparable for teaching order; patience; humility; and for thoroughly eradicating the last trace of the Old Adam in whoever pursues it."* Poole's response, published in the following issues of *The Nation,* unmasked the anonymous

writer who criticized his work, but also addressed the criticism with an intensity and humor appropriate to the whole episode: *"To cast odium or ridicule on work so useful to students and literary men as the indexing of books was the last thing which one would occur to so good a man. It seems, therefore, that for once Mr. Browne wanted to be funny; and his success was that of the elephant who attempted to dance a hornpipe. We accept the explanation, and record it among the curiosities of humor."*

2   Phone interview with Shannon Hysell, Senior Editor, *American Reference Books Annual (ARBA)*. Ms. Hysell indicated that, since 1997 approximately 8,500 subject encyclopedias and similar scholarly compendia have been received by ARBA for review.

3   Paratext's own *Reference Universe* service employs a proprietary system to match any libraries holdings to the *Reference Universe* bibliography. These matches also matched against *Books in Print* from Bowker. Our non-exhaustive analysis indicates that specialized reference works cost libraries, on average, approximately $300 a volume. This aggregates single-volume titles as well as multi-volume sets. Electronic equivalents may involve even higher costs, if the titles are 'leased' or subscribed to, rather than acquired outright by the library.

4   Agosto *et.al.*, deserves scrutiny by those interested in the role of traditional finding aids, as well as diminished role that the teaching of traditional reference sources has within a substantial sampling of the 57 ALA-accredited LIS programs. One respondent to a survey summed it up this way: *I totally agree that you're right in the sense that [keyword searching] solves most needs, but I feel that part of my responsibility as an educator is the help this future generation. That is what they get a master's degree for. Having that heritage of what the development of these tools is and [knowing] the history and the rich work and dedication through brought them to this place where they can have all these online tools is part of what graduate education is."*

5   Current statistics of the usage of *Reference Universe* among libraries indicates that the typical library possesses 8 print subject encyclopedias on any given topic to one in electronic form, as of May, 2011.

Chapter 15
Open Web Capture for Libraries:
Reinventing Subject Encyclopedias for the Open Web

John G. Dove
Credo Reference, USA

Ingrid Becker
Credo Reference, USA

ABSTRACT

One of the principle purposes of reference, especially subject encyclopedias, is to facilitate a new learner's approach to a field of study by providing context and vocabulary for the effective use of the rest of the library. Some have even referred to the subject encyclopedia as the "Rolls Royce of the Library" (East, 2010). With the economic pressures on libraries and the dramatic changes in usage patterns brought on by the shift from print to electronic content, subject encyclopedias must be re-invented if they are to embody their intended function. While print reference has been overshadowed by information on the Web, studies on student research habits show that the need for context, which reference provides, is higher than ever before. This chapter will argue for the contemporary relevance of the subject encyclopedia in response to student research needs in the information age and explore current and possible visions for the transformation of the subject encyclopedia to suit digital media and the open Web in particular.

INTRODUCTION

David Kronick, a librarian and information scientist in the 1970s, introduced the distinction between "primary" and "secondary" sources in academic work (McArthur, 1986). Others later added "tertiary" to handle the differences between commentary ("secondary") and summary or overview sources. Most reference works, such as subject encyclopedias, subject dictionaries, or biographical dictionaries are either "secondary" or "tertiary." Entries in reference books are distinctive from other types of sources for a number of reasons: they are atomic, self-contained; they

DOI: 10.4018/978-1-61350-308-9.ch015

are, by design, easily digestible in a discrete amount of time; and they are often linked by cross-references to other entries and by citations to further resources, providing an excellent launch point for a learner's inquiry.

The transition from print to electronic content means that print subject encyclopedias have been overshadowed by the vast array of information available online. Most of us are familiar with a sense of being overwhelmed that is symptomatic of internet use. "Information overload" is a frequent frustration for anyone searching the open Web. Social networking expert Clay Shirky (2008) points out, however, that since the invention of the Gutenberg Press there has been more information available to any one person than he or she can possibly consume in a lifetime. Some even argue that information overload existed much earlier (Blair, 2010). In any case, this advent of indigestible amounts of information has forced society to develop various filtering methods to narrow the field of information to that most relevant to the learner. Shirky gives the example of a spam filter on an email client. He also points out that despite our efforts the spam keeps coming, forcing us to reconfigure our filters again and again. Confronted by the transmission of information that the Internet allows, traditional filtering methods are breaking down. What we are dealing with is not information overload, but what Shirky calls "filter failure." The solution to the problem of filter failure does not lie in merely tweaking the filters currently available, but in creating new structures specifically adapted to the Web (Shirky, 2008).

The subject encyclopedia acts as a kind of information filter. The traditional print encyclopedia facilitates learning for someone new to a field, who can browse through headings, as well as the expert, who can go directly to content with a high degree of specificity or learn about an unfamiliar portion of their field. A given entry is crafted by authors and editors to accommodate a prescribed audience level of depth and coverage, so that only the most important aspects of the topic are covered. The electronic encyclopedia, although it can be browsed in the manner of a static e-book, is currently designed the way the rest of the Web is designed: to be searchable with keywords and linkable with links. This format does filter out entries that are less relevant to the inquiry term. However, it is likely to confuse the exploratory researcher, who does not yet know what she is searching for.

Subject encyclopedias are being re-envisioned and re-deployed for use on the free Web to the benefit of students and other end users. Subject encyclopedias have the potential to relieve confusion caused by "filter failure," information overload, and other difficulties that face researchers today. In order to accomplish this, these books need to be reconfigured and revitalized for a new online digital life. Electronic subject encyclopedias must retain their ability to supply a learner with appropriate levels of context and guidance for specific stages of inquiry while migrating to the open Web.

The rest of this chapter begins by discussing the state of subject encyclopedias and academic research in the digital age, highlighting student use of the open Web, especially Wikipedia, and drawing out the challenges presented to researchers during this process. The authors describe how subject encyclopedias can help address these challenges and propose some ways in which subject encyclopedias are being reinvented in order to do so. Examples of current models for this reinvention are identified, and the chapter concludes with an exploration of future development and research opportunities.

THE VALUE OF SUBJECT ENCYCLOPEDIAS

Twenty-five years ago, most academic research was carried out within the confines of the physical library, or with the use of print resources obtained directly from the library. The traditional value of subject encyclopedias is evident in their treatment in print libraries of the past. Academic libraries have always retained certain books on reserve. Some have used the term "reference books" to describe any book that was *so valuable* to *so many people* that they were *permanently on reserve* and not allowed to circulate outside of the library. Subject encyclopedias typically were, and sometimes still are, among the titles on permanent reserve.

Throughout the twentieth century, these encyclopedias grew in popularity and were published more intensively, attaining multiple levels of specialization and diversity of topic (East, 2010). Since then, however, the nearly ubiquitous shift to digital information of many types—ejournals, ebooks, newspapers, and e-reference—has been accompanied by significant changes in the research habits and information literacy skills of all searchers and researchers. We are now capable of indexing and storing resources on a scale larger than anything the space of a physical library could hold. In this increasingly digital research environment, what is the current value and state of vetted reference? In an age where so many researchers turn to free content on the Web, is there a place for the subject encyclopedia? Or, to state the question more severely, is reference dead?

There is plenty of support for the idea that traditional forms of reference, broadly defined, are outdated and facing complete renovation. Given the scale of university full time enrollment, for example, face-to-face reference interviews can no longer be the only form of instruction. The ratio of students to librarians means that only a tiny fraction of a given student body can be guided in this manner. While reference interviews are still worthwhile, changing circumstances require that reference services adapt. Indeed, the emergence of reference interviews conducted via chat, email, or text attests to the creative capabilities of reference to re-invent itself for the digital age. Electronic formats present a whole slew of opportunities: "Reference works are finding a home online because the technology permits mind-bending

integration of databases that you can't do in print" (Beam, 2011).

John East (2010), in his recent essay "The Rolls Royce of the Library Reference Collection," emphasizes the need for a reinvention of the subject encyclopedia for an online research context. He claims that the content of subject encyclopedias is, even now, of great import, pointing out that these texts are still produced and purchased in large numbers. East notes that 66 such titles were reviewed in *Reference User Services Quarterly* in 2009, averaging nearly $270 each, while 63 were reviewed in 1999. These figures suggest that even as digital collections become more and more essential, print encyclopedias remain consistently valuable to libraries. Of the 66 titles reviewed in 2009, 45 were also available digitally on e-reference platforms: the reference industry is actively working to keep pace with the changing research habits of their readers. A number of reference aggregators have emerged over the past decade, including Credo Reference, Gale Virtual Reference Library, STATREF, Knovel, as well as reference platforms from prolific reference publishers such as Sage Reference Online, Oxford Reference Online, and many others. Some of the innovations include visual browsing tools, interlinking among different reference sources, and outbound linking to other library and Web resources. Despite the provision of these resources via libraries' websites, students are by and large beginning their research somewhere else: on the open Web.

A 2005 OCLC study of international scope investigated the tendency of "information consumers," including academic users and the general public, to pursue information through a wide range of avenues. Of particular interest is the primacy of open Web search: users making a reference query and a restaurant reservation begin in the same space. The study found that 84% of survey respondents began an information search with a search engine on the open Web; just 1% began on a library website (Connaway & Dickey,

2010). A related 2006 study surveying only college students found that they were twice as likely to have used library websites and e-journals as the general public. When asked, however, about where they began an information search the results were strikingly consistent: 2% started out on their library websites, compared to 89% who reported they started with search engine queries. This data suggests that although library websites are perceived as useful and are frequently engaged as study tools, students do not use them as kick-off points for their research.

Library websites and OPACs are competing with search engines. Reference books, and subject encyclopedias in particular, are likewise competing with Wikipedia. Many arguments can be and are made about the benefits of electronic subject encyclopedias compared to Wikipedia: one is vetted by experts and authoritative publishers, and the other is vetted by the collective knowledge of a collaborating readership; one is citable in academic papers, while citation of the other is discouraged; one focuses on pre-defined audiences of specific levels and specific subjects, while the other has a more general purpose; one is often obscured by the barriers of logins and firewalls, while the other is one click away from Google. Both, admittedly, have their benefits. Yet Wikipedia, it will be shown, is used more frequently. It is also used in response to research needs that a subject encyclopedia is better designed, and can be even better redesigned, to fulfill.

If vetted subject encyclopedias are underused, it is not necessarily because researchers have found suitable substitutes. Subject encyclopedias are simply less visible, less discoverable, to students. The research needs and behaviors of students are also less visible to libraries, making it more challenging for librarians to adapt their resources to the digital age. This mutual opacity is caused by the migration of students out of traditional library spaces. They retrieve information on their mobile devices and write papers on laptops in coffee shops, park benches, and in their pajamas. They are not in the library, and they are not regularly visiting their library's website (Connaway & Dickey, 2010). They are unaware of many of the benefits the library has to offer.

THE PROBLEM OF GETTING STARTED: SUBJECT ENCYCLOPEDIAS AND CONTEXTS

A recent series of studies, conducted by Alison Head and Michael Eisenberg of the Information School at the University of Washington, explore user behavior at different stages of both "course-related" and "every-day life" research. Their ongoing investigation Project Information Literacy (PIL) examines the challenges that arise during a Web search and the solution-oriented strategies that users consequently develop. They present strong evidence of what some would deem a surprising paradox, given the amount of wireless information at our fingertips: "Research seems to be far more difficult to conduct in the digital age than it did in previous times" (Eisenberg & Head, 2009, p. 2). The beginning of the research process was reported to be the most difficult:

For over three-fourths (84%) of the students surveyed, the most difficult step of the course-related research process was getting started. Defining a topic (66%), narrowing it down (62%), and filtering through irrelevant results (61%) frequently hampered students in the sample, too. Follow-up interviews suggest students lacked the research acumen for framing an inquiry in the digital age where information abounds and intellectual discovery was paradoxically overwhelming for them. (Eisenberg & Head, 2010b, p. 2)

These early steps of the research process—defining a topic, narrowing it down, and filtering through irrelevant results—are the same starting points at which students tend to use search engines. The challenge of research in the digital age is related, then, to the disparity between the needs of these students and the functions of metasearch. The long list of results returned by a search engine requires additional work on the part of the user to narrow it down—in other words, it requires the "research acumen" mentioned above. Researchers unfamiliar with a topic lack filters, or research acumen, adequate to the task of gathering and organizing reliable information at the right level for their inquiry. To compensate, many open Web researchers seek out quick, convenient resources where some sort of additional filter has already been applied.

In a further study, Head and Eisenberg (2010a) polled undergraduates about their Wikipedia use. They found that students turned to Wikipedia to help them overcome the first, and biggest, hurdle in the research process. PIL recounts that 76% of students used Wikipedia because *it helps to get them started on a research paper.* A weighty 82% claimed they used it to "obtain a summary," and 67% used it to gain an understanding of the relevant vocabulary. Wikipedia was labeled by one student as a "presearch tool" used to delineate a topic (Eisenberg & Head, 2010a). Interestingly, the most pervasive reasons for Wikipedia use correspond almost exactly to what we can imagine as solutions to the most difficult steps in the research process. A student having trouble defining a topic for a course paper can go to Wikipedia to have it summarized, discovery related terms, and find links to related information. Lim (2009) found that over the course of a semester, a far larger percentage of college students used Wikipedia with frequency than reported that they used their library database with frequency.

These studies show that students on the open Web turn to Wikipedia to fill a crucial space in their research tool kit. Subject encyclopedias, however, have the potential to be far more powerful instruments. To demonstrate that this is the case, a more specific investigation of the challenges facing contemporary undergraduate researchers is necessary. PIL has determined several major

reasons for user frustration during course-related research, including: a lack of context under which students carry on research; a failure to find desired resources; and an inability to access found materials (Eisenberg & Head, 2009). At the risk of simplification, we can restate the issue in terms of three key steps of the online research process: contextualization, discovery, and delivery. The last of these is an important issue for libraries to focus on, but it will not be addressed in the scope of this chapter. Discovery can be significantly improved by the reinvention of reference on the open Web, which will be discussed below. We will deal first and foremost with the issue of context, since the most important role of the subject encyclopedia as intermediary manifests itself here.

Context is "a key to understanding how students operationalize and prioritize their...research activities" (Eisenberg & Head, 2009, p. 5). Contextualization was continually cited by surveyed students "as the most laborious, yet requisite, part of the research process" (Eisenberg & Head, 2009, p. 5). Based on the striking frequency of such a response, Head and Eisenberg develop a typology of contexts, the lack of which limit information literacy skills of the researcher and hinder her discovery of useful resources. Two of these contexts are especially relevant here: the "big picture context," and the "language context."

Big picture context, according to Head and Eisenberg, is characterized by an understanding of the boundaries that define a topic, the various perspectives within this topic, and how the topic is related to a more expansive field, e.g. the course curriculum. Big picture context facilitates the early stage of "synthesizing and delineating a topic" (Eisenberg & Head, 2009, p. 6). It imparts knowledge of how and where to start research and of the right questions to be asking of resources. It is often most essential for undergraduates writing their first few essays for an introductory course. The lack of big picture context can be held largely responsible for the challenging nature of early stages of research.

Language context is also a requirement for students navigating the information field of a subject. Language context, a guide to "what things are called and what they mean" (Eisenberg & Head, 2009, p. 8) situates a learner within the professional vocabulary, defining key terms and demystifying technical jargon. Without this context, a student can be entirely misdirected in their approach to the literature afforded by the various journal databases and e-book collections of their library. For example, the novice health student who does not know that "myocardial infarction" is another word for heart attack will not recognize many useful articles. When asked where students get stuck, librarians will often respond that students get lost when, ignorant of a new subject's language context, they guess at keywords. Then they cannot properly assess the returned results, or they miss seeing results which would have been the most appropriate for their topic of interest.

Context is in demand, a demand which Wikipedia fulfills, but only to a limited extent. Subject encyclopedias are far better prepared to provide big picture and language contexts. They offer a number of benefits that Wikipedia does not. Firstly, they are backed by the authority of recognized experts and respected academic publishers. Most students are aware of Wikipedia's weakness in this regard: only 17% of students polled by PIL valued Wikipedia because it was more credible than other sources available online. Therefore, they are not choosing it because of its guaranteed expertise. In fact, most students recognize that it is not acceptable to their professors or institutions, and do not cite Wikipedia articles on academic papers even if they visited the site (Eisenberg & Head, 2010a). If students have had positive experiences with Wikipedia, they still question its reliability, expecting to find reasonably good information rather than the best or most trustworthy information (Lim, 2009). Subject encyclopedias are also well equipped to provide key contexts because a given title has been selected by a user's

librarian to suit a distinctive institution, program, and degree level. Students who consult librarians during the research process are actually less likely to use Wikipedia. They cited librarians, especially reference librarians, as "sense-makers" helping them to navigate and contextualize the resources at hand (Eisenberg & Head, 2009). By providing the big picture and language contexts, as well as being sensitive to a range of audiences, subject encyclopedias are also a kind of "sense-makers."

Authoritative subject encyclopedias are put together by editors who have access to the leading thinkers and educators within a particular field, scholars with a whole life devoted to topical study. These subject encyclopedias are meant to serve as a guide to the landscape, the schools of thought, and the boundaries of research in the field. They are constructed with a view to the needs of users with limited knowledge of their content, and their purpose is to orient these readers in relation to this and other relevant content. They are facilitative intermediaries between a researcher and the body of knowledge of a field, crafted to be at just the right level of depth and scope to save the time and effort of researchers.

Given the many benefits of subject encyclopedias and their presence in the majority of electronic library collections, why do so many students still choose Wikipedia? Recall that 89% of college students began searches, including academic ones, on the open Web. Students who use Google are 10 times more likely to use Wikipedia to serve their course-related research needs (Eisenberg & Head, 2010a). Most students reach Wikipedia via Google rather than a bookmark (Lim, 2009). The connection with Wikipedia to search engines is very strong. Equipped with this knowledge, librarians and publishers can reinvent the subject encyclopedia, repurposing it for the space of search engines to connect students with the deeper information of the library.

SOLUTIONS AND RECOMMENDATIONS

An effort to increase the discoverability of library resources is evident in the development of tools both inside and outside the library. Although discovery initiatives that work only inside the library will not reach the user at her point of need, a few are worth mentioning as attempts to improve the discoverability of subject encyclopedias: a suggestion that reference publishers make more extensive use of DOI at the entry level; Reference Universe, a service that indexes reference headwords; and the inclusion of reference content on Web scale discovery services.

DOIs, or Digital Object Identifiers, are intended to provide consistent and persistent digital identifications of content. At a meeting of the RUSA Reference Publisher Advisory Committee at ALA Midwinter 2010, a suggestion was made that having DOIs assigned to entries of reference works would facilitate the inclusion of links to such content in catalogs and other discovery systems of a library. One barrier mentioned was the cost to the publisher of purchasing so many DOIs for a single work. While this idea might be practical and useful for some reference books, such as biographical dictionaries or collections of professional papers, it is questionable whether DOI assignments to every entry of a subject encyclopedia would actually be useful to the end user.

Another option is to index the headwords of reference entries. Paratext takes this approach with its product, Reference Universe. The service indexes the headwords of almost 30,000 reference works, both print and electronic. Through a search in Reference Universe a user can discover reference entries and get links to those hosted electronically or get pointed to the print book at her institution's library. Yet even within the library, a wider net can be cast to uncover entries in subject encyclopedias.

Recently developed Web scale discovery services are made to provide "deep discovery within a vast ocean of content" (Vaughan, 2011, p. 5). Services such as Serials Solutions Summon, EBSCO Discovery Services, and Ex Libris Primo Central allow researchers to search, in a single box, up to over half a billion items of content, including reference books, journal articles, monographs, audio files, and many others. Results offer users an awareness of what exists in their local libraries as well as in libraries around the world.

These are tremendous achievements for improved discovery, but they do not address some important research needs. Firstly, the user searching a library's catalog or discovery tool still has to know where on the Web to begin—although these services show the reader what resources exist at their disposal, the reader must first know that these services exist in the first place. This is not only a contemporary challenge: in 1961 Ranganathan noted that "many readers are not aware of the existence of encyclopedias in subjects of such narrow extension. They have to be brought to their notice by the reference librarian" (Ranganathan, 1961, p. 277). While a library might have a great discovery tool, how will the discovery tool itself get discovered when many students are not consulting librarians at all? What all of these in-the-library initiatives miss out on is the key challenge and opportunity presented by positioning reference content at the point of need of the user. This point is outside the library, outside the firewall, and in places where the students do not know about their library's systems and capabilities: on the open Web. Ideally, the electronic subject encyclopedia entry would be discoverable on the first page of a Google search or cited in Wikipedia, attracting the attention of researchers who didn't even know they were looking for it.

In addition, while discovery tools focused on better searches of the catalog can successfully link students to library resources, they do not provide the much-needed contexts previously discussed. Summon, for example, searches across both full-text and metadata, returning, by default, results sorted by accessibility from the user's library and by relevancy. The user has the option to expand results to additional libraries or limit results by specifying content type, publication date, language, etc. (Vaughan, 2011). Algorithms for surfacing the most appropriate items are constantly being improved, and one can anticipate that some of these discovery tools will see the advantages of displaying reference content separately and prominently in query results so that students can get the contexts they need for effective research.

A distinction between two types of searches is helpful here. The first is a search for a known item, for example a specific article that a student is aware of and hopes to read. In this case, Web scale discovery is an excellent tool, and provided the discovery service has indexed the article, it will be able to locate this text for the student immediately. However, there is also the type of search this chapter has been discussing: an exploratory search conducted by a student who doesn't know exactly what she is looking for. Such a student can find the results returned by discovery tools overwhelming. To make an analogy, if metasearch is sometimes a drink from a fire hose, a Web scale discovery service might feel to such a student like a drink from 100 fire hoses at once.

It is useful to imagine multiple domains of the discovery process, each with its own problems and possibilities for growth. The local catalog comprises the smallest sphere of discovery, even though its content is in fact some of the most important for students to discover. In the next sphere we have Web scale discovery services. Another, wider sphere is the entire open Web and its search engines. How can students entering a keyword in a Google search box be led to resources of their local library? More specifically, how can a subject encyclopedia provide a seamless pathway from search engine results into a *contextualized* database of scholarly literature?

The idea of using subject encyclopedia entries on the open Web to draw users into libraries is very new. Even so, there is some evidence that points to the success of similar practices. Google,

a 2009 study found, is a key discovery tool for e-journal articles, which usually contain specialized information, that is, information needed *after* the surrounding contexts are understood by a researcher. Monitoring e-journal use in the UK, the study reported that one third of the traffic to Elsevier ScienceDirect over a four month period came from Google, as did over half of the traffic to Oxford Journals over the span of a year (Connaway & Dickey, 2010). JSTOR, too, has collaborated with Google Scholar to increase the visibility of full-text content available to the subscribing user (JSTORNEWS, 2010). By opening up the discovery of their journals to Google, these platforms attracted open Web searchers who might not have otherwise known such a resource was even available.

Search engines can also be used to draw users into OPACs. WorldCat Local, for instance, forged a deal with Google in 2008 that "helps expose WorldCat records within a Google Book search, and expose Google digitized books within WorldCat" (Vaughan, 2011, p. 18). The first of these functions takes the form of a link on a "Get this Book" list labeled "Find in a library." Other links in the list are usually websites for purchase, but this link directs the user to WorldCat and thus, her local libraries. A user, for example a freshman writing her first college-level research paper,, unaware of WorldCat's existence, can begin her search on Google and end up in her library's catalog in just a few clicks.

These are both promising efforts to drive users into libraries. But in each case students can be drawn into the midst of professional literature that they are unequipped to handle. If the article that the user found on Google was a reference entry that provided her with context as well as discovery options, she would be able to optimize the potential of her library website with better keywords, assess e-journal content with alacrity, and overall conduct a less frustrating and more fulfilling search. The challenge here is to reinvent the subject encyclopedia so that it exists in the open Web but is programmed with the expertise of university librarians.

Credo Reference "Topic Pages," released in 2010, exemplify one possible approach. Credo is an online reference service with a multi-publisher platform. It describes a Topic Page as "an all-in-one starting point for students to begin their research process [that combines] quality resources, images and videos, and additional library resources to promote information literacy and improve research effectiveness" (Credo Reference, 2010). These pages, built dynamically, are composed of three main components that exist in the realm of the open Web. First, the page features a full exposition and definition of the term or phrase from authoritative content from subject dictionaries and subject encyclopedias, which Credo and its partner publishers have agreed to use in this manner. Secondly, it creates links to open Web resources such as images, news, and video, many of which are geographically localized sources. Thirdly, for users who are identified as subscribers to Credo's service, a set of dynamically selected results from any of more than 600 popular library databases and electronic resources will appear. Topic pages are customizable, so that librarians at subscribing institutions choose which resources show up, and are able to choose them by their appropriateness to the subject area a given topic lies within. If the user is not connected to a library already, Topic Pages locate and suggest nearby libraries, allowing the user to identify these or others to which they would prefer to be linked.

Topic Pages are designed specifically for the user beginning her research. They are built to provide big picture and language contexts and direct the user towards further resources. They are also designed to meet the user at her point of need, appearing on the open Web where she is likely to be looking. Because they are customizable, Topic Pages display resources that a librarian has chosen for a particular audience level, program, or even course: they contextualize resources at the moment a student clicks from Google to an entry link. A

user experience for a student on a laptop in the Medical Education Library at Northern Virginia Community College will then be very different from that of student doing an MFA in Fashion and Society at Parsons at The New School of Design in Manhattan. These library resources are two clicks away from a Google results page, and bring the user as seamlessly as possible from the open Web to the library. Credo has nearly 10,000 Topic Pages and these numbers are growing. This is an encouraging model of a re-invented subject encyclopedia; reliable reference information appears where most students pose their first research queries, and provides the context as well as the gateway for them to continue on to their specific library with its specifically chosen resources.

Oxford Bibliographies Online is another reference product that, by putting some of its content on the free Web, can draw users into libraries. Although O.B.O. is not a subject encyclopedia per se, it performs a similar role, and is worth mentioning here. In addition, any discussion of ways to reconfigure the subject encyclopedia for the Web demands openness to genre overlaps and transformations. O.B.O. describes itself as "a starting point for organizing a research plan, preparing a writing assignment, or creating a syllabus" (Oxford University Press, 2011). Like Credo Topic Pages, this product seeks to meet the beginning researcher at the point of need and guide her into the library and towards relevant scholarly content. Like an entry in a subject encyclopedia, these bibliographies are designed to help contextualize research. Open Web content consists of a brief summary of the topic, followed by a list of annotated resources, orienting a researcher within the literature. Subscribers can click through from search engine results to a guide to scholarship and right on to their library's catalog. O.B.O., however, does not give just-in-time results, nor can it be customized based on the skill level or institution of its user.

Re-inventing the subject encyclopedia may also involve using Wikipedia itself to increase discovery. Wikipedia's citation feature allows contributing authors to direct readers to published sources, including reference content. Casper Grathwohl of Oxford University Press, in a panel at the Annual Charleston Conference in 2010, recounted an instance in 2006 where OUP noticed a significant increase in the traffic to Grove Music Online. Seeking the reason for this, the publisher determined the likely cause: an academic had made a suggestion to the American Musicological Society listserv that musicologists contribute to Wikipedia in an effort to get the best information possible to learners on the subject. This catalyzed many conversations on the listserv, including the proposal of an imperative that faculty make Wikipedia contribution a part of their curricula. *The Grove Dictionary of Music* is a key subject encyclopedia for musicologists, and Grove Music Online already had a high level of traffic; still, following the creation of more citations on Wikipedia, traffic saw an increase of 43% over a 12-month period.

This example calls into question Wikipedia's principle to "strive for articles that advocate no single point of view" ("Wikipedia: Five Pillars," 2011). Do experts have a bias in directing users to specific published materials? On the other hand, as user-generated content Wikipedia should provide high quality peer-reviewed reading for seekers of knowledge. Whether the Wikipedia community will approve of such measures is yet to be determined, but the musicologists' success in directing readers to a subject encyclopedia is an exciting example of a way that free, user-generated content can cooperate with vetted reference.

Birds of North America, a project run by the Cornell Ornithology Lab, is also worthy of note as subject encyclopedia re-invented; it carves out an electronic space where both experts and the general public can collaborate on the creation and recreation of reference content. The print encyclopedia is 18 volumes. The online community of subscribers that contributes photos, corrects species accounts, and generates its own conver-

sations around the subject enlarges the scope of the text much further. Birds of North America is a specialized resource that may not be particularly useful to most undergraduates, but its dual format of content generated by users and experts should be considered as a model for other online subject encyclopedias.

These examples, taken together, outline some desirable methods of recreating electronic reference to fulfill the research needs of students. In summary, the Web-adapted subject encyclopedia should have the following properties: visibility on the open Web, just-in-time results that can be tailored using librarian input to accurately match the workflow of the student, an intuitive interface with seamless linkage to library websites and resources, content created collaboratively by experts and learners wishing to participate in the dissemination of knowledge, and, like a traditional print subject encyclopedia, the ability to provide context to the exploring student.

FUTURE RESEARCH DIRECTIONS

The role of the subject encyclopedia in Web capture as a part of information discovery and contextualization is only beginning to be fulfilled. By promoting reference on the open Web, the information is presented at the point of need of the user, appearing when they want context and subject-specific vocabulary. One librarian names the current generation of students the "Information Now Generation" (Jacobs, 2009). Researchers of today expect to get information when they need it, wherever they are. Access to subject encyclopedias on the open Web is just the first step here. E-reference platforms need to be available as mobile applications, so that students can search subject encyclopedias when they are inspired on the walk from a lecture to their dorm, on a bus or train or even at a party.

Gale's *AccessMyLibrary* application for mobile phones (Android, iPhone, iTouch, and iPad) allows users to search for libraries within a 10-mile radius of their current geographical location. Users can then access information about the library or search any electronic resources Gale services for these local libraries. It would represent a big step in the reinvention of the subject encyclopedia if all publishers and aggregators made e-reference platforms available as mobile apps.

The development of new platforms and applications are often driven by research studies, which can offer many new insights on the needs of users. ProQuest sponsored the Head and Eisenberg studies of undergraduates at a wide variety of academic institutions, which have delivered many insights about the challenges facing today's students. A great follow-on study would be extending the investigation of current research practices along the lines of what Peter Pirolli (2007) proposes in his book *Information Foraging Theory*. By researching the information gathering behaviors of the best performing students, and contrasting them with the behaviors of average students, it might be possible to determine a set of successful behaviors that could be encouraged by online reference systems to the benefit of all students.

Other exciting possibilities include developing discovery tools that act like the reference librarian with the knowledge of where or who the user is. Google can detect a lot of information about users, their preferences, and their needs. The search engine knows what places a user likes to travel to, what types of restaurants she likes, what health issues she has, whether she is a student or a professional, and many other details. All of this data is used to provide better results to one's queries in the Google search box. Yet a reference librarian has knowledge of the student's specific research needs that Google doesn't.

One can envision a reference service that acts like Google tailored ads, discovering data about its users in order to provide them with information they don't even know they are looking for. This would require capturing librarians' expert knowledge about the best resources for a particular subject, degree level, or even course. Imagine encyclopedia entries acting as Web-based "adwords" that suggest the most appropriate resources for a certain set of college students based on the recommendations of their college's librarians. Instead of a company advertising its product on Google, librarians could advertise the resources of libraries on entries discoverable by Google. In a sense, that is what Credo Reference Topic Pages are doing today.

CONCLUSION

Students conducting academic research in the digital age face more challenges than ever before. These new difficulties are related to the amount of largely unfiltered information available on the Web. In response, students have developed research strategies that include high usage of search engines and Wikipedia. Although students do not regard information from Wikipedia to be the best available, it is easy for them to find and helps them with the most difficult part of the research process: getting started.

Librarians are also facing new challenges. The rapid rate of shift from print to electronic resources have allowed libraries to index hundreds of millions of items of content across different media, but making this information visible to researchers is an ongoing effort. Librarians, publishers, and vendors have themselves developed strategies for web discovery and instruction to try and serve students outside the library, but still have trouble reaching them at their point of need.

Subject encyclopedias, because they provide essential contexts for understanding, represent a space where the needs of students and the expertise of librarians intersect. Electronic subject encyclopedias with content on the open Web, searched by Google and cited on Wikipedia, represent a space where the open Web strategies of students and of librarians also come together. Students can get the contexts they need to get started on their research, and librarians can get resources for further study discovered.

Credo Reference Topic Pages and similar tools presented by other library vendors empower librarians to apply their subject knowledge to the academic search environment of their end users. The result is beginning to uncover new and exciting opportunities to facilitate undergraduate research. Electronic subject encyclopedias will look different in the future – entries may have sections where experts and amateurs alike can collaborate in the dissemination of knowledge, or may even pop up on search engine home pages like advertisements – but as long as they guide researchers into a contextualized field, they will retain their fundamental value.

REFERENCES

Beam, A. (2011, January 28). The definition of change. *The Boston Globe*. Retrieved from http://www.boston.com/lifestyle/articles/2011/01/28/a_word_about_dictionaries_and_other_reference_books__in_print_and_online/

Blair, A. (2010). *Too much to know: Managing scholarly information before the modern age*. New Haven, CT: Yale University Press.

Connaway, L. S., Dickey, T. J., & OCLC Research. (2010). *The digital information seeker: Report of the findings from selected OCLC, RIN, and JISC user behaviour projects*. Retrieved January 5, 2011, from http://www.jisc.ac.uk/media/documents/publications/ reports/2010/digitalinformationseekerreport.pdf

East, J. (2010). "The Rolls Royce of the library reference collection": The subject encyclopedia in the age of Wikipedia. *RUSQ, 50*(2). Retrieved January 19, 2011, from http://www.rusq.org/2010/12/29/"the-rolls-royce-of-the-library-reference-collection"-the-subject-encyclopedia-in-the-age-of-wikipedia

Eisenberg, M. B., & Head, A. J. (2009). *Finding context: What today's college students say about conducting research in the digital age. Project Information Literacy progress report*. Retrieved January 14, 2011, from http://projectinfolit.org/pdfs/PIL_ProgressReport_2_2009.pdf

Eisenberg, M. B., & Head, A. J. (2010). How today's college students use Wikipedia for course-related research. *First Monday, 15*(3). Retrieved January 16, 2011, from http://www.uic.edu/htbin/cgiwrap/bin/ ojs/index.php/fm/article/view/2830/2476

Eisenberg, M. B., & Head, A. J. (2010). *Truth be told: How college students evaluate and use information in the digital age. Project Information Literacy progress report*. Retrieved January 14, 2011, from http://projectinfolit.org/pdfs/PIL_Fall2010 _Survey_FullReport1.pdf

Grathwohl, C. (2010). *The tower and the open Web: The role of reference*. Retrieved January 7, 2011, from http://www.katina.info/conference/video_2010_openweb.php

Jacobs, M. L. (2009). Libraries and the mobile revolution: Remediation = relevance. *RSR. Reference Services Review, 37*(3), 286–290. doi:10.1108/00907320910982776

JSTORNEWS. (2010). Enhancing discovery: JSTOR collaborates with Google Scholar. *JSTORNEWS, 14*. Retrieved from February 8, 2011, from http://news.jstor.org/jstornews/2010/03/march_2010_vol_14_issue_enhanc.html

Lim, S. (2009). How and why do college students use Wikipedia? *Journal of the American Society for Information Science and Technology, 60*(11), 2189–2202. doi:10.1002/asi.21142

McArthur, T. (1986). *Worlds of reference*. Cambridge, UK: Cambridge University Press.

Oxford University Press. (2011). *Oxford bibliographies online*. Retrieved February 4, 2011, from http://www.oup.com/online/us/obo/?view=usa

Pirolli, P. (2007). *Information foraging theory: Adaptive interaction with information.* Oxford, UK: Oxford University Press. doi:10.1093/acpr of:oso/9780195173321.001.0001

Ranganathan, S. R. (1961). *Reference service.* Bombay, India: Asia Publishing House.

Reference, C. (2010). *Credo Reference topic pages.* Retrieved February 2, 2011, from http://corp.credoreference.com/images/ PDFs/credo_topic_pages_2010.pdf

Shirky, C. (2008). *It's not information overload. It's filter failure.* Web 2.0 Expo NY. Retrieved January 7, 2010, from http://web2expo.blip.tv/file/1277460/

Vaughan, J. (2011). Web scale discovery: What and why? *Library Technology Reports, 47*(1), 5–11.

Wikipedia. (n.d.). *Wikipedia*: *Five pillars.*

ADDITIONAL READING

Dunford, C. E., & Lally, A. M. Using Wikipedia to Extend Digital Collections. *D-Lib Magazine 13*(5/6). Retrieved February 7, 2011, from www.dlib.org/dlib/may07/lally/05lally.html

Janes, J. (2003). *Introduction to Reference Work in the Digital Age.* New York, NY: Neal Schuman Publishers.

Krug, S. (2000). *Don't Make Me Think!: A Common Sense Approach to Web Usability.* Indianapolis, IN: New Riders.

McArthur, T. (1986). *Worlds of Reference.* Cambridge: Cambridge University Press.

Morville, P. (2005). *Ambient Findability.* Sebastopol: O'Reilly.

Shirky, C. (2008). *Here Comes Everybody: The Power of Organizing Without Organizations.* New York, NY: Penguin Press.

Weinberger, D. (2002). *Small Pieces Loosely Joined.* New York, NY: Basic Books.

West, K., & Williamson, J. (2009). Wikipedia: Friend or Foe? *RSR. Reference Services Review, 37*(3), 260–271. doi:10.1108/00907320910982758

KEY TERMS AND DEFINITIONS

Filter Failure: A term coined by Clay Shirky to describe the phenomenon that is elsewhere called information overload. He maintains that, in response to having access to more information than we can humanly handle, we have devised filters (processes, ways of working, even specific tools) to keep out of our span of attention things we don't have time or attention to handle.

Information Overload: An overabundance of information, often associated with the internet, that results a person's inability to comprehend an issue or make decisions.

OPAC: An Online Public Access Catalog.

Open Web: Those set of webpages which are freely available to anyone on the internet without requiring them to log in, register, or be defined as a computer user within the firewall of any particular institution. Such webpages are, by their nature, indexable and searchable by search engines such as Google, Yahoo, Bing, etc. All users in the world have access to such pages. Some make the distinction between the Open Web and the Invisible Web to describe those resources which are not available to all web users.

Open Web Capture: A term of our own devising to describe the situation in which a user on the Open Web is enticed to link into an otherwise restricted set of webpages such as a university's provision of proprietary web content. The publishing industry is not consistent with its use of the terms subject dictionary and subject encyclopedia. Both are distinct from general encyclopedias and dictionaries in that they cover the terms and concepts important to a particular field of study. As used in this paper we define:

Subject Encyclopedia: A reference work which contain essay length explanations of the core concepts, theories, schools of thought, and important people, places, and events important to an understanding of the field.

Subject Dictionary: A reference work which principally contains definitions of terms and phrases in a particular subject.

Chapter 16
Acquiring, Promoting, and Using Mobile-Optimized Library Resources and Services

Chad Mairn
St. Petersburg College, USA

ABSTRACT

Although the reasons vary, it is apparent that the majority of library users prefer electronic reference content primarily because information provided in that format is easier to find and use; plus, much of this content is accessed via mobile devices. This chapter will discuss best practices for acquiring, promoting, and using mobile-optimized library resources and services including reference content -- although most Ready Reference print collections have disappeared because of the ease of finding factual information thanks to Google, Wikipedia, and others. A report on mobile library surveys and vendor usage statistics regarding the use and future aspects of mobile-optimized library reference resources and services will also be discussed in order to provide a snapshot of what is working in this emerging technology that is impacting most everyone today. The chapter also will attempt to answer questions to determine if promoting mobile-optimized content is helping users discover oftentimes hidden library reference content while they are on the go.

DOI: 10.4018/978-1-61350-308-9.ch016

INTRODUCTION

Over the past several years, statistics have shown that mobile access to Web-based resources and services is growing exponentially. In fact, in 2010 the International Telecommunication Union estimated that there would be 5.3 billion mobile subscriptions by the end of the year. In 2011, there will be almost 7 billion people on earth, meaning that close to 80 percent of the world's population will have access to mobile devices and will eventually attempt to access authoritative information found in libraries. These numbers are staggering and should provide a compelling incentive for libraries to move into this mobile space. Mobile devices certainly are evolving beyond simple cellular phones: they are becoming connections to a world of information for users on the go who want instant access to information. In this new digital world, it is crucial for libraries to strive to have their resources and services mobile-optimized so as to be in their users' pockets at the instant they are needed.[1]

The *Horizon Report* (2010), a research project that identifies and describes emerging technologies likely to have a large impact on teaching, learning, or creative inquiry on college and university campuses (but could easily include public and special libraries), includes a chapter on mobile computing in which the report states that the projected time for mainstream use is less than one year. Interestingly, "mobile phones create new kinds of bounded places that merge the infrastructures of geography and technology, as well as techno-social practices that merge technical standards and social norms," so what will happen to our information culture when more than seven billion people gain access to high-quality information wherever and whenever they want it? (Moll, 2007, p.12). It will be an amazing and instantaneous way to access and share information globally, and since communication helps define what it means to be human, these "mobile devices [will] support communication in new and exciting ways" (Nagel, 2011). Again, it is imperative for libraries and other information providers to strive to include high-quality research materials and services and to merge the library as place (i.e., social aspect) with pertinent resources and services (i.e., technology) for mobile devices.

Within the last couple of years, several research studies have been published demonstrating what librarians have known instinctively -- that many library users do not use authoritative library resources such as subscription databases. Instead they turn to what is simple and, to be frank, good enough for personal research and for the "research" required of most college students. OCLC's 2006 report, "College Students' Perceptions of Libraries and Information Resources" concluded that twenty-first century academic librarians "need to better understand the interests, habits and behaviors of college students using libraries—or not—in a time of information abundance" (De, R. C., & OCLC, 2006). Although the report focused on academic librarians, this is not the only group of information professionals who need to be aware of these changing research behaviors. The trend impacts all libraries, and this information abundance is even more profound now that users have access to information anytime and from anywhere. In other words, it impacts anyone participating in the information age.

It is also known and well reported that traditional reference collections in public, academic, and special libraries are being used less these days primarily because users feel overwhelmed and perhaps think that these collections are both outdated and more difficult to use. Consequently, library users have altered their research habits to consider that whatever they find is simply "good enough" (Prabha, 2007). All of these factors should change the way reference collections in libraries are built, promoted, discovered, and used. Although the reasons for this trend vary, it is apparent that the majority of library users, especially if they are required to use library resources for school or work, prefer to use electronic rather than print reference content primarily because they perceive it is easier to find and use. Additionally, many library users are continuously connected to their entire social network and to a wealth of information using their mobile devices, and they expect library resources to be as easy to find and use as are the mobile versions of Google, Wikipedia, Facebook, and other "open" Web resources. As of today, it appears that many mobile users are not conducting rigorous research while they are on the go. As one Kent State University student mentioned, "If it occurs to me that I need to look for something in particular and I'm not near my computer, I could find the links and e-mail them to myself so I could go and find them again later" (Seeholzer & Salem, 2011). This may change, however, once mobile devices become more sophisticated and start incorporating tools such as highlighting, annotation, sharing notes, and citations, as many popular e-reading devices already do. Seeholzer and Salem compiled results from a student focus group at Kent State University, and they showed that participants were interested in using mobile-optimized databases, the library catalog, and reference services, including text messaging.

What follows is a discussion of best practices for acquiring, promoting, and using mobile-optimized library resources and services including reference content -- although most Ready Reference print collections have disappeared because of the ease of finding factual information thanks to Google, Wikipedia, and others. A report on various mobile library surveys and vendor usage statistics regarding the use and future aspects of mobile-optimized library reference resources and services will be discussed in order to provide a snapshot of what is working in this emerging technology that is impacting most everyone today. The chapter also will attempt to answer questions to determine if promoting mobile-optimized content is helping users discover oftentimes hidden library reference content while they are on the go or, for example, while waiting in line when a question

arises and they want it answered immediately before forgetting it. Or is having basic information literacy skills the major factor in successfully finding and using information? More than likely, it is a combination of both having high-quality library resources and services easily findable and having the skills to determine whether a particular piece of information is useful and authoritative.

Library Journal Mobile Libraries Survey 2010

There are reports and Web analytic data that reveal less than impressive usage thus far from those libraries who have already implemented mobile-optimized library resources and services. This low usage statistic will more than likely change for the better when more libraries offer a mobile presence, as library vendors produce mobile-optimized content, and when libraries promote and encourage library participants to utilize the mobile resources and services that they have carefully constructed. In the meantime, however, low mobile usage in libraries will be an important issue that will require serious attention so that libraries can focus on the future applicability of mobile library resources and services and develop appropriately to help successfully expand library usage into the mobile environment. Conducting an environmental scan in order to determine how library users are actually using mobile technologies now to access and use non-library resources and services will prove to be an invaluable exercise for any library planning to optimize these for use via mobile devices.

To gain a better understanding of mobile services and technologies used in libraries, *Library Journal* conducted a survey in 2010. Data from the 483 respondents showed that "44% of academic libraries and 34% of public libraries currently offer some type of mobile services" and that "two out of five libraries of all types are planning to 'go mobile' in the near future" (Thomas, 2010). Mobile-optimized versions of library websites, catalogs, and research databases; mobile access to patron accounts; Short Message Service (SMS), often referred to as texting, reference services and notifications; Quick Response (QR) codes to help guide mobile users from physical items to digital items; and e-book access were the main mobile resources and services that both public and academic libraries wanted to explore in the near future. In addition, Thomas reported that augmented reality, location-aware services, audio and video library tours, mobile marketing, and integration with major social media services such as Facebook and Twitter were other mobile initiatives that would likely be considered in the future once the other "priority" mobile resources and services were implemented and thoroughly tested.

QR codes, two-dimensional square barcodes that can have a variety of encoded information, are an easy way to promote mobile library resources and services. Mobile users with QR reader software can either take a photo of the code or use a barcode scanner in order to decode the QR code. They then are directed from a physical object to something digital. Libraries of all types are using QR codes to promote mobile-optimized resources and services. Other industries use QR codes too. For example, the Center for the Studies of Archaeological and Prehistoric Heritage (CEPAP) at the Autonomous University of Barcelona has started starting "using QR codes to ID and track ancient artifacts, from kraters to potsherds" (Hopkins, 2011).

With any new and emerging technology there are several issues to consider before planning, developing, and implementing a new mobile library resource or service. Perhaps one of the most difficult things to consider is whether or not to develop a native application or a web application (often called apps). Once this is determined, who will develop the app? Will it be developed within the library or through an outside development firm? To muddy the water some, it seems that the "openness of the Web" and the fact that "closed

platforms have turned many developers away from popular native platforms like the iPhone and iPad" may lead to Web-based apps becoming the mobile development choice in the future, but only time will tell (Cameron). The *Library Journal*'s "Mobile Libraries Survey" mentioned that 39 percent of all libraries "reported not having any services existing or planned for handheld devices" and that budgeting for "hardware, software, training, staffing, management, and time for research and development" would prove difficult (Thomas, 2010). Other issues Thomas raised in the report include lack of interest by less than savvy computer and mobile users, a deficiency in library staff's technical ability to develop mobile technologies in-house, and difficulty in justifying the need for mobile-optimized library resources and services to library leaders and stakeholders. The issues raised in *Library Journal's* "Mobile Libraries Survey" are significant, but it seems that many libraries are able to be creative while thinking outside the box in order to overcome obstacles and make these changes work for their users.

Although the "Mobile Libraries Survey" did not include special libraries or high school media centers, these types of libraries are building mobile-optimized library resources and services and are also experiencing low usage statistics. There are several health and law libraries, for example, utilizing mobile technologies because their users are frequently on the go and need high-quality, up-to-date information.

Mobile-Optimized Library Web Pages

The more popular that mobile access to non-library resources and services becomes and the more that people expect this content to be easily available via their mobile devices, the safer it is to assume that library vendors will be compelled to develop apps and mobile-optimized content for libraries because usage will undoubtedly go up. Libraries should not wait for this to happen. Instead, libraries should find ways to at least design mobile-optimized Web pages and/or apps now so that they are ready to link to mobile-optimized content when it is available from their vendors. Libraries with mobile-optimized websites usually include hyperlinks to common resources and services and also create hyperlinked telephone numbers and email addresses so that mobile users can easily contact professional librarians when they need help.

An important thing to consider when designing a mobile-optimized Web page is to know, as Ballard states, that "mobile refers to the user, not the device or application" (2007, p.3). Furthermore, your library's resources and services will be of little value to your mobile users if the design of the mobile Web page or app ignores the context in which it is being used. Keeping this in mind, it is essential to observe how your users find, access, and utilize your content with their mobile devices as well as when using desktop computers and to design your library's mobile Web pages and apps appropriately. Discovering what is relevant to your users and the tasks, problems, and needs that they may encounter while being mobile is also an important consideration when designing for mobile (Moll, 24). It can be helpful to also provide mobile library users with a list of recommended mobile apps that work on a variety of mobile operating systems and help with discovering content, brainstorming topic ideas, note taking, bibliographic citation management, "Web 2.0" sharing tools, and much more. It is important to understand that most mobile users are busy and probably accessing data while they are on the go and doing other things such as drinking a cup of coffee, which would make it difficult to accomplish complex tasks. Furthermore, mobile users may only be seeking directions or a phone number to your library, so it is crucial to develop appropriately for these users.

Using focus groups is an excellent method when planning to design anything, especially a mobile website, because you can learn precisely what your users expect from the site and, ideally,

provide answers to their questions and act on their recommendations. It is also possible to use a Web analytic tool, such as Google Analytics, to determine what links your users choose most often. It then makes sense to include the most popular links, if feasible, on your mobile-optimized Web page. It is essential to observe focus group members using your mobile Web page. Ask them what they think about using it and what they would like to see included, and then get it to work. If a new mobile-optimized website is created, be sure to include the JavaScript code that Google Analytics provides so you can measure the site's success. Google Analytics will provide invaluable information such as the type of operating system, browser, and screen resolution used to access your site, will highlight what links were clicked on the most, will calculate how long a user stayed on the website, and more.

Before releasing a mobile-optimized website to the public, it is important to design Web pages that are mobile-compliant to ensure that all the Web pages display well on a variety of mobile browsers. Although mobile device emulators are excellent tools to use while designing mobile-optimized Web pages, testing a new mobile-optimized website should be done on as many different mobile devices as possible. Going further, the World Wide Web Consortium (W3C) has a mobileOK Basic Tests document (http://www.w3.org/TR/mobileOK-basic10-tests/) that has extensive documentation to help design a mobile Web page that is compliant (i.e., mobileOK) according to industry best practices and standards. A W3C mobileOK Checker (http://validator.w3.org/mobile/) allows a designer to copy and paste a website's Uniform Resource Identifier (URI) into the empty field in order to determine "its level of mobile-friendliness" (W3C, 2010). "Mobile Web Application Best Practices" (http://www.w3.org/TR/mwabp/) and "Mobile Web Best Practices" (http://www.w3.org/TR/mobile-bp/), both written by the W3C in 2010, are essential readings because they warn against harmful design practices, highlight best practices, and offer guidelines for designing apps and mobile-optimized websites. Ready.mobi (http://ready.mobi) offers mobile conformance analysis, various mobile device emulation previews, estimated data costs for transferring data back and forth from server to mobile device, and speeds for mobile users, and is another excellent tool to help Web developers design mobile-compliant Web pages.

As mentioned previously, several tools and services are available to help transform desktop websites so that they can be viewed and/or tested on mobile devices and compatibility issues identified and resolved. One example is the mobile version of Wikipedia, which is powered by the HAWHAW Toolkit. HAWHAW, which stands for *HTML and WML hybrid adapted Webserver,* makes it easier to create a mobile website or app because a "programmer can rely on the accumulated experience of many running mobile applications" when developing a new application (HAWHAW, 2010). Web Developer 1.1.8, developed by Chris Pederick, is an extension for Firefox and Chrome browsers that provides an amazing set of tools for Web developers and includes a Small Screen Rendering option. This option displays any Web page viewed on a desktop computer as if rendered in an emulated mobile format.[2] Automatic mobile rendering software can automatically make your website appear to be mobile-optimized. Mowser. com is a site that will make any website mobile-optimized, but a mobile user would have to visit mowser.com first and then input the URL to be mobilized; Mowser then does the work. Opera Mini and Mobile browsers (http://www.opera.com/mobile) will open a full website; then, before displaying it on a mobile device, Opera will mobilize the full website through its servers and redisplay it in a mobile-optimized format. The process is quick and seamless. WordPress, the popular blogging platform, provides WordPress Mobile Pack (http://wordpress.org/extend/plugins/wordpress-mobile-pack/) which is a complete toolkit to create a mobile-optimized

version of one's blog or website. Although these mobilizing tools and many others on the Web are useful, it is still a good idea to design a mobile-optimized version of one's full website in order to gain more control of the site's features.

One popular mobile Web design option is to use the jQTouch framework. Its template makes it fairly easy to create a mobile Web page that responds to user interaction (i.e., touch) similar to the way a native app would work on a supported mobile device such as the iPhone, iPod, or Android phones. A native app is a computer program that must be executed within a particular mobile operating system (e.g., iOS, Android, webOS, etc.). jQTouch, on the other hand, is a Web-based app or, more specifically, a mobile Web page that utilizes Hypertext Markup Language (HTML), Cascading Style Sheets (CSS), and JavaScript to create a more interactive experience analogous to the way native apps work. jQTouch has gained a lot of popularity for mobile Web development primarily because it is easy to create a mobile website that acts like a native app. Also, updating Web content is exactly like updating a Web page and is easier than going through the review process to add an application to various stores such as iTunes, Android Marketplace, BlackBerry App World, et cetera.[3]

St. Petersburg College Libraries has developed a mobile-optimized website using jQTouch (http://www.spcollege.edu/central/libonline/touch). Designed for users on the go, it includes library locations with one-touch access to Google Maps, library telephone numbers, and hours of operation; access to mobile-optimized research databases and the library catalog; new library releases, resources, and services including the mobile version of Florida's Ask-a-Librarian virtual reference and its SMS reference service; selected research tools for a variety of operating systems including Android, Blackberry, iOS (Apple's iPhone), WebOS, Symbian, and Windows; and external links to the library's full website. The full website for the St. Petersburg College Library also includes a PHP script that determines first what kind of device or browser is being used to access the full website, and then displays a web page that gives the user the option to use either the full website, a minimal text-based version, or the "touch" mobile-optimized version. As yet, there does not seem to be a mobile "redirect best practice" because there is no consensus as to whether or not users should have the option to choose their interface or if the mobile-optimized version of the website should automatically display for the mobile user and then allow the mobile version to be turned on or off. Regardless, it is a good idea to provide a link to the mobile version of one's full website near the top of a web page so that mobile users can see the link before scrolling through a lot of text in order to find what they need.

The Massachusetts Institute of Technology (MIT) has developed a mobile-optimized web suite (http://m.mit.edu), which is more than a site and continues to push the boundaries of what can be accomplished using mobile technologies (Figure 1). Included are, among many other features, a people directory, campus map, shuttle schedule, events calendar, and emergency information. MIT's Mobile Web Open Source Project provides all of its source code as a zip file and can be downloaded at http://mitmobileweb.sourceforge.net/.

HTML5, an enhanced Web authoring markup language, is eliminating the need for many browser plug-ins. Multimedia will be much easier to display in Web pages that are written in HTML5, and innovative tools such as group collaboration, offline storage, and access to electronic content while not be connected to the Internet, will be possible with HTML5, which is a perfect markup language for mobile browsers. Although many Web pages are enhanced using HTML5, a prime example being Google's Gmail for mobile, there is no date for it to become standardized, according to the World Wide Web Consortium.

Wired magazine stated in "The Web is Dead. Long Live the Internet" that people are "aban-

Figure 1. [MIT Mobile]. (© 2010], [Massachusetts Institute of Technology] Used with permission.).

doning [the web] for simpler, sleeker services that just work" and are using mobile apps for distinct purposes such as reading a newspaper, browsing Facebook, and listening to a podcast instead of doing all of these things from within a web browser (Anderson & Wolff, 2010). In fact, thousands of mobile apps are being developed each year, and in April 2009 Apple's App Store had its one-billionth app downloaded. This is clearly an eye-opening statistic. Recently, Android App Inventor was made available for free and this tool makes it possible for people who are not computer programmers to build mobile apps for the Android operating system. The App Inventor interface is designed to function like a puzzle: the designer clicks and drags blocks of information and connects them to other blocks. In addition, the app can be tested in real-time using a USB-connected Android device before packaging it for the masses. However, tools like jQTouch are making mobile-optimized Web pages act like native apps where the interface acts much like an app for an iPhone or other type of mobile device. But unlike most apps, the website is entirely Web-based and requires no downloads or updates.

Although this section cannot discuss all the intricacies involved in designing a mobile-optimized Web presence for a library, resources to help start the process are available, and a listing of these will be provided in the recommended resources section at the end of this chapter.

Mobile-Optimized Content

Several well-known library vendors have developed mobile-optimized versions of their resources and services and the list continues to grow. This section will highlight a small selection of popular mobile reference apps that are currently available.

EBSCO*host*® Mobile™

EBSCO has developed a mobile-optimized website (Figure 2) that resembles its desktop database offerings. The mobile website includes basic searching, HTML and PDF full text, search limiters, image quick views, the option to email articles and set user preferences, multiple database searching, and library branding.

St. Petersburg College's mobile-optimized website has a referring URL that links to EBSCO*host*® Mobile™. Authenticated users can search individual databases or select multiple databases. The databases that are mobile-optimized for St. Petersburg College are Academic Search Complete; Business Source Complete; CINAHL Plus with Full Text; Education Research Complete; ERIC; GreenFILE; Health Source – Consumer Edition; Health Source – Nursing/Academic Edition; History Reference Center; Library, Information Science, and Technology Abstracts; Literary Reference Center Plus; MAS Ultra-School Edition; MEDLINE with Full Text; Military and Government Collection; psycARTICLES; and Regional Business News. Every day, other databases are becoming mobile-optimized and referring URLs are created and then added to the mobile-optimized website. If database vendors and other content providers could agree on a

Figure 2. [EBSCOHost Mobile]. (© 2010], [EB-SCOHost] Used with permission.).

"geolocation standard for licensing content," authenticated users could stay logged in to a mobile-optimized site using their location instead of their user IDs and passwords (Griffey, 2010, p.92). This would be a great benefit, especially for mobile users because they would not have to input any text on the typically small and awkward keyboard.

Encyclopedia Britannica Mobile Edition

The Encyclopedia Britannica (http://m.eb.com/) has developed a mobile-optimized website that includes entries from its popular reference title and that can be viewed on most any mobile device with Web access. The encyclopedia's interface is simple, and search results load quickly. Using this mobile encyclopedia is analogous to using Ready Reference and in many cases is much quicker. Having the Encyclopedia Britannica Mobile

Edition in a librarian's pocket would be a great "roaming reference" resource that would give the librarian or researcher an entire encyclopedia set when browsing the library bookshelves or when helping users. Although the Web-based mobile version of the encyclopedia is free, mobile applications for iPhone and Android that eliminate the advertisements are available for a fee.

Gale Cengage Learning™

Gale Cengage Learning™ offers AccessMyLibrary Public Edition, AccessMyLibrary School Edition, and AccessMyLibrary College Edition apps to provide mobile access to a user's local library resources. The apps utilize Global Positioning System (GPS) receivers found in most every cellular phone to locate the nearest library within a ten-mile radius. As of this writing, only Android, iPhone, iPod Touch, and iPad devices are supported for the AccessMyLibrary Public Edition, but other mobile platforms will be developed for the other apps in the future. Users can visit the Android Marketplace or Apple's App Store to download and install these apps. Conveniently, the Cengage website provides a QR code that can be scanned or photographed; encoding software will then guide the user to the appropriate file for easy downloading and installation on the mobile device (Figure 3).

Installing the app on Android, for example, is simple. Once the app is run, the GPS component will search for the nearest library. If it finds your local library, the user simply clicks on the "Continue" button. AccessMyLibrary Public Edition will then provide mobile access to several Gale resources that the library subscribes to, such as its Fine Arts and Music Collection, Business Economics and Theory, and Nursing and Allied Health Collection to DemographicsNow Library Edition, Small Business Resource Center, and much more. If a person's local library is not found, the user would then select from a list of other libraries appearing on a Google Map.

According to Mark Springer, Director of Usage Services and Analytics at Cengage Learning, in 2010 "Cengage-Gale has released three mobile apps for library resources on the Apple iOS platform (iPhone, iPad and iPod Touch) and one for the Android platform"; these apps "average around 80 downloads per day in total" (Personal communication, January 11, 2011). In the last five months of 2010, Springer said that Cengage-Gale library resources "recorded more than 55,000 visits and 256,000 page views from mobile devices"; however, "as a percentage of Cengage-Gale's total library usage, mobile traffic is small (less than 1%) but growing fast: in the past six months, visits from mobile devices have increased 67% and page views have increased 92%, with the iPad leading the way." Mobile access to the Web

Figure 3. [QR Codes for AccessMyLibrary apps (© 2010], [Gale Cengage Learning™] Used with permission.).

Get the free *AccessMyLibrary Public Edition* mobile app for your device using one of the QR codes or links below.

For Android™   For iPhone®, iPod Touch®, iPad®

What's this?   What's this?

is in its infancy stage, so these low usage statistics for mobile-optimized resources and content will undoubtedly increase in the coming years.

LexisNexis

LexisNexis, a well-known legal resource, has an iPhone application called LexisNexis Get Cases & Shepardize. At the time of this writing there were no other operating systems supported; however, its Web page dating back to 2004 did mention that a BlackBerry service can be established via subscription. The iPhone app provides access to the case law collection and citation service, but a subscription to LexisNexis is required in order to access the content. Libraries offering proxy access to LexisNexis may find it difficult to share the institution ID so that users can access the resource. And although Apple's App Store says the app is free, during installation a "buy" option was displayed and was misleading even though the app did install without the need to pay for it.

Wikipedia

Wikipedia is a free online encyclopedia with millions of articles written in several languages that can, in most cases, be edited by anyone. Although Wikipedia and other research tools are not perfect, they do provide a good first step in finding topic ideas and key concepts to help build specific research topics. Now that Wikipedia has a mobile presence online (http://en.m.wikipedia. org/) and is being integrated into many e-reading devices, e-reading software and apps, and other electronic reference apps (e.g., add-on for Color-Dict dictionary app) on mobile devices it seems desirable for libraries of all types to help edit and subsequently enhance Wikipedia articles with their library resources. For example, providing links to books via WorldCat Mobile or another mobile-optimized library catalog can bring more visibility to the rich collections to which libraries and their users have access; users would have choices other

than Amazon.com and other for-profit services. Wikipedia Mobile has an attractive and uncluttered interface and returns searches quickly, displaying article entries in an easy-to-read format so that users can show or hide certain parts of the article.

WorldCat Mobile

Having mobile Web access to WorldCat, the "world's largest library catalog" is an outstanding way to bring more visibility to libraries around the world. Considered beta, the interface (http://www.worldcat.org/m) is currently available only in English and is optimized for iOS and Android operating systems (Figure 4). However, World-Cat's Web page mentions that other mobile devices will be supported in the near future. Searching the mobile interface is simple; results are displayed quickly and it is possible to email the record's link or citation. However, as of this writing, the citations appear to be formatted in HTML (e.g., <p class="citation_style_APA">APA
Fern, T. E., & Castillo, L. (2008). <i>Buffalo music</i>. New York: Clarion Books. </p>) and

Figure 4. [Search Results from WorldCat Mobile] (© 2010], [OCLC] Used with permission.)

would need some user modification in order to be in a genuine citation style such as APA or MLA. Furthermore, a mobile user who selects the "Find in a Library" link is then prompted to input his or her ZIP code in order to search libraries nearby; a drop-down menu with choices for local libraries is then displayed. After the user selects the closest library, WorldCat would display the records for items in or near that library. It is likely that the next iteration of WorldCat Mobile will utilize the GPS function within each mobile device so there would be no need for the user to input any text. Library telephone numbers, email addresses, and websites should be hyperlinked within the interface so users can select the hyperlink and be guided to the resource.

Blackboard Mobile vs. iMobile U

Blackboard Mobile, which competes with MIT's iMobileU, is creating a mobile app for colleges that will include a campus map, searchable directory of faculty and staff, and college news; however, Blackboard Mobile's annual fee is around $30,000 depending on the size of the college. With iMobileU, the institution must provide support for the app; with Blackboard Mobile, however, the vendor's staff manages and supports the app, but institutions must pay for it.

Creating a library app can be difficult for many reasons and there are several questions that should be asked first. For example, should the app be created for various operating systems or only for the iPhone? Does the library have a technically proficient staff member or members who can develop an app in-house or will the library need to outsource the work? App development from third parties can be expensive, and most libraries lack the money to hire outside companies to build a mobile app, so what should be the priority? The answer will depend on one's expected users, so perhaps asking users to complete a survey in order to gauge their interest in having a library

mobile app should be a first priority. Are there widely accepted criteria to consider when building a mobile app or mobile-optimized website? There are, and some are more useful than others. Visiting the W3C website (http://www.w3.org/) and reading its recommendation documents is a good first step. Should the library do nothing and hope its existing website renders well on a mobile device? Probably not, but answering these questions can be difficult and not every library or user base is the same; however, being ready and understanding the needs of your users when they start using mobile technologies is essential for success.

appMobi (http://www.appmobi.com/), a mobile app development company, provides a complete platform for mobile development for free, but it also offers a Pro account that allows developers to add their app to Apple's App Store and includes consulting and training. Using free tools like appMobi or Android's App Inventor are excellent ways to try and develop a mobile app for your library without having much experience.

Again, the list of library vendors and other content providers that are optimizing their content for mobile devices is growing quickly. Since not all could be covered in this chapter, the recommended resources section includes a website that will act as a "living" document to help keep current with these advances.

Mobile-Optimized Services

Mobile-optimized content is essential for libraries to provide their users with high-quality information whenever and wherever they want it, but library services can also be mobile and just as important as the library content. Librarians themselves are considered resources and frequently help their users make sense of all this information, so it is logical to provide mobile-optimized services too.

Although many "ready-reference" collections are not as popular as they were a few years ago and some have disappeared completely because of Google, Wikipedia, and other search engines and easily accessible online resources, these collections were designed to answer questions quickly, and mobile reference services should strive to do the same. Short Message Service (SMS), often referred to in the United States as "text messaging," is a communication system that allows mobile devices to send short text messages to other mobile devices. The system allows only 160 characters so the messages, as the acronym suggests, are short and concise. SMS Reference can become a mechanism to keep "ready reference" alive. Over the last few years, several libraries have added SMS reference services to their arsenal of research tools available to their users at their point of need.[4]

One successful SMS Reference example is that of Florida's Ask-a-Librarian Virtual Reference Service. In late 2010, Ask-a-Librarian implemented an SMS Reference Service using Twilio's (http://www.twilio.com) Application

Programming Interface (API). An API is a way for companies to share programming instructions so that software applications can communicate with one another. APIs make it easier to write software applications because certain functions from another piece of software can be "borrowed" and used in another.

A small group of Florida librarians and a programmer were able to modify Twilio's SMS API and offer text messaging reference for the entire state of Florida for less than 2¢ per message. A user texting a question to the service is not charged by Ask-a-Librarian (Figure 5). It is free, unless the mobile carrier charges for the text message. Most users, it seems, have an unlimited texting plan, so this is not usually a problem. The SMS Reference system was configured so a user could include a three-letter keyword and have a text message go to a specific library within the email queue. If a user does not include the keyword, the text message goes to a collaborative queue where any librarian staffing the statewide virtual

Figure 5. [Ask-a-Librarian SMS Texting Widget] (© 2010], [Tampa Bay Library Consortium] Used with permission.)

reference desk can answer the question. ATG Live Help, formerly Instant Service, has provided the Software-as-a-Service (SaaS) solution for the chat portion of Ask-a-Librarian for eight years. Within the software interface, a texting Web page widget was incorporated in order to help librarians stay within the 160- character limit; it also included a URL shortening option to conveniently include links in the text message reply. Ask a Librarian's "Text Us" initiative started on October 25, 2010, and in only the first three weeks, the service answered 458 questions. Ask-a-Librarian is an extremely successful virtual reference service, and so far the SMS reference service has proven to be an important extension to help quickly answer users' questions wherever and whenever needed.

One issue regarding SMS reference is that of following up on reference transactions. For example, if a user texts a question to the virtual reference desk and a librarian replies with a follow-up question and then logs off, the user's reply can be vague to a librarian taking over the shift from the one who just logged off. Procedures and policies can be written, but it is beneficial to make the process seamless and easy for both the librarian and the user. Also, text messages are limited to 160 characters, so in-depth research questions cannot be answered this way. Instead, a user would want to use instant messaging (i.e., chat), voice calling using their cellular network or voice over internet protocol (VoIP), or even video chat/conferencing. Having all these functions on a mobile device is a great advantage, especially when one technology cannot accomplish a certain research or reference goal.

Twitter, the popular microblogging service, is analogous to scanning a newspaper's headlines that users themselves create. As the world has seen, it can become much more than that. For example, in early 2011 Twitter helped the Egyptian people communicate and share their experiences with others outside the country even though access to the Internet was severed. Going further, Twitter can become a mobile platform to help promote

resources and to act as a mobile "reference desk," playing a significant role in reference transactions for mobile users. Twitter can be used to send links to library users because it can be easier to point the user to, for instance, twitter.com/yourlibrary to get a more complex link instead of trying to articulate each character of a URL. Perhaps in the future every mobile user will have access to a mobile device with Bluetooth functionality that can send information wirelessly, but this is not true today, so using Twitter can help make reference transactions much easier. Although it originally referred to communication devices, Metcalfe's law states that "communications networks increase in value as they add members" and librarians using social media, such as Twitter, can be proactive and help answer questions within their networks (Briscoe et al., 2006).

Promoting and Using Mobile-Optimized Library Resources and Services

After developing anything that helps bring more visibility to library resources and services, it is essential to promote that new resource or service so that it gets used. If, for instance, a mobile-optimized website was created, a simple flyer highlighting the new features with an inserted QR code to help link it to the new site would be a great start- the mobile user would not need to input a URL into the device's browser. Using Twitter, Facebook, YouTube, and many other social media services can be highly effective ways to promote new library resources and services as well. In addition, being active in these social media networks and simply being available for your users when they need it most is good practice. Of course, word of mouth is an excellent promotional tool, too.

It is good practice to initiate a pre-launch promotion of a new library app or a mobile-optimized library resource or service so that you can get initial feedback from users before you submit an "official" press release on your new mobile tool.

Then you can promote the "beta" version of the new tool, asking users to provide feedback so that you can accumulate a list of enhancements that your users want, making sure to implement these changes as soon as possible.

EBSCOhost, for instance, provides multiple ways to promote its online resources by product and by market (e.g., academic libraries, corporate, government, medical, public libraries, and school libraries) including product buttons and logos, ads, customizable posters, a search box builder and more. Using vendor-supplied promotional tools like EBSCO's can save valuable staff time while providing more visibility for library resources and services.

The Seattle Public Library placed an image in a prominent position on its website linking to its mobile app and included a detailed video explaining the features and how to use the app. The video includes a link to the app (spl.boopsie. com) and explains how to find it in Apple's App Store and Android's Market. An iPhone emulator demonstrates how to access one's library account; search the catalog with smart prefix searching; put items on hold; access the calendar of events; chat, email, call, or text a librarian; and use the library locations feature, which will show the closest location if a user's GPS feature is enabled on his or her mobile device. The app is well designed, and the video shows users exactly how it will help them get the most out of their public library. Not only does the Seattle Public Library provide users with a fantastic resource, it has also put that resource in the spotlight so that it can be easily found and used.

The University of Illinois at Urbana-Champaign's University Library has created a mobile-optimized website that includes links to Mobile Labs, a section for "experimental library iPhone apps," which should seemingly pique the interest of students. The Mobile Labs includes Infopoint, a location-based tour of the main library, a video tour of the library for undergraduates, and new library acquisitions. The beta mobile-optimized

site includes "access to a core set of basic library services customized for successful use on mobile devices" as well as the library's Text a Librarian service (University Library, 2010). In early 2010, the University Library announced the mobile site on its News and Events blog with a clever "start your homework on your phone" catchphrase. As the University Library demonstrated, remembering who your audience is will be essential when promoting new library resources and services.

North Carolina State University Libraries created WolfWalk, an augmented reality app that allows mobile users to "explore North Carolina State University's campus history on your phone" and includes "information on 90 different sites on campus, with images that trace the site's history, courtesy of the NCSU Libraries Special Collections Research Center" (WolfWalk, 2011). The possibilities for using augmented reality, or data superimposed over reality, to help promote library resources and services are huge and exciting. Augmented reality can be a tool for mobile learning, too. Imagine having course notes, faculty lecture podcasts, mobile-optimized research databases with persistent links to articles, and other subject-related data superimposed over a specific section of the library bookshelves! Not only would this enhance a user's understanding of that section, but this type of innovative technology would be an amazing promotional tool to help share the richness of the library's as well as the institution's supporting resources.

Geocaching is a digital scavenger hunt in which tiny containers called geocaches are hidden; players search for and locate them using GPS-enabled devices and share their discoveries online. One interesting example of using geocaching was the Calgary Public Library's co-sponsorship of an event called the Geocaching Challenge. From May until August 25, 2010, geocaches were placed in Calgary parks. Prizes were offered for participating. This "game" brought many people into the Calgary Public Library because the library allowed anyone with a valid library card to borrow a GPS unit for use in the challenge, which also promoted exploration of the city's parks (Geocaching Challenge, 2010). Although Geocaching is a game, there seem to be some innovative ways to experiment with hiding the caches in library resources as incentives for visiting the building. In one instance, a library user came in to the Shoshone Public Library in Idaho with GPS coordinates "N 42° 56.160 W 114° 24.514." There she found a hollowed-out book containing a token that she replaced with a similar item and then added her name to a logbook. The Shoshone Public Library created "Get a clue at your library" where the library started using geocaching with its community in order for the library to connect with their existing users while creating a "low-cost opportunity to draw in new community members" (Funabiki, 2009).

Mobile Learning

According to a report titled "US Market for Mobile Learning Products and Services: 2009-2014 Forecast and Analysis," the United States will take the lead in mobile learning by 2014, and since libraries are considered centers for discovery and learning, this should be a perfect fit for libraries to play an integral role (Adkins, 2010, pp. 6-7). Going further, public spaces including libraries "are an important source of exposure to diverse ideas, issues and opinions -- as well as meeting places for interacting with social ties" (Pew Research Center, 2009). Although many mobile users throughout the United States will continue to use their libraries, many will go beyond the library's walls and classrooms in order to access information, all the while expecting to have instantaneous contact with their social networks including their communication systems and collaboration tools. As a result, libraries should strengthen their bonds with schools and, more importantly, their users and their potential users, so as to be ready for the explosion in mobile use.

If the above forecast and analysis report proves to be true, all libraries will need to have an understanding of the various content providers' role in offering mobile-optimized content and will need to become adept at helping users acquire, transfer, and use this content successfully regardless of what mobile device or operating systems they use. Going further, libraries should empower their users to discover and subsequently to learn from any medium. The question remains as to whether or not libraries should acquire mobile devices to help enhance their users' learning or if they should simply remain device agnostic, not being concerned with the device itself but able to help their users learn in any fashion.

A leader in providing digital course materials is CourseSmart, a joint venture among major educational publishers including Pearson, Cengage Learning, McGraw-Hill Education, Bedford, Freeman & Worth Publishing Group, Macmillan, and John Wiley & Sons. CourseSmart is selling "mobile learning directly to students" while bypassing bookstores and app stores completely (Nagel, 2010). Should libraries feel obligated to help their users succeed in this ever-evolving mobile environment, especially when users can bypass the library or their school's bookstore? The answer from this author's perspective is a resounding yes. Users come to libraries because they think librarians know everything about books. They may or may not know everything about books, but they do know a great deal about things other than books. Nonetheless, librarians should strive to know as much as possible about acquiring, transferring, and using books, e-books, e-reference materials, and other electronic research tools no matter what format they are in. It seems that the e-textbook and other e-resource offerings will continue to thrive for many reasons primarily because they provide instant access to materials, are less expensive, and are more lightweight, but the determining factor will be whether or not students can adapt to using completely electronic texts for rigorous research and study. One Yale

University student said about the iPad that the "book reader saves money because I don't need to buy as many books, and is lightweight and much easier to carry around than multiple textbooks" and being "able to keep all class notes together in one place and send notes via email, and use the calendar to keep track of exams, meetings and events" is "very helpful for me as a student" (Personal communication, February 8, 2011).

Duke University's Global Health Institute has been testing iPads in the field in order to provide their students with "a toolset that allows them to make the most of their time in the field" and imagines high-quality library resources and services being an integrated part of this toolset (Schaffhauser, 2010). Marc Sperber, the main consultant for the Duke University iPad project, says that "with an iPad a student may collect, organize and display data while in the field, allowing them to immediately engage in analyzing and interpreting that data when and where it has greatest meaning (Schaffhauser, 2010). Libraries, again, should foster the discovery and sharing process, and initiatives like these will help bring library resources and services into the spotlight where they belong.

Mobile devices can also be used to engage students during library instructions or lectures, allowing them to vote or interact with content on the projector screen. For example, Polleverywhere. com can be integrated into PowerPoint or Keynote slides in order to poll a class via text messaging, Twitter, or submission through a Web page. The results can be seen by the instructor and the participants in real-time, similar to the way clickers work. The free version of Polleverywhere allows for 30 submissions and includes a simple reporting feature; the polling questions can be used as many times as necessary. Engaging students with technologies that they are already using will certainly keep them interested in the content that is being delivered.

Twenty-first century learners, including library users, will expect to have information whenever and wherever they are, and they will also become more mobile. As mobile technologies evolve and become less expensive and more intuitive to use, the digital divide will shrink, and these learners will expect to have the library in their pockets at all times. According to Elliot Soloway, a professor at the University of Michigan, within the next five years "every K-12 student in America will be using a mobile handheld device as a part of learning"; "smart phones are the one technology that can eliminate the digital divide," because they are affordable; it is "conceivable that every child, rich or poor, can have one." (Nagel, 2011). K-12 students, Nagel says, can use skills "they have developed outside of school inside of school" to help enhance their learning because, for one thing, it is more meaningful to them. Soloway goes on to say that "portability enables relating abstract concepts in the classroom to concrete items in the world" and this can be a profound tool for enhanced learning (Nagel, 2011). John Dewey once said that "if we teach today's students as we did yesterday's, we are robbing them of tomorrow." If this is true, it would be extremely unfortunate for future generations.

If libraries are not ready for this explosion in mobile technologies, their users will undoubtedly turn to something else besides their physical and perhaps even their digital libraries. This is unfortunate, but library users are already moving towards Google, Wikipedia, and other free online resources because they are easier to use and are available all the time without any restrictions. Libraries need to continue working with their vendors and other stakeholders to negotiate changes in subscription models, authentication systems, and other information access issues to better mirror resources such as Google. Users are getting accustomed to the simplicity of instant access; libraries need to be aware of this while continuing to focus on information literacy in order to help their users make sense of the torrent of information streaming at them every day. Although information literacy is vital, communication is key for success. Local libraries should communicate better with one another and share resources and responsibilities so that they do not lose sight of their mission statements and their visions for the future.

Libraries can learn from Barnes and Noble where, for example, Nook display tables are constructed where knowledgeable employees sit to help customers use their Nooks. Free wireless is promoted so users can browse new books for possible purchases while they are in the store. Obtaining books that library users must purchase first in order to read and promoting only one e-reading device is where libraries differ obviously from Barnes and Noble, but they can still learn from Barnes and Noble's customer service model. Libraries that demonstrate value to their users while creating the most visible and usable resources and services will thrive in society. It is the library system that is unprepared for technological advances and its users' evolving needs that can easily cease to exist. Thanks to a struggling economy, libraries are being absorbed by other departments while seeing deep financial cuts. This is a serious problem that cannot be overlooked.

Future Considerations

The future of mobile technologies will depend on many variables. This section will highlight some future considerations that developers will need to understand in order for these technologies to become more powerful and truly ubiquitous.

Broadband must continue to be developed and implemented because more data is required for mobile library resources and services, such as multimedia streaming. If data cannot quickly be transferred, users will forgo these heavy services. Long Term Evolution (LTE) and Fourth Generation (4G) cellular network technologies are expanding bandwidth and are critical upgrades if the cellular infrastructure is to be able to handle the richness of mobile library apps, resources, and services in the future. Small mobile screens will not be a hindrance in the future. In fact,

many mobile devices today can project a 60-inch screen onto a wall. GPS (Global Position Satellite) is an essential component in most, if not all, mobile phones so technologies can be configured to "sense" when a user is in or near your library physical location and automatically provide updates or promotional materials to these users while they are on the go. Again, if database vendors and other content providers could agree on a "geolocation standard for licensing content" then library services could query a user's location and provide seamless access to a library-owned resource or service (Griffey, 2010, p.92). When a Nevada State College student did not have reliable Internet access for a few months, she relied on her iPhone to register for classes and check e-mails, saying that she "used it all the time, for everything" (Keller, 2011). This anecdote and others like it will soon be commonplace, and libraries need to be ready. Apple received its first patent for solar powered portable devices in 2011; this is a critical advance for mobile devices that are always on and utilizing many resources, which can drain battery power quickly (Eaton, 2010). Reliable solar power for mobile devices is several years away, so libraries should consider including more electrical outlets that can be easily accessed or set up charging stations. According to the Kent State University focus group results, mobile users would like to be able to "customize their Web experience" and in particular to be able to "pick their favorite databases or choose their own top ten links to see on a mobile website" (Seeholzer & Salem). This customization trend has been popular for traditional Web resources and services for quite some time, so it makes sense to see customization requests for various mobile technologies.

With Bluetooth and other near-field mobile technologies it is already possible for mobile devices to send files "over the air" to a variety of devices such as printers, storage disks, other mobile devices, automobile entertainment systems, and home entertainment systems. Imagine library resources and services becoming available "over the air" or preloaded within some of these systems. It is theoretically possible for users to have access to their local library within, for example, a popular gaming console like the Wii. When connected to the Internet, a Wii can determine a user's location; simply entering one's library registration credentials would gain access to that library from within the Wii gaming console similar to the way Netflix works today, or already have instant access to an e-audiobook from within one's car stereo system. Again, with library reference resources and services becoming mobile-optimized, information will be more discoverable anytime because users will want to access high-quality information whenever the desire strikes. It is essential for libraries to be ready for this emerging (perhaps disruptive) trend and to become more visible and accessible to their mobile users.

To get a glimpse of the future of mobile technologies, Japan may be a good place to start because "keitai denwa" (Japanese for *mobile phones*) are an "integral part of modern Japanese life in that there are more services and functions relating to mobile phones there than nearly anywhere else in the world" (Griffey, 2010, pp. 93-94). Griffey highlights some common tasks that keitai can accomplish ranging from watching live television and navigating by GPS to crime prevention buzzers that report directly to the police and e-money services. With mobile technologies it will be easier to have a roving reference model allowing reference librarians to move away from the Reference Desk and help their users who are lost in the library stacks or to be able to check out a few books for them on the spot. Polaris and other integrated library systems now allow users to send item records directly to their mobile devices using SMS, a service that will become commonplace within the next couple of years.

Are acquisition and promotion enough for today's library users to use mobile-optimized library resources and services successfully? Transliteracy,

according to the Transliteracy Research Group, is "the ability to read, write and interact across a range of platforms, tools and media from signing and orality through handwriting, print, TV, radio and film, to digital social networks" (Transliteracy Research Group, 2010). This seems to be a perfect concept for librarians and information professionals to focus on, primarily because, as the introduction stated, in 2011 close to 80 percent of the world's population will have access to mobile devices and will eventually attempt to access authoritative information found in libraries. With the increase in information available on mobile devices, librarians are more valuable today than ever before because they can help users make sense of the information and teach them how to use it wisely. Equally important, however, librarians should be familiar with the various mobile devices and tools available on the market so that they can help empower their users to be successful information consumers well into the twenty-first century. Educators, including librarians, should be striving for a "21st century education in the same ways we are doing 21st century commerce" and to not use "19th century technology and fooling ourselves that we are teaching 21st century skills and content" because it is "doing our students a huge disservice" (Nagel, 2011).

Many libraries by now have embraced the "Web 2.0" philosophy primarily because the discovery and sharing aspects of "Web 2.0" have fit well into their missions, their vision for the future, and their everyday workflows. Consequently, it seems that libraries will continue to take long gazes into their future and see that it clearly includes mobile technologies. It will be an interesting landscape to watch, for sure, and if librarians and other information professionals keep their fingers on the pulse of these emerging technologies, especially the mobile technologies described in this chapter, then the library will remain in focus and clearly visible and viable, even essential, as a center for discovery and learning.

REFERENCES

Adkins, S. (2010). *The US market for mobile learning products and services: 2009-2014 forecast and analysis.* Retrieved November 30, 2010, from http://www.ambientinsight.com/Resources/Documents/ Ambient-Insight-2009-2014-US-Mobile -Learning-Market-Executive-Overview.pdf

Ballard, B. (2007). *Designing the mobile user experience.* Chichester, UK: Wiley. doi:10.1002/9780470060575

Briscoe, B., Odlyzko, A., & Tilly, B. (2009). *Metcalfe's law is wrong.* Retrieved February 7, 2011, from http://spectrum.ieee.org/computing / networks/metcalfes- law-is-wrong

Calgary Public Library. (2010). *Geocaching challenge: CPL news.* Retrieved November 30, 2010, from http://blog.calgarypubliclibrary.com/ blogs/cplnews/archive/2010/05/06/ Geocaching.aspx

Cameron, C. (2010) *Will mobile Web apps eventually replace native apps?* ReadWriteWeb.com. Retrieved 12/1/2010, from http://www.readwriteweb.com /archives/will_mobile_web_apps_eventually_replace_native_apps.php

De Rosa, C., & OCLC. (2006). *College students' perceptions of libraries and information resources: A report to the OCLC membership.* Dublin, Ohio: Online Computer Library Center.

Eaton, K. (2011). *Apple's solar power patent: Sun powered mac, iPods, iPhones in the future.* Retrieved January 11, 2011, from http://www.fastcompany.com/1716322 /apples-solar-power-patent-sun-powered -mac-ipods-iphones-in-the-future

Funabiki, R. (2009). *Geocaching: Hide and seek at your library.* Retrieved February 8, 2011 from http://www.idaholibraries.org/idlibrarian /index.php/idaho-librarian/article/view/25/81

Griffey, J. (2010). *Mobile technology and libraries.* New York, NY: Neal-Schuman Publisher.

HAWHAW. (2011). *Toolkit.* Retrieved November 30, 2010, from http://www.hawhaw.de/

Hopkins, C. (2011). *Spain pioneers QR codes to track ancient artifacts.* Retrieved January 14, 2011, from http://www.readwriteweb.com/archives /spain_pioneers_qr_codes_to_track_ ancient_artifacts.php?utm_source= feedburner&utm_medium=feed&utm _campaign=Feed:+readwriteweb+ (ReadWriteWeb)

International Telecommunication Union Newsroom. (2010). *Press release.* Retrieved November 2, 2010, from http://www.itu.int/net/pressoffice / press_releases/2010/39.aspx

Keller, J. (2011). *As the Web goes mobile, colleges fail to keep up.* Retrieved February 8, 2011, from http://chronicle.com/article/ Colleges-Search-for-Their/126016/

Moll, C. (2007). *Mobile Web design: A Web standards approach for delivering content to mobile devices.* Salt Lake City, UT: Cameron Moll.

Nagel, D. (2010). *Report: E-readers, LMS driving growth in higher ed mobile learning.* Retrieved February 2, 2011, from http://campustechnology.com/ articles/2010/08/31/report-e-readers- lms-driving-growth-in-higher-ed- mobile-learning.aspx

Nagel, D. (2011). Will smart phones eliminate the digital divide? *THE Journal.* Retrieved February 1, 2011, from http://thejournal.com/Articles /2011/02/01/Will-Smart- Phones-Eliminate-the-Digital-Divide.aspx

Pew Research Center. (2009). *Social isolation and new technology: How the Internet and mobile phones impact Americans' social networks.* Retrieved January 31, 2011, from http://pewresearch.org/pubs/1398/ internet-mobile-phones-impact-american -social-networks

Prabha, C., Silipigni Connaway, L., Olszewski, L., & Jenkins, L. R. (2007). What is enough? Satisficing information needs. *The Journal of Documentation, 63*(1), 74–89. doi:10.1108/00220410710723894

Seeholzer, J., & Salem, J. A. (2011). Library on the go: A focus group study of the mobile Web and the academic library. *College & Research Libraries, 72*(1), 9–20. Retrieved from http://vnweb.hwwilsonweb.com/hww /jumpstart.jhtml?recid=0bc05f7a67b 1790e0b52b53f9c-3da90e40fc1718e 75a19bb5c9f8fd67b98c-1903c9b320 b1b256c29&fmt=HPDF.

The New Media Consortium and EDUCAUSE Learning Initiative. (2010). *2010 Horizon report.* Retrieved November 2, 2010, from http://wp.nmc.org/horizon2010/

Thomas, L. C. (2010). *Gone mobile? (mobile libraries survey 2010).* Retrieved November 23, 2010, from http://www.libraryjournal.com/lj/ ljinprintcurrentissue/886987-403/gone_ mobile_mobile_libraries_ survey.html.csp

Transliteracy Research Group. (2011). *Transliteracy.* Retrieved February 2, 2011, from http://nlabnetworks.typepad.com /transliteracy/

WolfWalk. (n.d.). *NCSU library service.* Retrieved February 1, 2011, from http://www.lib.ncsu.edu/wolfwalk/

ADDITIONAL READING AND RESOURCES

Since mobile technologies are changing every day, an online version of the recommended resources section was created and is available at: http://www.scribd.com/doc/48662166/Recommended-mobile-Resources.

SELECT APPS AND APP DEVELOPMENT RESOURCES

AirPAC. http://www.iii.com/products/airpac.shtml

Blackboard Mobile. http://www.blackboard.com/Platforms /Mobile/overview.aspx

Lone Star Apps. http://www.lonestarapps.com

MIT's iMobileU, http://www.imobileu.org/

Mobile WebO. S. P.http://mobilewebosp.pbworks.com/

Molly Project. http://mollyproject.org/

Straxis Technology. www.U360mobile.com

University Web Developers Mobile Group. http://cuwebd.ning.com/group/mobile

SELECT LIBRARY MOBILE-OPTIMIZED RESOURCES AND SERVICES

Harvard, http://m.harvard.edu/

MIT. http://m.mit.edu/

Stanford University. (non-Blackboard), http://stanford.edu/m/

Stanford University (Blackboard). http://m.stanford.edu/

University of Washington. http://m.uw.edu/

West Virginia University. http://m.wvu.edu/

SELECT MOBILE-OPTIMIZED RESOURCES AND SERVICES

Read, Write, Web, http://m.readwriteweb.com/

Wolfram Alpha, http://m.wolframalpha.com/

ENDNOTES

[1]   "Mobile-optimized" here refers to content that is formatted to fit within the confines of small screens.

[2]   More information on Web Developer 1.1.8 can be found at http://chrispederick.com/work/web-developer/

[3]   To see a jQTouch demonstration and to download all the files visit the website at http://jqtouch.com/

[4]   To see an extensive list of libraries using SMS Reference Services visit Library Success: A Best Practices Wiki at http://www.libsuccess.org and search for SMS.

Chapter 17
The Semantic Web:
History, Applications and Future Possibilities

Darrell Gunter
Gunter Media Group, USA

ABSTRACT

The Semantic Web provides a common structure that allows data to be shared and reused across a variety of applications. The history and terminology of the Semantic Web, examples of STM achievements with semantics, an examination of semantic technology companies, and future possibilities for reference publishers are discussed and examined in this chapter. Cooperation between publishers will be imperative if we are to fully benefit from the advantages of the semantic technology.

INTRODUCTION

The promise of the Semantic Web needs to be balanced with patience, rules, freedom, structure, innovation, standards, creativity, and a sense of boldness. As there have been mini gains in the information industry, we are beginning to see gains in reference publishing with regard to the Semantic Web. This is an exploration of how semantic technology will not only enhance reference publishing but also put it at the forefront due to significant gains that will be achieved by researchers.

Since the publishing of Tim Berners-Lee's article on the Semantic Web in *Scientific American* in May 2001 (Berners-Lee, 2001, p. 3), the World Wide Web community has been holding its collective breath waiting for the big announcement—the announcement that would change the way that we conduct business, interact with one other, research for cures, and more importantly, how we put context into our search content.

DOI: 10.4018/978-1-61350-308-9.ch017

Tim Berners-Lee predicted that the Semantic Web, which "provides a common framework that allows data to be shared and reused across application, enterprise, and community boundaries," would connect all of the disparate pages from the Web and put the context in this vast sea of content. For example, imagine conducting a search for a specific disease to determine the latest research, top researchers, prestigious medical facilities that are known to treat the disease, and the doctors who are on the cutting edge of treating the disease. In today's world, several searches would have to be conducted to get the answers to these questions. However, in a semantic world, a single search can now accomplish this task due to the innovative tools and improved algorithms now available.

This chapter explores this capability and many more possibilities that the Semantic Web offers to the information industry, specifically to reference publishers. Included in the discussion is the history of the Semantic Web, an overview of semantic technologies, examples of publisher achievements in this area, an examination of semantic technology companies, and last but not least, the future possibilities.

BACKGROUND

The Semantic Web was conceived by Tim Berners-Lee, the inventor of the World Wide Web, in his landmark article "The Semantic Web" (Berners-Lee, 2001). Lee explored in the article all of the possibilities that the Semantic Web would be able to provide. While the Semantic Web advances have been painstakingly slow compared to other Web progress, there have been some key developments in many areas and industries. In his "Project 10X's Semantic Wave 2008 Report: Industry Roadmap to Web 3.0 & Multibillion Dollar Market Opportunities" (Davis, 2008), Mills Davis explored the development of the Semantic Web in four phases: Phase 1, "the Web"; Phase 2, "the social Web"; Phase 3, "the Semantic Web"; and Phase

4 (the future), "the ubiquitous Web." Phase 1 (the Web) is about connecting information and getting access to the Web. Phase 2 (the social Web) is about connecting people. As we have seen with the development and growth of social media sites like Facebook, MySpace, LinkedIn, Plaxo Xing, UniPHY.org, BiomedExperts.com and Naymz, connecting people from all walks of life and all parts of the world (i.e., Phase 2) has been accomplished. Phase 3 (the Semantic Web) is about connecting knowledge. Phase 4 (the ubiquitous Web) will allow us to connect intelligence.

Mills explains the three planes that have been developed over time to allow the Semantic Web to become a reality. The Operating Plane is the foundation layer of the three planes. It consists of the information, infrastructure, applications, and user interface. The second plane is the Internet. The third plane, the Knowledge Plane, is where the Semantic Web has its beginnings, developments, and breakthroughs. And a successful development of the Semantic Web requires the use of many tools, including, to name only a few, tagged collections, dictionaries, taxonomies, thesauri, and ontologies. These tools need to be understood fully to be able to navigate the semantic waters as they assist the algorithms in providing the accuracy in the result set.

In online computer systems terminology, a *tag* is a non-hierarchical keyword or term assigned to a piece of information (such as an Internet bookmark, digital image, or computer file). This kind of metadata helps describe an item and allows it to be found again by browsing or searching. Tags are generally chosen informally and personally by the item's creator or by its viewer, depending on the system (Tag, Wikipedia, 2010).

There are many definitions of *ontology*. Wikipedia defines it as the hierarchical structuring of knowledge about things by sub-categorizing them according to their essential (or at least relevant and/or cognitive) qualities. This is an extension of the previous senses of ontology, which has become common in discussions about the difficulty of maintaining subject indexes (Ontology, Wikipedia, 2011).

A *taxonomy*, or taxonomic scheme, is a particular classification ("the taxonomy of..."), arranged in a hierarchical structure. Typically this is organized by supertype-subtype relationships, also called generalization-specialization relationships, or less formally, parent-child relationships. In such an inheritance relationship, the subtype by definition has the same properties, behaviors, and constraints as the supertype plus one or more additional properties, behaviors, or constraints. For example: a car is a subtype of vehicle, so any car is also a vehicle, but not every vehicle is a car. Therefore a type needs to satisfy more constraints to be a car than to be a vehicle. Another example: any shirt is also a piece of clothing, but not every piece of clothing is a shirt. Hence, a type must satisfy more parameters to be a shirt than to be a piece of clothing (Taxonomy, Wikipedia, 2011).

A *thesaurus* is a dictionary of synonyms and antonyms. For example, if a student has written a paper about volcanoes in Africa, then her paper would be tagged with terms that would define volcanoes, Africa, lava, rough terrain, et cetera.

DEFINITION OF SEMANTIC WEB

The World Wide Web Consortium (W3C) states "the Semantic Web provides a common framework that allows *data* to be shared and reused across application, enterprise, and community boundaries." Wikipedia defines *semantics* as the study of meaning (Semantics, Wikipedia, 2010). The word "semantics" itself denotes a range of ideas, from the popular to the highly technical. It is often used in ordinary language to denote a problem of understanding that comes down to word selection or connotation. *Semantic search* is a process used to improve or conduct online searching by using data from *semantic networks* (Semantic Networks, Wikipedia, 2010) to disambiguate queries and Web text in order to generate more relevant results.

The Semantic Web requires us to go beyond documents and think of content as data. The resource description framework (RDF) data model, a language for representing information about resources in the World Wide Web (Resource Description Framework, Wikipedia, 2011), is similar to classic conceptual modeling approaches such as Entity-Relationship or Class diagrams, as it is based upon the idea of making statements about resources (in particular web resources) in the form of subject-predicate-object expressions. These expressions are known as *triples* in RDF terminology. The subject denotes the resource, and the predicate denotes traits or aspects of the resource and expresses a relationship between the subject and the object. For example, one way to represent the notion "The sky has the color blue" in RDF is as the triple: a subject denoting "the sky," a predicate denoting "has the color," and an object denoting "blue." RDF is an abstract model with several serialization formats (i.e., file formats), and so the particular way in which a resource or triple is encoded varies from format to format (Resource Description Framework, Wikipedia, 2011).

The semantic layer is an evolution of traditional Web metadata. It is a consistent, rules-based information layer for computer logic parsing. It is a method for exposing the meaning of data so the computer can perform more sophisticated cognitive tasks.

The taxonomy is the framework for the semantic layer and semantic tagging—crucial for concept normalization and hierarchies. Thanks to industry standard taxonomies, they help with the integration of concept across different subject areas. As taxonomies are always fluid and never stale, it is imperative that taxonomies be maintained by humans.

To achieve precision within the Semantic Web framework, the algorithms need the following attributes: stemming, lemmatization, normalization multi-lingual, synonyms, and disambiguation of homonyms and abbreviations.

Stemming, lemmatization, and normalizing allows for interpretation of going from plural to singular, past to present, and vice versa. The multi-lingual function allows you to interpret a word in different languages. For example: Gripe → Griep → Influenza. With the synonym capability it will capture all words that have a common point of reference, such as earth and globe. The disambiguation of homonyms is very important as it will distinguish correctly between concepts that are similar in some respects and could confuse a search result. For example, you could have a life science researcher that is conducting research on Dolly the sheep. Without the advent of disambiguation of homonyms, the search result set will include Dolly Parton the entertainer. Abbreviations allow for the interpretations of short /long form abbreviations; i.e. SARS → Severa Acute Respetory Syndrom (SARS). Last, but not least, are the inclusion Phrases (meaningful and coherent utterances). Being able to intrepret the term "blackwater fever" ensures that the researcher would achieve the precise definition.

With these capabilities contextual integration is possible. The use of a shared vocabulary or taxonomy will allow you the opportunity to integrate content from a variety of sources (e.g., journals, books, videos, images, training). In the healthcare field, there are a number of taxonomies, such as: MeSH, SNOMED, ICD-10, Read Codes, Silverchair Cortex, and about 100 more. The Unified Medical Language System (UMLS) is a place to start for health care integrations.

Semantic tagging is the future of true metadata. Tagging is the insertion of semantic information in the XML, whose smallest unit is called a tag. Tagging can also be placed in database tables and header files if the content is inaccessible (such as images and videos). Human indexers are the most accurate taggers for high-value content, but computer routines can help them tag or tag extremely formulaic content. Community tagging/ author tagging seems attractive, but it can also be risky due to inconsistency.

BENEFITS OF SEMANTIC TECHNOLOGY

There are many benefits of semantic technology, of which precision in discovery is the most important. Precision in answering user queries is a key component of an application's usability and user satisfaction rating. The semantic layer provides an application with a concise guide to the content in a language it can understand. It can now provide more accurate results. Computable, contextual relationships create a rich matrix of linking for your users using the semantic layer. These links never have to be updated by a person—semantics enable instantaneous, automated relationships whenever new content is added. What's more, semantic reports give a unified view to integrated sites and can help guide collection development (Semantics, Wikipedia, 2010).

Gale/Cengage's recently-launched PowerSearch tool—like those by several other publishers—has many benefits for precision in discovery, but it falls short of what a true semantic technology application can provide. Its four key new features include Search Assist, Enhanced Results, Language Customizability and Enhanced Subject, and Publication Search. The Search Assist feature states that it will save users time and provide Web search-functionality similar to Yahoo and Google. It is quite apparent that Gale/Cengage is using semantic technology to help researchers save time, as the use of semantic technology is visible in the background. But, they have not yet taken the next step to aggregate and visualize the results in a more effective manner. For example, in Figure 1, the search results detail the various keywords, but do not provide a weighted visualization of these concepts to point out which concepts have more relevance. (See Figure 1.) Taking semantics a step further, by aggregating, weighting, and visualizing results offers a value-added search feature for users, ultimately to provide precision in content discovery. In Figure 2, the Collexis FingerPrint, which provides a view of the weighted concepts of

Figure 1. © Gale/Cengage Learning, Used With Permission

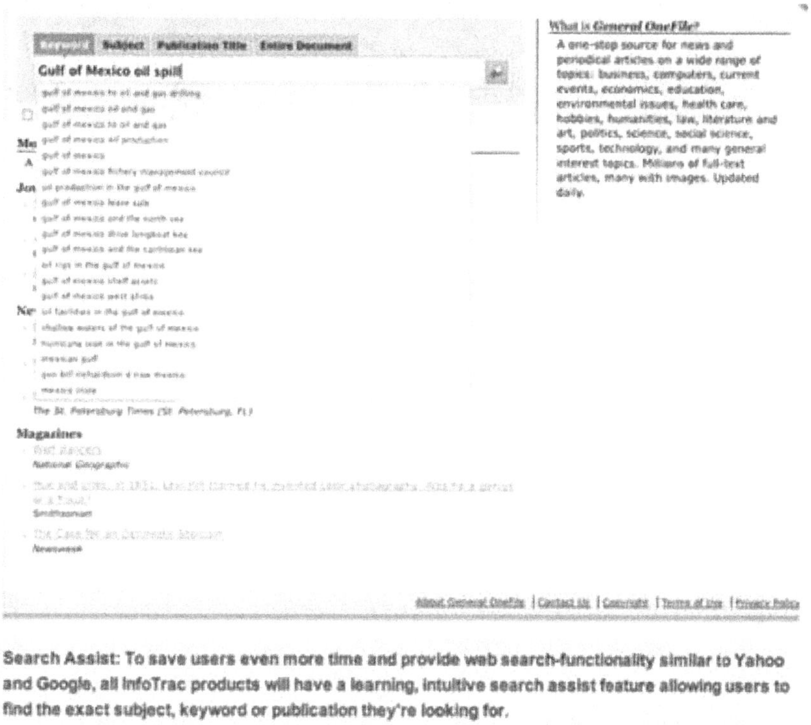

Search Assist: To save users even more time and provide web search-functionality similar to Yahoo and Google, all InfoTrac products will have a learning, intuitive search assist feature allowing users to find the exact subject, keyword or publication they're looking for.

a search result, demonstrates this next step in the semantic process. The benefit of this visualization is that it allows the researcher to see the weighted relevant concepts of their search result that allows them to see the concepts they recognize and others they don't recognize. This allows them to explore new areas of research.

Unfortunately, many reference publishers are still presenting search results in the traditional vertical list format. We know that researchers are not looking beyond the top ten search results and in most cases not looking past the first page. This is the appeal of semantic technology, coupled with aggregation and visualization. Semantic technology allows you take huge amounts of data, aggregate and organize it, and then visualize the results with clear links to key data. This will be the next development phase for publishers and producers of reference content. If they choose not to move in this direction, they could find them-

selves and their products obsolete in less than five years.

One reference aggregator has moved in this direction, taking a positive step in the use of semantic technology. Credo Reference has recently added a feature to their online reference service called topic pages. Topic pages are created using a semantic ontology. Credo started with an ontology called Yago, developed by the Max-Planck-Institut Informatik (http://www.mpi-inf.mpg.de/yago-naga/yago/), which includes category information from Wikipedia and word information from Wordnet. Credo extended the ontology using their own data. The ontology is used to select topics from Credo's 3+ million entries, select the articles, and select the definitions and images for display on each topic page. The ontology also is used to provide a set of related topics. This enables Credo to present the user with a coherent set of information about each topic along with links to

Figure 2. © Elsevier, Used With Permission

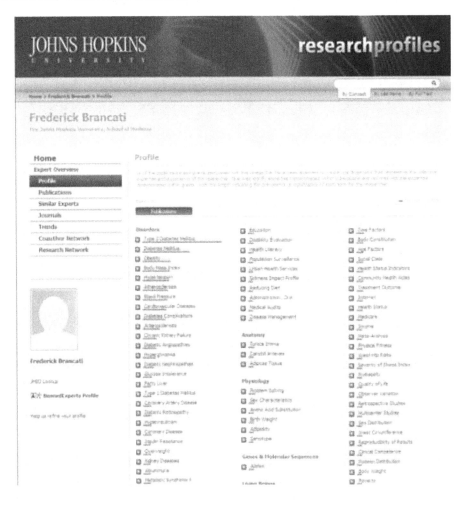

related topics, each of which is also generated using the ontology.

The example in Figure 3 shows the topic page for DNA. To generate this page, the topic "DNA" is chosen from the ontology, the main article is then selected, using various quality measures, and a definition, additional entries and relevant images are chosen. All of these choices are based on information in the ontology and reflect information about the topic itself. The ontology is then used to suggest different, but closely related topics for display in the related topics tag cloud. This degree of relatedness was determined from the ontology and reflected in the font size.

By using a semantic approach, Credo has been able to move away from a simple list of research results and present a more organized set of material about each topic on a single page. At present, there are over 9,000 topic pages in the Credo Reference product.

SEMANTICS & STM PUBLISHING

In 2010 Elsevier acquired the assets of Collexis Holdings, Inc. Collexis was founded in 1999 and had established itself as one of the leading semantic technology companies by the adoption of their Expert Profiles, BiomedExperts.com and

Figure 3. © 2011, Credo Reference, Used With Permission

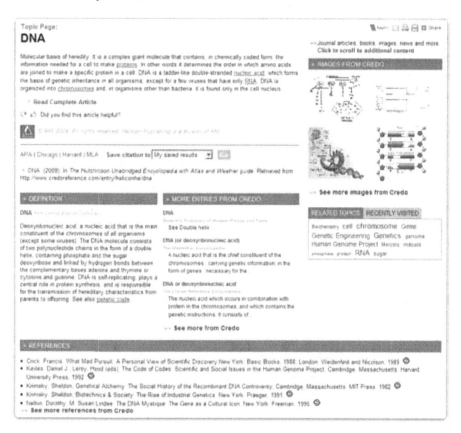

the Collexis Reviewer Finder. The backbone of the Collexis technology is their capability to create digital fingerprints of a corpus of documents. From those fingerprints, a researcher is able to determine the expert in a given disease category, within a department, an institution, a state, or a country.

The Collexis technology is able to aggregate large amounts of structured and unstructured data and then organize it into digital fingerprints. The visualization of the data allows the reader to take in vast amount of data by focusing on key concept topics and sub topics. From here, the researcher is able to select a specific search topic either to expand or contract their search.

The second example of semantic technology at work is Portland Press' project Utopia. The vision for Utopia is to blend the best of the Semantic Web with the ease of use, stability, and elegance of PDFs. Articles remain as stable Versions of Record while being dynamic, interactive, and evolving repositories of knowledge. At the 2010 SSP Annual Meeting & Charleston Conference, Adam Marshall provided the attendees with a first-hand look at Utopia.

Utopia enriches the document metadata as it able to read a PDF much like a human would. It recognizes the content of a document by the known sources (e.g., title, author, keywords, citations, references). It also identifies important features such as materials and methods Citations and references are automatically linked to online repositories. Utopia also allows you to interact with document content by bringing a static PDF to life. It has interactive visualizations. For example, molecules can be realized as 3D rotating images; protein sequences become live and interactive; tables of data become live spreadsheets; graphs generated on the fly are linked to source data, and the researcher is able to dynamically include data/text-mining results. A full demonstration of Utopia is available at http://www.biochemj.org/demo.

All STM publishers are now actively pursuing not only the understanding of semantic technology but the implementation of it into their publishing processes. In the next two years, publishers like Wiley, Springer, Wolters Kluwer, and Informa and a host of other society publishers will announce their plans for implementations of semantic technology and applications. Beyond the STM realm, large media houses like McGraw Hill, Thomson Reuters, and the BBC are also utilizing semantic technology to improve their user community's experience because it allows them to regain their prominence as these new semantic search and information dashboards allow the user to navigate large corpus of data from many different publishers faster than ever before.

To help bring about this new dramatic change, there are several semantic technology companies that will be ready to help the STM publishers take the next steps. They include the following (listed in no particular order):

- **Parity Computing** (http://www.parity-computing.com/web/index.html): This company's unstructured data management and knowledge discovery solutions transform disparate data and content into a knowledge network of actionable profiles and linked relationships.
- **Silverchair** (http://www.silverchair.com): Silverchair develops products by combining their Silverchair Content Manager platform with customizable functionality and interfaces designed for optimal user value. It collaborates with a variety of STM publishers to help them create information applications optimized for the Web as well as portable devices.
- **Fairview Research** (http://www.fairviewresearch.com/pr/temp-home-page.aspx): This company provides a set of products and services that support the development and maintenance of highly customized information retrieval solutions, from simple data enhancement to a full solution implementation.

- **Textwise** (http://textwise.com): TextWise developed the first scalable, automated semantic similarity search technology that enabled the Web to move from matching keywords to a meaning-based foundation.
- **Molecular Connections** (http://www.molecularconnections.com/home): This discovery services company specializes in information abstraction services, literature curation and annotation in the area of biomedical, chemistry, and patent literature.
- **Access Innovations / Data Harmony** (http://www.accessinn.com): This company's services include design, construction, and maintenance of databases, taxonomy construction, metadata planning, and content management, to name a few. Quality control is performed throughout production.
- **TEMIS** (http://www.temis.com): Temis's Luxid® for Scientific Discovery solution brings answers to the challenges of information discovery and knowledge extraction from unstructured data. It is designed to meet the content management requirements of innovation-driven companies, giving access to non-obvious information and delivering industry-specific knowledge.
- **NextBio** (http://www.nextbio.com/b/nextbio.nb): NextBio develops innovative global discovery platform for life sciences data. Corporate and individual researchers' data from diverse experiments can be imported, integrated with public data, and explored within relevant biological and clinical context.

CONCLUSION

What does the future hold for semantic technology? Over the next three to five years, there will be a number of great advances. We have already seen the power of the Collexis Fingerprint and how it is able to aggregate, organize and visualize the requested data requested from the researcher. From the PubMed database, Collexis was able to create BiomedExperts.com, the world's first pre-populated professional network for life science researchers. BiomedExperts.com now contains 1.4 million profiles of life science researchers and their more than 20 million co-author connections. In addition, their institutional application Expert Profiles is being utilized by John Hopkins, The Mayo Clinic, the NIH, and University of Miami, to name a few.

Similarly, Portland Press has successfully launched Utopia, and the Royal Society of Chemistry has entered the game with Project Prospect. The Nature Publishing Group has introduced an Open Text Mining Interface (OTMI). In addition to acquiring Collexis, Elsevier has used Parity Computing to address the author disambiguation project for Scopus. It has also introduced Illumin8 and has an agreement with NextBio.

All of these examples point to the exciting developments underway. In the future we can expect to see traditional reference publishers and vendors—including, among others, Gale/Cengage, ProQuest, and EBSCO—enhancing their products with these technologies to stay competitive and to serve their readers. Imagine being able to conduct a search over a corpus of data that includes journals, books, reference works, grey literature, video, and podcast and for that data to be aggregated, organized, and visualized in a manner that allows you to see either a one-page dashboard or a digital fingerprint consisting of the key concepts. The technology is already there, and it is only a matter of time before this kind of an application becomes a reality.

Cooperation between publishers will be imperative if we are to fully benefit from the advantages of the semantic technology. This big win will happen only when competing publishers open their databases to each other to allow the user to conduct a search on a given topic across all their products and platforms. While the promise of this new technology has taken years to come to fruition, we are still in the very early stages of the semantic wave. It will take patience, innovation, more investment, sharing, and partnership before the ultimate goal is reached: to reduce the number of clicks needed to get to the information as seamlessly as possible.

REFERENCES

Berners-Lee, T., Hendler, J., & Lassila, O. (2001). The Semantic Web. *Scientific American, 284*(5), 34. doi:10.1038/scientificamerican0501-34

Davis, M. (2008). *Project 10X, semantic wave report: Industry roadmap to Web 3.0 and multibillion dollar market opportunities*. Retrieved August 20, 2009, from http://www.project10x.com/

Lasilla, O., & Swick, R. (1999). *Resource description framework (RDF) model and syntax specification*. W3C. Retrieved November 12, 2010, from http://www.w3.org/TR/PR-rdf-syntax/

Wikipedia, The Free Encyclopedia. (2011). *Ontology*. Retrieved February 28, 2011, from http://en.wikipedia.org/w/index.php?title=Ontology&oldid=416410140

Wikipedia, The Free Encyclopedia. (2011). *Resource description framework*. Retrieved February 19, 2011, from http://en.wikipedia.org/w/index.php?title=Resource_Description_Framework&oldid=420026139

Wikipedia, The Free Encyclopedia. (2011). *Semantic network*. Retrieved August 20, 2010, from http://en.wikipedia.org/w/index.php ?title=Semantic_network& oldid=420472897

Wikipedia, The Free Encyclopedia. (2011). *Semantics*. Retrieved August 20, 2010, from http://en.wikipedia.org/w/index.php ?title=Semantics&oldid =420586324

Wikipedia, The Free Encyclopedia. (2011). *Tag (metadata)*. Retrieved February 19, 2011, from http://en.wikipedia.org/w/index.php ?title=Tag_ (metadata)& oldid=419544900

Wikipedia, The Free Encyclopedia. (2011). *Taxonomy*. Retrieved February 19, 2011, from http://en.wikipedia.org/w/index.php ?title=Taxonomy& oldid=420078840

Chapter 18
Hooligans in the Archives:
Easing Restrictions and Partnering with the Users

Laurie Gemmill
LYRASIS, USA

Jane Wildermuth
Wright State University, USA

ABSTRACT

Archival reference has changed dramatically with the advent of the Web, which challenged archivists to rethink their role as gatekeepers of archival materials. Traditionally, archival reference tools and materials were difficult to gain access to or required meditation by archivists. Archivists moved from gatekeepers to innovators, by putting reference tools and digital surrogates of collections online. But as with any new step, there are challenges. The traditional archival tension in trying to balance access and preservation has morphed. As access has changed, preservation concerns have given way to control concerns. Archivists are now poised to take the next step by engaging the users, sharing control over collections, and potentially empowering the users to become true partners in the reference and research experience.

INTRODUCTION

Online access has radically changed the nature of archival reference. In a few short years archivists moved from a traditional framework of controlled access of archival reference tools and collections to a new mindset of making materials more accessible online. With the onset of digitization, archivists debated whether they should make digital surrogates of collections available online since it was counter to their traditional role as gatekeeper to collections. Archivists worried that the online world would inhibit their ability to maintain the safety and intellectual control of the original items.

DOI: 10.4018/978-1-61350-308-9.ch018

Archivists soon learned that digitization helped protect collections from frequent handling while allowing them to reach a worldwide audience. With some preservation concerns subsiding, focus shifted into control concerns.

Over time, there has been increasing pressure to make more collections available online and allow more user interaction. In this new climate archivists need to balance their traditional concerns of maintaining physical and intellectual control over their collections with the changing nature of user expectations and curation of digital objects and collections. Users are demanding and expecting increased access to and interactivity with the collections. Archivists now need to expand their approach and create tools to empower users to find, use, and engage the archives.

BACKGROUND OF ARCHIVAL REFERENCE

Prior to the Internet, archival reference was typically a one on one, personal interaction that was highly controlled. Archivists served as the gatekeepers of archival materials. While providing reference assistance to researchers, archivists knew who, when, and for what purpose materials in their repositories were being used. Those interested in collections were typically required to physically visit the repository. During a visit, access to materials was mediated by archivists through special appointments, strict security, and supervised interaction with the materials. Rules and regulations helped archivists strike a balance between preservation of and access to archival materials. It is the archivists' duty to preserve archival materials to ensure our history can be researched and studied now as well as by future generations. The online environment has radically changed archival reference and the traditional role of archivist as gatekeeper by figuratively opening up the gates and allowing unmediated access to collections on the Web via digitization.

ARCHIVAL REFERENCE MOVING TO ONLINE ENVIRONMENT

Early Development of Online Archival Reference Tools

With the advent of the Internet, archivists began to move print reference materials to the online environment. One of the first archival reference tools that moved online was the National Union Catalog of Manuscript Collections (NUCMC). NUCMC was created in 1958 to provide the location of and bibliographic information for manuscript collections. From 1959 to 1993, 29 volumes were printed and provided descriptions of approximately 72,300 collections in 1406 repositories (National Union Catalog of Manuscript Collections [NUCMC], 2009). Researchers could go to their local library and page through the volumes of NUCMC to learn about manuscript collections throughout the country. Now available online, NUCMC has over 1.5 million records for archival and individual manuscripts and is available to the public for free through OCLC WorldCat (NUCMC, 2010). Moving this reference tool to an online environment allowed researchers to discover archival collections more easily; however the brief bibliographic information provides only a glimpse at the content contained in collections comprised of hundreds and even thousands of cubic feet of materials.

Finding aids are another example of a print reference tool used in archival repositories that moved to the Web. They describe the scope and provenance of collections and list the contents according to the physical arrangement of the collection. Typically finding aids were available in the reading room and were used as a starting point for the researcher and a means of controlling access to/preservation of the collection for archivists. A researcher would not have to browse through an entire collection to see what is contained within. Rather, they browse the finding aid and then request particular boxes. Some archives would provide visitors with a paper copy of a finding aid prior to their visit, or for significant collections one could purchase a bound copy of the finding aid. As websites for archives became commonplace, archives began to put to finding aids online into HTML. Researchers could simply use a search engine to find their topic in a manuscript collection contained within an archives they never knew existed. Archivists soon realized that although the increased and easier access to findings aid helped researchers, standardization was needed. Finding aids varied from repository to repository and even within repositories. Archivists realized the need for researchers to be able to search online finding aids in a uniform way. EAD (Encoded Archival Description) allowed for the formalization and standardization of finding aids within and across repositories. It was an early step in using the web to improve the researchers' experience when using archival materials. Many archivists began converting their finding aids into EAD and began depositing them into EAD repositories. Although EADs improve searching, it is still cumbersome to researchers. In 2004, Elizabeth Yakel explained in *Encoded Archival Descriptions: Are Finding Aids Boundary Spanners or Barriers for Users?* that EAD often acted as a barrier to the researcher, emphasizing a reliance on archival jargon and the reliance of the researcher's prior understanding of hierarchical finding aids (Yakel, 2010).

These early projects allowed researchers to locate and gain a better understanding of the holdings in repositories. One early project that allowed researchers to perform research remotely was the Ohio Historical Society's Ohio Death Index Project. Volumes of indexes of Ohio death records came to the Ohio Historical Society in 1996 from the Ohio Secretary of State. Genealogists from around the state began requesting research to be performed for them or came to the Ohio Historical Society (OHS) to use these printed reference materials. In 1996 OHS decided to scan, OCR (Optical Character Recognition), and make available on the Web the Ohio Death Index

through a grant from the State Library which was supported by the OHS, and Ohio Public Library and Information Network (OPLIN). By giving researchers access to the index remotely, it lessened the need to handle the originals by researchers and staff. By providing the full text (via OCR), users could perform much more effective searches. It also decreased the work load for OHS staff since researchers could ask for the specific death records by volume and page number. This project was the perfect balance of opening up access to records which in turn helped preserve the original. It also did not conflict with the gatekeeper role of the archivists. Researchers had access to the indexes, but to view the actual death record, they still had to make contact with the Ohio Historical Society. The online index is available at: http://ohsweb. ohiohistory.org/death/.

Developing Online Collections: Considerations and User Impact

As the Internet developed and computers storage and speed increased, archives had the ability to not only put reference tools online, but digital images of actual collections such as manuscripts and photographs. Some archivists were reluctant to put digital images of the materials online, fearing they would give up control of the materials for which they were responsible. Archivists worried that researchers would no longer need to come to visit their archives which might lead to reduction in funding and staffing. Some archivists worried that digitization of the materials would damage the materials and that preservation of the item outweighed giving access to researchers worldwide. This attitude changed as equipment improved and lessened the fears of damaging materials, digitization standards and procedures were developed, and archivists realized that by putting materials online they increased access to materials while at the same time lessening the need to handle those original materials. During this time there was a great deal of experimentation in determining what repositories should do and what users expected. Standards and best practices for technical considerations such as DPI, resolution, and file formats soon evolved. The Library of Congress (http://memory.loc.gov/ammem/about/techIn.html) and the Collaborative Digitization Program (now available at: http://www.lyrasis.org/Products-and-Services/Digital-and-Preservation-Services/Digital-Toolbox.aspx) pioneered efforts in this areas and provided widely used best practices. While the technical decisions were easing, other workflow issues such as selection and metadata were more complicated.

Selection

Manuscript/photograph/government collections can be massive. Some collections consist of a few physical items but many include hundreds of thousands of individual items. Once archivists realized the value of putting materials online, the enormity of the issue hit them. They had potentially millions of items to put online. Where should they start?

Many early digitization projects focused on "cherry picking" individual items, including especially significant items such as individual photographs or "samples" of a manuscript collection. In doing the *African American Experience in Ohio* for the Library of Congress/Ameritech's National Digital Library Competition (American Memory) the Ohio Historical Society staff chose specific items relating to the African American experience in Ohio (http://dbs.ohiohistory.org/africanam/). In this project, staff selected individual manuscript items or folders and specific photographs that would be especially notable. They provided context for these by including serial and newspaper materials. Projects had to develop selection criteria as a way to determine what to digitize because it would take substantial time and resources to digitize all collections or even all of one collection. The selection criteria helped focus the digitization to be done, but a

new problem arose. Archivists found themselves spending substantial amounts of time researching items to be digitized to be sure they met the selection criteria.

Copyright is another major consideration in selection. Even though materials are held by a repository, that does not mean the institution has the right to publish the materials on the Web. A manuscript collection can have numerous copyright holders within it. For example, in a collection of letters sent to one person, the copyright belongs to the authors of the letters, not to the possessor or receiver of the letters. Many archives focus on materials in the public domain or have contacted the copyright holder to gain approval to place materials online.

Metadata

At the same time, the actual process of digitizing and putting collections online was bringing up other issues. Traditional processing focused on providing folder level access. But when putting items online, there is a desire to treat and thus describe each item, letter, or photograph individually. When spending a great deal of time and attention on an item, archivists want to ensure the user finds it and realizes its significance. Putting an entire collection online but not providing access points to individual items seemed problematic. Without specific metadata to help users narrow their search, how would researchers find the item that would be most useful to them?

Initially, projects used traditional cataloging standards such as MARC records when creating information to access the item. But MARC records are designed for collections, not for individual items such as a singular photograph. In addition, following traditional cataloging practices can be time consuming and resource intensive.

While many institutions were trying to determine what metadata would be most appropriate to create, many early efforts were stymied by lack of options. Institutions had long used MARC records but sought more flexible and less time consuming options. Dublin Core (http://dublincore.org/), initiated at a workshop hosted by OCLC in Dublin, Ohio in 1995, was created in an effort to address concerns with different metadata standards being used. The Dublin Core Metadata Initiative's purpose "is to provide simple standards to facilitate the finding, sharing, and management of information" (Dublin Core Metadata Initiative [DCMI], 1995- 2010). It was intended to be a flexible, simple way of having core metadata (simple and implementable descriptions) for a wide variety of materials. That flexibility is a great strength and encourages wide adoption but can also lead to difficulties. For example, the title field is described as: "The name given to the resource. Typically a title will be a name by which the resource is formally known." This can be fairly straightforward if the item is a book but with a photograph, ideas about the "name" can differ widely. Variants could include:

- Photograph of Man in Hat
- Man in Hat Photograph
- Man in Hat in Black and White Photograph
- Man in Hat Outside
- Man in Hat, 1934

This variation can be especially problematic for collaborative projects where many institutions may be describing different media types including photographs, manuscripts, and 3 dimensional objects. Some projects such as the Collaborative Digitization Program (formerly Colorado Digitization Project) and the SENYLRC's Hudson River Valley Heritage (HRVH) project implemented style guides in an effort to provide some consistency within projects. Examples can be seen at: HRVH Metadata Style Guide http://www.hrvh.org/about/standards_bestpractice.htm and CDP's guide http://www.lyrasis.org/Products-and-Services/Digital-and-Preservation-Services/Digital-Toolbox/Metadata.aspx. The development of standards and consistency is important so that

users can effectively search across a wide number of items and find the most useful resources.

In the early days of digitization, institutions experimented with different approaches. Three different approaches include those by the Georgia Archives, the Ohio Historical Society's Ohio Memory program, and West Virginia University Library.

The Georgia Archives was an early innovator in making substantial collections available via their "George's Virtual Vault" (http://cdm.sos.state.ga.us/index.php). In their initial projects they were interested in getting a great number of materials online quickly. They digitized and put items online with minimal metadata with the objective to go back and create more metadata later as necessary but in the meantime, items were at least accessible (Georgia Secretary of State, 2007-2010).

Another approach taken in metadata creation was with Ohio Memory (http://www.ohiomemory.org/). It is a collaborative program, coordinated by the Ohio Historical Society, designed to make historical materials from all over the Ohio available online. In this program, which began in 2000, institutions submitted materials which were then reviewed by program staff against various criteria including historical significance and copyright. Many institutions found that what they knew about their own collections was frequently undocumented. In creating submissions, staffs researched materials and were able to document their items much more thoroughly. A great deal of metadata was generated in this review process; once it was created, it was important to include it in the digital library so that others benefited from the information. Thus the digital collection has fairly extensive metadata for materials included the collection (Ohio Historical Society, 2008).

In 2005, the West Virginia University Library embarked on another method of metadata creation with their project to digitize more than 25,000 historical photographs. With such a large collection of individual items to work with, they developed an innovative way to reduce costs but accelerate workflow. They utilized student workers who prepared initial metadata with the assistance of drop down menus of pre-selected terms. The project manager reviewed each item, and once approved, the item went online. At that point, it also went into the queue for the cataloger to review it. Items went online before a cataloger did their final review but were made available in a much timelier fashion than could have happened otherwise. While it is important to ensure metadata is thorough and accurate, it can be difficult to make progress without a dedicated cataloger. This process ensured that materials were made available quickly and the cataloging review would not serve as a bottleneck (Cuthbert, 2008).

Over time these concerns over selection, copyright, and metadata lessened as standards evolved and were widely adopted. As those considerations ebbed, users were becoming more and more accustomed to online research and finding and using online collections. The next stages focused on changing user expectations and use of materials.

Empowering the Users: Example

A tremendous benefit of putting materials online is enabling the user to have more control over their discovery during the research process. An illustrative example is found in Wright State University's pre-eminent Wright Brothers Collection. In 2002, Special Collections and Archives staff began working to put the photographs from this collection online. Prior to digitization, handling a reference request for Wright Brothers photographs was labor intensive and required regular handling of the original photos in the collection by archival staff. A typical request might be, "Please send us some sample photos of the Wright Brothers wearing hats." The finding aid to the collection would not indicate which of the over 4,000 photos included the brothers with hats. Archivists would have to leaf through the substantial collection, find a sampling they felt might be appropriate,

photocopy those images, fax the photocopies to the researcher, and wait to hear feedback. If they ordered a photo, a copy negative would need to be made from the original print by a Wright State photographer. The archivist could not leave such a valuable item with the photographer. So an appointment was set and the archivist watched as the photographer did his work. Then after the negative was developed, a print was made and sent to the researcher. If a similar request is made today, the user would simply go the photographic collection online (http://core.libraries.wright.edu/handle/2374.WSU/827) and search the word "hat." They are immediately presented with numerous examples from the collection. Next, they provide the archivist with the item number and a master high quality, high resolution image would be posted later that day for download from a server. This was an early and important step in allowing the user more direct access to the collections. Two very different examples of images with a Wright brother in a hat are shown in Figures 1 and 2.

These two widely divergent images demonstrate the value of enabling users to view and determine which image is most suitable for their purpose.

NEXT STEPS

As online collections developed, users were finding more and more content. However, over time, it became clear that researchers were not aware that selection was being done by archivists. Underfunded repositories and overworked staff did not suddenly have sufficient resources to digitize and put entire collections online. But with the growing number of online resources, many users assumed *everything* was online or worse, if it was not online, that it was unimportant. Like everyone else, researchers are struggling to do more with less, so they will use what is easiest and more convenient to access including poor resources that are easily accessible rather than an item with

Figure 1. L'Aero-cap Chapeau Extra Leger. © 1908, Courtesy of Wright State University Special Collections & Archives. Used with permission.

high research value that is unavailable online. To many researchers, research begins and ends online.

At the same time more content was being made available, the Web was continuing to develop. For many institutions, their early websites were "brochure-ware," that included operating hours, contact information, maps, et cetera. As time went on, putting collections online become the norm. But expectations continued to evolve in a Web 2.0 environment. It was no longer enough to have access; users were becoming accustomed to doing much more online. In non-archival online settings they were making friends, creating art, gaming, dating, forming relationships, and creating virtual worlds. In this context, just "viewing" the materials wasn't enough. Users wanted to *interact* with the materials. Initially they wanted to be empowered to download it, use it in a PowerPoint, and then they wanted to interact with it – tag it, colorize it, get involved with it.

In the past few years there has been a great deal of experimentation among archives regarding how much access and thus control to give to users. Many institutions have been extremely cautious and continue to restrict access. Most have

Figure 2. Wright Brothers walking at Belmont Park. © 1910, Courtesy of Wright State University Special Collections & Archives. Used with permission.

at minimum started to digitize and provide some limited online access. As it noted in the recent Taking Our Pulse: The OCLC Research Survey of Special Collections and Archives report, "half of archival collections have no online presence" but "user demand for digitized collections remains insatiable" (Dooley & Luce, 2010).

Users want to engage with the materials. This is intrinsically threatening to the traditional gatekeeper mindset. Not long ago archivists would require an interview with a researcher before that researcher was allowed to touch an item, even with gloves in a supervised reading room with security cameras. The age-old tension between access and preservation has since developed into a tension between access and control. The idea of giving the public some degree of control is threatening to many archivists. An excellent summary of concerns and responses to these concerns was presented at the 2009 IMLS WebWise conference in Washington DC. Michael Edson, Director of Digital Media Strategy at the Smithsonian, gave an overview of the concerns many archivists have. More information about this presentation can be found at Edson's blog *Using Data* at http://using-data.typepad.com/usingdata/2009/03/web.html. Edson outlined many of the concerns archivists have including: legal issues, potential confusion for users, limited staff available for additional work, and concerns whether users will come to the institution if the materials are available online. One of the preeminent concerns is: What happens if you allow users to contribute metadata and they get it WRONG? (Edson, 2009).

Archivists get it wrong too sometimes. Archivists are not experts in all subjects. In addition, collections have their own histories. Many times there are notes written on the backs of items. In viewing the notes it is typically unclear who wrote them. For example, the text "Fred Jones" may be written on the back of a photograph. It is unclear who wrote that. Did someone who knew Mr. Jones write it? Did a volunteer/curator see other photographs of Fred Jones, notice he appeared to

be the same person and note it? Even when notes are verified, they are subject to misinterpretation. In looking at the back of a photograph with the note "Mount Vernon" one might think it was a photograph of a picture of a home in Mount Vernon, Ohio. Instead it might be a picture of George Washington's home Mount Vernon in Virginia.

As Michael Edson reminds us, "Most of the experts don't work for you" (Edson, 2009), and archivists do not have the control they think they do. Many institutions have very knowledgeable staff and experts on many subjects. But they cannot know everything, and many of the knowledgeable specialists outside of the institution are willing to help. In a time of reduced budgets and limited staff, the idea of having knowledgeable people volunteer their expertise and contribute to the general knowledge about collections is appealing. Another consideration is that when the public tags items online, it is usually clear that it is the public tagging them. The viewer can see the item and the metadata contributed and make their own evaluation of it.

Some preeminent institutions, such as the Library of Congress (LC), have taken the lead by experimenting with ways to let the user interact with and even gain some "ownership" of collections. In 2008 LC took an innovative step in the area of shared metadata. They undertook a pilot project with Flickr to share photographs. This resulted in the Flickr Commons being launched on January 16, 2008. Flickr has more on the project at: 'Many hands make light work" http://blog.flickr.net/en/2008/01/16/many-hands-make-light-work/. LC undertook the project to "help address at least two major challenges: how to ensure better and better access to our collections, and how to ensure that we have the best possible information about those collections for the benefit of researchers and posterity." In putting the materials online, they found that "all that work that we've put in has contributed to making something greater than the sum of its parts: an organic Information System." They indicated that "the real magic comes when the power of the Flickr community takes over. We want people to tag, comment and make notes on the images…which will benefit not only the community but also the collections themselves. For instance, many photos are missing key caption information such as where the photo was taken and who is pictured. If such information is collected via Flickr members, it can potentially enhance the quality of the bibliographic records" (Raymond, 2008). LC has blogged on this project; more info is available at the preceding link. Pilot info including summary and full reports is at: http://www.loc.gov/rr/print/flickr_pilot.html

The fact that the Library of Congress was willing to take steps to share their material and let the public tag items was a quantum leap forward. As a preeminent institution demonstrated its willingness to allow the public to tag library items, the library provided a model for the library/archival/museum community to follow. The Brooklyn Museum became an early adopter when it joined Flickr in May 2008. The museum staff wrote that by "sharing these images we will support a better understanding of the cultures that have created the great art that is held by this Museum" (Lawrence, 2008).

In a presentation at the 2009 WebWise conference, Shelley Bernstein, Chief of Technology from the Brooklyn Museum, spoke about their experience. They found that putting the materials online resulted in a flood of interest from the public. The response was rewarding but initially resulted in additional work as the public wanted to know more about the materials. However, over time, staff found new users in the community that wanted to help. Many experts that worked outside of the museum were able to contribute information about the museum's resources. The staff did not accept everything as correct without review, but were able to verify information about their collections which was more efficient than doing original research. This "crowd" sourcing proved

to be a valuable way to enhance the collection metadata and grow the museum's community (Bernstein, 2009).

CONCLUSION

Archivists have grown from gatekeepers to innovators in a relatively short period of time. They have been in the forefront in putting unique resources online, adding not only reference tools, but collections themselves to the online world. Now is the time for the next steps in archival reference. Archivists need to continue to find innovative ways to enable and facilitate interactivity for the user. Models include creating shared metadata and updating records, accepting verified user generated information, and treating the users as partners in information sharing.

Reaching out to "the crowd" is a necessary step in growing the contextual information and access points, but also to grow the community of those interested in and invested in these materials. Archivists need to provide the collections and user-generated tags to researchers and let them decide their value. This is the model followed in the reading room for decades – provide the source to the researcher and let them evaluate it and make a decision about meaning and significance for themselves.

What is the purpose of protecting and preserving archival materials if they are not used, studied, researched, and engaged with? Those institutions that do not encourage or even allow their users to engage with collections do so at their peril. Without meeting the needs of their users, these institutions will cease serving their community and risk a diminished base of users. It is time "open the gates" and let the hooligans into the archives if they are to become true partners in the reference and research experience.

REFERENCES

Bernstein, S. (2009). Session 1: Online communities and the institution. *WebWise 2009 Digital Debates Conference Proceedings*, (pp. 13-17). Retrieved from http://www.imls.gov/pdf/ WW09_Proceedings.pdf

Cuthbert, J. (2008). *West Virginia history on view: The evolution of a big digital project with a tiny budget.* Retrieved from http://www.wvla.org/conference/2008/postcon/presentations/cuthbert.pdf

Dooley, J. M., & Luce, K. (2010). *Taking our pulse: The OCLC research survey of special collections and archives.* Dublin, OH: OCLC Research. Retrieved from http://www.oclc.org/research/ publications/library/ 2010/2010-11.pdf

Dublin Core Metadata Initiative. (1995-2010). *Mission and principles.* Retrieved from http:// dublincore.org/about-us/

Edson, M. (2009). Session 1: Online communities and the institution. *WebWise 2009 Digital Debates Conference Proceedings*, (pp. 13-17). Retrieved from http://www.imls.gov/pdf/ WW09_Proceedings.pdf

Georgia Secretary of State, Georgia's Virtual Vault. (2007-2008). *Georgia's virtual vault.* Retrieved from http://cdm.sos.state.ga.us/index.php

Lawrence, D. (2008, May 28). *Flickr commons: Begin at the beginning.* [Web log post]. Retrieved November 19, 2010, from http://www. brooklynmuseum.org/ community/blogosphere/ bloggers/2008/05/ 28/flickr-commons-begin-at-the-beginning/

Library of Congress, National Union Catalog of Manuscript Collections. (2009). *Frequently asked questions.* Retrieved from http://www.loc.gov/ coll/nucmc/newfaqs.html

Library of Congress, National Union Catalog of Manuscript Collections. (2010). *NUCMC program annual report.* Retrieved from http://www.loc. gov/coll/ nucmc/NUCMCFY10.pdf

Ohio Historical Society, Ohio Memory Project. (2008). *About the Ohio memory project.* Retrieved from http://www.ohiomemory.org/custom/ ohiomemory/om/index.php?About

Raymond, M. (2008, January 16). *My friend Flickr: A match made in photo heaven.* [Web log post]. Retrieved November 19, 2010, from http:// blogs.loc.gov/loc/2008/01/ my-friend-flickr-a-match-made-in-photo-heaven/

Yakel, E. (2004). Encoded archival description: Are finding aids boundary spanners or barriers for users? *Journal of Archival Organization*, *2*(1/2), 63–77..doi:10.1300/J201v02n01_06

Section 5
Case Studies

Chapter 19
E–Reference in Public Libraries:
Phoenix Public Library Case Study, Our Website is Your 24/7 Reference Librarian

Ross McLachlan
Phoenix Public Library, USA

Kathleen Sullivan
Phoenix Public Library, USA

ABSTRACT

This case study offers insight into how Phoenix Public Library attempts to meet customer's needs for 24/7 access to Library information and services. Strategies to achieve quality results, successful and failed initiatives, and lessons learned are presented.

INTRODUCTION

The concept of e-reference was born in the early 1990s, with the advent of fledgling subscription databases in CD-ROM format, which contained many periodical indexes and only a small number of full text articles. These resources supplemented and expanded individual libraries periodical holdings, held the potential of solving storage issues, and augmented reference staff search capability with their multiple search engines.

Today, e-reference products comprise many tens of thousands of full-text periodical titles going back multiple decades; entire libraries of reference and research materials in a single database, with some having a limited subject focus and others covering a spectrum of disciplines; downloadable e-books, e-audio, and e-video; and integrated learning tools for self-paced customer use. In recent years, many producers have also embellished their products with hyperlinks to relevant Web-based resources, both subscription-based and free, social networking and blogging capabilities, and/or daily updates that help keep the content as current as possible.

DOI: 10.4018/978-1-61350-308-9.ch019

Unlike academic libraries, which make their selection of e-reference products based on clearly defined campus curricula needs, public libraries face a unique set of challenges when building and maintaining their selected e-reference library from the entire vendor spectrum. They must not only select the products that best fits the needs of the communities they serve, but also integrate them as a core function of their websites, make them easy to find, and market them to the customer.

The following is a case study of the Phoenix Public Library's e-reference experience.

BACKGROUND

To put Phoenix Public Library in to context for this case study, it is a system of 16 branches[1] and a large central library serving a population of 1.5 plus million in a metro area of 4.5 million. The metro area also includes 11 independent (some multi-branch) systems and a county library system serving the unincorporated parts of the county. In fiscal year 2009/10, the library housed 1,736,000 items; offered 78 subscription databases; circulated 14,447,111 items; counted 230,822 active customers (card used in the last year); had 850,940 customer-initiated public Internet PC sessions; provided 4,111 programs attended by 102,242 customers; and staff taught regular basic computer classes in five library training classrooms. They did this with a total staff of 330 FTE of which 22 percent were librarians.

The Phoenix Public Library approached the development of its e-reference library using a staff-developed ten step methodology. The process has been refined over the last 15 years, but the basic concepts have not changed.

- Know your community's needs. Facts and figures are better than assumptions and anecdotes.
- Develop an ideal collection development plan; review it annually.

- Review the marketplace which will take the plan from ideal to "what is available now."
- Arrange for both staff and public testing of the resources. Testing must also be done by the IT staff whose input will help eliminate any technical implementation pitfalls.
- Evaluate for content quality, ease of use (intuitive use without training to access the most relevant information), and technical/ maintenance issues.
- Select resources based on a set of defined criteria. Criteria will evolve over time.
- Implement, bring the resource(s) live on the library website.
- Market every product to both the public and staff.
- Continually evaluate both from the usage/ cost per search perspective and public satisfaction. This equals your return on investment (ROI).
- Repeat the process continually.

Another key component of the Phoenix Public Library's corporate philosophy is the maintenance of the best possible relationship with library vendors. In practical terms, this translates into being an active partner with the vendors. As an example, the Deputy Director for Technical Services has served on both the Advisory Boards of ProQuest and EBSCO products for the past ten years. The Collection Development staff has also served on a number of publisher boards (e.g., Emerald Press, Sage Publications, and Rosen Press). This ensures that the vendors and producers of content understand the needs of our customers and that their searching interface meets the rigorous standards that our customers have come to expect. By serving on these boards, staff brings the experience and expertise of Phoenix professional staff directly into the product development and search engine refinement processes.

Like most public library websites in the mid 1990s, ours was rudimentary. Staff was essential

Figure 1. Annual Cost/Search ROI²

Fiscal Year	Customer Satisfaction	Fiscal Year	Customer Satisfaction
2008/09	73%	2001/02	83%
2007/08	86%	2000/01	85%
2006/07	88%	1999/00	91%
2005/06	80%	1998/99	76%
2004/05	89%	1997/98	88%
2003/04	90%	1996/97	87%
2002/03	94%	1995/96	85%

Figure 2. Annual Customer Satisfaction ROI³

Fiscal Year	Cost Per Search	Fiscal Year	Cost Per Search
2008/09	$0.29	2001/02	$0.97
2007/08	$0.34	2000/01	$0.48
2006/07	$0.39	1999/00	$0.73
2005/06	$0.38	1998/99	$0.63
2004/05	$0.93	1997/98	$0.35
2003/04	$0.53	1996/97	$0.43
2002/03	$0.73	1995/96	$0.32

to both selling and marketing these new resources and guiding customers in their use. Each vendor had a different search engine and type of controlled searching vocabulary. Specialized training was needed by staff to effectively use the products. In retrospect, it was a mess. Despite these drawbacks, the library implemented the first online e-reference collection in 1995 to coincide with the opening of the new Burton Barr Central Library. Since that time, annual evaluations of the suite of resources for annual usage, cost per search, and public satisfaction have been conducted (see Figure 1 and Figure 2). The annual reports were delivered to Library management with recommendations for additions, drops, and an update of the electronic collection plan.

Over the next six years, the library labored to continually evolve the website and e-resources to make the best tool possible for customers. However, there was one flaw with the out-of-the box systems. Library websites were designed by librarians for librarians, and thus they were still not easy for customers to use without staff assistance.

In an effort to correct this, the library put together in 2002 a group of staff members representing all staff levels, viewpoints, and technological aptitudes. With a facilitator, they were sent off to plan a path for website development *designed specifically for Phoenix customers*. Several months

later, the executive team's report and plan was approved by the City Librarian. The core principals of that reports are still viable today:

- Make the library website fast, intuitive and easy to use.
- Provide a "one box search" for all library resources (print and electronic) everywhere on the website.

With these recommendations, Phoenix Public Library admitted that Google and Yahoo had won the Internet war and we had to adapt our website using standard Web functionality to remain relevant to our community.

Following that concept, in 2003 a new type of library website was launched to a 92 percent public approval. In 2004, *Library Journal* published an article heralding the website as "Phoenix Gets It Right" (Klein, 2004). A key component was the marketing of library resources, services, and programs. In 2007, another new website was launched with a 95 percent public approval rate. The following year, the website received the 2008 Outstanding Achievement in Local Government Award from the Alliance for Innovation[4].

The major improvements between the 2003 and 2007 websites were:

- Abandoning the Library's ILS catalog search engine and implementing the Endeca search engine.
- Using BISAC (Book Industry Standards and Communications) subject headings as the search engine's subject vocabulary.
- Maximizing the power of the MARC record by including not only a record for all databases, but for databases offering searchable or downloadable e-materials with direct access to the products offered the 856 41 $u URL (4 – HTTP, 1 – version of the resource and/or 856 40 $u URL 4-HTTP, 0 – for the resource itself).

To fulfill the core principal of "make the library website fast, intuitive and easy to use," the Endeca search engine was chosen, after a marketplace review, to replace the library's ILS catalog search engine. Endeca was selected because it is a retail search engine giving the Library complete control over the search experience and greatly expanding the ability to cross promote "things owned," "things leased (e.g., subscription databases)," programs, and services. In other words, if you liked this, you may also like the following books, electronic resources, programs, and/or services.

The Library also used "people speak" (BISAC subject headings) as the searching vocabulary rather than "library speak" (Library of Congress Subject Headings). For instance BISAC utilized the term "vegan" long before it was established as an official LC subject term. Working with OCLC and our book vendors, all bibliographic records were populated with BISAC subject headings. BISAC is the vocabulary developed by the publishers and book retailers to sell to the public and working with our partners at OCLC is now a standard MARC record field (695 00 $a Description $b Code or the OCLC version uses the 072 02 $a Three letter $u extension $2 bisacsh and the 650 02 $a Subject $2 bisacsh).

All databases and e-materials have a MARC record with a link in the URL field and BISAC field(s). If the database allows download or use of full text book materials, vendors are required to provide OCLC MARC records with an URL field. Many customers initially discover resources they need by using our catalog rather than knowing that the database exists.

ISSUES, CONTROVERSIES, PROBLEMS

Access

For Phoenix library website customers, every click beyond the one box search is a potential failure unless each click serves to quickly refine the search using standard Web searching conventions just like Google, Yahoo, Amazon.com, et cetera.

As the number of e-reference resources grew, the major problems faced by our customer were deciding which database to use and becoming familiar with the different search engines and searching vocabularies. The first glimmer of hope came in 2001/02 with the development of aggregated / federated search engines. In theory, the aggregated / federated search engine would sit on-top of all the databases and guide the customer to the most relevant article or e-reference resource without having to perform multiple searches and knowing exactly which database to use. Without going into a detailed history of this technology and the multiple vendor products (e.g., WebFeat, Serials Solutions, Autographics, etc.), suffice it to say that it worked in theory better than in reality. These first-generation federated search engines products had a slow response time and usually produced a bewilderingly complex set of search results screens; however, it was a step in the right direction.

Undeterred by the shortcomings, in 2005 the library implemented WebFeat using every available customization option to make it a "self service" access to the databases and learning tools. It did achieve some success for the undaunted, doggedly resourceful customer and received a customer satisfaction rate of 86 percent in 2006/07. The library website also employed every Web convention to make this as seamless a self service as possible.

A major improvement appeared on the horizon in 2008 when ProQuest bought both WebFeat and Serials Solutions and planned to combine them into a new and improved product. The result was Summon, which came into the marketplace in 2009. We purchased the product in fiscal year 2009/10.

Naturally, the library is taking a different approach to its implementation. The first phase was executed in mid 2010 as a simple replacement for WebFeat with Summon. The plan for fiscal year 2010/11 is the true implementation. Simply put, if possible, Summon will be integrated with Endeca and the dream will become a reality of the true: "one box search" which will guide the customer to the most relevant books, magazine and newspaper articles, e-reference resources, downloadabales, and library programs. The result for the customer will be an enhanced service that easily guides them to the best of any resource in any format via the one box search using "people speak" and standard Web conventions familiar to all.

Training

After years of training provided by the database vendors for staff and our customers, most of the major vendors have made the leap to providing online tutorials that can be linked to the library's public and staff websites. In the early years, our public service staff devoted much time and energy in training staff to train the public, creating training competencies that all public service staff had to complete and update annually. The public training for the most part has been on a one-to-one basis during the reference interview. When the library built public training facilities in multiple locations throughout the system beginning in 1999/00, the public training curricula included a component on using the e-reference databases. In the last few

years, the library has developed online tutorials to assist customers in effectively using e-reference resources and online learning tools. Over the years, this has reached thousands of customers, but in relationship to serving a city with a population of 1.5 plus million in a metro area of 4.5 million, it is only a drop in the bucket. Technology had to be the solution for easy access, and the Endeca and Summon integration into a one box solution is today's hoped-for answer.

Return on Investment (ROI)

Determining the cost per search has been difficult. Vendors do not standardize their statistics. Each library has developed different methodologies to derive a cost per search that worked for them. At Phoenix, we accepted the fact that not all searches were counted the same, but we used the vendor's usage figures and the annual cost of the database to determine the cost per search. It was not perfect, but it was the reality of the moment.

Finally, in the past few years a standard was created that enabled database vendors to develop various products that could then be used to normalize all of the vendors' data, which now will give libraries a much more accurate figure. This was Project COUNTER (Flemming-May, 2010), and Phoenix uses the ProQuest product to perform this task.

This represents only one portion of the ROI. What about customers' input into the quality of our product selection? Phoenix began with paper surveys bribing customers with extended Internet PC time to complete the often lengthy survey. Now there are multiple software survey programs available that can do this for libraries including the one we use: Survey Monkey with short pop-up surveys. That is short both in terms of the length of survey (one to two questions only) and the duration it is live on the website (two to three days and possibly as long as a week at a time). Multiple surveys are then combined and analyzed at the end of the year to paint a clearer picture of customer satisfaction. The ROI is a factor that goes into the annual evaluation of e-resources.

Evolution of E-Reference and the Impact of Self Service

Nationally, the genesis of e-reference began in the 1970s by providing reference service to remote customers at their convenience in the form of telephone reference.

Since the early 1980s, with the establishment of our Telephone Reference Center, Phoenix has sought ways to help reference customers obtain the service they need without a visit to a local branch. By 2002, with a major reduction in service, the Telephone Reference Center became the only telephone contact for customers, eliminating local calls to individual facilities. This led to the development of the Call Center, which fielded all calls for all branches in one location. Soon, both Call Center staff and frontline staff were reporting that customers were requesting the ability to ask questions and receive information electronically.

While "chat" options were investigated, the financial situation allowed for only a basic, home-grown e-mail option to be inaugurated in 2000. Originally staffed by a few librarians at the Burton Barr Central Library, soon reference, collection development, and circulation staff throughout the system were made part of the "Contact Us" teams and were assigned "online desk hours."

By 2001, approximately 70 reference questions per month were answered via "online desk hours." After a "Contact Us" button went live on the library's website in January 2002, the volume of customer requests via e-mail increased one hundred percent.

By 2003, the types of questions received via e-mail were categorized as:

- 24% Reference
- 21% Library Operations/Employment
- 14% Circulation

- 11% Complaints and Compliments
- 11% Junk mail
- 9% Collection Development
- 6% Website or technical problems
- 2% Facts to Go! – A fee based service in which customers could pay to receive research help and documents related to their search.

Phoenix also investigated options to provide 24x7 e-reference services. The library tried unsuccessfully to create a countywide consortium for its funding and staffing. However, in order to effectively track queries, ensure that all questions were answered, and build a FAQ database to be used by staff, QuestionPoint was purchased in 2006. The product was chosen because it would allow the library to consider expanding to 24x7 services if a local consortium could be developed.

Also, using grant funds, the library provided online live chat sessions for middle and high school students utilizing Tutor.com. While a noble experiment, the hours of service the library could afford were too limited, staff intervention and marketing too costly, and use so low that the library abandoned the initiative. In order to effectively utilize this product, we would have had to commit to "homework help" as a major service initiative, and the library was committed to other initiatives.

Meanwhile in 2002/03, Collection Development staff worked successfully with Maricopa County Library District, the Arizona State Library, and other local library systems to successfully cooperate in the purchase of online databases. A small Phoenix Public Library E-Resources team was formed to assist with the management of a growing library of databases, as well as the advent of downloadable technology. Team members include public services, collection management, cataloging, and IT staff. It tests all products not just for content and ease of use, but also for the item's ability to operate in the library's technical environment. The team annually sets the collection goals, gathers statistics, and makes recommendations on selection and retention of products.

By 2003/04, 119 online databases were available for customer use. Although the number of overall databases has since been reduced to 78 for fiscal year 2010/11, use of the remaining products has continued strong for both customers and staff. The eliminated products were those with the highest cost per search, were not available remotely, could not provide adequate statistics, received low customer satisfaction ratings, or overlapped with other more highly used databases.

In 2004, eight local library systems formed the Greater Phoenix Digital Library (GDPL) to supply downloadable e-materials through OverDrive.[5] Having expanded to ten systems in 2008/09, the use of these materials continues to be among the highest in the nation. In that year, GDPL became the highest circulating e-materials library in the country.

CIRCULATION OF E-MEDIA IN OVERDRIVE: PHOENIX AND THE GREATER PHOENIX DIGITAL LIBRARY (GPDL)

For the Call Center and the Contact Us teams, the popularity of these products meant more questions on how to troubleshoot the technology involved rather than answering traditional reference questions. To help offset this influx of questions, staff produced training modules for the public website to assist with accessing and using downloadable products. Training and FAQ's were also developed to help staff assist customers.

With all e-book related products, whether downloadable or database based, the library learned the *essential* lesson that full MARC bibliographic records with linked URLs were critical to driving customers to use these resources.

Figure 3.

Fiscal Year	Phoenix	GPDL
2004-2005	5,279	NA
2005-2006	18,664	22,384*
2006-2007	42,238	82,081
2007-2008	83,983	189,933
2008-2009	116,964	279,502
2009-2010	143,288	351,759
*First year GPDL Includes PPL Figures		

Starting in 2003, the new Phoenix website also offered customers the ability to search specifically for e-content by providing navigational tabs for both downloadable products and online full text research and learning tools. Thus, the design and functionality of the library's website continue to be of critical importance in helping customers to help themselves.

During this same period, customer self service options blossomed. Briefly they included the following:

- Self check implemented in 2002 and converted to RFID in 2008.
- Customer managed reading lists as a standard website service in 2003.
- Customized RSS feeds and online newsletters in 2005.
- Online library card registration in 2006.
- Expanded number of learning databases (e.g., typing master, Learning Express, Books 24 x 7, Auralog – learning a foreign language, etc.).
- Online fee/fine payment in 2008.
- "My Account" features on the website that include remembering your searches, renewal of materials, and the ability to e-mail a friend your favorite book, magazine, article, downloadable, or program.

FUTURE AND EMERGING TRENDS

Access and Self Service

ILS (Integrated Library Systems) vendors are being forced to overhaul their online catalogs due to the growing number of libraries that are choosing library open source options and customizing their entire system, libraries demanding as contract deliverables enhancements to the "search," and libraries like Phoenix that are integrating non-standard products into their website to totally control the customer experience which allows customers to choose how to access information and products.

The larger ILS vendors are also developing components of their systems that can be sold separately to any library as a "plug and play" option (e.g., Integrated Interfaces Inc.'s federated search engine, TLC's acquisition system, etc.).

Libraries of all sizes with the technology resources have entered into a world where they have the possibility of meeting their customer's expectation in the electronic environment. This is a risky step for some as it entails listening to their customers, gathering data, and walking away from the concept of librarians knowing what is best for their community and designing a tool for librarians. Librarians and reference paraprofessionals are being used more and more to work with technical staff to market resources, develop and expand discovery tools, and teach customers technical literacy.

In the last three years, the number of libraries that are taking control of the customer experience themselves and/or in cooperation with vendors or other libraries is increasing. This will continue to push vendors to develop new products, enhance existing ones, and bring new players into the library marketplace. It promises to be an interesting future and one the Phoenix Public Library will continue to embrace.

Keeping it Relevant

At Phoenix Public Library, the success or failure of e-reference or any other customer service is based on the customer's ability to help themselves and find what they need independently. As an example, part of the function of the Call Center and Contact Us teams is to identify where customers are consistently "stuck"; where they don't know about resources that are already available to them from the Library; or they don't know how to access them. Passing this information on the marketing team, Library IT, Circulation, Collection Development, vendors and all other affected groups helps those teams to develop solutions so that customers can easily and effectively get to the content they need.

Phoenix staff is currently working with vendors to:

- Adjust pricing to better reflect actual use patterns; this price must be reflected in pennies per use, not dollars
- Encourage vendor relationships that combine many needed resources by different publishers under the same umbrella (e.g., Gale Virtual Reference Library)
- Improve functionality, particularly with "federated search" products OR (and this is what Phoenix prefers) giving the library the code so we can make it work with our own search engine.
- Provide easily accessible training videos and products (24/7) that customers and staff can use to maximize product use.
- Make the ordering of materials more seamless. For instance, being able to order downloadable and/or searchable e-media form standard book vendors at the same time the physical items are selected (e.g., Baker & Taylor now has agreements with the Gale Virtual Reference Library and NetLibrary to do this).

- Find ways to better plan, evaluate, and maximize collection purchases.

For librarians to remain relevant in this environment they must act as leaders of teams, initiatives, and services in their libraries. Libraries and their staff must offer quality assistance to customers in their quest for answers and materials **when** and **where** and **how** the customer needs it. This must be their goal.

CONCLUSION

This case study clearly illustrates the following key factors in ensuring the successful implementation of e-reference:

- Have a dynamic selection / retention process and follow it as part of an e-collection plan.
- Develop a ROI process for your e-resources.
- Partner with vendors and publishers; participate in focus groups, boards, and committees to influence product development and searching capabilities.
- Be relevant to the community and be able to prove it to your funding source.
- Continue to exploit any technology that will improve the website to make it a self service, customer-centric tool.
- Exploit the full potential of your bibliographic database to include direct links to resources and introduce "people speak" (BISAC) as part of the bibliographic record.
- Invest in building your IT resources and fully integrate them into the library environment.
- Always remember that your website is for many your reference librarian and, at the same time: (a.) make it easy for customers to provide feedback and find personal help they need and (b.) use feedback from cus-

tomers to design 24/7 website solutions to common issues and problems (registering for cards, paying fees, disputing overdue fees, etc.).
- Be willing to invest in experiments that may fail, learn from the experience, and share with colleagues and vendors
- Accept the fact that the challenges will never go away, only change over time.

REFERENCES

Flemming-May, R. (2010). Measuring e-resource use. *American Libraries*, *41*(9), 22.

Klein, L. R. (1976). Phoenix gets it right. *Library Journal*, *129*(12), 34–36.

ADDITIONAL READING

Price, B. (2008). *The best service is no service: how to liberate your customers from customer service*. San Francisco, California: Jossey-Bass.

ENDNOTES

[1] The 16th branch will open in August 2011 as a 150,000 sq. ft. joint use library with the South Mountain Community College.
[2] Cost per search is only for databases paid for by Phoenix Public Library.
[3] 2008/2009 statistics were for Spanish Language database only.
[4] The Alliance for Innovation is an international network of progressive governments and partners committed to transforming local government by accelerating the development and dissemination of innovations. They seek out innovative practices, challenge existing business models, exchange knowledge, and

provide products and services that help our members perform at their best. Together with their partners, International City/County Management Association (ICMA) and Arizona State University (ASU), they promote excellence in local government and build a community of practice in local government innovation.

[5] The Library had offered online e-books for customers through NetLibrary since 1998. However it was not until the advent of a circulation model that these resources garnered significant customer use. OverDrive has been fully implemented by Phoenix since 2002/03 and it was through that initial investment that the other seven libraries could join with minimal start-up costs in 2004-2005.

Chapter 20

Changes in Customer Behavior:
A Case Study in Reference Service at the Santa Monica Public Library

R. Wright Rix
Santa Monica Public Library, USA

ABSTRACT

Today's library customers exhibit a decreasing tendency to regard the public library as the primary local repository of research information. The rise of the Internet is at the root of this and many other changes that have taken place in public libraries during the past twenty years. Customer preferences have shifted away from print tools in favor of the simplest available online tools. A pervasive user expectation is that information access should be free, easy, and immediate. Information literacy issues continue to occupy a growing portion of librarians' time. As customer needs and expectations evolve, so must the library's services and products.

INTRODUCTION

The goal of this case study is to explore how reference services over the past two decades have evolved at the Santa Monica Public Library. It begins with an overview of the library, the reference department, and its services. It describes changes in expectations and experiences of both staff and customers. Changes prompted by the popularization of the Internet and World Wide Web receive special consideration. Other areas covered include computer literacy classes, the reference interview, print vs. online reference tools, collection development, and the creation of digitized local history resources. Primary objectives are to provide context by outlining evolving practices in one reference department, to presage future trends, and evaluate priorities.

DOI: 10.4018/978-1-61350-308-9.ch020

HISTORY AND CONTEXT

As the adult collection grew in size and complexity, residents needed more assistance in using the library, and reference service became an important part of the overall service. At first librarians helped users choose and find books in the local collection. Then they provided answers from library reference books to those in need of information. Later they were able to locate materials anywhere... and produce them via interlibrary loan. Today they are able to research complex questions through a sophisticated network of information and referral sources, both inside and outside the library... and still provide the basic service of helping users find the books they want. (Braby & Hunt, 1990, p. 50)

When these words were published just over 20 years ago, the Santa Monica Public Library (SMPL) Reference Department had an established reputation as a provider of top quality reference service, including dedicated telephone and email service points. Santa Monica is a city of 94,000 occupying 8.3 square miles in the western part of the Greater Los Angeles Metropolitan Area. The library system offers free public library services to all California residents. It consists of one main library and three branch libraries, currently housing approximately 430,000 items. The reference department is located in the Main Library.

SMPL has been fortunate in the level of sustained support it has received from the city and in the sense of stewardship demonstrated by successive library directors. To date there have been only eight directors in the course of the library's 120-year history. This has resulted in a high degree of continuity that has fostered an atmosphere of stability, supportiveness, and innovation. The library consistently ranks near the top of the scales of measures published by the California State Library in its annual *California Library Statistics*. Examples of these measures are fulltime staff and materials budget per capita.

While never shy about innovating, the SMPL Reference Department has a long history of sustaining the tradition of providing free, high quality one-on-one reference service directly to library customers. The work group focuses intently on such actions as practicing active listening skills, asking open-ended questions to "get at the question behind the question," and conferring with colleagues about improving reference services. What happens as the interview progresses, however, has changed noticeably in recent years.

Prior to the popular ascendancy of the Internet in the mid-1990s, it was essential for reference librarians to master the content, structure, and navigation of myriad print reference sources. Following a reference interview during which relevant resources were determined, staff was expected to spend time orienting the customer in the use of the given work(s). Examples of large reference sets maintained at SMPL at that time were the *Facts On File News Digest*, the *National Cyclopaedia of American Biography*, and the *SIRS Social Issues Resources Series*. (The print editions of all three of these sets are no longer part of the collection. The library continues at this time to subscribe to an online version of *Facts On File*.) When the situation warranted, the librarian would undertake a potentially costly DIALOG online search or refer the question to a second-level reference center managed by the California State Library.

Reference staff also created and maintained offline ready reference files of hard-to-find information. One popular example was a file of the current and historical value of the Consumer Price Index for All Urban Consumers and for the Los Angeles-Long Beach-Santa Ana Metropolitan Statistical Area. This kind of information was cumbersome to access and maintain. It was typically beyond the reach of all but the most determined individuals. The reference staff received dozens of requests for CPI quotes alone each year. This is but one example from an extensive set of so-called "vertical files" that occupied at least five filing cabinets. These files were liquidated in 2003 when the Main Library facility was vacated and razed to make way for a new Main Library, which opened in January 2006.

The telephone reference service occupied a dedicated workspace away from the public floor. New employees were not permitted to work at telephone reference until they had acquired ample experience at the main reference desk. Whereas work at the reference desk often consisted of leading people to resources and ultimately leaving them to wend their way, telephone callers routinely demanded a precise answer. The librarian had to have the ability to select the requisite reference works and extract the answer from them quickly. Most days the telephone rang constantly from the moment the library opened. While many callers had simple needs, such as the desire to place a hold on a popular book, others routinely required more time and a higher level of assistance.

THE INTERNET ARRIVES

When Internet PCs for public use arrived, many things changed. Public access Internet workstations were installed at the Main Library in 1997, attracting a new clientele of avid computer users. Meanwhile, the Internet had already begun to enable growing numbers of the reference department's traditional customer base to do self-service fact checking and other research at home. This trend would lead to the demise of the vertical file.

Library staff initially showed some reluctance to assist the new and rapidly growing segment of the customer base, those whose chief interest is in using the public Internet computers. Incredible as it may seem, there was a widespread sense that troubleshooting at computer workstations was somehow an inappropriate task for librarian staff. After observing this reluctance at first hand, management staff concluded that this feeling was a reflexive response to the shock of the new. The

needs of the new public library computer users differed from those of traditional public library customers. Many of the new customers showed little interest in the traditional library resources, most of which continued to enjoy devoted constituencies of their own. In fact, the new computer workstations and their clientele caused anxiety among frontline service staff throughout the system. This was partly due to the tense demeanor of some Internet customers who wanted to use a workstation for longer than their allotted time. Some customers developed a sense of territoriality about their timeslot at the computer. Sometimes heated disputes about timeslots were adjudicated by library staff.

The library's administrative unit responded to the situation by seeking options to automate the sign-up procedure for computers and by leading a series of staff development sessions. These acknowledged the disorienting effect of rapid change, and explored managerial and individuated strategies for dealing constructively with the specific new challenges brought by the Internet. By 1998, reference staff had begun teaching information literacy classes about the basics of the Internet. Classes on topics such as setting up a free email account and creating a basic word processing document were soon to follow. The thinking at the time was that demand for such classes would dwindle in a few years, once the older cohort of the populace had become more computer savvy. In fact, the opposite occurred.

REFERENCE SERVICES TODAY AND TOMORROW

Computer Literacy Classes and One-to-Many Services

The computer literacy classes remain in heavy demand. Instead of waning, the classes have steadily increased in number and popularity since the introduction of computer classes at the library. The intervening years have shown that many adults still possess minimal to nonexistent basic computer skills. A large number of the people on the far side of the "digital divide" are not well-equipped to produce a simple word processing document, much less navigate cyberspace. When a triggering mechanism occurs, these individuals often head straight to the nearest public library. For example, since late 2008 many midlife jobseekers who had not needed to develop computer skills in order to apply for jobs earlier in their careers have now made their way to the library. Events and classes on the subject of job-seeking drew capacity crowds to the library throughout 2010. In addition to a seemingly endless stream of people seeking to develop basic skills, there are those who need help keeping abreast of burgeoning trends in computing and online resources. Classes on subjects such as digital image editing and cloud-based computing appeal to a different audience altogether. Classes are routinely full.

The advent of inexpensive videocasting and of social networking tools such as Facebook and Twitter have aided the library's ability to communicate on a one-to-many basis. Today, the reference staff regularly makes instructional videocasts posted to YouTube. These videos, information about librarians' participation at library at local events, and more are promoted via the library's Facebook page and Twitter feed.

While staff continue to serve library customers who prize one-on-one interactions with librarians, staff has realized that one-to-many communication, such as that afforded by videocasting and social networking tools, enables the organization to propagate knowledge widely and economically to countless customers beyond the library's walls. As with many service innovations, a key challenge is time management: how to incorporate new services while maintaining preexisting ones. That is a topic worthy of exploration in another study.

One-to-One Services and Print Reference

Immediacy is increasingly an essential component of information delivery services in the public library. This falls in line with changes in the broader culture brought about by the availability of instant online access to a variety of resources. One constant is that reference librarians spend a significant amount of time every workday providing one-on-one reference service in-person, by phone, and by email. Fee-per-search database options such as DIALOG are no longer offered at SMPL, but ready reference service using text messaging has been added to the mix. SMPL reference staff also provides interactive Internet-based chat reference as part of OCLC's QuestionPoint service. In 2000 the library served as a beta site for the Library of Congress' Collaborative Digital Reference Service Initiative, which ultimately became QuestionPoint.

Longtime librarians, meaning those who entered the profession prior to the popular ascendancy of the Internet, are unanimous in acknowledging the following. There has been a marked shift away from the use of print reference resources over the past twenty years. Library customers have largely lost the patience required to navigate unwieldy reference tomes and the inclination to spend the requisite in-library hours consulting them. Despite many veteran librarians' abiding nostalgia for classic resources such as the *Dictionary of American Biography (DAB)*, it now appears that most customers were only ever reluctant users of such works. Most customers' eyes will glaze over when staff attempts to lead them to a print resource. They will request online alternatives. Librarians are apt to recommend a subscription database such as Gale's *Biography in Context* or *Literature Resource Center*, which contains content from the *DAB* series. Self-directed customers in the library's Computer Commons or on their own laptops connected to the library's Wi-Fi network can be observed gravitating toward free alternatives, often of dubious authority such as *Wikipedia*. In their haste, ease of access and speed trump authority and depth.

Discoverability, or lack thereof, is a factor discouraging potential use of both print reference resources and subscription databases. Even many of the customers who take it upon themselves to use the online catalog often come away empty handed. A user-experience and expectation chasm has grown between Google-type searching on the one hand, and combined forces of library online catalog search architecture and standard cataloging practices. Customers living in a world of Google tend to enter the narrowest possible search terms, whether using Google or a library's online catalog interface. Applying this approach in online catalogs virtually guarantees the customer will fail to retrieve listings of relevant works properly cataloged at a more general level. For example, someone entering the search terms "Central Asian Art" in the online catalog will not retrieve the title record for the Grove *Dictionary of Art* (1996), even though that masterly reference work contains over 140 pages on the subject.

Customers have evidently forgotten, if they ever knew, many basic pre-Internet research skills. It is distressing to report a near complete absence of interest in computer literacy classes geared to the use of the library catalog. Such classes are exceptional in the lack of customer interest they generate. The prevailing notion is that the online catalog should be intuitive to use and thus should not require a classroom session. Yet practically speaking, the current situation creates an environment in which many library resources, including print reference titles, often remain unknown to their presumed target audience. In this situation, staff transactions have become a primary means by which customers learn about print resources. Of this subset of customers, a great number still balk at print resources and request online alternatives.

Faced with these circumstances, staff has worked to pare down the print reference collec-tion significantly during the past five years and to cancel over a third of the library's standing orders for print resources. Purchase of new print reference titles is practically nil, with the major exception of works relating to local history. A recent survey of newer generation integrated library systems, along with innovative database products such as EBSCO's NoveList Complete, which can insert readalike recommendations into a title record, provide some hope that the library catalogs of the future are tardily becoming more useful to today's computer users. One constant that pertains is that individual users, whether in surveys or on library comment forms, consistently praise and value the quality of their one-on-one transactions with librarian staff.

Online Resources

When recommending online resources, most librarians value the greater authority and precision of licensed content providers such as EBSCO, Elsevier, and Gale-Cengage, to name a few. The importance of these attributes often eludes customers, many of whom lack awareness of such products. In effect, the superior value of licensed content has to be sold twice -- first to the institution and then to its customers. The library advertises these products on posters and signs in its facilities and promotes them on its Web page and through its social media tools. The increasing simplicity of some content providers search interfaces has been promising. However, insufficient marketing by the companies themselves and lack of general brand awareness remain concerns.

Because of their high cost, online resources are keenly scrutinized by management staff. Like many public libraries, Santa Monica's investment in online reference resources has been largely in standard public library databases such as *OneFile* (formerly *InfoTrac*) and *ReferenceUSA*, or in interactive tools such as the *Mango Languages* learning tool. Purchase of stand-alone e-books has been limited to popular reading materials, fiction, and nonfiction bestsellers. This is consistent with customer suggestions and demand. The number of customers interested in and demanding access to leisure-based online content continues to surge. Whether for scholarly pursuits or recreational ones, customers demand simplicity in the search interface.

Budgets and Collection Development

Over the past several years, collection management staff responded to the steady decline in demand for print reference sources by cutting its budget allocation. Purchases of major new print reference titles have been virtually nil over the past few years. Every budget cycle brings fresh cuts to the list of print reference titles on standing order. In 2006, SMPL opened a new Main Library that is double the size of its predecessor. However, the amount of linear shelf space devoted to print reference resources was not increased. On the contrary, the allotted space continues to shrink in direct correlation with declining customer demand. The budget allocation for reference materials has decreased by 20 percent since 2006, the year the new Main Library opened.

Collection development of print, nonprint, and online resources continues to be a major responsibility of reference staff. In 2003, collection development of all the library's adult collections was centralized at the Main Library. Reference staff became responsible for developing and maintaining Main and branch collections, thereby reducing duplication of effort by branch staff. This change was enabled, and has since been enhanced by, advances in automation and ordering processes both within the library and with major vendors of library materials. Customer demand for all formats, including popular e-books, continues to surge. Circulation rates are, at present, higher than they have been at any time in SMPL's history.

Local History and Digital Assets

SMPL's Reference Department has a long history of preserving materials of local historical interest, in particular local newspapers and photographs of the area. In recent years the library has embraced the creation of digitized content, ideally in a Web-accessible format. In 1996, the library secured funding to digitize the Santa Monica Image Archives, a collection of thousands of historical photographs of the area. The digitized images were initially available from a single workstation at the Main Library. In 2000, the collection went live on the Internet as a SIRSI/Dynix module linked to the library's online catalog. In 2008 staff secured a Library Services and Technology Act grant to digitize the years 1875-1910 of the microfilm editions of the local newspaper, the *Santa Monica Outlook*. During this time, the library also migrated its growing Image Archives to a CONTENTdm-based website called *Imagine Santa Monica* (digital.smpl.org). By late 2009, the photographs and newspaper data were fully searchable and freely available worldwide to anyone with an Internet connection. In addition, MARC records for the historical images collection have been harvested by WorldCat. This makes the images discoverable through Google searches. In sum, the reference department is dedicated to preserving local history materials and making them broadly available via today's technology. Customers, many of whom live in other states and nations, actively seek out this content, which is otherwise rare or impossible to find elsewhere.

CONCLUSION

The public's appetite for print reference sources has ceded pride of place to a preference for online tools. Customers are less patient and less inclined to view the reference librarian as an oracle or even to accept her or him as an expert. The one-on-one transactions are still popular, although the trend is to view the librarian more as a consultant. Being perceived as an effective interlocutor now carries as much weight as being perceived as an expert.

As attested to by the thousands of questions SMPL reference librarians answer each year, the public continues to visit public libraries and to value the availability of reference service to meet their information needs. Many of today's customers self-disclose that they are seeking the assistance of reference librarians because the Internet has failed to meet their information needs. Publishers and content providers would benefit by taking note of and catering to the specific needs driving people to libraries. Education, employment, health, and legal concerns are all key needs. The most relevant proprietary online tools for the public library market continue to be licensed databases, supplemented by free websites. Moving some print reference resources into the circulating collections increases their value to customers. The self-help legal titles published by Nolo Press make excellent examples. The ability to access Web-based content for most ready reference questions significantly reduces the need to warehouse collections of print reference materials.

The priorities of reference departments and library management teams should be to listen actively to their customers, assess their needs, and then exceed expectations. Libraries must find ways to give customers what they want, while recognizing that customer needs will continue to evolve. In publicizing resources and reaching out to new customers, libraries should heed all opportunities presented by new, affordable online trends such as the recent surge in social media tools.

Reference staff will continue to value guidance from professional organizations and societies in how best to meet those changing needs. Reference departments, and libraries as a whole, must focus on providing experiences and materials that are either available no place else or for which the library can provide a singularly satisfying access point. Uniqueness counts. Increasing access to local history resources is an area of growth. Digitizing rare or unusual historical content will increase the library's value as a community-based resource. It is worth mentioning that free services also need to be sold (i.e., promoted). The provision of free reference service on-demand is a defining, even a unique element of the American public library. Putting well-trained professional staff on the frontline will lead to the creation and development of a supportive community base.

REFERENCES

Aldrich, S. (2010). *California library statistics.* Sacramento, CA: California State Library.

Braby, E., & Hunt, J. (1990). *The Santa Monica Public Library, 1890-1990.* Spokane, WA: Arthur C. Clark Co.

Turner, J. (1996). *The dictionary of art.* New York, NY: Grove.

Chapter 21
Embedded Librarianship:
A High School Case Study

Buffy J. Hamilton
Creekview High School, USA

ABSTRACT

This case study chronicles the learning experiences of 10th grade Honors Literature/Composition students who participated in a 2009-10 learning initiative, Media 21, at Creekview High School. This program, spearheaded by school librarian Buffy Hamilton and English teacher Susan Lester, provided students a learning environment facilitated by both Hamilton and Lester in which Hamilton was "embedded" as an instructor. Media 21, rooted in connectivism, inquiry, and participatory literacy, emphasized students creating their own research "dashboards" and portals, the creation of personal learning networks to help students engage in their learning experiences, and to evaluate a diverse offering of information sources more critically.

INTRODUCTION

Media 21 (http://portal.cherokee.k12.ga.us/ departments/technology/media/default.aspx), a technology endorsement program for Cherokee County School District school librarians, is a local initiative designed to provide school librarians support for enhancing the learning environment of the library and increasing the level of technology integration into collaboratively designed learning activities between school librarians and classroom teachers. Participants take courses on learning pedagogy and technology tools for learning; the capstone project is the culminating learning experience in which each school librarian develops an information literacy project in his/her school.

Hamilton utilized her participation in the program to initiate a collaborative partnership with Susan Lester in which she was embedded into the daily life of two sections of 10th Honors World

DOI: 10.4018/978-1-61350-308-9.ch021

Literature and Composition for approximately 120 of the 180 days of the academic year. Hamilton's Media 21 initiative at Creekview High School provided students a unique opportunity to be part of a collaborative partnership between teachers and students in which collective intelligence, the crowd sourcing of research and learning experiences, and inquiry took center stage in a participatory environment. Hamilton and Lester functioned as sponsors of traditional transliteracy as they scaffolded students' efforts to build their ability to read, write, and create content across multiple forms of media. The chapter explores how students used an assortment of tools and resources for learning, reflection, and content creation as part of the class research experiences as well as personal information seeking needs. The chapter also examines how students used traditional, authoritative sources of information as well as emerging forms of social scholarship for research and content creation of personalized research portals.

BACKGROUND AND LITERATURE REVIEW

In 1989 the American Library Association defined information literacy as "a set of abilities requiring individuals to recognize when information is needed and have the ability to locate, evaluate, and use effectively the needed information" (Association of College and Research Libraries, 2009). While these fundamental skills are still at the heart of information literacy instruction, the nature of that information and the strategies for evaluating it are rapidly changing; the Read/Write Web and Web 2.0 technologies are disrupting many traditional, long-held concepts of authority. We are now in what Michael Jensen calls the "era of information abundance," as a result of this abundance, Jensen asserts, "…we are witnessing a radical shift in how we establish authority, sig-

nificance, and even scholarly validity" (Jensen, 2007, p. B6).

Social networking and social media are responsible for these shifts in which any author may be valued as an "expert" in the production of scholarly knowledge. What does this mean to librarians and our interpretation of "information literacy?" Laura Cohen says, "We can no longer be content to train students to understand the difference between peer-reviewed journals and popular magazines, to appreciate the value of books, newspapers and reference sources, and to understand how to evaluate garden variety Web sites" (Cohen, 2007).

The debate over what counts as authoritative information parallels similar arguments about what counts as literacy and reading. Literacy is no longer confined to traditional print materials as we now recognize multiple formats. In their American Educational Research Association paper, "Towards a Transformative Pedagogy for School Libraries 2.0," Asselin and Dorion maintain, "Within multiliteracies, 'new literacies' refers to new forms of texts—or post-typographic (digital) forms—and new ways of using text to shape new ways of thinking such as wikis, mash-ups, zines and scenario planning but may include media literacy and digital literacy…" (Asselin & Doiron, 2008). Henry Jenkins defines new media literacies as "…social skills developed through collaboration and networking. These skills build on the foundation of traditional literacy, research skills, technical skills, and critical analysis skills taught in the classroom" (Jenkins, 2006, p. 4).

School library media specialists function as sponsors of literacy (Brandt, 2001, p.19) by promoting traditional forms of information literacy—as well as new literacies—to encourage many voices of discourse and representations of information. Our conversations about authority and information evaluation reflect my personal paradigm shift and resulting effort to position new literacies as an integral element of learning. To embed information literacy as an essential standard in every subject area, we must collaborate with subject-area teachers to foster an inquiry-based approach to learning that dovetails perfectly with the use of social networks, new media, and information commons as part of students' personal learning networks and syntheses of these information streams. By responding to the changes that are occurring in today's information culture, school librarians can facilitate learning experiences that situate information literacy as a fundamental literacy shaped by today's society, culture, and ever-evolving technologies.

The arguments of authority and literacy ultimately lead back to how media specialists help students navigate both traditional and nontraditional information. How have these changes in the information landscape affected our commitment to practice an expanding definition of information literacy? Two theoretical lenses, *participatory librarianship* and *connectivism*, inform how one may cultivate an inquiry driven and participatory learning environment facilitated by the school library program in collaboration with classroom teachers and students. This environment seeks to provide students opportunities to access information through multiple mediums, to evaluate, organize, and filter those information sources in meaningful ways, and to create content to represent key learnings through traditional and emerging literacies. These theories embrace an innovative, organic approach to information literacy integration and value the power of social media and learning networks that are an essential element of evolving information literacy concepts.

Participatory librarianship positions librarians as agents of change in their learning communities. Rooted in conversation theory, participatory librarianship suggests that if people must engage in some form of conversation to acquire knowledge, and if librarians are in the knowledge business, then librarians should be in the conversation business by engaging patrons and providing access to an information-rich environment by providing multiple points of access to

that knowledge (Lankes 2007). Librarians seek to create conversations about learning and all aspects of library programming go back to the essential question, "How does this decision impact and create a conversation for learning?" (The Information Institute of Syracuse, n.d.).

Consequently, librarians should think about how we can facilitate these conversations about information literacy with learners using social media and cloud computing. Helping students create their own personal learning environments and information dashboards for engaging in these conversations for learning with themselves as well as peers within and outside the immediate classroom environment is critical in teaching students how to navigate today's information landscape and giving them the learning tools they need to initiate their own conversations for learning.

The second lens for envisioning these conversations for learning in my library program is **connectivism**, a theory that explains how technology influences learning in a digital world. George Siemens, who developed this learning theory, describes connectivism: "[The] starting point of connectivism is the individual. Personal knowledge is comprised of a network, which feeds into organizations and institutions, which in turn feed back into the network, and then continue to provide learning to individual" (Siemens, 2004). This theory lends itself to the idea of a personal learning network, a set of resources to go to for new information, strategies, and ideas. Students can also add RSS feeds from their teachers' blogs.

In today's mashup world of information, a plethora of resources are available via the Internet, including podcasts, blogs, social bookmarks, social networks, videos and video streaming, wikis, and RSS feeds through a favorite feed aggregator. The premise behind participatory tools used to build these information dashboards and personal learning environments is to model ethical and informed information-seeking behavior for our students. Students learn how to connect with other learners and entities to build knowledge and solve information-search problems ("Networked Student," 2008). Information literacy instruction must include helping students learn to pick and evaluate the best resources for their personal learning networks from print, subscriptions, and emerging forms of authoritative information via social media streams.

THE EMBEDDED LIBRARIAN PROGRAM

The Collaborative Process: School Librarian and Classroom Teacher

In March 2009, Hamilton approached Susan Lester, one of Creekview High School's English teachers, with an idea for a collaborative project grounded in connectivism and participatory librarianship. For her Media 21 Capstone project (please see http://portal.cherokee.k12.ga.us/departments/technology/media/default.aspx), Hamilton wanted to create a nine to twelve week long learning experience that would help students learn how to use social media and cloud computing for learning and as a means of cultivating a personal learning network. In addition, Hamilton wanted students to engage in learning through collective knowledge building and inquiry. After sharing the resources and research she had collected to support this vision of learning, Lester agreed to take a leap of faith and join Hamilton on this journey of teaching and learning. Together, the two outlined content based and information literacy performance standards we wanted students to master; they also collaborated to draft a list of learning activities and tools they wanted to implement, as well as a master list of materials. The materials purchased by Dr. Eddy, school principal, and the Cherokee County School District included 12 sets of nonfiction and fiction books related to issues in Africa for students to read in literature circles (we had purchased quite a few print book sets the previous year on veterans' issues, so new print materials were not need for

that unit of study); Gale Global Issues in Context and Gale History Resource Center databases to support the topics in our units of study and to provide students unlimited 24/7 access to these virtual reference materials; an additional 16 station wireless laptop lab to facilitate group work and other classes in the library; and two additional Flip video cameras. Additional print reference materials were not purchased since the new virtual resources (in conjunction with existing virtual reference materials) and existing print resources would be sufficient for students' research needs.

Over the summer, Hamilton and Lester collaborated in person and via email to fine tune their plans. Consequently, they were prepared at the beginning of the school year in early August 2009 to launch the 10th grade Honors World Literature and Composition course sections together running together. For two periods a day for an entire semester, Hamilton and Lester worked as a team to co-teach the two sections on a daily basis, creating and facilitating mini-lessons, providing group and individual instruction, designing lesson plans, co-creating assessment rubrics, facilitating the course blog, course website, and course wiki, and assisting with the formative and summative evaluation of student learning artifacts. Both Hamilton and Lester fielded questions via students via email and provided feedback on the class blog and individual student learning blogs.

During the first semester (Fall 2009), students engaged in units of inquiry about ways people can use social media and then actually used social media and cloud computing tools as tools for facilitating learning and creating content as well as actual information sources. In this eight-week unit, students explored the use of social media for educational uses and as a form of authoritative information. We also explored the use of social media for social good, exploring examples of real world uses of social media for social justice and charitable causes; in addition, we participated in the blogathon for the Louisville Free Public Library at the end of August. While students relied heavily on websites, videos, and news articles available for free on the Web because of the currency of the topic, students did use some periodical articles and viewpoint essays from Gale Opposing Viewpoints, SIRS Researcher, and Academic Search Complete. The unit culminated in students composing persuasive essays that either argued the case for social media in the classroom or the limitation of social media as an educational tool in K12 schools. To explore the research guides for this unit, please see http://www.theunquietlibrary.libguides.com/wikis-media21, http://www.theunquietlibrary.libguides.com/google, http://www.theunquietlibrary.libguides.com/socialmediaforsocialgood, and http://www.theunquietlibrary.libguides.com/media21home for the research pathfinders that supports this collaborative effort.

In late September of 2009, classes began a ten week unit in which students engaged in inquiry about issues in Africa, such as the civil war in Sudan, genocide in Rwanda, and the HIV epidemic. For this unit, Hamilton and Lester students now used their learning tools, such as blogs and wikis, to share their reflections to the readings in their literature circles and their individual research on an issue in Africa depicted in the literature circle reading. Students engaged in metacognition by composing research reflection blog entries in which they discussed research strategies and information evaluation techniques. Students also blogged reader response posts about their fiction or nonfiction work; in addition, students shared literature circle meeting notes and responses to those meetings on their literature circle group wikis with Google Sites to encourage sharing and for students to see research and reading as forms of deeper inquiry and learning. Students also learned how to bookmark articles of interest to the class Diigo account so that quality articles could be shared with students in both course sections. Students met in literature circles two days a week, so instructional mini-lessons and time

for research were provided during the remaining three days each week.

Mini-lessons focused on evaluating all information sources, including Wikipedia, websites, videos, virtual reference, and print nonfiction materials for timeliness, relevance to the research task, and credibility. Additional mini-lessons were provided on how to search database resources, such as SIRS, Gale Global Issues in Context, and titles in Gale Virtual Reference Library, effectively to find articles related to their research questions. Students also learned how to customize their Google News pages to add sections related to their research topics; in addition, students learned how to set up Google News alerts.

Learning artifacts for this extended unit of study included a traditional research paper and a learning/research portfolio created with Google Sites. In this portfolio, students included links to their blogs, their embedded research papers in Google Docs or an attached Word version of their paper, and multigenre learning artifacts that were incorporated. The multigenre learning artifacts provided students alternative ways of representing the key ideas from their readings and research; artifacts included artwork, songs, poetry, videos, skits, Glogster electronic posters, VoiceThread creations, games, and collages. Please see http://goo.gl/rZNvt and http://goo.gl/Se1Xz for the research pathfinders that support the skills and learning activities of this unit.

A culminating learning activity in which students learned about "presentation zen" style for public speaking and presentations was the final collaborative unit of the semester. Students learned how to use images and minimal to convey key ideas and learning, effective public speaking skills, and how to use Creative Commons licensed photos in their slidedecks to create a final presentation to represent their journey of learning in the Issues in Africa unit. This final learning activity was the first presentation experience for most of our students, and for all students in the cohort, the first in which they could not use bullets and merely copy/paste information. As one student, "Beth", observed, "Using the 'presentation zen' style, I actually had to understand my findings. Because I couldn't use bullets in my power point, I was forced to really connect to my research to talk about it during my presentation." Please see for supporting materials for this unit at http://goo.gl/AYTbF and http://goo.gl/Yz3k7.

From March through mid-May 2010, Hamilton and Lester worked together again as librarian, students, and teacher to engage in inquiry of issues and challenges our veterans face (http://goo.gl/IWKXQ). Students again maintained their blogs for their reading journals and research reflections; students also created a new Google Site portfolio to reflect four multigenre learning artifacts, blog posts, a narrative of their research journey, and a new element: a Netvibes information dashboard.

Hamilton and Lester introduced *Netvibes* to students in March 2010 to give them a way to digitally showcase their information sources, tools for learning and research, and learning artifacts. The purpose of incorporating Netvibes as a learning tool was to give students a means for creating an information dashboard for organizing all of their information sources (RSS feeds from blogs, online news sources, or saved database searches, widgets for databases, Google Books or Google Books versions of print materials, videos). This decision was inspired by Howard Rheingold's concept of **infotention** and his assertion that "Knowing how to put together intelligence dashboards, news radars, and information filters from online tools like persistent search and RSS is the external technical component of information literacy. Knowing what to pay attention to is a cognitive skill that steers and focuses the technical knowledge of how to find information worth your attention" (Rheingold, 2009).

Many students liked Netvibe's extensive gallery of widgets they could use in addition to the diverse range of themes for a custom look and feel; several students also commented that they found it easy to add content and embed more types of Web code to showcase their learning tools and artifacts. Students also enjoyed using the news widgets available in Netvibes for discovering news articles on their research topic. While students were provided a list of required elements for their Netvibes information portals/learning dashboards, they also had flexibility and creative license in choosing additional content to incorporate and paint a digital story of their research process. By creating these information dashboards, students could easily access their information sources and were cultivating their own information fluency by constructing their own individualized research guides for their topics.

In addition, many students used Netvibes as a space for publishing their learning artifacts related to their research project, such as Glogsters, videos, VoiceThreads, poems, artwork, skits, and written narratives. "Jonathan" conceptualized Netvibes as an essential research tool, sharing that "Netvibes has really helped me as I continue working on my research project. It gives me a great place to combine information and research together in one, easy-to-use place. I enjoy using it and I can't wait to implement it in my every day routine. Netvibes is easily an essential tool for me. I'm on it each class period and every night I get home. If I'm not using it for a basis for research, then it's a portal for links and RSS feeds." A video of students describing their initial efforts with Netvibes is available at http://theunquietlibrarian.wordpress.com/2010/03/26/in-their-own-words-students-provide-a-video-tour-of-their-netvibes-learning-portals/.

Hamilton and Lester also introduced another new tool, *Evernote*, a social bookmarking tool that can clip virtually any information source, including Web pages, blog entries, database articles, images, audio memos, and emails (important for this project since many did email interviews with experts on their topics). Evernote can run on a PC, Mac, or in the cloud on the Web, which makes it accessible in any environment; in addition, some students chose to use the Evernote app for their smartphones and iPod Touches. Once a source is clipped, students can take notes while adding tags to easily search for notes they have created; in addition, notes can be organized in folders and published to the Web for sharing with others. While students still used the district subscription to NoodleTools for creating MLA style citations, they chose to use the notetaking feature in Evernote over the NoodleTools electronic notecards. Students overwhelmingly chose to use Evernote instead of Diigo, our first semester bookmarking tool; students cited the ease of use and the ability to clip multiple forms of information as the primary reasons for***. You can read more about their response to Evernote on the Unquiet Library blog at http://theunquietlibrarian.wordpress.com/2010/03/29/the-verdict-is-in-media-21-students-love-evernote/.

One other new element of the Spring unit of study on veterans' issues was the requirement that students **interview an expert** on their research topic. Because this research skill was new to all students, Hamilton and Lester provided mini-lessons on how to identify potential experts by identifying authors of credible articles they were using or identifying experts quoted in these information sources (news articles on the Web, bloggers who were writing about veterans' issues, and journal, magazine, and news articles from databases). For information sources with a bibliography, students learned how to locate information sources from these bibliographies and to identify additional potential scholars for interview. Hamilton and Lester also provided mini-lesson on vetting the credibility of each person on this list of potential experts.

Students learned how to search Google and Google Scholar to find out information about each candidate's scholarship and credentials as well as contact information. Some students who wanted to interview an actual veteran of the Iraq or Afghanistan war identified local resources they knew through family, friends, or community activities and then evaluated if that person's experiences were relevant to their research task. In some cases, students connected with experts who had commented on their blogs. In one instance, an expert for the U.S. Army's Advanced Prosthetics and Human Performance Research Program at the Telemedicine and Advanced Technology Research Center commented on the blog of a student, Nolan, who was investigating bionic prosthetics. Through the blog connection, Nolan then discovered Turner's Google Reader RSS feed of interesting resources he was sharing publicly on research and advancements in prosthetics for wounded veterans; Nolan then added the Google Reader RSS feed to his Netvibes page to keep an ongoing stream of potential information sources at his fingertips. Eventually, Nolan interviewed Turner for his research project as well. Once a list of potential experts had been identified, students learned how to write a letter of inquiry and request an interview; students had the option of conducting the interview via email, in person, or Skype. In some cases, a potential expert declined an interview for various reasons but provided additional names and contact information of other experts he/she felt would be a good fit for the interview. Developing meaningful interview questions and composing a thank you letter were additional skills students learned in this process. At the end of the semester, students identified the skills in identifying and interviewing an expert as some of the most valuable they had acquired the entire school year and praised the value of using this kind of primary source in the research process.

Through these collaborative units of study, students learned:

- How to effectively use social media tools, such as blogs, wikis, and social bookmarking to reflect, share, and collaboratively construct knowledge.
- How to use cloud computing and social media tools to organize information resources, to collaborate with classmates,

and to share their learning process within and outside of our school community.

- How to create their own subject guides or "research pathfinders."
- How to represent key learnings through traditional texts and new media.
- How to evaluate traditional and emerging authoritative information sources
- How to use writing as a tool for reflection and metacognition through the individual blogs.
- How to demonstrate digital citizenship through the ethical use of information and through the use of tools like Creative Commons licensed media.
- How to engage in inquiry based learning as a community of learners who shared and collaborated their learning efforts.

Hamilton and Lester are currently working with a second cohort of Media 21 students through two sections of 10th Honors World Literature/Composition. While many of the learning activities have been the same during the first semester, one significant difference in the 2010-11 implementation of the initiative has been greater use of Google Documents. Students have composed all work in Google Docs and have collaborated to compose group created research papers. This collaborative research paper has led to more conversations about the selection and rationale of information sources, material incorporated into the paper, and writing strategies. Many students enjoyed using the Google Chat feature incorporated into Google Docs for real time conversations about their papers while on and off campus.

Another shift for the 2010-11 cohort was to provide more scaffolding for students in their research reflection blog entries. While Hamilton and Lester were reluctant to be more prescriptive with the directions for writing and reflection, they realized most students come with little prior experience in actively reflecting on the research process: the information literacy skills they're acquiring

and using, strategies for evaluating information sources, and decision-making processes as they engage in inquiry. The experience of articulating the how and why of information seeking behaviors and participating in active self-assessment of how they are demonstrating standards for learning and specific information literacy skills is one that has also required some more intense scaffolding in Fall 2010 because most students had limited experience in participating in self-assessment and identifying work that exemplified information literacy standards they were mastering. The research reflection blog posts have also encouraged students' participation literacy in being active agents in the research process rather than passive beings who aren't being purposeful in their information seeking behaviors. In addition, these blog posts have served a springboard to annotations they composed for each information source on their final Works Cited page created in NoodleTools.

Three new research tools have also been incorporated into the research experience for the 2010-211 cohort: SweetSearch, NewsTrust, and the Facts on File video database. SweetSearch is a search engine geared toward K-12 students and returns results for approximately 35,000 websites vetted by teachers, librarians, and research experts with Dulcinea Media, whose mission is to help students discover high quality Web resources (Dulcinea Media, Inc., 2010). NewsTrust is a journalism portal and nonprofit news service that provides "...a wide range of tools that empower citizens to access quality news and information -- and learn to separate fact from fiction about important public issues. We promote good journalism, news literacy and civic engagement -- and we welcome donations to support our service" (NewsTrust, 2011). Although students are still required to evaluate each information source from both of these free search engines/news portals, the results returned are of a higher quality, and students do not have to sift through as many results as they might with a search engine like Google or Bing. The third resource, Facts on File, is a subscription service provided by the Cherokee County School District and gives students access to educational video clips across multiple curriculum areas. Since students cannot access YouTube during the school day at this time, Facts on File provides students another means of discovering information in multimedia format (few databases outside of Gale Global Issues in Context provide this "container" of information") and a bank of high quality, educational video clips. While students can still access videos from news services like CNN, Facts on File provides an alternative pool of video clips that cover topics beyond current news.

In her efforts to model the transparency and spirit of sharing with a learning community with students in Media 21, Hamilton's blog posts on the Media 21 initiative at Creekview High School are available at http://theunquietlibrarian.wordpress.com/category/media-21/, and a resource page housing videos, photos, archived webinars, and links to student work are available at http://theunquietlibrarian.wikispaces.com/media21capstone-buffy.

SCHOOL LIBRARY MEDIA CENTER RESOURCES USED IN PROJECT IMPLEMENTATION

Students accessed computer hardware, database materials, and print materials to engage in this collaborative learning experience. As a participant in the Media 21 Capstone project, Hamilton received an additional 16 station wireless laptop set and cart to facilitate student learning not just for the Media 21 cohort students but for all classes utilizing the media center. Hamilton and Lester also made extensive use of the library's teaching lab, which houses 30 desktop computers, Gale Global Issues in Context and History Resource Center, the laptop lab for working in the commons area during group activities, and the twelve novel and nonfiction sets of books for literature circles, all to support student learning.

In addition to the materials purchased for this project, students used existing resources, such as Gale Virtual Reference Library and SIRS Researcher, as information sources. We also accessed many of our free and integral tools through the Internet, including Google Documents, Google Sites, Gmail, Google News, Wetpaint wikis, LibGuides (for research pathfinders), Wordpress blogs, Flickr, Twitter, TeacherTube, YouTube, Netvibes, Evernote, and RSS feeds from a variety of information sources. While some students utilized print materials, most found it easier to use the virtual equivalent available through one of our databases or Google Books; others found that a print material did not lend itself to the information seeking task because the print materials were not as timely or relevant to the students' research questions. The expansion of authoritative information sources transcended the traditional print and database materials as "Nolan", one of our students, observed, "In this new learning environment, my learning environment is the world."

Lester and Hamilton also used the physical space of the commons area of the library for reading, group activities, literature circle meetings, and collaborative learning activities. The class essentially met every day in the library either in the lab or the commons area for the semester. In addition, the library's large projection screen and overhead LCD projector with integrated sound were instrumental resources for the students' culminating presentations each semester.

The library resource that students used most, however, was Hamilton, the school librarian who was an integral resource in designing, teaching, and facilitating the unit on a daily basis for an entire semester. As Hamilton began the school year with a learning activity using PollEverywhere (http://alalearning.org/2010/02/11/engaging-learners-with-poll-everywhere/) requiring students to text their responses via their cell phones to participate in the poll, one student wondered aloud, "What kind of teacher are you?" Students quickly came to regard Hamilton as more than the librarian;

she was their co-teacher with Lester. The students perceived the two as a team who worked together to provide them learning experiences that are uniquely different from any other in their school experience at Creekview High School because of the blended emphasis on technology integration as a tool for inquiry and learning.

ASSESSMENT: GOALS AND STANDARDS MET IN AASL STANDARDS FOR 21ST CENTURY LEARNERS

The mastery of Georgia Performance Standards and *AASL Standards for 21st Century Learners* were assessed through two primary means: teacher and librarian generated rubrics and student self-assessments. Students demonstrated the accurate and effective use of information in the research papers, research/learning portfolios, individual blog posts, and class presentations. They showed growth in their ability to create original research questions and to formulate their opinions on issues based on the research they engaged in. Students demonstrated excellence in information seeking and knowledge generation by exceeding our and their own expectations with the written portion of the research project using more than the minimum number of information sources required and writing double the number of minimum pages required. Students demonstrated exemplary skill in group participation through the literature circle group wikis, peer editing/writing groups, and in helping each other with their digital research portfolios; additionally, many students worked together to provide feedback and suggestions as they worked on their individual presentations.

At the beginning of August 2009, students were used to answering basic comprehension questions and working in isolation. Through this project, that mode of learning was disrupted as they became part of a community of learners in which sharing, dialogue, and questioning were valued. Students learned how to seek out information and to share their findings in creative and transparent ways that helped inform our understandings as a group.

We used a variety of tools to collect data and evaluate student work, including rubrics, student narratives posted on their Google Sites and/or blogs, and Google Forms. With the 2010-11 cohort, students are taking on even more participation in directly evaluating their own work as well as that of their classmates. Students now blog and reflect on how their learning artifacts represent how they are meeting or exceeding a course content Georgia Performance Standard or AASL Standard for 21st Century Learners. Students also participated in evaluating and providing written and virtual feedback on each others' digital portfolios hosted at Wikispaces in the fall of 2010.

In reviewing the student reflections and self-assessments, several patterns emerge. First, students demonstrated a greater awareness of the concept of authority when choosing information sources, whether they are looking at traditional resources like print materials and databases or emerging forms of social scholarship such as blogs and videos. Students also showed improved skill in evaluating and determining the best information sources in the context of the research topic and questions. Students also shared that the process of publishing information dashboards, blog entries, digital portfolios, public presentations, and collaboratively created documents forced them to synthesize and evaluate information rather than merely copying and pasting information. They demonstrated a shift from being mere consumers of information to producers of content and thoughtful users of information. Students also indicated that participatory learning and the use of cloud computing tools engendered a sense of empowerment because their work was shared not just with peers but also with the world at large; many students indicated that they felt their work might make a difference to another student.

Most importantly, the use of diverse information sources to inquire deeply into a research task and the conversations for learning created in this participatory environment was "eye-opening" for many students and expanded their world view. One student, "Nicole" wrote, "I can actually say that I have changed for the better. I have never had such a life changing research topic and this definitely has changed my life. I couldn't believe how much this research project affected me. It definitely forced me to look at myself and made me ask myself what I could do better in my life to help impact other people. I feel that this research that I have done will make a huge difference to others because they too will see what they can do to help others. I hope that by reading my essay, others will decide to devote their time and life to helping those that are in need." Another student, "Ben," reflected, "I realized that we all need to be more aware of things going on in places other than our backyard. We should be concerned with the wellbeing of everyone and not just the people within our borders. I think I, in particular, should be more aware of other countries and try to help in any way I can. I've heard the phrase 'it only takes one person to make a difference' my whole life. But, I've never considered myself to be that one person. And I've just been waiting for someone else to do something. I believe that most of Americans are like that. However that needs to change."

Hamilton and Lester believe that the insights gained by students and improvement in information literacy skills would not have been possible in a traditional learning environment in which the research project is a one shot, isolated activity rather than an integrated, organic, and ongoing process of the larger learning experience. This participatory environment posits research as the centerpiece of learning and provides students a greater sense of agency as learners. This belief is reflected in the words of the students, including "Kristen," who shared, "I definitely, without a doubt learned more in the Media 21 learning environment. It allowed me to research things that interest me, which made me work more

diligently and work more in depth. I did not learn more because I was forced to do a whole lot of busywork assignments. I learned because Ms. Lester and Ms. Hamilton made me want to learn more about my topics, and, also, to work hard to produce quality projects."

In our final exit survey, students were asked to respond to a series of questions; the results included:

- When asked, "Think about the Media 21 learning experience of collaborative learning, networked learning, and using technology to access, manage, and create content. Would you want to have this kind of learning experience again? Why or why not?"
  - 25 students responded "yes"
  - 4 students responded "no"
  - 9 students responding "maybe" citing both pros and cons of this learning environment
- When asked, "Do think you will use any of the skills and/or tools you have learned in this class this past year in your classes next year even if not required by your teachers? If so, which tools or skills?"
  - 33 students responded yes
  - 4 students responded no
  - 1 student responded with an off-topic response
  - Skills and resources cited by students included: research databases, Evernote, Google Docs, Noodletools, Netvibes, Google Sites, presentation zen skills, information evaluation and searching strategies, interviewing skills, Gmail, Google News, iGoogle, Google Books, Google News, Diigo. Interestingly enough, no students identified their Wordpress blogs even though they indicated in previous blog posts this tool was one of value.
- When asked, "Would you like for more of your teachers to work closely with the li-

brary staff next year as Ms. Lester has in 2009-10? Why or why not?"

- ◦ 26 students responded "yes"
- ◦ 4 students responded "no"
- ◦ 8 student responded with split responses of both "yes" and "no"
- ◦ Most students who indicated some reservations or "no" shared they expected the course to consist more of classical literature and to be a literature based with less emphasis on research, use of technology, information sharing, and public speaking; these same students also indicated they felt they performed better when they learned from worksheets and books in a teacher centered classroom rather than a learning or student centered classroom.

Challenges

Disruption of Traditional Models of "School"

While not all students embraced the "connected learner" model, the majority of students demonstrated an improvement in the quality of their writing, their creation of multigenre elements, information literacy skills, and digital competencies. In spite of our efforts to actively scaffold each student, some did not demonstrate engagement or an improved ability to manage their own personal learning environments. While most students welcomed the opportunity to take on greater responsibility for their learning, others found this freedom overwhelming. This participatory model of learning via inquiry, collective intelligence, collaboration, and connectivism disrupted some students' previous concept of "schooling"; most students were accustomed to a traditional model in which they were receptacles of information and the teacher was the "sage on the stage." Some students never felt comfortable taking ownership

and responsibility for their learning and the teachers acting as a facilitator of learning.

While students showed improvement in many of the AASL Standards for 21st Century Learners, Hamilton and Lester have incorporated a greater emphasis on information evaluation skills in 2010-11 by providing direct instruction and practice for students to support their skills in more critical evaluation of Web-based or social media sources of information.

We have to remind ourselves that inquiry often does disrupt comfort zones, and that the process of working through that discomfort, whatever it may be, is unique for each person. We try to balance our expectations of these students as learners (because we *do* believe they will rise to whatever expectations you set forth) and our desire to help them find ways to tap into their "cognitive surplus" with the reality that they come with unique previous experiences and temperaments that may impact how they work through the assorted disruptions and where they are as learners. While the idea of incorporating transliterate practices and privileging many forms of literacy into the act of creating a personal learning environment is familiar to us, it is not to these students. Consequently, our challenge is respecting the process of making the unfamiliar familiar. Ultimately, the process of moving from a spectator to a participant in a learning community is a unique journey for each person.

In addition, Hamilton and Lester learned that while the participatory environment centered in inquiry and supported by the use of cloud computing tools engaged most students in learning more than ever before, "...there were those who still could not handle the responsibility of managing their learning even with these tools because of their inability to finish projects they started. The point is that even though engagement may increase with this model of learning, it is not an overnight "no cure" for a lifetime of deficient work habits for some students." (Hamilton, 2010, May 28) Lester and Hamilton feel that if this type of learning environment were established earlier and more consistently across all grade levels and content areas, student curiosity and time management skills could be cultivated more effectively.

The Limitations of the Traditional Model of School Library Staffing

For Hamilton, balancing her own participation as a teacher and learner with the other responsibilities and demands on her time as the lead and primary instructional librarian in her program. Although the school library is staffed by Hamilton and a second certified school librarian, Hamilton has wrestled with preserving her commitment to the Media 21 cohort and the demand for instructional services of the learning community that consists of 1800 students and over 100 faculty. As other teachers have learned of the success of Media 21, more faculty are requesting Hamilton's collaborative services to take their first steps to incorporate elements of Media 21 into their own classrooms. While this challenge is a joyful one, it is nonetheless frustrating at times for Hamilton to feel challenged in terms of time and human resources to meet everyone's needs.

However, because of the success of Media 21, Hamilton's primary focus as an instructional librarian in 2011-12 will be as an embedded librarianship with a multi-disciplinary team of teachers who will form a professional learning community that will engage in deep collaboration with Hamilton as a co-teacher and instructional partner. This shift in her instructional responsibilities will allow her to continue her duties as program administrator while enabling her to focus on her role as an embedded librarian with multiple teachers across different subject areas.

Solutions and Recommendations

Media 21 has provided students a unique opportunity to be part of a collaborative partnership in which collective intelligence, crowd sourcing research and learning, and inquiry have taken center stage in a participatory environment. Hamilton and Lester have incorporated multiple literacies as they scaffolded students' efforts to build their ability to read, write, and create content across multiple forms of media. They strongly believe that the learning experiences of the students will go with them and be the seeds of their ability to see transact with the world of information in more powerful ways for both academic as well as personal information seeking needs.

What factors are conducive to this kind of collaborative partnership between a librarian and academic instructor? First, the librarian and teacher shared similar philosophies about teaching and learning. Without this shared vision of learning goals, the trust needed to cultivate this partnership would not have been possible. Another important element in this case study was the teacher's willingness to open up the possibilities of the physical spaces of the classroom. The class, which met primarily in the library, was able to establish a sense of community fairly quickly because of the collaborative and transparent nature of the course; in addition, the students, librarian, and classroom teacher were able to communicate virtually after class hours through blogs, wikis, and email. Another important factor in this case study was the teacher's willingness to share ownership of content, pedagogy, and assessment practices that helped established the librarian as a true co-teacher of the course. Students recognized quickly that the librarian was not there just to provide ancillary support or just to teach information literacy skills, but that both Hamilton and Lester were facilitators of the learning activities and practices.

Another factor in the success of this model has been Hamilton and Lester's willingness to focus on conversations about the concept of authority with students and to engage in inquiry about how and why information sources are appropriate for information seeking tasks. In addition, Hamilton and Lester scaffolded students' independence and information fluency during 2009-10 by moving them from librarian-teacher created research pathfinders to student created subject guides created by students themselves with Netvibes. The school administration's support of their efforts to incorporate free cloud computing tools for learning and the transparency of the project on the part of the students as well as Hamilton with the public and open nature of their work. In addition, the district's progressive filtering policy gave students greater access to a broader range of information sources and search tools that supplemented the traditional research databases.

Most importantly, the school administration supported this vision of the librarian "embedded" into the classroom and the deep level of collaboration between Hamilton and Lester because it supported student learning and achievement. While the librarian's role as a teacher was vital in this project, so was her expertise as an information specialist and her knowledge of the expanding universe of authoritative information sources. The extended integration of the librarian into the classroom helped both her and the classroom teacher be more responsive to the needs of the students and better assess gaps in understanding in both content knowledge as well as information literacy skills. Had the librarian not been embedded into this classroom for the extended time period, students would not have gained the depth and diversity they did in their research skills. This immersion experience incorporated the evaluation of information as a regular part of classroom life and learning experiences in authentic contexts as opposed to the traditional model of a fixed, isolated research experience in which students receive very little depth, experience, or personalized guided instruction in research processes. In addition, the broad range of learning tools incorporated into this learning model would have been difficult to implement and manage for just one person; through this collaborative partnership, Hamilton and Lester were able to share the responsibility for folding these skills and learning tools into classroom life seamlessly and purposefully, particularly given the reality that most students came with little to no prior knowledge of the digital literacies addressed, as well as minimal information literacy skills.

FUTURE RESEARCH DIRECTIONS

One possibility for future research is examining the impact of the embedded librarianship model on high school students' information literacy skills and attitudes. *Project Information Literacy*, a research study facilitated by the University of Washington's Information School (http://projectinfolit.org/about/), poses three primary research questions that are relevant to the Media 21 model:

1. How do early adults (in their own words) put their information literacy competencies into practice in learning environments in a digital age, regardless of how they may measure up to standards for being information literate?
2. With the proliferation of online resources and new technologies, how do early adults recognize the information needs they may have and in turn, how do they locate, evaluate, select and use the information that is needed?
3. How can teaching the critical and information literacy skills that are needed to enable lifelong learning be more effectively transferred to college students? (University of Washington's Information School, 2011).

By replicating this research framework, I would collect and analyze data on students in grades 9-21 in an embedded librarian cohort team; I'd also like to compare that data to data collected from a cohort not participating in an embedded librarian team at Creekview High School to better understand the impact of the embedded librarianship in relation to these three key research questions.

Another research model would be to replicate an ethnographic study of high school students exploring how they acquire and use digital, information, and new media literacies and incorporate those skills into academic and personal information seeking tasks. Using Dr. Deborah Brandt's *Literacy in American Lives* (http://writing.wisc.edu/podcasts/transcripts/wc_brandt3.pdf) as an ethnographic research model, I would like to explore how today's students are acquiring information and digital and media literacies against the changing information landscape of today's digital world; I am especially interested in seeing how public, school, and academic libraries function as what Brandt calls *sponsors of literacy*, which are "any agents, local or distant, concrete or abstracts, who enable, support, teach, and model, as well as recruit, regulate, suppress, or withhold literacy---and gain advantage by it in some way… sponsors are delivery systems for the economies of literacy, the means by which these forces present themselves to—and through---individual learners. They also represent the causes into which people's literacy usually gets required"(Brandt, 2001, p. 19). This kind of ethnographic study could help librarians explore: what roles, and to what extent, do librarians play these roles in the learning communities, and how students acquire and use information and digital and new media literacies?

The *Undergraduate Scholarly Habits Ethnography Project* (http://ushep.commons.gc.cuny.edu/) is another ethnographic research model that could yield valuable insights. This research project, led by Maura A. Smale of New York City College of Technology, CUNY and Mariana Regalado, Brooklyn College, CUNY, seeks to answer three primary research questions:

- What are faculty expectations for student scholarly work and assignments?
- How do students study, research, and complete their assignments?
- How do students use the library for their coursework (and, if they don't, why not)? (CUNY Academic Commons, 2011).

An ethnographic study of the learning strategies and information seeking behaviors of students in an embedded librarianship cohort as well as a non-embedded librarianship cohort group; by comparing the results of both groups, librarians could compare behaviors and look for patterns that might not only improve the embedded librarianship model but expand our concepts for how libraries can better facilitate conversations for learning with patrons. In addition, a similar ethnographic study of faculty and teachers who participate in an embedded librarianship model could improve our understanding of the impact of those collaborative relationships on student learning as well as the impact of embedded librarianship on the scholarship of a learning community.

CONCLUSION

In most K-12 schools, a school is lucky to have one, possibly two, certified school librarians at most. Because school librarians are trying to take on the roles of leader, teacher, instructional partner, information specialist, and program administrator, they rarely have the opportunity to cultivate partnerships like the one between Hamilton and Lester in *Media 21*. This current model of school librarianship is simply not *scalable* in its *current* incarnation as Hamilton has discovered in her work through Media 21. These kinds of intense and ongoing collaborative efforts require a tremendous investment of time during the school day as well as after hours; it is physically impossible for Hamilton to replicate a Media 21 type experience beyond one to two additional teachers at this time, because there simply is not enough of her as a human resource to meet the demand. While Hamilton and Lester are thrilled with the progress and growth they have seen in their students, they can't help but wonder how much more students could evolve if they could have the kinds of learning experiences they provide them across the curriculum and with their co-taught team approach. This model, however, could be easily replicated in an academic library, where larger staff makes it easier to attach multiple staff members to a number of faculty or a single academic department.

For school and academic libraries to truly represent the qualities rooted in a participatory, inquiry driven learning environment, school districts must be willing to let go of the traditional model of school librarianship and grasp one that is bolder in *scope* and *practice*. The model of the solitary librarian (who might be lucky to have an additional partner) toiling in a piecemeal effort to infuse information literacy skills into the curriculum and to be a true collaborative partner to a disproportionate ration of teachers and students is in direct conflict to the model of 21st century classrooms that value learning focused on collective intelligence and collaborative knowledge building as a community of learners. How much more seamless and authentic would research, content creation, and evaluation of information be if school librarians were embedded in a team of classroom teachers by grade level or discipline? The Media 21 embedded librarian model would help teachers, students, and school librarians engage in conversations about multiple forms of literacy, and consequently, position information literacy as an essential and integrated literacy into content area instruction. Research, information seeking and evaluation, and creation of content would no longer be an isolated activity students engaged in once or twice or year, but instead, a regular learning experience.

Media 21 represents a model of librarianship that can greatly improve the profession's ability to establish and cultivate rich **relationships** with faculty and students. The foundation of successful teacher, student, and librarian collaboration is building meaningful relationships; we cannot ask others to have faith in us, to trust us, to let us become part of their world of teaching and learning without building a relationship that has depth and substance. The importance of trust and

these relationships is reflected in the "Truth Be Told: How College Students Use and Evaluate Information in the Digital Age" report from The Information School at The University of Washington, in which Head and Eisenberg found that "Nearly half of the students in the sample (49%) frequently asked instructors for assistance with assessing the quality of sources for course work—far fewer asked librarians (11%) for assistance" (Head & Eisenberg, 2010, p. 3).

The Media 21 also embodies an effective approach to integrating information literacy skills into content area instruction and instruction rather than an isolated skill set that is only used on occasion. How much more effectively could we build our "tribe" and lead through example if we were embedded into an academic department or interdisciplinary team? Librarians cannot be content to "settle" and accept the limitations funding cuts impose upon our potential as catalysts in our learning communities. Librarians must wave the banner for a new model of librarianship that ultimately is an investment in our learning communities.

REFERENCES

Asselin, M., & Doiron, R. (2008, March 26). *Towards a transformative pedagogy for school libraries 2.0*. Retrieved January 2, 2009, from http://asselindoiron.pbwiki.com/AERApaper

Association of College and Research Libraries. (2009). *Information literacy competency standards for higher education*. Retrieved January 2, 2009, from http://www.ala.org//////.cfm

Brandt, D. (2001). *Literacy in American lives*. New York, NY: Cambridge University Press.

Cohen, L. (2007, October 31). *Information literacy in the age of social scholarship* [Web log message]. Retrieved from http://liblogs.albany.edu///_literacy_in_the_ag.html

Hamilton, B. J. (2010, March 25). Sponsors of literacy in contemporary culture: An e-interview with Dr. Deborah Brandt [Web log post]. Retrieved from http://theunquietlibrarian.wordpress.com///of-literacy-in-contemporary-culture-an- e-interview-with-dr-deborah-brandt/

Hamilton, B. J. (2010, May 28). *Guest post: Susan Lester reflects on Media 21* [Web log post]. Retrieved from http://theunquietlibrarian.wordpress.com/ 2010/05/27/guest-post-susan-lester- reflects-on-media-21/

Jenkins, H. (2006). *Confronting the challenges of participatory culture: Media education for the 21st century*. Retrieved from http://newmedialiteracies.org/// NMLWhitePaper.pdf

Jensen, M. (2007, June 15). The new metrics of scholarly authority. *The Chronicle Review, 53*(41), B6. Retrieved from http://chronicle.com////b00601.htm

Knight Commission on the Information Needs of Communities in a Democracy. (2009, October). *Informing communities: Sustaining democracy in the digital age*. Retrieved from https://secure.nmmstream.net/.newmediamill//.pdf

Lankes, R. D. (Producer). (2007). *Participatory librarianship* [Motion picture]. United States. Retrieved from http://www.youtube.com/?v=7TyuVJ4vENo

Networked student. [Motion picture]. (2008). Retrieved from http://www.youtube.com/?v=XwM4ieFOotA

Rheingold, H. (2009, September 1). *Mindful infotention: Dashboards, radars, filters* [Web log post]. Retrieved from http://www.sfgate.com/bin//?entry_id=46677

Siemens, G. (2004, December 12). *Connectivism: A learning theory for the digital age*. Retrieved January 3, 2009, from http://www.elearnspace.org //.htm

The Information Institute of Syracuse. (n.d.). *The participatory librarianship starter kit: Introduction*. Retrieved January 2, 2009, from http://ptbed.org/.php

University of Washington's Information School. (2011, January 26). *Project information literacy: A large-scale study about early adults and their research habits*. Retrieved from http://projectinfolit.org//

Chapter 22
Making an Impact:
Digital Resources for Teens

Roger Rosen
Rosen Publishing, USA

Miriam Gilbert
Rosen Publishing, USA

ABSTRACT

In this case study, Roger Rosen and Miriam Gilbert describe the creation of Rosen Publishing's award-winning, critically acclaimed Teen Health & Wellness: Real Life, Real Answers database. They focus on how Rosen was able to offer a unique value proposition both to teens and librarians, craft age-appropriate and credible content, and build an interactive site that offers an engaging, dynamic user experience. They review the process of creating a resource that had no barrier to finding information, made the discovery process fast and easy, and supported different styles of learning and information-seeking behavior. They discuss the challenges of ensuring that Teen Health & Wellness remains relevant and current in today's crowded digital landscape, and share the successes in building a unique health and wellness resource that is indispensable to teens and librarians alike.

MAKING AN IMPACT: DIGITAL RESOURCES FOR TEENS

Whether content is on clay tablets, papyrus, the printed page or online, the eternal verity embedded in the compact between reader and information provider is that the content be authoritative, accurate, unbiased, vetted, and, ideally, age appropriate.

DOI: 10.4018/978-1-61350-308-9.ch022

This basic principle has guided Rosen Publishing's e-decisions as we negotiate and innovate in these revolutionary times.

Rosen Online's goal is to create a "digital experience" and bring critical, often life-saving, information to the place that teens turn most often: online. To that end, we strove to create a resource that works both in an authoritative and in a personal, peer-to-peer fashion. We recognize that the online experience is a dynamic, mutual one, and aim to provide a vehicle not just to give teens static information but also to allow them to share that information and filter it through the lens their personal experiences.

Notwithstanding the common ground to be found in the editorial process between our 1969 book *The Teenager and VD* (Deschin, 1969) and the eleven articles on STDs in the Rosen Publishing's 2011 database Teen Health & Wellness: Real Life, Real Answers (Rosen Publishing, 2011), there are innumerable challenges, decisions and opportunities that impact the dissemination of information in the 21st century. These issues include the competition against unvetted sources, helping students who struggle with information overload, providing context when other sources fail to do so, aiding discoverability, dynamizing interactivity, and providing continual updates for currency.

In January 2007, Rosen Publishing launched its first online database for middle school and high school students—Teen Health & Wellness: Real Life, Real Answers. Our goal was to provide an age-appropriate, up-to-date, authoritative health resource that would be the go-to site for teens to consult with their questions and needs. We wanted this site to be direct, intuitive, easy, seamless, and engaging, such that any user or learner could be immediately successful. A pivotal goal was to make the process simple for users to find the information that they were seeking as well as to encounter other material that might be of interest to them. We wanted to provide a resource that had no barrier to finding information, made the discovery process fast and easy, and supported different styles of learning and information-seeking behavior.

Rosen felt it was critically important to put information online in the format and modality that teens look to most frequently when seeking answers. Discoverability and ease of search and browse was key, because we were cognizant that teen users would have limited time in the library and not all would have computers at home.

We conducted extensive testing with both teen and librarian users at the beta stage of site development. We observed user behavior on the site and asked for feedback on specific features and function to ensure that we were building a site that met their needs and complemented their online behavior.

Teen Health & Wellness: Real Life, Real Answers—the award-winning, critically acclaimed online resource—provides middle school and high school students with nonjudgmental, straightforward, standards-aligned, curricular and self-help support. Topics include diseases, drugs, alcohol, nutrition, mental health, online safety, suicide, bullying, green living, financial literacy, and more.

Rosen cast the definition of "health and wellness" as broadly as teens themselves define health. This concept includes far more than simple physical and mental health, but the health of relationships with family, friends, and significant others as well as the health of the school, local community, and larger world. Key features of Teen Health & Wellness: Real Life, Real Answers include the following:

- Instant translation into 50 languages, including Spanish, French, Chinese, Russian, Arabic, and Haitian Creole.
- Site optimized for Smartphones to connect anytime, anywhere.
- Social bookmarking allows users to share article links with friends and family.
- Videos throughout, including student-created videos, add a sense of personal connection for teens.
- Customizable hotlines connect users to local community resources as well as national organizations.
- Engaging photos, illustrations, and charts.
- Health calculators, including body mass index (BMI), budget, blood alcohol content, and more for personalized tips.

Teen Health & Wellness: Real Life, Real Answers is an ever changing and evolving resource. Maintaining currency of both topical coverage and technology is a challenge for all electronic publishers. The Teen Health & Wellness team works closely with our community of advisors from school and public libraries to ensure we are including the content and features that teens need most.

To understand why Teen Health & Wellness has been described as "setting the standard for interactive databases" (Brisco, 2010) for young adults, this chapter will examine the ongoing development and collaboration with librarians, teachers, and students that has ensured that Teen Health & Wellness has remained the vital resource upon which teens have come to depend.

Librarians are at the forefront in training students to become an informed citizenry, in part by teaching them how to gather information and recognize its quality. Sheila Schofer, Coordinator of Young Adult Services, and Michael Santangelo, Electronic Resources Librarian, at the Brooklyn Public Library, an independent library system with 60 branches that serve a population of 2.5 million people, have had great success using the Teen Health & Wellness database to reach their diverse community of patrons:

Our librarians like to point kids to Teen Health & Wellness (THW) because it's one comprehensive resource rather than a lot of resources to remember. It's easy for kids to use—they just type in what they're looking for and they'll find it… Many teens, regardless of socioeconomic background, do not necessarily feel they have someone to go to in order to ask questions about their bodies or the changes they are experiencing… THW helps out here and offers kids a resource they can use in the library, at school or from home if they have access to an internet-enabled computer. It also offers privacy and never comes off as patronizing to teens. (Santangelo & Schofer, 2009)

At Brooklyn Public Library, Teen Health & Wellness acts not only as a convenient source

of accurate and age-appropriate information for teens, but also as a comprehensive resource for adults who are perplexed by the delicate nature of offering honest answers to controversial questions broached by their teenage patrons:

Teen Health & Wellness (THW) fills a niche for information on real life issues. It covers health, but it's also about wellness in the broadest sense. Kids can find information on topical subjects like tattoos and piercings. Teen Health & Wellness gives our youth librarians a good way to address sensitive topics without crossing the line into giving advice. A group of girls approached one of our YA librarians to request a girls-only teen time to talk about sexuality and health issues. The librarian arranged the program and showed them how to find solid, credible information using THW. She asked the girls to write down questions that the group researched together on THW. Throughout the BPL system, other librarians have now embraced this program. Once kids have seen the database, they are more comfortable using it on their own (Santangelo & Schofer, 2009). With such highly controversial, constantly evolving topics covered as when a parent is gay, bullying, and human papillomavirus--HPV, for example, it is essential for librarians to be able to offer input into the development of content:

Rosen Publishing is very responsive in enhancing the content based on feedback from users. We have made suggestions where we have seen gaps in coverage and they have filled those gaps quickly with excellent information (Santangelo & Schofer, 2009).

It is also important in these situations that teens come to recognize the high-stakes of assessing the distinction between vetted and unvetted information. Direct participation through interactivity reinforces relevance and ownership of the subjects considered. Comments from two librarians, the first the librarian/media specialist at a rural middle/high school in Ohio and the other library director for a central New York BOCES (Board of Cooperative Educational Services) speak to the success of online resources developed with the input of librarians and teens:

In a small school, with a limited budget, potential resources are carefully weighed and selected with quality, curricular needs, students' personal needs, accessibility, and teen-appeal in mind. Excellence is a starting point in the decision-making process, but it is not enough; our resources have to meet student needs on many levels. Teen Health & Wellness earns its place in our collection. Teen Health & Wellness combines current, authoritative, in depth, written specifically for teen information, with Web 2.0 cool tools and access. Whether a student is searching from home or at school for answers to a personal question, or researching for a health, psychology, or biological science class, Teen Health & Wellness is a first stop and top choice. During the past three weeks, I have watched students use Teen Health & Wellness in a variety of ways. One student explored her disability and became excited and empowered as she contemplated writing her own person anecdote for the database. After a frustrating search through other databases and online catalogs, seniors in Government class turned to Teen Health & Wellness and found information on a Supreme Court case. One group of students in a Sociology class explored a cultural group through Teen Health & Wellness. These students are doing more than finding, selecting and learning content; our students are learning to make decisions about where to search, how to search and navigate, how to select information, and how to combine information from a variety of resources to create and communicate their own information projects. Our students are learning invaluable 21st century skills. (Deb Logan, personal correspondence, November 10, 2010)

It is extremely accessible and the information provided is "hip," up-to-date, and grounded in science and medicine. Students can also submit essays on issues that deal with pertinent issues

such as death, suicide, and friendship. ...I really think that, by including student voices in the database, the purely fact-driven database model recedes and a more interactive, end-user interface is created. ...Many of our regional student library systems have picked up the database and have seen great responses from teaching staff, librarians, and students. (Charles O'Bryan personal correspondence, June 15, 2010)

Interactivity is certainly one of the great and dynamic points of departure from the printed book. Our research has shown that site features can build community in a network of users. With our Personal Story Project, students are able to submit and post (first-name only) compelling personal life experiences, and with our calculators, students can get personalized health information. The ability to write to our staff psychologist, to cast one's vote in online polls, and to submit student-made PSAs to our video section, all contribute to participation and empowerment in a safe environment that could not be similarly guaranteed with a general Web search. Marcie Mann, library/media specialist and Heather Amidon, health teacher at LaFayette Junior Senior High School in LaFayette, New York attest to this effectiveness:

LaFayette JSHS has embraced the move from traditional print resources to online resources. But it presents many challenges, particularly in the field of health where many sites in school are blocked because they are about things like "breast" cancer, marijuana or addiction. Vetted online sources are often written for an adult audience, far above what students in grades 7-12 can handle. Also, many other online options are just not authoritative, trusted sources.

LaFayette JSHS purchased Rosen's Teen Health & Wellness two years ago. The first thing we noticed about it was that it was written for its intended audience: teens. This has made the research process in health class a lot easier and more successful. Prior to THW, students googled information on their topics and we checked it for authority, since most of the health databases were written for professionals. This is unwieldy and frustrating for students. Now searches are simple and successful, by keyword or subject, and everything is in one place. The personalization of resources in our community has also been a great addition. Most importantly, the quality of finished research projects has improved. Our health class is adding a new dimension to the research project on illegal drugs that they do each semester. This year, at the end of the project, they will script and produce PSAs using the information from THW and a flip camera. This combination research using an authoritative database, creativity and a national audience has taken a good research project and made it a great one. (Marcie Mann and Heather Amidon, personal correspondence, November 4, 2010)

It is also vital in the creation of any online resource that users can get to it easily and effectively. Librarians face significant challenges in making visible and promoting the online resources that they provide to users. Many online resources can be enhanced by publishers to increase exposure and to put the resource in the students' everyday search path. Teen Health & Wellness has utilized RSS feeds, social book marking (Twitter, Facebook), site-optimization for smart phones, Google Translate, content indexing with Google, and widgets. Additionally, we have built a unique feature that allows patrons to share our content via social networking in the same way that they would have shared a Xerox copy twenty years ago, or an email five years ago. This tool allows students to post articles from our database in a way that allows friends and family to read our proprietary content without having to log into the site.

Also, Teen Health & Wellness provides advertising collateral to help librarians get out the word, including bookmarks, access cards, posters, and Web banners, buttons, and widgets. Librar-

ians can distribute access cards and bookmarks to users and can display posters to raise awareness of the site. Web buttons and banners give teens immediate access into the database from a school library Web page or public library teen page. They also make it quick and easy for librarians to promote the resource in an engaging, graphic, and teen-friendly way. Web widgets allow users to search the contents of Teen Health & Wellness from anywhere on the library website. The librarian at Spring Branch ISD, an urban school district in Houston, Texas, had this to say about its effectiveness:

We do training on our databases and the various ways to use them. This includes our LA teachers; we show them the options of using images, quotes, cartoons and "in the news" as writing prompts for spontaneous writing in Middle and High school.

The database is linked on our library resources pages as well as several campus library Web pages so that it is easy to get to. We also use the cards that THW provides to give to our councilors and nurses and they give these out to students. The card had the website URL and the log in information so that the student can access the database from wherever and whenever. They really like the cards; it is an unobtrusive private way to help students without embarrassing them or making them feel self-conscious about their questions.

We have used Teen Health & Wellness in Spring Branch ISD since the spring of 2007. It has proved to be an essential tool for the health and well-being of our students, especially in Middle and High School grades. Our councilors and nurses use the database to both teach students about the changes they are experiencing as they grow and mature, and as a resource for students to access privately when they need answers about personal issues that they aren't comfortable asking about. Our Health Fitness department uses THW to teach fitness, nutrition, and health, and one of their favorite resources is the personalized BMI index based not only on height and weight but also age! This tool is so useful for teaching students what is a good weight for their age and size, and they can refer back to the index as their bodies grow and change. Even our Language Arts department has used the Dr. Jan questions and the "in the news" section as writing prompts in high school classrooms, as well as Science classes studying Biology.

This database is targeted at a subject that is becoming one of the most difficult issues for schools to deal with; it helps our students with issues like depression, weight, physical appearance, puberty, and sexual issues. The information is invaluable both at the teaching level and on a personal level for our teenagers, and as the database continues to grow and update the information will only become more valuable because it offers a place for teenagers to get truthful, honest answers about hard questions! (Liz Phillipi, personal correspondence, November 12, 2010)

Producers of vetted online databases have tremendous resources at their fingertips to help libraries disseminate crafted content to specialized constituencies. Unlike the vast majority of other health information available online, Teen Health & Wellness has been developed specifically for teens, with their unique concerns and perspective in mind. It features age-appropriate, developmentally appropriate content that is crafted at an accessible reading level for teens. Librarians can be comfortable directing users to the site knowing that it is free of advertising, up to date, credible, and without an agenda. The site eliminates the guesswork and potential danger of surfing the open Web and serves "as a one-stop self-help resource and a fully interactive online community center for teen health and wellness" (Roncevic, 2007). [8]

"Today's youth continue to be the internet gurus and technology and media experts of our time,"

reports Harris Interactive's YouthPulse (Crane & Pieters, 2010). "In addition to economic concerns, getting good grades or that someone close to them will die, are some of the top worries for at least half of today's youth.... Four in ten teens and young adults worry about how they look or about their weight." (Crane & Pieters, 2010) With the right medium and message, Teen Health and Wellness connects with teens in the digital language they understand about the central issues of their lives.

Teen Health and Wellness prides itself on its relevancy and currency. The site is updated on an ongoing basis: The homepage is updated weekly and as breaking health news occurs from across North America. Articles are updated throughout the year as part of an editorial review cycle, as breaking news happens, and as new personal stories, Dr. Jan Q&As, videos, and reading list suggestions are submitted by users. The fact that Teen Health & Wellness is continuously updated and enhanced by the creative work of its users guarantees its relevance in the midst of the crowd-clamor of unregulated noise that can also be a part of students' exposure to the Internet.

For Rosen Publishing—and indeed for all digital publishers--an ongoing challenge is to keep pace with advances in technology and delivery methods. For example, we have recently optimized the site for Smarthones to connect anytime anywhere. We are working closely with social media including Twitter, Facebook, and YouTube, and we are constantly searching for new ways to reach, engage, and inform our teen users. With increasing competition for teens' time and attention, our goal is create an ever-more dynamic, timely, and relevant resource.

REFERENCES

Brisco, S. (2010, June 16). *Database*. [Msg 00420]. Message posted to LM-Net, archived at http://lmnet-archive.iis.syr.edu/ LM_NET/2010/ Jun_2010 /msg00420.html

Crane, L., & Pieters, A. (2010). Youth Pulse 2010. *Harris Interactive: Trends & Tudes, 9*(2). Retrieved from http://www.harrisinteractive.com/vault/HI_TrendsTudes_2010_v09_i02.pdf

Deschin, C. S. (1969). *The teenager and VD: A social symptom of our times*. New York, NY: R. Rosen Press.

Roncevic, M. (2007, February 15). Rosen's e-venture. *Library Journal*. Retrieved from http://www.libraryjournal.com/lj/ ljinprintcur-rentissue/850312-403/ rosens_e-venture.html.csp

Rosen Publishing. (2011). *Sexuality and sexual health*. In Teen Health & Wellness: Real Life, Real Answers.

Santangelo, M., & Schofer, S. (2009). *Teen health & wellness story: Brooklyn Public Library, NY*. Retrieved from http://teenhealthfiles.rosenpub.com/ Educator_Resources_files/LessonPlans / THW_Brooklyn_FINAL.pdf

Chapter 23

From 'Gateway Site' to Reference Content:
The Role of Bibliographies in Research and a Case Study of Oxford Bibliographies Online

Rebecca Cullen
Oxford University Press, UK

Robert Faber
Oxford University Press, UK

ABSTRACT

It is suddenly axiomatic that today's researchers, faculty, and students alike begin their research online. The gateway sites (e.g., Google Books, Wikipedia) may provide a user-friendly and serendipitous search-ing experience, while simultaneously keeping the most authoritative and vetted content out of sight. This chapter will examine the research chain as it is currently understood, as well as discussing the planned and actual role of Oxford Bibliographies Online within this shifting research context.

INTRODUCTION

Web use and online searching have become much more usual in daily life. However, from being a manageable collection of informational pages, the Web has become a trackless wilderness. Present day students and researchers represent themselves as "drowning in content."

There is now so much information online that both faculty and students are overwhelmed, and often uncertain which search terms to use in order to find the good quality information they are sure is available. The gateway sites currently provide only a partial solution, precisely because they are

DOI: 10.4018/978-1-61350-308-9.ch023

exclusive of subscription content. With research beginning more often on the free Web than in the walled garden of the library catalog, students at all levels are faced with the ironic situation of seeing too many search results which may yet not include the most authoritative and vetted scholarly materials that they really need.

At the same time, the reference market demands that more information should transition online because that is now the medium in which research takes place. So how are publishers to fulfil market and user needs without either augmenting the existing problem of information overload or of adding to the stockpile of hidden content?

As a further factor, in this research environment, discoverability and accessibility are significant drivers. Librarians are keen to encourage use of both their online and print collections, and researchers at all levels want a clear link between finding a pointer to content and finding the content itself. In order to be noticed in the first place, publisher provided material has to participate and compete in the arena of the free Web, where only the first page of Google results counts.

The focus of this chapter will be to dig deeper into the current research chain, describing the use of a nexus of search tools, sites, and content. While students are aware of the importance of using vetted resources, they often turn to the gateway sites, such as Google Books, Google Scholar, and Wikipedia for their perceived speed, ease of use, and simply because there is increased overlap between the tools individuals use as part of their daily life and those they use in scholarly research. In fact, familiarity may become an even more important factor in the future for those students who have grown up with the resource of the free Web to hand, and have therefore never had to bother developing any other research habits.

We will then discuss the role of bibliographies in an online environment and outline the rationale behind the development of *Oxford Bibliographies Online*. Finally, we will provide some preliminary

evaluation of its place in the scholarly research toolkit based on feedback to date.

BACKGROUND

Several articles of late have examined aspects of undergraduate and postgraduate students' research behavior and the overall results are encouraging, in that students do use course readings, scholarly databases, and library OPACS, as well as gateway sites (Head, 2007; Head and Eisenburg, 2009). Wong (2009) found that students adopt a mixed search strategy, using a combination of free Web and scholarly resources.

One of the most well-known, as well as most controversial of the gateway sites, Wikipedia, has now been around for 10 years. During that time, attitudes to it have moved along a trust continuum: from initial mistrust and benchmarking against traditional reference materials, as in the 2005 *Nature* comparison between Wikipedia and *Encyclopedia Britannica*; to tacit acceptance and limited use among undergraduate students (Head, 2007, p.2); to the present day's active and acknowledged use by both faculty and students.

Particularly for undergraduate students, the gateway sites fulfil an unmet need in the research process by enabling them to begin to build the context within which their search *should* happen. Head and Eisenburg reported that students "described finding context as laborious, often frustrating, yet essential to most of their research" (2009, p.7).

Wikipedia is regarded as an efficient tool with which to fill in gaps in knowledge so that these students can acquire the appropriate vocabulary and mental map of a subject that they need in order to be able to tackle the scholarly research databases; one focus group attendee used the term "presearch tool" (Head and Eisenburg, 2010, p.4), and this is a useful concept to take forward in understanding the current multi-step research process.

Despite fears among both librarians and publishers that a reliance on search engines means research is dumbing down, Head and Eisenburg (2010) found that in fact undergraduate students are well aware of potential credibility issues. However, in the early stages of research, they demonstrate willingness to compromise on authority in favor of "coverage, currency, convenience and comprehensibility" (Head and Eisenburg, 2010). Students are, in fact, ruthlessly efficient in conducting research, and their attitude to the importance of authority and credibility seems to vary depending on the ultimate effect of getting the information wrong. With regard to Wikipedia, for example, students may take the pragmatic approach of double checking any references to which it leads them, and when they have really begun to evaluate content rather than simply to find it, they will conduct some fact checking of information as well (Rieh and Hillgoss, 2008).

Head and Eisenburg also found that online research habits followed a similar routine, regardless of the context of whether the research was being conducted for school or daily life (2010). Users at all research levels automatically turn to the Web as the primary source from which to gain information, and they then bring the aggregate expectations of all their online activity to their research. Given that neither faculty nor students conduct their research in any regular hours, and often from outside the library or any academic environment, such consistency in behavior is unsurprising.

Two important points to take on board, then, in thinking about the research chain are:

1. That scholarly research should be viewed in the context of overall Web use, rather than as specialized activity;
2. That undergraduate and postgraduate students, and faculty who are conducting scholarly research, are not a breed apart from regular Web users, but inhabit the same mental space, depend on some of the same tools, and utilize the same search strategies.

Of course, the likelihood with both Wikipedia and Google is that no search is going to fail entirely, thus circumventing any mental discomfort. Familiarity and reliability are key factors in driving repeated use of a search tool, to a greater extent than the perceived authority of the site (Wong et al, 2009). Basically, once students have identified a core group of research tools and resources that works for them, which may happen early in their academic careers and is most likely to consist of a combination of scholarly databases and gateway sites, they set an on-going research pattern based around those same tools. Searching is a "skill learned by rote" rather than an ability that evolves in response to the students' changing research needs (Head, 2007).

The identification of those core tools can be a fairly random process: undergraduate students may get recommendations from librarians when first introduced to the library, but will rarely ask for help subsequent to that; they will take suggestions from peers; and recommendations from professors are highly valued although not always forthcoming (Head and Eisenburg, 2009). Regardless of source, the setting of artificial parameters is a way in which undergraduate students tackle the problem of information overload. It puts them in a comfort zone, from where they can bring to bear "predictive judgment," because they have learned what to expect from the resources on which they repeatedly depend (Rieh and Hillgoss, 2008). As a result, students may not be using the most appropriate resources for their particular research topic, but they prefer to stay with the tools they know and understand.

RESEARCH CONTENT IN THE MULTI-STEP RESEARCH PROCESS

Both undergraduate and postgraduate students employ an array of sophisticated search techniques as they progress through their information seeking sessions (Wong, 2009). The current research chain is one that may start with a fairly top level query that is then progressively refined as students identify more specific or appropriate search terms that will generate meaningful search results. Part of the "presearch" work lies in contextualization of the topic in order to gather enough background understanding accurately to define these terms. The need for such contextualization has been outlined above.

For students at this early stage of research, scholarly databases may be perceived as obstructive, because the student must first understand the scope and taxonomy of each individual site before they can navigate it (Wong, 2009). Perception is therefore an important psychological factor in determining research behavior, in that the perceived complexity or difficulty of a site may turn users away, even when they are fully aware that they are giving up on an effective resource. This is sometimes the case with regard to library OPACs, which may seem to require specialist skills in order to navigate them. The same hesitancy that makes undergraduate students chary of asking a question at a reference desk, may also see them preferring to avoid the uncomfortable feeling of struggling with a resource that they ought to be able to use, but which they feel demands some investment of time in order to learn how to use it (Fast, 2004, p. 143).

Even if a user has started their search within a library-held resource, frustration with that resource may take them back to Google to get grounded again, exhibiting "phase shifting behaviour" (Wong et al, 2009). Fortunately, this phase shifting can be bi-directional. For example, one student participating in Wong's survey chose to research on Google Scholar, note the results, and then download the articles via a library site (Wong, 2009, p. 67). This example speaks to the fact that use of the gateway sites is embedded in users' search behavior.

So students first turn to sites that they have previously used with a degree of success, looking for a quick win. Rather than aiming at the best results, researchers display satisficing behavior, in that they will settle for what is good enough. They are usually aware of the limitations of the resource and prepared to accept those limitations in order to get their search started. Search terms may be refined by using the auto-population fields in quick search boxes, by picking out terms displayed in search results sets, and by scanning resulting content to develop a subject specific vocabulary. As the search terms evolve, the student simultaneously builds up a mental map of the subject, identifying potentially appropriate content along the way, to which they may then return.

In fact, there has been a gradual evolution in search terms, which we see as concurrent with a greater dependence on increasingly sophisticated search engines. Whereas undergraduate researchers used to limit their search term to just one or two words (Fast, 2004), analysis of referrals to *Oxford Islamic Studies Online* in 2010 showed that users input the entire title of their research paper as a quick search term on Google and were subsequently directed to the *OISO* site via a search results hit.

In general, searching is not a linear process and may begin without a specific objective in mind. Students will shift back and forth between scholarly databases and gateway sites, but the danger is that their frustration with the available search tools, results sets, or content sets will more often drive them from the former to the latter. Students are aware that the scholarly sites or library OPACs have greater credibility, but this is something they will give up on for ease and speed of use. They can be directed back to those more authoritative sites if results from Google, Google Scholar, or Google Books point them there, but that may be dependent on just what content has been made available for Web indexing.

THE ROLE OF BIBLIOGRAPHIES IN RESEARCH

In the research context, a bibliography is a listing of titles that are relevant to a particular subject, and which includes as wide a range of materials as is appropriate to that subject (because, let's face it, not all disciplines are down with podcasts). A bibliography may be appended to a monograph or other work, in which case it allows the reader of that work to follow up on the author's references and potentially to pursue their own research. Alternately, it may exist as a stand-alone resource, usually intended as a survey of all research in a particular field over a particular time. In introductory texts, a bibliography may be purposely constructed to pick out the major landmarks of research in a field and is then of extra use in providing a helpful starting point to someone finding their way through a subject. Thus, typically, a bibliography provides a pre-compiled list with a certain purpose; the titles listed within it have already been useful (to the author) and/or offer a survey of works that *may* be of further use (to the researcher).

Taking the bibliography as an early step in a traditional research chain, the next activity is usually to identify those titles that seem of particular interest and then to track them down. In the print world, a flat bibliography accessed in a library where the works that it lists are mostly to hand to be evaluated is a powerful tool. In the online environment, bibliographies are competing for users' attention alongside all the other scholarly resources, as well as the gateway sites. The traditional bibliographic format did not transition well to online publication, with the expectations of immediate gratification that the medium brings with it. Three core problems may be identified:

1. Bibliographies are usually static when in print, or updated at a rate slower than the pace at which new works are published;

2. They are flat lists that are organized by topic but provide little or no explanatory context for either the topic or the work cited;

3. Bibliographies do not link through to full text (unless via OpenURL linking to online library holdings, where available)

In many respects, information is now delivered to us via a variety of "push" functions (RSS, email, Twitter); we don't go looking for it, and when we do, we don't look very hard. As we have already discussed, academic research happens in the same context as any other searching and is subject to the same set of expectations. Thus, researchers expect to find and access content without necessarily leaving their desks, and are impatient of obstacles. Undergraduates, postgraduates, and scholars are increasingly impatient with the need to visit a library at all, let alone troll shelves.

OXFORD BIBLIOGRAPHIES ONLINE

In 2007, Reference Editorial staff within Oxford University Press US began talking to faculty members, librarians, postgraduate, and undergraduate students about the types of reference resources they felt were needed. One message that came back loud and clear was, in fact, the same as that which can be interpreted from assessment of the current research process: the requirement for a tool that can help researchers get oriented in a new research topic.[1]

In particular, with regard to bibliographies, librarians expressed dissatisfaction with the currency and level of information provided in existing resources, as well as the fact that they were too much a reflection of their print original. It was felt that these bibliographies did not best tie in with contemporary research habits nor maximize opportunities for linking to the sources they included. Finally, identifying the *what* in terms of scholarly resource no longer seemed to be enough. There was also an articulated need to explain *why* a particular resource was relevant or important. Providing more context around the titles included in a bibliography enables the researcher to make a well informed assessment with regard to its potential usefulness, without the need to find a version of the content itself. This suits the power browsing and grazing behavior that online researchers often display.

Another issue to be addressed was that of accessibility. With all levels of researchers increasingly reluctant to visit the library, and an ever growing amount of content available digitally, it was felt that an online bibliography should maximize the possibilities of linking to library catalogs, OCLC's WorldCat, and Google books, as well as including Digital Object Identifiers (DOIs) where available. Researchers felt very strongly that they did not want to be led down a path towards content which they then could not obtain.

Shortly after the launch of *Oxford Bibliographies Online*, Oxford University Press launched a year-long research program into user expectations, use, preferences, and future needs. This program is still underway, but some general points may be extracted from the preliminary findings.

As might be expected, undergraduate and postgraduate students and faculty are all comfortable with the basic premise of an online bibliography that has pared down its citations to key resources. The site is used as a starting point for research, predominantly by undergraduate students who are more focused on completing course assignments and specific projects. This use is consistent with JISC findings with regard to student use of library resources in general, and suggests that use of *Oxford Bibliographies Online* within that particular demographic will display significant peaks and troughs depending on course requirements.

Postgraduate students use the site for their own research, as do faculty to a lesser degree. Faculty members refer both students and colleagues to the site, and faculty and postgraduate students use the site for creating course syllabi. This is a secondary use that was not entirely unforeseen, and may

eventually create a loop in which recommended resources are drawn from *Oxford Bibliographies Online*, to which students then return in order to find the resource itself.

The site is also used for pure exploration, about which more data will be teased out in the second half of the program. One possible explanation for this is that, due to the hybrid encyclopedic-bibliographic nature of the content, users are bouncing around following general information, much as they might with a regular reference work. The entry introductions, which offer basic contextual information around the subject of a particularly bibliography, are regarded as a valuable component of the site and lend themselves well to this type of behavior.

There is clearly more work to be done to develop a clearer picture of how *Oxford Bibliographies Online* is being used, and how it must continue to develop to match evolving user research requirements.

CONCLUSION

Academic research has moved online and is forcing the pace of online content provision. Research has already moved too far down the path of the free web to be brought back within the institution and neither library service providers nor publishers are likely to be in a position to offer a search experience comparable to Google. Consequently, the discoverability of content will continue to be heavily dependent on the free Web, and in fact, the pressure has already started to shift beyond that. It will soon no longer be enough merely to point to a source for content; the demand will be for a seamless transition from search result to content. For good or bad, it is possible to research entirely outside the confines of the academic library. There is, in fact, a wealth of good material available, but it takes more effort to find it, as the research process for this chapter illustrated to us.

REFERENCES

Fast, K. V., & Campbell, D. G. (2004). "I still like Google": University student perceptions of searching OPACS and the Web. *Proceedings of the 67th ASIS&T Annual Meeting, 41*, (pp. 138-146).

Head, A. J. (2007, August 6). Beyond Google. How do students conduct academic research? *First Monday, 12*(8).

Head, A. J., & Eisenburg, M. B. (2009). *Lessons learned: How college students seek information in the digital age. Project Information Literacy progress report*. The Information School: University of Washington.

Head, A. J., & Eisenburg, M. B. (2010, March 1). How today's students use Wikipedia for course-related research. *First Monday, 15*(3).

Nicholas, D., Williams, P., & Rowland, I. (2010). Researchers' e-journals use and information seeking behavior. *Journal of Information Science, 36*(4), 494–516. doi:10.1177/0165551510371883

Nicholson, P. J. (2006). The changing role of intellectual authority. *Proceedings of the 148th Meeting of the ARL* 247, August.

Nielsen, J. (2010). *Alertbox: Mental models*. Retrieved on October 20, 2010, from http://www.useit.com/alertbox /mental-models.html

Rieh, S. Y., & Hillgoss, B. (2008). College students' credibility judgments in the information seeking process. In M. J. Metzer & A. J. Flanigin (Eds), *Digital media, youth and credibility* (pp. 49-72). The John D. and Catherine T. MacArthur series on digital media and learning. Cambridge, MA: MIT Press.

Silipigni, L., & Dickey, T. J. (2010). *The digital information seeker: Report of findings from selected OCLC, RIN and JISC user behaviour projects*. JISC.

Wong, W. (2009). *User behavior in discovery: Final report*. JISC.

ENDNOTES

[1] Rebecca was closely involved with the *Oxford Bibliographies Online* project from around Summer 2008 to Spring 2010. However, the preliminary research pre-dates her time with OUP, and she has had no involvement with the on-going, post-launch research program.

Compilation of References

Adkins, S. (2010). *The US market for mobile learning products and services: 2009-2014 forecast and analysis.* Retrieved November 30, 2010, from http://www.ambientinsight.com/Resources/Documents/Ambient-Insight-2009-2014-US-Mobile -Learning-Market-Executive-Overview.pdf

Agosto, D. E., Rozaklis, L., MacDonald, C., & Abels, E. (2010). Barriers and challenges to teaching reference in today's electronic information environment. *Journal of Education for Library and Information Science, 51*(3), 177–186.

Aked, M. J., Phillips, J. C., Reiman-Sendi, K., Risner, K., Voigt, K. J., & Wiesler, J. (1998). Faculty use of an academic library reference collection. *Collection Building, 17*(2), 56–64. doi:10.1108/01604959810212444

Aldrich, S. (2010). *California library statistics.* Sacramento, CA: California State Library.

Alpert, J., & Hajaj, N. (2008). We knew the Web was big…. *The Official Google Blog,* Retrieved February 5, 2011, from http://googleblog.blogspot.com/2008/ 07/ we-knew-web-was-big.html

American Medical Association. (2011). *Continuing medical education.* Retrieved January 27, 2011, from http:// www.ama-assn.org/ama/pub/ education-careers/continuing-medical-education/frequently-asked-questions.shtml

Anderson, T. D. (2006). Uncertainty in action: Observing information seeking within the creative processes of scholarly research. *Information Research, 12*(1). Retrieved September 14, 2010, from http://infomrationr.net/ir/12-1/paper283.html

Asher, A. (2010, November). *The changing role of libraries in discovery.* Presented at the Ithaka Sustainable Scholarship Conference, New York, NY.

Asselin, M., & Doiron, R. (2008, March 26). *Towards a transformative pedagogy for school libraries 2.0.* Retrieved January 2, 2009, from http://asselindoiron.pbwiki. com/AERApaper

Association of College and Research Libraries. (2009). *Information literacy competency standards for higher education.* Retrieved January 2, 2009, from http://www.ala.org//////.cfm

Baldwin, R. G. (1998). Technology's impact on faculty life and work. *New Directions for Teaching and Learning, 76,* 7–21. doi:10.1002/tl.7601

Ballard, B. (2007). *Designing the mobile user experience.* Chichester, UK: Wiley. doi:10.1002/9780470060575

Barrett, A. (2005). The information-seeking habits of graduate student researchers in the humanities. *Journal of Academic Librarianship, 31*(4), 324–331. doi:10.1016/j. acalib.2005.04.005

Beam, A. (2011, January 28). The definition of change. *The Boston Globe.* Retrieved from http://www.boston.com/ lifestyle/articles/2011/01/28/ a_word_about_dictionaries_and_other_reference_books__in_print_and_online/

Bennett, D. B., & Buhler, A. G. (2010). Browsing of e-journals by engineering faculty. *Issues in Science and Technology Librarianship, 61.* Retrieved September 14, 2010, from http://www.istl.org/10-spring/refereed2.html

Berners-Lee, T., Hendler, J., & Lassila, O. (2001). The Semantic Web. *Scientific American, 284*(5), 34. doi:10.1038/ scientificamerican0501-34

Bernstein, S. (2009). Session 1: Online communities and the institution. *WebWise 2009 Digital Debates Conference Proceedings*, (pp. 13-17). Retrieved from http://www. imls.gov/pdf/ WW09_Proceedings.pdf

Bhanoo, S. N., & Post, S. T. W. (2009, May 19). New tool in the MD's bag: A smartphone. *The Washington Post*, pp. HE01.

Blair, A. (2010). *Too much to know: Managing scholarly information before the modern age*. New Haven, CT: Yale University Press.

Borgman, C. L., Smart, L. J., Millwood, K. A., Finley, J. R., Champeny, L., Gilliland, A. J., & Leazer, G. H. (2005). Comparing faculty information seeking in teaching and research: Implications for the design of digital libraries. *Journal of the American Society for Information Science and Technology*, *56*(6), 636–657. doi:10.1002/asi.20154

Boudreau, J. (2010, September 26). Doctors rely on iPhones to guide treatment: "We want the data right at our fingertips." *Times-Picayune (New Orleans)*, pp. B 12.

Braby, E., & Hunt, J. (1990). *The Santa Monica Public Library, 1890-1990*. Spokane, WA: Arthur C. Clark Co.

Brandt, D. (2001). *Literacy in American lives*. New York, NY: Cambridge University Press.

Branin, J. (2000). The changing nature of collection management in research libraries. *Library Resources & Technical Services*, *44*, 23–32.

Brisco, S. (2010, June 16). *Database*. [Msg 00420]. Message posted to LM-Net, archived at http://lmnet-archive. iis.syr.edu/ LM_NET/2010/Jun_2010 /msg00420.html

Briscoe, B., Odlyzko, A., & Tilly, B. (2009). *Metcalfe's law is wrong*. Retrieved February 7, 2011, from http:// spectrum.ieee.org/computing /networks/metcalfes- law-is-wrong

Brown, C. (2005). Where do molecular biology graduate students find information? *Science & Technology Libraries*, *25*(3), 89–104. doi:10.1300/J122v25n03_06

Brown, J. S., & Duguid, P. (2000). *The social life of information*. Cambridge, MA: Harvard Business School Press.

Brunton, C. (2005). The effects of library user-education programmes on the information-seeking behavior of Brisbane College of Theology students: An Australian case study. *Journal of Religious & Theological Information*, *7*(2), 55–73. doi:10.1300/J112v07n02_05

Burns, V., & Harper, K. (2007). Asking students about their research. In Foster, N. F., & Gibbons, S. (Eds.), *Studying students: The undergraduate research project at the University of Rochester* (pp. 7–15). Chicago, IL: Association of College and Research Libraries.

Calgary Public Library. (2010). *Geocaching challenge: CPL news*. Retrieved November 30, 2010, from http://blog.calgarypubliclibrary.com/ blogs/cplnews/ archive/2010/05/06/ Geocaching.aspx

Cameron, C. (2010) *Will mobile Web apps eventually replace native apps?* ReadWriteWeb.com. Retrieved 12/1/2010, from http://www.readwriteweb.com /archives/will_mobile_web_apps_ eventually_replace_native_apps.php

Campbell, J. (2006). Changing a cultural icon: The academic library as a virtual destination. *EDUCAUSE Quarterly*, *41*(1), 16–31. Retrieved October 17, 2010, from http://www.educause.edu/apps/eq/eqm01/eqm014.asp

Carlucci, T. L. (2010). Gone mobile? Mobile libraries survey 2010. *LibraryJournal.com*. Retrieved from http://www.libraryjournal.com/lj/ljinprintcurrentissue/886987-403/ gone_mobile_mobile_libraries_survey.html.csp

Carpenter, J., Wetheridge, L., Smith, N., Goodman, M., & Struijvé, O. (2010). Researchers of tomorrow: A three year (BL/JISC) study tracking the research behaviour of "Generation Y" doctoral students. Retrieved September 14, 2010, from http://explorationforchange.net/index. php/rot-home.html

Carr, N. (2010). *The shallows: What the Internet is doing to our brains*. New York, NY: Norton.

Cassell, K. A., & Hiremath, U. (2009). *Reference and information services in the 21st century: An introduction* (2nd ed.). New York, NY: Neal-Schuman.

Chu, S. K., & Law, N. (2008). The development of information search expertise of research students. *Journal of Librarianship and Information Science, 40*(3), 165–177. doi:10.1177/0961000608092552

Cohen, L. (2007, October 31). *Information literacy in the age of social scholarship* [Web log message]. Retrieved from http://liblogs.albany.edu/ / /_literacy_in_the_ag.html

Connaway, L. S. (2008). *Expectations of the Screenager Generation* [PDF document]. Retrieved from http://www.oclc.org/programs/events/2008-11-05c.pdf

Connaway, L. S., Dickey, T. J., & OCLC Research. (2010). *The digital information seeker: Report of the findings from selected OCLC, RIN, and JISC user behaviour projects.* Retrieved January 5, 2011, from http://www.jisc.ac.uk/media/documents/publications/ reports/2010/digitalinformationseekerreport.pdf

Cook, W. R. (2004). Assisi. In Kleinhenz, C. (Ed.), *Medieval Italy: An encyclopedia.* New York, NY: Routledge.

Crane, L., & Pieters, A. (2010). Youth Pulse 2010. *Harris Interactive: Trends & Tudes, 9*(2). Retrieved from http://www.harrisinteractive.com/vault/HI_TrendsTudes_2010_v09_i02.pdf

CrossRef. (2011). DOI Resolver. Retrieved May 18, 2011, from http://www.crossref.org.

Cullen, K., Kaminski, K., & Seel, P. (2003). Technology literate students? Results from a survey. *EDUCAUSE Quarterly, 26*(3), 34-40. Retrieved August 1, 2010, from http://www.educause.edu/ir/library/pdf/eqm0336.pdf

Cuthbert, J. (2008). *West Virginia history on view: The evolution of a big digital project with a tiny budget.* Retrieved from http://www.wvla.org/conference/ 2008/postcon/presentations/ cuthbert.pdf

Daly, J. (2004). George Lucas: Life on the screen. *EDUTOPIA, 1*, 34–40. Retrieved June 14, 2010, from http://www.glef.org/magazine/ ed1article.php?id=art_1160&issue=sept_04

Davis, P. M. (2002). The effect of the Web on undergraduate citation behavior: A 2000 update. *College & Research Libraries, 63*(1), 53.

Davis, P. M. (2003). Effect of the Web on undergraduate citation behavior: Guiding student scholarship in a networked age. *Libraries & the Academy, 3*(1), 43.

Davis, P. M., & Cohen, S. A. (2001). The effect of the Web on undergraduate citation behavior 1996-1999. *Journal of the American Society for Information Science and Technology, 52*(4), 309–314. doi:10.1002/1532-2890(2000)9999:9999<::AID-ASI1069>3.0.CO;2-P

Davis, M. (2008). *Project 10X, semantic wave report: Industry roadmap to Web 3.0 and multibillion dollar market opportunities.* Retrieved August 20, 2009, from http://www.project10x.com/

De Rosa, C., & OCLC. (2006). *College students' perceptions of libraries and information resources: A report to the OCLC membership.* Dublin, Ohio: Online Computer Library Center.

De Rosa, C., Dempsey, L., & Wilson, A. (2004). *The 2003 OCLC environmental scan: Pattern recognition - Social landscape* (A. Wilson, Ed.). Retrieved from http://www.oclc.org.htm

Dempsey, L. (2009). Always on: Libraries in a world of permanent connectivity. *First Monday, 14*(1). Retrieved September 5, 2010, from http://firstmonday.org/htbin/cgiwrap/ bin/ojs/index.php/fm/article/view/2291/2070

DeRosa, C., Cantrell, J., Hawk, J., & Wilson, A. (2005). *College students' perceptions of libraries and information sources: A report to the OCLC membership.* Dublin, OH: OCLC.

Deschin, C. S. (1969). *The teenager and VD: A social symptom of our times.* New York, NY: R. Rosen Press.

Dolan, P. L. (2009, December 21). Smartphones becoming clinical tools. *American Medical News.* Retrieved November 17, 2010, from http://www.ama-assn.org/amednews/2009/ 12/21/bica1221.htm

Dolan, P. L. (2010a, February 22). iPad stoking doctor interest in tablet computers. *American Medical News.* Retrieved November 17, 2010, from http://www.ama-assn.org/amednews/2010/ 02/22/bica0222.htm

Dolan, P. L. (2010b, August 23). Physician smartphone popularity shifts health IT focus to mobile use. *American Medical News.* Retrieved November 17, 2010, from http://www.ama-assn.org/amednews/ 2010/08/23/bil10823.htm

Dolan, P. L. (2010c, October 4). Doctors, patients use smartphones, but can't make mobile connection. *American Medical News*. Retrieved November 17, 2010, from http://www.ama-assn.org/amednews/2010/10/04/bil21004.htm

Dooley, J. M., & Luce, K. (2010). *Taking our pulse: The OCLC research survey of special collections and archives*. Dublin, OH: OCLC Research. Retrieved from http://www.oclc.org/research/publications/library/2010/2010-11.pdf

Doraswamy, M. (2009, June). The relationship of academic role and information use by engineering faculty. *Library Philosophy and Practice, 11*(1), 1–9.

Dublin Core Metadata Initiative. (1995-2010). *Mission and principles.* Retrieved from http://dublincore.org/about-us/

Dunham, J., & Neylon, C. (2010, September 8). *The future of search and discovery: Empowering researchers to accelerate science.* Presented at the Elsevier Webinar. Retrieved from http://mediazone.brighttalk.com/event/ReedElsevier/d7b76edf79-4207-intro

Duster, T. (2006). Comparative perspectives and competing explanations: Taking on the newly configured reductionist challenge to sociology. *American Sociological Review, 71*(1), 1–15. doi:10.1177/000312240607100101

Earp, V. J. (2008). Information source preference of education graduate students. *Behavioral & Social Sciences Librarian, 27*(2), 73–91. doi:10.1080/01639260802194974

East, J. (2010). "The Rolls Royce of the library reference collection": The subject encyclopedia in the age of Wikipedia. *RUSQ, 50*(2). Retrieved January 19, 2011, from http://www.rusq.org/2010/12/29/"the-rolls-royce-of-the-library-reference-collection"-the-subject-encyclopedia-in-the-age-of-wikipedia

Eaton, K. (2011). *Apple's solar power patent: Sun powered mac, iPods, iPhones in the future.* Retrieved January 11, 2011, from http://www.fastcompany.com/1716322/apples-solar-power-patent-sun-powered-mac-ipods-iphones-in-the-future

Edson, M. (2009). Session 1: Online communities and the institution. *WebWise 2009 Digital Debates Conference Proceedings*, (pp. 13-17). Retrieved from http://www.imls.gov/pdf/WW09_Proceedings.pdf

Eisenberg, M. B., & Head, A. J. (2009). *What today's college students say about conducting research in the digital age. Project Information Literacy progress report.* Retrieved July 15, 2010, from http://projectinfolit.org/pdfs/PIL_ProgressReport_2_2009.pdf

Eisenberg, M. B., & Head, A. J. (2009). *Finding context: What today's college students say about conducting research in the digital age. Project Information Literacy progress report.* Retrieved January 14, 2011, from http://projectinfolit.org/pdfs/PIL_ProgressReport_2_2009.pdf

Eisenberg, M. B., & Head, A. J. (2010). How today's college students use Wikipedia for course-related research. *First Monday, 15*(3). Retrieved January 16, 2011, from http://www.uic.edu/htbin/cgiwrap/bin/ojs/index.php/fm/article/view/2830/2476

Eisenberg, M. B., & Head, A. J. (2010). *Truth be told: How college students evaluate and use information in the digital age. Project Information Literacy progress report.* Retrieved January 14, 2011, from http://projectinfolit.org/pdfs/PIL_Fall2010_Survey_FullReport1.pdf

Ellis, D. (1989). A behavioural approach to information retrieval system design. *The Journal of Documentation, 45*(2), 171–212. doi:10.1108/eb026843

Ellis, D. (1993). Modeling the information-seeking patterns of academic researchers: A grounded theory approach. *The Library Quarterly, 63*(4), 469–486. doi:10.1086/602622

Ellis, D., Cox, D., & Hall, K. (1993). A comparison of the information seeking patterns of researchers in the physical and social sciences. *The Journal of Documentation, 49*(4), 356–369. doi:10.1108/eb026919

Entwistle, N., McCune, V., & Scheja, M. (2006). Student learning in context: Understanding the phenomenon and the person. In Verschaffel, L., Dochy, F., Boekaerts, M., & Vosniadon, S. (Eds.), *Instructional psychology: Past, present and future trends.*

Estabrook, L., Witt, E., & Rainie, L. (2007). *Information searches that solve problems.* Washington, DC: Pew Internet and American Life Project. Retrieved on February 13, 2011, from http://www.pewinternet.org/Reports/2007/Information-Searches-That-Solve-Problems.aspx

Fast, K. V., & Campbell, D. G. (2004). "I still like Google": University student perceptions of searching OPACS and the Web. *Proceedings of the 67th ASIS&T Annual Meeting, 41*, (pp. 138-146).

Feeman, M., & Wilson, J. (2010). *Apple seminar: IPad in health science education.* Unpublished manuscript.

Fischer, K. S., Barton, H., Wright, M., & Clatanoff, K. (2010). *Give 'em what they want: Patron-driven collection development.* Paper presented at the Charleston Conference, Charleston, South Carolina. Retrieved November 18, 2010, from http://ir.uiowa.edu/lib_pubs/61/

Fister, B., Gilbert, J., & Fry, A. R. (2008). Aggregated interdisciplinary databases and the needs of undergraduate researchers. *portal. Libraries and the Academy, 8*(3), 273–292. doi:10.1353/pla.0.0003

Flaxbart, D. (2001). Conversations with chemists: Information-seeking behavior of chemistry faculty in the electronic age. *Science & Technology Libraries, 21*(3/4), 5–26. doi:10.1300/J122v21n03_02

Flemming-May, R. (2010). Measuring e-resource use. *American Libraries, 41*(9), 22.

Fletcher, W.I., Hartford Connecticut. (1883). Letters. *Library Journal, 8*, 73–74.

Foley, M. (2002). Instant Messaging reference in an academic library: A case study. *College & Research Libraries, 63*(1), 36–45.

Frost, W. J. (2005). *The reference collection: From the shelf to the web.* Binghamton, NY: Haworth Information Press.

Funabiki, R. (2009). *Geocaching: Hide and seek at your library.* Retrieved February 8, 2011 from http://www.idaholibraries.org/idlibrarian/index.php/idaho-librarian/article/view/25/81

Gabridge, T., Gaskell, M., & Stout, A. (2008). Information seeking through students' eyes: The MIT photo diary study. *College & Research Libraries, 69*(6), 510–522.

Gamble, K. H. (2010). Wireless tech trends 2010. Trend: Smartphones. *Healthcare Informatics: The Business Magazine for Information and Communication Systems, 27*(2), 24, 26-7.

Gardner, E. (2011, January). Moving target: New mobile devices offer opportunities and headaches for healthcare CIOs. *Health Data Management*, 62.

George, C., Bright, A., Hurlbert, T., Linke, E. C., St. Clair, G., & Stein, J. (2006). Scholarly use of information: Graduate students' information seeking behavior. *Information Research, 11*(4). Retrieved September 14, 2010, from http://informationr.net/ir/11-4/paper272.html

Georgia Secretary of State, Georgia's Virtual Vault. (2007-2008). *Georgia's virtual vault.* Retrieved from http://cdm.sos.state.ga.us/index.php

Gibbons, S., & Reeb, B. (2004). Students, librarians, and subject guides: Improving a poor rate of return. *Portal: Libraries and the Academy, 4*(1), 123–130. Retrieved October 2, 2010, from http://muse.jhu.edu/journals/portal_libraries_and_the_academy/toc/pla4.1.html

Gielen, N. (2010). *Handheld e-book readers and scholarship: Report and reader survey (White Paper No. 3).* New York, NY: The American Council of Learned Societies. Retrieved from http://www.humanitiesebook.org/HEBWhitePaper3.pdf

Gorz, A. (2010). *The immaterial.* Ithaca, NY: Seagull Books.

Grafstein, A. (2002). A discipline-based approach to information literacy. *Journal of Academic Librarianship, 28*(4), 197–204. doi:10.1016/S0099-1333(02)00283-5

Grathwohl, C. (2010). *The tower and the open Web: The role of reference.* Retrieved January 7, 2011, from http://www.katina.info/conference/video_2010_openweb.php

Grathwohl, C. (2010, November). *The tower and the open Web.* Presented at the Charleston Conference, Charleston, SC.

Griffey, J. (2010). *Mobile technology and libraries.* New York, NY: Neal-Schuman Publisher.

Groen, F. K. (2007). *Access to medical knowledge: Libraries, digitization, and the public good.* Lanham, MD: Scarecrow Press.

Guthrie, K., & Housewright, R. (2008). Attitudes and behaviors in the field of economics: Anomaly or leading indicator. *Journal of Library Administration, 48*(2), 173–193. doi:10.1080/01930820802231369

Guthrie, K., Kirchoff, A., & Tapp, W. N. (2003). The JSTOR solution, six years later. In Hodges, P., & Lougee, W. P. (Eds.), *Digital libraries: A vision for the 21ˢᵗ century* (pp. 100–121). Ann Arbor, MI: Scholarly Publishing Office, The University of Michigan University Library.

Hamilton, B. J. (2010, March 25). Sponsors of literacy in contemporary culture: An e-interview with Dr. Deborah Brandt [Web log post]. Retrieved from http://theunquietlibrarian.wordpress.com// //of-literacy-in-contemporary-culture-an- e-interview-with-dr-deborah-brandt/

Hamilton, B. J. (2010, May 28). *Guest post: Susan Lester reflects on Media 21* [Web log post]. Retrieved from http://theunquietlibrarian.wordpress.com/ 2010/05/27/ guest-post-susan-lester- reflects-on-media-21/

Hargittai, E., Fullerton, L., Mancen-Trevino, E., & Yates Thomas, K. (2010). Trust online: Young adults' evaluation of Web content. *International Journal of Communication, 4*, 468-494. Retrieved November 20, 2010, from http://ijoc.org/ojs/index.php/ijoc/article/view/636/423

Harley, D., et al. (2006). *Use and users of digital resources: A focus on undergraduate education in the humanities and social sciences.* Berkeley, CA: Center for Studies in Higher Education, University of California Berkeley. Retrieved December 30, 2010, from http://cshe.berkeley.edu/research/digitalresourcestudy/report/

Harris, M. H. (1999). *History of libraries in the western world* (4th ed.). Lanham, MD & London, UK: Scarecrow.

HAWHAW. (2011). *Toolkit.* Retrieved November 30, 2010, from http://www.hawhaw.de/

Head, A., & Eisenberg, M. B. (2010). *How college students evaluate and use information in the digital age.* Seattle, WA: The Information School, University of Washington.

Head, A. J. (2007, August 6). Beyond Google. How do students conduct academic research? *First Monday, 12*(8).

Head, A. J., & Eisenburg, M. B. (2010, March 1). How today's students use Wikipedia for course-related research. *First Monday, 15*(3).

Head, A. J., & Eisenberg, M. B. (2010). *Truth be told: How college students evaluate and use information in the digital age. Project Information literacy progress report.* Seattle, WA: The Information School, University of Washington. Retrieved from http://projectinfolit.org/pdfs/ PIL_Fall2010_Survey_FullReport1.pdf

Head, A. J., & Eisenberg, M. B. (2010). *Project Information Literacy progress report: "Truth be told": How college students evaluate and use information in the digital age.* The Information School, University of Washington. November 1, 2010.

Head, A. J., & Eisenburg, M. B. (2009). *Lessons learned: How college students seek information in the digital age. Project Information Literacy progress report.* The Information School: University of Washington.

Head, A., & Eisenberg, M. (2010). *Truth be told: How college students evaluate and use information in the digital age. Project Information Literary progress report.* Retrieved November 1, 2010, from http://projectinfolit.org/pdfs/PIL_Fall2010_Survey_FullReport1.pdf

Heinstrom, J. (2000). The impact of personality and approaches to learning on information behaviour. *Information Research, 5*(3).

Heinström, J. (2006). Fast surfing for availability or deep diving into quality - Motivation and information seeking among middle and high school students. *Information Research, 11*(4), 265. Retrieved from http://InformationR.net/ir/11-4/paper265.html

Hellman, E. (2010, May 30). Book expo, digital book 2010, and e-book messes. Retrieved from http://go-to-hellman.blogspot.com/2010_05_01_archive.html

Hemminger, B., Lu, D., Vaughan, K. T. L., & Adams, S. J. (2007). Information seeking behavior of academic scientists. *Journal of the American Society for Information Science and Technology, 58*(15), 2205–2225. doi:10.1002/asi.20686

Hersh, W. R. (2003). *Information retrieval: A health and biomedical perspective* (2nd ed.). New York, NY: Springer.

Heyd, M. (2010). Three e-book aggregators for medical libraries: NetLibrary, Rittenhouse R2 Digital Library, and STAT!Ref. *Journal of Electronic Resources in Medical Libraries, 7*(1), 13–41..doi:10.1080/15424060903585693

Holmes, J., Robins, D., Zhang, Y., Salaba, A., & Byerly, G. (2006, May 22). *Report on the usability and effectiveness of SirsiDynix SchoolRooms for K-12 students.* Retrieved from http://www.schoolrooms.net_KentState.pdf

Hopkins, C. (2011). *Spain pioneers QR codes to track ancient artifacts*. Retrieved January 14, 2011, from http://www.readwriteweb.com/archives / spain_pioneers_qr_codes_to_track_ ancient_artifacts. php?utm_source=feedburner&utm_medium=feed&utm _campaign=Feed:+readwriteweb+ (ReadWriteWeb)

Horowitz, M. C. (2005). *New dictionary of the history of ideas*. New York, NY: Charles Scribner's Sons.

Hysell, S. (2010, November 16). Telephone interview.

INFOhio and SchoolRooms. (2009, June 29). Retrieved February 10, 2011, from http://www.infohio.org.html

INFOhio. (2009, August 14). *About INFOhio*. Retrieved February 2, 2011, from http://www.infohio.org//.html

INFOhio. (2010, August 30). *DIALOGUE model for information 21st century skills - inquiry and the knowledge building process*. Retrieved February 9, 2011, from http:// www.infohio.org.html

INFOhio. (2011). *Website*. Retrieved February 9, 2011, from http://www.infohio.org

INFOhio. (n.d.). *INFOhio & 21st century learning skills*. Retrieved February 9, 2011, from http://learningcommons.infohio.org

Instruction and Information Literacy Committee Task Force on Information Literacy Standards. (2008). *Information literacy standards for anthropology and sociology students*. Chicago, IL: Association of College and Research Libraries. Retrieved December 30, 2010, from http://www.ala.org/ala/mgrps/divs/acrl/ standards/ anthro_soc_standards.cfm

International Telecommunication Union Newsroom. (2010). *Press release*. Retrieved November 2, 2010, from http://www.itu.int/net/pressoffice /press_releases/2010/39.aspx

Ismail, L. (2010). What net generation students really want: Determining library help-seeking preferences of undergraduates. *RSR. Reference Services Review, 38*(1), 10–27. doi:10.1108/00907321011020699

Jacobs, M. L. (2009). Libraries and the mobile revolution: Remediation = relevance. *RSR. Reference Services Review, 37*(3), 286–290. doi:10.1108/00907320910982776

Jamali, H. R., & Nicholas, D. (2008). Information-seeking behavior of physicists and astronomers. *Aslib Proceedings: New Information Perspectives, 60*(5), 444–462.

Jenkins, H. (2006). *Confronting the challenges of participatory culture: Media education for the 21st century*. Retrieved from http://newmedialiteracies.org/// NML-WhitePaper.pdf

Jensen, M. (2007, June 15). The new metrics of scholarly authority. *The Chronicle Review, 53*(41), B6. Retrieved from http://chronicle.com////b00601.htm

JISC. (2009). JISC national e-books observatory project: Key findings and recommendations. *JISC*. Retrieved from http://www.jiscebooksproject.org/wp-content/ JISC-e-books-observatory-final-report-Nov-09.pdf

Johnson, E. D. (1970). *History of libraries in the western world* (2nd ed.). Metuchen, NJ: Scarecrow Press.

Johnson, A., Sproles, C., & Detmering, R. (2010). Library instruction and information literacy 2009. *RSR. Reference Services Review, 38*(4), 676–768.. doi:10.1108/00907321011090809

Johnson, C., McCord, S. K., & Walter, S. (2003). Instruction outreach across the curriculum: Enhancing the liaison role at a research university. In Kelsey, P., & Kelsey, S. (Eds.), *Outreach services in academic and special libraries* (pp. 19–38). Binghamton, NY: Haworth Press.

Jones, S. (2002). *The Internet goes to college: How students are living in the future with today's technology*. Washington, DC: Pew Internet and American Life Project.

JSTORNEWS. (2010). Enhancing discovery: JSTOR collaborates with Google Scholar. *JSTORNEWS, 14*. Retrieved from February 8, 2011, from http://news.jstor.org/jstornews/2010/03/ march_2010_vol_14_issue_enhanc.html

Kamin, C., Souza, K. H., Heestand, D., Moses, A., & O'Sullivan, P. (2006). Educational technology infrastructure and services in North American medical schools. *Academic Medicine: Journal of the Association of American Medical Colleges, 81*(7), 632–637. doi:.doi:10.1097/01. ACM.0000232413.43142.8b

Katz, B. (1998). *Cuneiform to computer: A history of reference sources*. Lanham, MD: Scarecrow Press.

Kayongo, J., & Helm, C. (2010). Graduate students and the library: A survey of research practices and library use at the University of Notre Dame. *Reference and User Services Quarterly, 49*(4), 341–349.

Keller, J. (2011). *As the Web goes mobile, colleges fail to keep up.* Retrieved February 8, 2011, from http://chronicle.com/article/ Colleges-Search-for-Their/126016/

Kelly, K. (2008). Better than free. *The Technicum.* Retrieved October 24, 2010, from http://www.kk.org/thetechnium/archives/2008/01/better_than_fre.php

Kenney, B. (2006, July 1). Keeping up with the Googles [Editorial]. *School Library Journal, 52*(7), 11. Retrieved from http://www.libraryjournal.com-427/_up_with_the_googles.html.csp

Kho, A., Henderson, L. E., Dressler, D. D., & Kripalani, S. (2006). Use of handheld computers in medical education. *Journal of General Internal Medicine, 21*(5), 531–537. doi:10.1111/j.1525-1497.2006.00444.x

Kilgour, F. G. (1998). *The evolution of the book.* New York, NY: Oxford University Press.

King, D. W., & Montgomery, C. H. (2002). After migration to an electronic journal collection: Impact on faculty and doctoral students. *D-Lib Magazine, 8*(12). doi:10.1045/december2002-king

King, D. W., Tenopir, C., Choemprayong, S., & Wu, L. (2009). Scholarly journal information-seeking and reading patterns of faculty at five U. S. universities. *Learned Publishing, 22*, 126–144. doi:10.1087/2009208

Kister, K. F. (Ed.). (1986). *Best Encyclopedias: A guide to general and specialized encyclopedias.* Phoenix, AZ: Oryx Press.

Klein, L. R. (1976). Phoenix gets it right. *Library Journal, 129*(12), 34–36.

Knight Commission on the Information Needs of Communities in a Democracy. (2009, October). *Informing communities: Sustaining democracy in the digital age.* Retrieved from https://secure.nmmstream.net/.newmediamill//.pdf

Kraft, M. A. (2010, November 17, 2010). E-books: The library catalog and federated searching, part 1. *The Krafty Librarian: Every librarian needs a bag of tricks.* Retrieved December 7, 2010, from http://kraftylibrarian.com/?p=834

Kraft, M. A. (2010b, November 18). E-books: The library catalog and federated searching, part 2. *The Krafty Librarian: Every librarian needs a bag of tricks.* Retrieved December 7, 2010, from http://kraftylibrarian.com/?p=839

Kraft, M. A. (2010c, June 16). iPad use in the hospital and IT departments. *The Krafty Librarian: Every librarian needs a bag of tricks.* Retrieved January 17, 2011, from http://kraftylibrarian.com/?p=633

Kriebel, L., & Lapham, L. (2008). Transition to electronic resources in undergraduate social science research: A study of honors theses bibliographies, 1999-2005. *College & Research Libraries, 69*(3), 268–284.

Krikelas, J. (1983). Information-seeking behavior- Patterns and concepts. *Drexel Library Quarterly, 19*(2), 5–20.

Kuhn, T. (1962). *The structure of scientific revolutions.* Chicago, IL: University of Chicago Press.

Kusche, K. (2009). Lessons learned: Mobile device encryption in the academic medical center. *Journal of Healthcare Information Management, 23*(2), 22–25.

Lanier, J. (2010). *You are not a gadget.* New York, NY: Knopf.

Lankes, R. D. (Producer). (2007). *Participatory librarianship* [Motion picture]. United States. Retrieved from http://www.youtube.com/ ?v=7TyuVJ4vENo

Lasilla, O., & Swick, R. (1999). *Resource description framework (RDF) model and syntax specification.* W3C. Retrieved November 12, 2010, from http://www.w3.org/TR/PR-rdf-syntax/

Lawrence, D. (2008, May 28). *Flickr commons: Begin at the beginning.* [Web log post]. Retrieved November 19, 2010, from http://www.brooklynmuseum.org/ community/blogosphere/bloggers/2008/05/28/flickr-commons-begin-at-the-beginning/

Leiding, R. (2005). Using citation checking of undergraduate honors thesis bibliographies to evaluate library collections. *College & Research Libraries, 66*(5), 417-429.

Lenhart, A., Simon, M., & Graziano, M. (2001). *The Internet and education: Findings of the Pew Internet & American Life Project*. Washington, DC: Pew Internet and American Life Project.

Liao, Y., Finn, M., & Lu, J. (2007). Information-seeking behavior of international graduate students vs. American graduate students: A user study at Virginia Tech 2005. *College & Research Libraries, 68*(1), 5–25.

Libraries Connect Ohio. (n.d.). Retrieved February 7, 2011, from http://www.librariesconnectohio.org/

Library of Congress and American Library Association. (1968). *The national union catalog, pre-1956 imprints: A cumulative author list representing Library of Congress printed cards and titles reported by other American libraries*. London, UK: Mansell.

Library of Congress, National Union Catalog of Manuscript Collections. (2009). *Frequently asked questions*. Retrieved from http://www.loc.gov/coll/nucmc/newfaqs.html

Library of Congress, National Union Catalog of Manuscript Collections. (2010). *NUCMC program annual report*. Retrieved from http://www.loc.gov/coll/nucmc/NUCMCFY10.pdf

Lim, S. (2009). How and why do college students use Wikipedia? *Journal of the American Society for Information Science and Technology, 60*(11), 2189–2202. doi:10.1002/asi.21142

Lippincott, S., & Kyrillidou, M. (2004). How ARL university communities access information: Highlights from LIBQUAL+. *ARL: A Bimonthly Report, 236,* 7-8. Retrieved October 10, 2010, from http://www.arl.org/newsltr/236/lqaccess.html

Lorbeer, E. R., & Mitchell, N. (2008). E-books in academic health sciences libraries. *Against the Grain, 20*(5), 30-34.

Lubans, D. (1998). *How first-year university students use and regard Internet resources*. Retrieved from http://www.lubans.org/docs/1styear/firstyear.html

MacNeely, I. F., & Wolverton, L. (2010). *Reinventing knowledge: From Alexandria to the Internet*. New York, NY: Norton.

Mann, T. (2005). *Oxford guide to library research*. Oxford, UK: Oxford University Press.

Mann, T. (2005). *Oxford guide to library research*. Oxford, UK: Oxford University Press.

Mansourian, Y., & Madden, A. D. (2007). Perceptions of the Web as a research tool amongst researchers in biological sciences. *New Library World, 108*(9/10), 407–423. doi:10.1108/03074800710823944

Martin, P. N., & Park, L. (2010). Reference desk consultation assignment: An exploratory study of students' perceptions of reference service. *Reference and User Services Quarterly, 49*(4), 333–340.

Massy, W. F., & Zemsky, R. (2004). *Thwarted innovation: What happened to e-learning and why*. West Chester, PA: The Learning Alliance at the University of Pennsylvania. Retrieved July 4, 2010, from http://www.thelearningalliance.info/ Docs/Jun2004/ThwartedInnovation.pdf

Maughan, P. D. (2001). Assessing information literacy among undergraduates: A discussion of the literature and the university of California-Berkeley assessment experience. *College & Research Libraries, 62*(1), 71–85.

Mayfield, T., & Thomas, J. (2005). A tale of two departments: A comparison of faculty information-seeking practices. *Behavioral & Social Sciences Librarian, 23*(2), 47–66. doi:10.1300/J103v23n02_03

McArthur, T. (1986). *Worlds of reference*. Cambridge, UK: Cambridge University Press.

McCarn, D. B. (1970). Planning for online bibliographic access by the Lister Hill National Center for Biomedical Communications. *Bulletin of the Medical Library Association, 58*(3), 303–310.

McEuen, S. F. (2001). How fluent with Information Technology are our students? *EDUCAUSE Quarterly, 24*(4), 8–17. Retrieved October 17, 2010, from http://www.educause.edu/apps/eq/eqm01/eqm014.asp

McKinney, K., Howery, C. B., Strand, K. J., Kain, E. L., & Berheide, C. W. (2004). *Liberal learning and the sociology major updated: Meeting the challenge of teaching sociology in the twenty-first century*. Washington, DC: American Sociological Association. Retrieved December 30, 2010, from http://www.asanet.org/images/teaching/docs/pdf/Lib_Learning_FINAL.pdf

Medical Library Association. (2010). *ABCs of e-books: Strategies for the medical library* (MLA webcast).

Meho, L. I., & Hass, S. W. (2001). Information-seeking behavior and use of social science faculty studying stateless nations: A case study. *Library & Information Science Research, 23,* 5–25. doi:10.1016/S0740-8188(00)00065-7

Miles, W. D., & National Library of Medicine. (1982). *A history of the National Library of Medicine: The nation's treasury of medical knowledge.* Bethesda, MD & Washington, DC: U.S. Dept. of Health and Human Services, Public Health Service, National Institutes of Health, National Library of Medicine.

Mill, D. H. (2008). Undergraduate information resource choices. *College & Research Libraries, 69*(4), 342–355.

Miller, S. (2008). *Encyclopedia Indexes in the digital age.* Unpublished Manuscript.

Mills, K. (2009). M-Libraries: Information use on the move (A report from the Arcadia Programme). *Arcadia@ Cambridge: Rethinking the role of the research library in a digital age.* University of Cambridge. Retrieved from http://arcadiaproject.lib.cam.ac.uk/docs/M-Libraries_report.pdf

Mirwis, A. N. (1999). *Subject encyclopedias: User guide, review citations and keyword index.* Phoenix, AZ: Oryx Press.

Moll, C. (2007). *Mobile Web design: A Web standards approach for delivering content to mobile devices.* Salt Lake City, UT: Cameron Moll.

Nagel, D. (2010). *Report: E-readers, LMS driving growth in higher ed mobile learning.* Retrieved February 2, 2011, from http://campustechnology.com/articles/2010/08/31/report-e-readers-lms-driving-growth-in-higher-ed-mobile-learning.aspx

Nagel, D. (2011). Will smart phones eliminate the digital divide? *THE Journal.* Retrieved February 1, 2011, from http://thejournal.com/Articles/2011/02/01/Will-Smart-Phones-Eliminate-the-Digital-Divide.aspx

Networked student. [Motion picture]. (2008). Retrieved from http://www.youtube.com/?v=XwM4ieFOotA

Newman, M. L. (2010). Collections strategies for electronic books. *Information Outlook, 14*(4), 10–12.

Newman, M. (2010). *HighWire press 2009 librarian e-book survey.* Palo Alto, CA: HighWire Press, Stanford University. Retrieved from http://highwire.stanford.edu/PR/HighWireEBookSurvey2010.pdf

Neylon, C. (2010 July). It's not information overload, nor is it filter failure: It's a discovery deficit. *Science in the Open Blog.* Retrieved November 22, 2010, from http://cameronneylon.net/blog/it%E2%80%99s-not-information-overload-nor-is-it-filter-failure-it%E2%80%99s-a-discovery-deficit/

Nicholas, D., Williams, P., & Rowland, I. (2010). Researchers' e-journals use and information seeking behavior. *Journal of Information Science, 36*(4), 494–516. doi:10.1177/0165551510371883

Nicholson, P. J. (2006). The changing role of intellectual authority. *Proceedings of the 148th Meeting of the ARL 247,* August.

Nicolas, D., Rowlands, I., & Wamae, D. (2010, November). *Are social media impacting on research?* Presented at the Charleston Conference, Charleston, SC.

Nielsen, J. (2010). *Alertbox: Mental models.* Retrieved on October 20, 2010, from http://www.useit.com/alertbox/mental-models.html

No child left behind act, 20 USC U.S.C. § 6301 (2002).

NOACSC, & Banks, J. (2010, August 13). *Introducing INFOhio Discovery Portal.* PowerPoint presented at INFOhio Technical Support, Lima, OH.

Nolan, C. W. (1999). *Managing the reference collection.* Chicago, IL: American Library Association.

OCLC. (2010). *OCLC adds more content accessible through WorldCat Local.* Dublin, OH: OCLC. Retrieved on December 11, 2010, from http://www.oclc.org/us/en/news/releases/2010/201059.htm

Ohio Historical Society, Ohio Memory Project. (2008). *About the Ohio memory project.* Retrieved from http://www.ohiomemory.org/custom/ohiomemory/om/index.php?About

Olmert, M. (1992). *The Smithsonian book of books* (1st ed.). Washington, DC: Smithsonian Books.

Online Computer Library Center. (c2006). *College students' perceptions of libraries and information resources: A report to the OCLC membership*. Dublin, OH: OCLC.

Online Computer Library Center (OCLC). (2002). How academic librarians can influence students' Web-based information choices. Retrieved June 15, 2010, from http://www5.oclc.org/downloads/ community/informationhabits.pdf

Ownes, D. (2010). Webcast report: Reference: The missing link in discovery. *LibraryJournal.com*. Retrieved November 22, 2010, from http://www.libraryjournal.com/article/CA6728783.html

Oxford University Press. (1989). *Oxford English dictionary*.

Oxford University Press. (2011). *Oxford bibliographies online*. Retrieved February 4, 2011, from http://www.oup.com/online/us/obo/?view=usa

Palmer, R. C. (1987). *Online reference and information retrieval* (2nd ed.). Littleton, CO: Libraries Unlimited.

Palmer, C. L., Teffeau, L. C., & Pirmann, C. M. (2009). *Scholarly information practices in the online environment: Themes from the literature and implications for library services development*. Report commissioned by OCLC Research. Retrieved September 14, 2010, from http://www.oclc.org/programs/publications/reports/2009-02.pdf

Paskin, N. (2010). Digital object identifier (DOI®) system. In Bates, M., & Maack, M. N. (Eds.), *Encyclopedia of library and information sciences* (3rd ed.). Boca Raton, FL: CRC Press.

Persell, C. H. (2010). How sociological leaders rank learning goals for introductory sociology. *Teaching Sociology*, *38*(4), 330–339. doi:10.1177/0092055X10378822

Pew Research Center. (2009). *Social isolation and new technology: How the Internet and mobile phones impact Americans' social networks*. Retrieved January 31, 2011, from http://pewresearch.org/pubs/1398/internet-mobile-phones-impact-american -social-networks

Pharow, P., & Blobel, B. (2008). Mobile health requires mobile security: Challenges, solutions, and standardization. *Studies in Health Technology and Informatics*, *136*, 697–702.

Pirolli, P. (2007). *Information foraging theory: Adaptive interaction with information*. Oxford, UK: Oxford University Press. doi:10.1093/acprof:oso/9780195173321.001.0001

Prabha, C., Silipigni Connaway, L., Olszewski, L., & Jenkins, L. R. (2007). What is enough? Satisficing information needs. *The Journal of Documentation*, *63*(1), 74–89. doi:10.1108/00220410710723894

Prgomet, M., Georgiou, A., & Westbrook, J. I. (2009). The impact of mobile handheld technology on hospital physicians' work practices and patient care: A systematic review. *Journal of the American Medical Informatics Association*, *16*(6), 792..doi:10.1197/jamia.M3215

PRNewswire. (2009, August 25). American Medical Association launches e-book strategy with iPublishCentral from impelsys; AMA inaugurates e-book offerings with bestselling clinical title. *PR Newswire*.

Pyatt, E., & Snavely, L. (2004). *No longer missing: Tools for connecting the library with the course management system*. Retrieved October 21, 2010, from http://www.syllabus.com/print.asp?ID=9094

Quigley, J., Peck, D. R., Rutter, S., & Williams, E. M. (2002). Making choices: Factors in the selection of information resources among science faculty at the University of Michigan. *Issues in Science and Technology Librarianship*, *34*, Spring. Retrieved September 14, 2010, from http://www.istl.org/02-spring/refereed.html

Radford, M. L., & Lankes, R. D. (Eds.). (2010). *Reference renaissance: Current and future trends*. New York, NY: Neal-Schuman Publishers, Inc.

Rafiq, M., & Ameen, K. (2009). Information-seeking behavior and user satisfaction of university instructors: A case study. *Library Philosophy and Practice*, *11*(1), 1–9.

Rand, A. D. (2010). Mediating at the student-Wikipedia intersection. *Journal of Library Administration*, *50*(7/8), 923–932. doi:10.1080/01930826.2010.488994

Ranganathan, S. R. (1961). *Reference service*. Bombay, India: Asia Publishing House.

Raymond, M. (2008, January 16). *My friend Flickr: A match made in photo heaven*. [Web log post]. Retrieved November 19, 2010, from http://blogs.loc.gov/loc/2008/01/ my-friend-flickr-a-match-made-in-photo-heaven/

Raynor, M., & Iggulden, H. (2008). Online anatomy and physiology: Piloting the use of an anatomy and physiology e-book–VLE hybrid in pre-registration and post-qualifying nursing programmes at the University of Salford. *Health Information and Libraries Journal*, *25*(2), 98–105..doi:10.1111/j.1471-1842.2007.00748.x

Reference, C. (2010). *Credo Reference topic pages*. Retrieved February 2, 2011, from http://corp.credoreference.com/images/ PDFs/credo_topic_pages_2010.pdf

Reitz, J. M. (2004). *Dictionary for library and information science*. Westport, CT: Libraries Unlimited.

Research Information Network. (2006). *Researchers and discovery services: Behavior, perceptions and needs*. Research Information Network. Retrieved from http://www.rin.ac.uk/system/files/attachments/ Researchers-discovery-services-report.pdf

Research Information Network and the British Library. (2009). *Patterns of information use and exchange: Case studies of researchers in the life sciences*. Retrieved from http://www.rin.ac.uk/system/files/attachments/ Patterns_information_use-REPORT_Nov09.pdf

Rettig, J. (1992). *Distinguished classics of reference publishing*. Phoenix, AZ: Oryx Press.

Rheingold, H. (2009, September 1). *Mindful infotention: Dashboards, radars, filters* [Web log post]. Retrieved from http://www.sfgate.com/bin //?entry_id=46677

Rieh, S. Y., & Hillgoss, B. (2008). College students' credibility judgments in the information seeking process. In M. J. Metzer & A. J. Flanigin (Eds), *Digital media, youth and credibility* (pp. 49-72). The John D. and Catherine T. MacArthur series on digital media and learning. Cambridge, MA: MIT Press.

Rogers, S. A. (2003). Developing an institutional knowledge bank at Ohio State University: From concept to action plan. *Portal: Libraries and the Academy*, *3*(1), 125–136. doi:10.1353/pla.2003.0018

Roncevic, M. (2007, February 15). Rosen's e-venture. *Library Journal*. Retrieved from http://www.libraryjournal.com/lj/ ljinprintcurrentissue/850312-403/ rosens_e-venture.html.csp

Rosen Publishing. (2011). *Sexuality and sexual health*. In Teen Health & Wellness: Real Life, Real Answers.

Rothstein, S. (1989). The development of the concept of reference service in American libraries, 1850-1900. *The Library Quarterly*, *23*(1), 1–15. doi:10.1086/617934

Rubin, Z. (2011, March 13). How the internet tried to kill me. *New York Times*, p. 11.

Ryan, J. (Ed.). (1989). *First stop: The master index to subject encyclopedias*. Phoenix, AZ: Oryx Press.

Salemi, M. K. (2009). Economics and liberal education: Why, where, and how. In Colander, D., & McGoldrick, M. (Eds.), *Education economists: The Teagle discussion on re-evaluating the undergraduate economics major* (pp. 99–106). Northhampton, MA: Edward Elgar.

Santangelo, M., & Schofer, S. (2009). *Teen health & wellness story: Brooklyn Public Library, NY*. Retrieved from http://teenhealthfiles.rosenpub.com/ Educator_Resources_files/LessonPlans/THW_Brooklyn_FINAL.pdf

Schell, L. (2011). The academic library e-book. In Polanka, S. (Ed.), *No shelf required: E-books in libraries* (pp. 75–93). Chicago, IL: The American Library Association.

Schlosser, R. W., Wendt, O., Bhavnani, S., & Nail-Chiwetalu, B. (2006). Use of information-seeking strategies for developing systematic reviews and engaging in evidence-based practice: The application of traditional and comprehensive Pearl Growing- A review. *International Journal of Language & Communication Disorders*, *41*(5), 567–582..doi:10.1080/13682820600742190

Schonfeld, R. C. (2003). *JSTOR: A history*. Princeton, NJ: Princeton University Press.

Schonfeld, R. C. (2005). JSTOR: A case study in the recent history of scholarly communications. *Program*, *39*(4), 337–334.

Schonfeld, R. C., & Housewright, R. (2010). *Faculty survey 2009: Key strategic insights for libraries, publishers, and societies*. Retrieved November 5, 2010 from http://www.ithaka.org/ithaka-s-r/ research/faculty-surveys-2000-2009

Seeholzer, J., & Salem, J. A. (2011). Library on the go: A focus group study of the mobile Web and the academic library. *College & Research Libraries*, *72*(1), 9–20. Retrieved from http://vnweb.hwwilsonweb.com/hww / jumpstart.jhtml?recid=0bc05f7a67b 1790e0b52b53f9c-3da90e40fc1718e 75a19bb5c9f8fd67b98c1903c9b320 b1b256c29&fmt=HPDF.

Shen, Y. (2007). Information seeking in academic research: A study of the sociology faculty at the University of Wisconsin-Madison. *Information Technology and Libraries, 26*(1), 4–13.

Shirky, C. (2008, September). *It's not information overload. It's filter failure.* Presented at the Web 2.0 Expo, New York City, NY. Retrieved from http://www.youtube.com/watch?v=LabqeJEOQyI

Shreeves, E. (2000). The acquisitions culture wars. *Library Trends, 48*(4), 877–890.

Siemens, G. (2004, December 12). *Connectivism: A learning theory for the digital age.* Retrieved January 3, 2009, from http://www.elearnspace.org //.htm

Silipigni, L., & Dickey, T. J. (2010). *The digital information seeker: Report of findings from selected OCLC, RIN and JISC user behaviour projects.* JISC.

SirsiDynix. (n.d.). Retrieved February 9, 2011, from http://www.sirsidynix.com

Smith, A. (2011). *Mobile access 2010.* Retrieved January 25, 2011, from http://www.pewinternet.org/Reports/2010/Mobile-Access-2010/Summary-of-Findings.aspx

Stead, W. T. (Ed.). (1901). *Review of Reviews: index to the periodicals of 1901.* London, NY: Review of Reviews.

Tenopir, C., King, D. W., Edwards, D., & Wu, L. (2009). Electronic journals and changes in scholarly article seeking and reading patterns. *Aslib Proceedings: New Information Perspectives, 61*(1), 5–32.

The Information Institute of Syracuse. (n.d.). *The participatory librarianship starter kit: Introduction.* Retrieved January 2, 2009, from http://ptbed.org/.php

The New Media Consortium and EDUCAUSE Learning Initiative. (2010). *2010 Horizon report.* Retrieved November 2, 2010, from http://wp.nmc.org/horizon2010/

Thelwall, M. (2005). Directing students to new information types: A new role for Google in literature searchers? *Internet Reference Services Quarterly, 10*(3/4), 159–166.

Thomas, L. C. (2010). *Gone mobile? (mobile libraries survey 2010).* Retrieved November 23, 2010, from http://www.libraryjournal.com/lj/ ljinprintcurrentissue/886987-403/gone_ mobile_mobile_libraries_survey.html.csp

Thomas, M., & Sun-Times, T. C. (2010, October 19). iPad functionality just what doctor ordered: Ultra-portable tablet becoming hospital fixture. *Chicago Sun Times,* pp. 14.

Thompson, C. (2003). Information illiterate or lazy: How college students use the Web for research. *Libraries & the Academy, 3*(2), 259. doi:10.1353/pla.2003.0047

Toninelli, A., Montanari, R., & Corradi, A. (2009). Enabling secure service discovery in mobile healthcare enterprise networks. *IEEE Wireless Communications, 16*(3), 24–32..doi:10.1109/MWC.2009.5109461

Transliteracy Research Group. (2011). *Transliteracy.* Retrieved February 2, 2011, from http://nlabnetworks.typepad.com /transliteracy/

Trautfetter, G. (2006, August 30). Arctic harvest: Global warming a boon for Greenland's farmers. *Der Spigel Online International.* Retrieved from http://www.spiegel.de/international/ spiegel/0,1518,434356,00.html

Turner, J. (1996). *The dictionary of art.* New York, NY: Grove.

U.S. National Library of Medicine and the National Center for Biotechnology Information. (2010). *NCBI bookshelf.* Retrieved November 18, 2010, from http://www.ncbi.nlm.nih.gov.ezproxy. libraries.wright.edu:2048/books

Ugaz, A. G., & Resnick, T. (2008). Assessing print and electronic use of reference/core medical textbooks. *Journal of the Medical Library Association, 96*(2), 145–147.. doi:10.3163/1536-5050.96.2.145

Unbound Medicine Inc. (2011). *Unbound Medicine: About us.* Retrieved January 24, 2011, from http://www.unboundmedicine.com/company

University of Washington Libraries. (2002). *Newsletter.* Seattle, WA: University of Washington Libraries.

University of Washington's Information School. (2011, January 26). *Project information literacy: A large-scale study about early adults and their research habits.* Retrieved from http://projectinfolit.org//

Van Scoyoc, A. M., & Cason, C. (2006). The electronic academic library: Undergraduate research behavior in a library without books. *Libraries and the Academy, 6*(1), 47–58. doi:10.1353/pla.2006.0012

Vasich, T. (2010). *Medicine's new wave.* Retrieved January 25, 2011, from http://www.zotzine.uci.edu/2010_11/imed.php

Vaughan, J. (2011). Web scale discovery: What and why? *Library Technology Reports, 47*(1), 5–11.

Wastawy, S. F., Uth, C. W., & Stewart, C. (2004). Learning communities: An investigative study into their impact on library services. *Science & Technology Libraries, 24*(3/4), 327–374. doi:10.1300/J122v24n03_07

Webster, K. (2010). Evaluating printed reference sources: Apostscript. *Refer, 26*(1)

Weiler, A. (2005). Information-seeking behavior in generation Y students: Motivation, critical thinking, and learning theory. *Journal of Academic Librarianship, 31*(1), 46–53. doi:10.1016/j.acalib.2004.09.009

Weiner, S. A. (2010). Information literacy: A neglected core competency. *EDUCAUSE Quarterly, 33*(1), 8.

Westbrook, L. (2003). Information needs and experiences of scholars in women's studies: Problems and solutions. *College & Research Libraries, 64*(3), 192–209.

When your carpet calls your doctor. (2010, April 10). *The Economist, 395*(8677), 65-66.

White, M. (2008). E-books in health sciences circa 2008-What have we got for our journey now? *Against the Grain, 20*(5), 26-30.

Whitmire, E. (2001). A longitudinal study of undergraduates' academic library experiences. *Journal of Academic Librarianship, 27*(5), 379–385. doi:10.1016/S0099-1333(01)00223-3

Whitmire, E. (2002). Disciplinary differences and undergraduates' information seeking behavior. *Journal of the American Society for Information Science and Technology, 53*(8), 631–638. doi:10.1002/asi.10123

Wiegand, W. A., & Davis, D. G. (1994). *Encyclopedia of library history.* New York, NY: Garland Pub.

Wikipedia, The Free Encyclopedia. (2011). *Ontology.* Retrieved February 28, 2011, from http://en.wikipedia.org/w/index.php? title=Ontology&oldid=416410140

Wikipedia, The Free Encyclopedia. (2011). *Resource description framework.* Retrieved February 19, 2011, from http://en.wikipedia.org/w/index.php?title=Resource_Description_ Framework&oldid=420026139

Wikipedia, The Free Encyclopedia. (2011). *Semantic network.* Retrieved August 20, 2010, from http://en.wikipedia.org/w/index.php?title=Semantic_network&oldid=420472897

Wikipedia, The Free Encyclopedia. (2011). *Semantics.* Retrieved August 20, 2010, from http://en.wikipedia.org/w/index.php?title=Semantics&oldid=420586324

Wikipedia, The Free Encyclopedia. (2011). *Tag (metadata).* Retrieved February 19, 2011, from http://en.wikipedia.org/w/index.php?title=Tag_(metadata)&oldid=419544900

Wikipedia, The Free Encyclopedia. (2011). *Taxonomy.* Retrieved February 19, 2011, from http://en.wikipedia.org/w/index.php?title=Taxonomy&oldid=420078840

Wikipedia. (2010, November 16). *About - Wikipedia, the free encyclopedia.* Retrieved November 23, 2010, from http://en.wikipedia.org/wiki/Wikipedia:About

Wikipedia. (n.d.). *Wikipedia: Five pillars.*

Wojick, D. (2010). Untangling the web of technical knowledge: A model of information content and structure. *Information Bridge.* Retrieved December 12, 2010, from http://www.osti.gov/bridge/product.biblio.jsp?query_id=0&page=0 &osti_id=991543&Row=0

WolfWalk. (n.d.). *NCSU library service.* Retrieved February 1, 2011, from http://www.lib.ncsu.edu/wolfwalk/

Wolters Kluwer Health. (2010). *UpToDate Inc.* Retrieved November 20, 2010, from http://www.uptodate.com/

Wong, W. (2009). *User behavior in discovery: Final report.* JISC.

Wright, A. (2008). *Glut: Mastering information through the ages.* Ithaca, NY: Cornell University Press.

Wynar, B. S. (Ed.). (1986). *ARBA: Guide to subject encyclopedias and dictionaries.* Littleton, CO: Libraries Unlimited.

Yakel, E. (2004). Encoded archival description: Are finding aids boundary spanners or barriers for users? *Journal of Archival Organization, 2*(1/2), 63–77..doi:10.1300/J201v02n01_06

Young, J. (2006, June 12). Wikipedia founder discourages academic use of his creation. *The Chronicle of Higher Education*. Retrieved from http://chronicle.com/blogs/wiredcampus/wikipedia-founder-discourages-academic-use-of-his-creation/2305

Zhang, Y. (2008). Undergraduate students' mental models of the Web as an information retrieval system. *Journal of the American Society for Information Science and Technology, 59*(13), 2087–2098. doi:10.1002/asi.20915

About the Contributors

Sue Polanka is Head of Reference and Instruction at the Wright State University Libraries in Dayton, OH. In her 20 years of library service, she has experienced the changing reference environment in public, state, and academic libraries. She has also served on Booklist's Reference Books Bulletin Editorial Board for over ten years and was Chair from 2007 to 2010. She moderates the award–winning eBook blog, No Shelf Required® and edited the 2011 ALA Editions book of the same name, No Shelf Required: E-Books in Libraries. She was named a Library Journal Mover and Shaker in 2011. Follow her on Twitter @spolanka.

* * *

Ingrid Becker is Content Analyst with Credo Reference. Ingrid Becker graduated with a Bachelor of Arts in English from Boston University in 2009 and a Master of Studies in 20th century English Literature from Oxford University in 2010. She presently works at Credo Reference, where she pursues her passion for books and the distribution of knowledge by helping to select the best possible reference works for inclusion in Credo's products. Ingrid lives in the Boston area.

Tom Beyer is Vice President of Publishing for iFactory and is responsible for leading iFactory's efforts in the publishing space. This has included online projects for OUP, SAGE Publications, Cengage Learning, RR Donnelly, the IMF, the World Bank, Rosen Publishing, and Bloomsbury Publishing, among others. Currently, Tom is leading the efforts for PubFactory, iFactory's new mixed content online publishing platform. Tom has a BA from Harvard and an MA in Computer Science from Brown where he concentrated on 3D graphics. He has worked in the industry on everything from decision support software, to Disney and Hasbro titles and a real-time strategy game, "Extreme Tactics."

Anh Bui is Executive Publication Manager, Books Products, HighWire Press, Stanford University, CA. In this role, she works to define, evolve, and implement HighWire's platform for hosting book content and other scholarly content published outside of journals. She brings to this work a background in literary scholarship, content analysis, and digital humanities, including experience managing digital editions for the Mark Twain Project at University of California, Berkeley (UCB). Bui holds a Ph.D. in English from UCB.

Eric M. Calaluca has been active in the development of scholarly Information Systems since 1987. After receiving the M.A. in Philosophy from the University of Dallas, he joined the publishing firm Chadwyck-Healey. He worked in sales and product development, becoming Executive Vice President in 1991. During his tenure there he had a major role in moving the company from microform-based publications to the production of full-text scholarly databases. He left in 1993 to found Paratext, where he and his colleagues have developed scholarly database applications in reference, classical studies, history, music, and government documents.

Ximena Chrisagis is Nursing Librarian at the Wright State University Libraries (WSUL) in Dayton, OH. She has been a reference, instruction, and collection development librarian in the health sciences disciplines at WSU since 1998 and was based at WSU's Fordham Health Sciences Library until June 2009. In addition to her librarian duties, she devotes time to WSUL's Special Collections and Archives Department. She holds an M.L.I.S. from the University of Illinois at Urbana-Champaign and a M.A. in public history from WSU.

Lettie Conrad is the Online Product Manager for SAGE Publications in Los Angeles, CA. She began her career at SAGE Publications in 2006 after four years managing the publications program for a think tank in Washington, DC. As the Online Product Manager, Lettie leads strategic, user-centered development for SAGE's award-winning Web-based content products and platforms, hosting inter-disciplinary reference materials and an international suite of more than 550 academic and professional journals. She is instrumental in launching new Web products, developing new online features and Web-publishing systems, and maintaining outstanding content quality on SAGE platforms. Lettie has a Master's degree in Mass Communication from California State University, Northridge.

Rebecca Cullen is currently Digital Product Manager at Oxford University Press in Oxford, UK. Prior to taking on this role, she was based in the New York office for two years, where she worked mainly on the development of Oxford Bibliographies Online. Now in the Oxford office, she is responsible for reviewing, creating, and implementing best practice processes with regard to online product development.

Terese DeSimio is a Science/Web Services Librarian in the Reference and Instruction Department at the Wright State University (WSU) Libraries. She holds an M.L.I.S. from Kent State University and a B.S. in Biomedical Engineering from WSU. Her prior publications include a co-authored chapter in ALA's Reference Sources for Small and Medium-sized Libraries, 7th ed. and an article for Booklist titled "Reference on the Web: Common Health Concerns."

John G. Dove is President of Credo Reference. In 1968, John Dove joined Interactive Data Corporation and helped produce the first end-user accessible online database of stock market information. In the early 90s he was on the executive team of a Boston area consulting firm, Symmetrix, which was instrumental in building learning organizations and electronic performance support systems to back them up. Subsequently, he was president and COO of SilverPlatter, a supplier of electronic and online bibliographic information to research libraries worldwide. Prior to joining Credo Reference in 2003, John worked with the Executive Education on E-Government project at Harvard's Kennedy School of Government.

Robert Faber is the Editorial Director, Reference, and Director of the Discoverability Program at Oxford University Press, Oxford, UK. Robert's role as an online publisher at OUP includes Oxford

Reference (published out of the UK) and the Oxford Dictionary of National Biography, for which he helped get 10,000 people to write 50,000 biographies on time, and organized simultaneous publication in print and online in 2004. He was also director of the Oxford English Dictionary through to the launch of its new online edition in December 2010, and now heads a major program to improve ways of finding and navigating content across OUP's global academic business.

Theresa M. Fredericka is Executive Director of INFOhio, the Information Network for Ohio Schools. She has also served as a library media services consultant for the Kentucky and Ohio Departments of Education, a Coordinator of Learning Resources and Technology for Lakewood City Schools, and as a school librarian for both Deer Park Community Elementary Schools and Findlay High School in Ohio. She currently serves on the Board of Trustees for OHIONET and is a past president of the Ohio Educational Library Media Association. Theresa has an undergraduate degree in library science from Bowling Green State University and an M.S.L.S. from University of Kentucky. She is active in state and national library organizations.

James Galbraith is Associate Director for Collections and Scholarly Resources at DePaul University, Chicago. He was previously OCLC's Member Services Consultant for the Midwest as well as Head of Collections at University of California, Irvine, and Head of Collection Development at Wake Forest University, NC. His primary interests are e-books, digitization of information, and academic collection development.

Laurie Gemmill is Mass Digitization Program Manager at LYRASIS. She is responsible for establishing the Mass Digitization Collaborative and working with members and business partners to broaden the array of digital services available to members. Previously, she was Senior Implementation Program Manager and Digital Projects Specialist for OCLC. While with the Ohio Historical Society, she served as the State Archivist and managed several award–winning digital projects for the Library of Congress' American Memory program, including the African-American Experience in Ohio. She holds an M.L.I.S. from UCLA.

Miriam Gilbert is a long-time leader in the publishing community. She is currently Director, Rosen Publishing Online. During a 30-year career in the publishing business, she has held a range of positions. Miriam was Associate Publisher, Westview Press, a Boulder-based academic publisher. She was Assistant Vice President, Global Licensing and Consortia Sales, at Marcel Dekker, Inc, a leading mid-sized STM (scientific, technical, and medical) publisher headquartered in New York and London. As NetLibrary's Senior Director of Publisher Relations, Miriam was responsible for forging relationships with the book publishing community and acquiring the content that serves as the foundation for NetLibrary's eBook collection. Miriam serves on the faculty of the Denver Publishing Institute and is a former Trustee of the Foundation for Boulder Valley Schools.

Darrell Gunter is a leading advocate of semantic technology and social media in the science, technical, and medical industry and is a frequent speaker/ moderator at many industry events. He is the Chief Commercial Officer for the American Institute of Physics and previously has served as a sales and marketing executive for Collexis, Elsevier, and Dow Jones. He is an Adjunct Professor at Seton

Hall University and serves on the Content Board of the Software Information Industry Association, Olin College of Engineering Library Advisory Board, Seton Hall University Advisory Council and the Women's Venture Fund. His radio program "Leadership" airs Saturday mornings at 9:00 am on WSOU HD 89.5 FM / WSOU.net.

Buffy J. Hamilton is the founding librarian of "The Unquiet Library" at Creekview High School in Canton, GA. She earned an Ed.S. in Instructional Technology and School Library Media at the University of Georgia and serves as Communications Coordinator for the Georgia Library Media Association, Social Media Chair for the AASL National Conference 2011 Committee, and is a member of the Interdivisional Committee on Information Literacy AASL/ACRL. In addition, Hamilton is one of Tech and Learning's 30 EdTech Leaders of the Future, Georgia (GLMA and GAIT) School Library Media Specialist of the Year 2010, one of the National School Boards Association's "20 to Watch" educators for 2010, and a Library Journal Mover and Shaker for 2011. Her media program at Creekview High School was also named one of two exemplary high school programs for the state of Georgia in 2010 and was an ALA Office for Information Technology Policy 2011 Cutting Edge Service Award winner.

Jackie Zanghi-LaPlaca has an academic background in education policy, history, and economics and has completed research projects at the University of Pennsylvania, a Rotary International Fellowship, as well as a NEH Fellowship. Jackie spent 10 years coordinating education non-profits, faculty professional development programs, and government projects with educational technology. Before her current position as a director for Credo Reference, Jackie was the Director of Library & Educational Relations for a STM publisher, IGI Global. A central focus of Jackie's current position is assisting libraries with their e-resources planning and developing the new Credo Reference Publisher and Subject Collection offering.

Ross W. McLachlan served as the Deputy Director for Technical Services at the Phoenix Public Library from 1990–2010. In this role he was responsible for coordinating all activities of the collection development, bibliographic services (acquisition/cataloging), processing, courier services, and library information systems center work units. He reviewed for Library Journal, Books Collectors Market, and Books of the Southwest and presented over 35 programs at ALA, PLA, Arizona Library Association, and regional/state library technology conferences. Ross has a B.A. and M.A. in History from the University of Arizona and an MLS from UCLA. He held positions at Yale University, the University of Arizona, and the Tucson Public Library throughout his extensive professional career.

Chad Mairn is Information Services Librarian at St. Petersburg College and an adjunct instructor who teaches, in both online and face-to-face formats, a variety of computer and information literacy courses. While an undergraduate studying Humanities at the University of South Florida (USF), Mairn was awarded a Library of Congress Fellowship archiving Leonard Bernstein's personal papers. During his Library and Information Science (LIS) graduate work, also at USF, he became a technology liaison between the Bill Gates Learning Foundation and Florida public libraries. Follow him on Twitter @cmairn.

Miriam Matteson is an Assistant Professor at Kent State University School of Library and Information Science. Her past professional experience includes library positions at Indiana University, Universidad Simón Bolívar in Caracas, Venezuela, and the University of Maryland University College. Her primary research area is library management, and she studies emotions in the workplace and small group communication. Other research interests include issues in academic librarianship. She teaches in the areas of library management, information sources and reference services, and academic librarianship. Miriam Matteson can be contacted at mmattes1@kent.edu.

Frank Menchaca is Executive Vice President and Publisher, Research Solutions, at Cengage Learning. He began his long publishing career with John Wiley & Sons and has since held positions in literary trade publishing at George Braziller, in educational magazine publishing at Weekly Reader Corporation, and in library publishing at Chelsea House and Millbrook Press. He holds degrees from New York University and Yale University and has authored two books of poetry, many reviews, and articles on topics ranging from literature and music to the information industry.

Jack O'Gorman is a reference and instruction librarian and Associate Professor at the University of Dayton's Roesch Library. There he is responsible for reference, library instruction, collection development, and liaison work in engineering, physics, math, and geology. With almost 30 years experience in university, government, and business libraries, Jack has an in-depth knowledge of reference sources. He has a Bachelor's degree in Mathematics from Walsh University and an MLS from St. John's University. He chaired the editorial board of Reference Books Bulletin from 2001-2004, and continued as a member of that board until 2010. He has served on the RUSA Outstanding Reference Sources Committee, and is the Chair of the Dartmouth Award Committee. He is co-editor of the third edition of Recommended Reference Books in Paperback (Libraries Unlimited, 2000) and editor of the 7th edition of Reference Sources for Small and Medium Sized Libraries, (ALA 2008), and a contributor to the Guide to Reference.

Jason B. Phillips is Coordinator of the Data Service Studio and Librarian for Sociology, Psychology, Gender & Sexuality Studies, and American Studies at New York University. He holds degrees from Long Island University (M.S.L.I.S.) and Harvard University (M.A.). He has published previously on issues related to both information literacy and thanatology. He is also active in the Anthropology and Sociology Section of the Association of College and Research Libraries having served on various committees.

Wright Rix is the Principal Librarian for Reference Services at the Santa Monica Public Library. Wright has held a variety of managerial position since arriving at Santa Monica Public Library in 1991. He currently serves on the advisory board for OCLC QuestionPoint and has chaired or served on committees for organizations such as the Metropolitan Cooperative Library System (now SCLC) and the California Library Association. Wright began his librarian career with the County of Los Angeles Public Library system. He earned a Master's degree in Library and Information Science from UCLA's Graduate School of Education and Information Science, and a Bachelor's degree from the University of Texas at Austin's College of Communications.

Roger Rosen is the President of Rosen Publishing, an independent publisher that has been providing supplemental educational books and materials to libraries and K-12 schools since 1950. Roger Rosen was named President, Rosen Publishing, in 1980 and has grown the publishing program to over 1,000 titles per year, across all curriculum areas. Imprints include PowerKids Press, Rosen Central, Rosen Young Adult, Windmill Books, and Editorial Buenas Letras. Rosen Publishing was the first educational publisher to bring content-driven graphic nonfiction to the school and library market. Rosen continues to be a market leader as this genre continues its fast-paced journey from marginal to mainstream, even, mainstay in today's educational publishing landscape. Under Roger Rosen's leadership, in 2007 the company launched a new digital division, Rosen Online. Its first database, Teen Health and Wellness: Real Life, Real Answers, has been named a Library Journal's Best Reference Sources, as well as been called a "Must Have" Product and Top 10 Digital Resource by School Library Journal. The company recently launched the PowerKids Life Science database, covering elementary and middle school life science. Initial enthusiasm and accolades have been tremendous, and PowerKids Earth & Space Science and PowerKids Physical Science will complete this science suite in 2012. Roger Rosen also spearheaded the launch of epointbooks, an e-book hosting platform offering over 3,000 nonfiction e-books for pre-K-12. In addition, Rosen Publishing has developed a program of innovative, multimedia interactive e-books.

Jennifer C. Schwelik is the PreK-12 Technology and Professional Development Manager for WVIZ/PBS & WCPN/NPR ideastream. She has also served as the project manager for TRAILS; as a consultant for INFOhio; as a school librarian for both Beachwood City Schools and Bay Village Schools; and as an English and Social Studies teacher for both Lorain County JVS and Polaris JVS. She currently serves on the LSTA Board for the State Library of Ohio. Jennifer has an undergraduate and M. Ed. from Kent State University. She is active in state and national library and educational technology organizations.

Kathleen Sullivan is the Collection Development Coordinator for the Phoenix Public Library in Phoenix, Arizona. She is interested in how public use of library materials is shifting and in future formats for materials delivery. She has supervised collection and reference services in public libraries in Arizona and California and trained other librarians in both services. She has also served on and chaired numerous ALA, CLA, and AZLA committees.

Peter W. Tobey is Director of Sales & Marketing at Salem Press. He is the author of nine books, a past publisher of both classroom and commercial fiction and nonfiction, and the editor and publisher of two national magazines.

Alix Vance is Founder and Principal of Architrave Consulting and Chief Operating Officer at The Center for Education Reform. She is a member of the Board of Directors of The Society for Scholarly Publishing, serves on the Editorial Board of Learned Publishing, and is co-author of the Webby Award–nominated technology blog, The Scholarly Kitchen. Previously, Vance was President of Paratext, a research content discovery company, Director of the Reference Information Group at CQ Press, a division of SAGE, and Vice President of Business Development for E-book Library, a subsidiary of e-books.com.

Jane Wildermuth is the head of the Digital Services Department at Wright State University (WSU) Libraries. She is responsible for managing digitization projects for the Libraries and campus. Wildermuth and her staff, with the assistance of OhioLINK, developed an institutional repository for WSU that was launched in October of 2008. She also serves as a member of the Libraries' Web Team, creating, developing, and maintaining the Libraries' web resources. Prior to her employment at WSU, she held several archival positions at the Ohio Historical Society. She earned her Master's degree in History from Miami University.

David E. Wojick is Senior Consultant for Innovation at the Office of Scientific and Technical Information (OSTI) of the U.S. Department of Energy. OSTI operates several of the world's largest technical reference portals, including www.science.gov and www.worldwidescience.org. Wojick's efforts focus on analyzing and modeling the structure and dynamics of technical information, then translating these findings into workable technological solutions. He holds a Ph.D. in Philosophy of Science, has served on the faculty of Carnegie-Mellon University and the staffs of the Office of Naval Research and the Naval Research Laboratory, and has written frequently for OSTI's blog.

Index

web search engine 23, 50, 52
WikiLeaks 63
Wikipedia 17, 21-22, 25, 32-33, 36, 41-44, 57, 64,
    66-67, 77, 81, 98, 128, 138, 140-141, 144-146,
    157-158, 162, 165, 167-170, 172-176, 178,
    180, 183, 187, 189, 193, 200-203, 207-208,
    234, 241, 261-263, 267

Wiley 115, 150, 192, 196, 206
Wolters Kluwer Health 117, 119, 125
WorldCat 5, 43, 45, 100, 171, 187-188, 210, 235

Y

YouTube 21, 32, 67, 93, 190, 233, 245, 253, 259